THE
ARCHITECT

THE ARCHITECT

KARL ROVE

and

THE MASTER PLAN FOR ABSOLUTE POWER

JAMES MOORE AND WAYNE SLATER

CROWN PUBLISHERS
NEW YORK

Published in the United States by Crown Publishers, an imprint of the Crown Publishing
Group, a division of Random House, Inc., New York.
www.crownpublishing.com

Crown is a trademark and the Crown colophon is a registered trademark
of Random House, Inc.

Library of Congress Cataloging-in-Publication Data
Moore, James, 1951–
    The architect : Karl Rove and the master plan for absolute power/James Moore and
Wayne Slater.—1st ed.
    Includes bibliographical references.
    1. Rove, Karl. 2. Rove, Karl—Influence.   3. Rove, Karl—Political and social views.
4. Political consultants—United States—Biography.   5. United States—Politics and
government—2001–.   6. Political corruption—United States.   7. Democratic Party
(U.S.) I. Slater, Wayne.   II. Title.
E840.8.R68M66 2006
973.931092—dc22
    [B]   2006011346

ISBN-10: 0-307-23792-3
ISBN-13: 978-0-307-23792-7

Printed in the United States of America

Design by Joseph Rutt

10 9 8 7 6 5 4 3 2 1

First Edition

For my mother,
Elizabeth Joyce Hiscock Moore,
in honor of her immigrant dreams of America.

—JCM

For Ouida Slater, who gave me life.
And for Etta Gluff, whose daughter, Dianne, gave my life meaning.

—WRS

Acknowledgments

O n late-night flights and during cocktail chatter, reporters traveling on presidential campaigns speculate about books they might write detailing the historical moment they're covering. Authoring a book seems far preferable to the mundane work of filing daily stories. Although books about the Bush presidency have long since jammed American bookshelves, during Bush's political ascension there was little to say beyond the obvious. We were only marginally interested in the president's story. As Texas journalists, we were too familiar with its predictable contours. Our fascination had long been focused on Karl Rove, who we knew was the reason George W. Bush was bound for the White House.

The president may become a historically tragic figure of great intrigue, but Rove's story continues—for us and many others—to be more engaging. From the time Rove set up shop on the limestone bluffs above Shoal Creek in Austin in the late 1970s, we've been interviewing him, writing about his skills and tricks. And like every other journalist he's known, we've also been a little bit used by the "big brained" strategist. For more than two-and-a-half decades, we've been building clip files, transcribing news-conference tapes, talking to his political opponents, and gathering every Rove info-nugget we could find. Our initial book, *Bush's Brain: How Karl Rove Made George W. Bush Presidential,* merely tapped some of that material—and certainly since that book's publication, Rove has merited even closer scrutiny.

Rove helmed the president's decisive 2004 reelection in spite of an unpopular war and a scandal a week involving his political party. In recent years, his role and importance have expanded in significance, and when federal investigators probed the leaking of a CIA agent's name to a reporter, we suspected Karl of using his time-tested practice of hiding behind a reporter's obligation to protect sources. Karl Rove wasn't someone we felt comfortable ignoring. We had experience dealing with him, and sources willing to talk, and we felt his story had only increased in relevance. No one, of course, ever sets out to be the biographer of a political consultant, but there's never been a political consultant like Rove.

Reporting on him hasn't been a simple task. The number of people willing to speak has often been limited by fear of retribution. Nonetheless, we found individuals, interested in facts, who provided information both on and off the record. Our debt to them is immense, and we hope their contribution to the historical record will be appreciated by more than these two writers from the Texas hill country.

Marc Schwartz told us of his meetings with Jack Abramoff and Karl Rove, while Linda Lipson patiently explained the trial lawyers' perspective on Rove's tort reform. David Swanson laid out the details of the Rove attack on unions, and John Ryan offered specifics from a union local in Cleveland. Rove's former colleague and friend Bill Israel gave patient and considered insight on Karl, the person. Richard Land helped us to understand the power of religion in GOP politics and how it motivates Karl. Bobbie Gobel explained the nascent enthusiasm among fundamentalists for George W. Bush. Patrick Guerriero helped us to appreciate the political fight of gay Republicans, and Kelly Shackleford offered a detailed rationale for the use of homosexuals as an issue—as did Ted Haggard. Former Texas Governor Ann Richards was gracious and forthright on her experiences with Karl Rove, as was Bush and Rove associate Don Sipple. Joe Perkins provided information on how Rove attacked in Alabama. Journalist Anne Marie Kilday told of an intimidating call from Rove to her home. Mark McKinnon consistently offered the positive view of Karl and Professor John Green of Akron explained how the gay issue worked in Ohio. David Barton of the Texas Republican Party spoke the truth about Rove's role in the election in Ohio, and the former head of the Texas GOP, Tom Pauken, still hasn't flinched from his beliefs, offering always candid comments. Pastor Dallas Billington provided insight on how gay marriage and religious values motivate voters, and Dan Trevas told us about how the Democrats in Ohio weren't paying close enough attention. Doug Wead and Ken Luce were open about their political relationships with Karl and the Bush family, and Ralph Reed offered time to understand his motivations. Reporter Ken Herman, who hates to be interviewed by fellow journalists, agreed to answer a few questions. Author Frederick Clarkson was a source of great material on the beginning of the political power of Christians in America, and Max Blumenthal showed a masterful grasp of how far they've come.

Eric Resnick's perspective regarding what it was like being a gay reporter covering an antigay campaign was invaluable. John Aravosis and Mike Rogers, who confront hypocrisy in all its forms, were outstanding interview subjects and sources. Canton, Ohio mayor Janet Creighton's enthusiasm for political accomplishment gave us the winner's point of view after a Rove-assisted win, and Matthew Dowd shared the numbers Karl read for guidance. Bob Klaffky and Doug Preisse, Ohio's leading GOP consultants, gave us time, knowledge, and strategic insight, and old friend Pieter Wykoff showed us the way across the Buckeye state. Bob Bennett, one of the Republican Party's most successful state leaders, invited us to receptions and fund-raisers and explained what he's done in his home state of Ohio. Herb Asher, an esteemed political thinker and Ohio State professor, gave us the big picture we didn't have, and Rocky Saxbe unveiled a dissident Republican voice in Ohio. Chad Clanton revealed what it was like for the Kerry people to be on the receiving end of a Swift Boat attack, while Jo Ann Davidson and Tom Erney impressed us with their frankness. Deal Hudson shared private moments with Karl and an understanding of how religious voters are animated, as did Pastor John Hays. Walter Dean Burnham's fine mind gave us the long historical view of Karl's work, and the decades of experience from Ohio reporter Lee Leonard were critical to grasping the state's political dynamics. Gary Marx acknowledged the facts behind claims that church directories were a valuable tool for an Ohio win, and Rob Schuler facilitated our understanding of what it is like to be a Christian soldier in a campaign.

Joseph Koons deserves special recognition for speaking so truthfully and openly about his personal life as a gay man and his long friendship with Louis Rove. Attorney George Parker Young, an early Bush supporter and donor in Texas, was a powerful source on the impact of tort reform. John Weaver, a former Rove colleague and political adversary, has experience we've always found important. Ken Vest, whose friendship is a steady strength, took us inside the trial lawyers' fight while Carlton Carl articulated the lawyers' cause, and pollster Ed Lazarus proved what the public was thinking about the issue. Ralph Wayne provided great information on how tort reform became a national issue in Texas, and Jon Opelt explained how the arms and legs of that movement went to work. Ty Runyan gave us an understanding of what it's like to own a company and deal with unions, and Jon Hiatt explained the struggle of a union trying to get fairness from a business, as did Per Bernstein. John Judis put it all into a historical frame.

Michael Ledeen, though reluctant to answer questions on the phone, agreed to consider e-mail queries. Karen Kwiatkowski shared her amazing experience as a career officer inside the Pentagon as facts were being manufactured to make the case for war, and Stephen Green's research, writing, and work with the United Nations presented some difficult truths about our country's relationship with Israel. Ian Masters and Louis Vandenberg of KPFK radio in Los Angeles are always way ahead of almost every journalist on the issues driving U.S. foreign policy and domestic politics, and they willingly shared sources. Former CIA agents Philip Giraldi and Vince Cannistraro communicated the anger of professionals who witnessed the undoing of their institution's reputation for accuracy. Texas political whiz Bill Miller connected the similarities between the early Karl and the White House version. Simon Rosenberg argued for a new approach for Democrats dealing with Rove and the GOP, and Reverend Richard Lee showed how the church and its voters can hope to keep winning.

This project would have been impossible without the steadfast support of editors Bob Mong, Mark Edgar, and Ryan Rusak of *The Dallas Morning News*, whose dedication to excellence in journalism has never wavered. There's no way to acknowledge all of the reporters and authors whose work has assisted the creation of this narrative, and we're certain to have slighted a few. Some, however, must be mentioned individually.

Stephanie Mencimer of *Washington Monthly* was the only reporter to see Rove's manipulations in the creation of a lawsuit and doctors' crisis. Joshua Micah Marshall, Laura Rozen, and Paul Glastris of that same magazine did some of the first and best journalism on the Niger forgeries and the unofficial work of Michael Ledeen. Jonathan Landay and Warren Strobel of Knight-Ridder stand out as journalists who were unafraid to write the unspun facts from the beginning of the White House's effort to create public support for the war. Larisa Alexandrovna's journalism reflects a high regard for the craft and has informed our own work, as has the writing of Michael Smith of the *Sunday Times* of London. In this regard, Seymour Hersh is in a class of his own. He always tends to lead the way and is followed closely by the indefatigable Murray Waas. We also owe great thanks to Carlo Bonini and Giuseppe d'Avanzo of Italy's *La Repubblica* for their groundbreaking work on the international campaign to deceive the world on Iraq and WMD. Sidney Blumenthal's relentlessness has been inspiring, and Ambassador Joseph Wilson's fearlessness goes to the heart of why we remain proud Americans. Arianna Huffington has been supportive since our first book was published, and her blog has been a wonderful place to test-drive ideas. We thank Joe Conansan for reading the draft manuscript, along with Marvin Olasky and University of Texas presidential scholar and author Bruce Buchanan. Greg Groogan has yet to stop saying encouraging things.

We've drawn repeatedly on our personal extensive files of notes, transcripts, and tape recordings with Karl Rove and President Bush, which we accumulated over the past twenty-five-plus years. There are also numerous others whose nameless insights delivered us material we'd have otherwise never acquired, and their requests for anonymity spoke loudly to the threatening style and power of Karl Rove and the Bush administration. Someone whose name deserves to be proclaimed widely, however, is our late colleague and friend Sam Attlesey, whose love of Texas politics and its national implications continues to inspire and energize our own work.

We're fortunate to be represented by Jim Hornfischer, who is an author, attorney, and literary agent; he constructs sentences as artfully as he does publishing deals. He led us to our editor, Rick Horgan, whose knowledge of books, politics, and the marketplace has guided us as ably as his red pencil. Rick and the authors have been helped immensely by

Julian Pavia. And we're, of course, grateful to Crown publisher Steve Ross, who gave us the resources to get the job done.

Finally, as always, we thank the members of our families, Mary Lou and Amanda and Dianne and Todd, who've indulged our political fascinations for many years. There are no words without the four of you.

James C. Moore
Wayne Slater
Austin, Texas, May 2006

Contents

*"As nightfall does not come all at once, neither does oppression.
In both instances, there is a twilight when everything remains
seemingly unchanged. And it is in such twilight that we all
must be aware of change in the air however slight,
lest we become unwitting victims of the darkness."*
—Justice William O. Douglas

INTRODUCTION

There is no more compelling subject in contemporary American politics, and perhaps in our country's electoral history, than Karl Christian Rove. In everything he's done, George W. Bush's senior political and policy adviser has had a transforming effect on how democracy functions in the United States. Rove's grand vision, complex strategies, and knock-down tactics exceed everything dreamed up by other consultants. Rove may just be very, very good at what he does, or he might exhibit genius.

The evidence argues in favor of the notion that Karl Rove is unique in both intellect and ambition and that his accomplishments have been transcendent for the American democracy. He is the architect not only of George W. Bush's political success but of a considerably larger goal—a generation of Republican hegemony. His arsenal of skills includes an ability to analyze and act under unexpected contemporaneous conditions while also managing a mid- and long-term strategy. What Rove does on a Monday is inextricably connected by design to what he'll be doing on another Monday four, six, and even eight years in the future. Nothing is without a plan. No detail is too small. All eventualities have been considered. Mistakes, though they have happened, are rarities.

Rove's ability to think and act in the moment while also seeing beyond the event horizon is the peculiar characteristic that makes it difficult to write and report about his many endeavors. If nothing else, it has informed our decisions regarding the construction of this narrative. Although this story does have a traditional arc, which carries it from Rove's early years in Texas with George W. Bush to the leak of a CIA operative's identity, Rove's approach to politics has necessitated a different narrative style.

The chapters that follow have not been arranged strictly by theme and subject matter, partly because Rove's history has never been simply linear. As an example, the decidedly pro-Israel attitude of almost every senior staffer in the White House and in the vice president's office is not simply a product of Rove and the president's making these hiring moves after taking office. This sort of "Israel-first" ideology took root for Rove and Bush back in their political salad days in Texas.

Understanding Rove and how he's guiding President Bush also requires backward glances even as the narrative follows contemporary events. For example, it's impossible to truly grasp the power of the gay-marriage controversy as a political wedge issue without looking back from the 2004 election to how Rove used homosexuality, not just as a wedge but as a bludgeon, when dealing with opponents earlier in his career. We consider the gay question in microcosm in Ohio and also study its implications for the national political debate. The early reporting in our narrative on this also helps deliver an insight into how Rove reached his conclusion that he had to both divide voters and motivate the conservative base by using homosexuality as a monster under the bed. This, too, requires looking forward to gain a picture of the contemporary landscape while also pausing for the occasional reminder of how we got to a particular political locale.

To the average voter, a political event, campaign, attack, or controversy that is Karl Rove's handiwork is something to be judged without context. Within Rove's universe, however, nothing occurs without prodigious planning and meticulous execution. In other words, voters should know that the exquisite feast of an election prepared by Karl Rove is the product of many, many years. Often, though, voters do not. Again, consider the theme of religion in this narrative. In Texas, Rove quickly understood the value of a motivated Christian voter, and he figured out how to get that support in Bush's gubernatorial races. While he was doing that, however, he was also taking the initial steps toward making Christian evangelicals and other social conservatives a powerful tool for the delivery of votes in the presidential contest he was preparing for his premier client. Therefore, religion, as a theme, will recur in our story because it explains so many successes at every point of the Rove and Bush alliance. In Ohio, the reader will be reminded of Texas, and in Texas, the reader will get a foreshadowing of what is to come in Ohio and beyond, though not always in a strictly linear sequence. Rove took specific, carefully considered measures beginning in Texas a decade earlier to make gay marriage and religion the wedge issues that helped Bush succeed in Ohio and nationally in 2004.

By visiting the early Rove in different time periods, we hope to more fully illuminate the Karl Rove of 2004 and 2005. By the time the reader approaches the final third of this narrative, it will be readily apparent that Karl Rove, through all of his preceding endeavors, was determined to protect all that he'd built in the Bush White House and, as a result, could be expected to do whatever was necessary to render critics and political detractors irrelevant. Within the context provided early in the book, the reader can easily reach a conclusion as to whether Karl Rove can be reasonably suspected of having leaked Valerie Plame's identity to Robert Novak as an act of vengeance. The evidence is not polemical and speaks loudly for itself.

Although, as we write, Rove is certainly exhibiting his talents on a much larger stage than during his Texas days, he still, nonetheless, has shown that he's willing to take almost any political, ethical, and even legal risk in pursuit of power. His record reflects this and prompts the question of whether the Bush administration, determined to invade Iraq, used Roverian deceptions in pursuit of that goal, including the acquisition of false documents to build a political case for war. Rove and Bush's proclamations of innocence require us to assume that the best and brightest of this administration and intelligence operatives with decades of experience were easily duped by bad forgeries. Rove's résumé demands that we analyze closely the possibility that he and the administration were collaborators in a colossal fraud.

By now it has become cliché in American political discourse to say that Karl Rove is unique and all-powerful, the "brain" that the president's accusers suggest he lacks. The truth is that the president is neither as intellectually challenged as his detractors insist nor as capable as his followers believe. Bush would, however, not be in the White House without Karl Rove, and no one knows that more intimately than the president himself. Perhaps no other political consultant has played such a close role in the ascension of a president. In the context of our most recent history,

Rove is without parallel among White House advisers, likely the most powerful unelected official of our time. In a sense, he created George W. Bush; gave him policies, politics, and strategies; and twice got him elected as a governor and then twice to the presidency. For all of his many and manifest political skills, the president, who is at his best in the retail side of politics, has relied on Rove to assist him in varying capacities. In the process, Rove has redefined the role of the adviser.

Historically, the presidential political adviser has maintained a certain distance as his newly elected client begins running the country. Counsel has been offered from an outside office. Generally, the adviser's insights are narrowly confined, in most cases, to politics. Rove, however, went into the White House on the federal payroll and eventually merged his political expertise with a considerable knowledge of policy to create an unprecedented hybrid creature. The political strategy Karl Rove helps George W. Bush execute is defined by the policy Rove and the president have determined will serve GOP goals. Rove is best suited to the martial arts of political combat and thus has pursued public policy as if it were a campaign rather than a public debate on the merits of any proposal.

Much as presidents leave legacies dissected by historians, Rove will leave a legacy. In many ways, Bush has served as a voice and face for the products Karl Rove has manufactured in his little shop of politics. One piece of that legacy is transforming government into a vestigial, almost debilitated entity, a change whose consequences might have hurt Rove and the president—and, by extension, their party—after Hurricane Katrina, but that remains a longer-term goal: government must be shrunk. The rolling back or elimination of regulations concerning the environment and business will have effects across decades. Programs to expand military reach, often at the expense of education and the poor, will profoundly define who we are as a nation, and it will only be later that we recognize Rove as the minstrel who sang us happy songs we chose to hum.

Ultimately, though, Karl Rove, we think, will be a man who's remembered for figuring out how to game the American political system. Under Rove, the politics of deception has become a conventional political tool. By drumming up the cash he needs from corporate supporters, Rove has been able to fill the ether with television and radio ads that create an alternative reality. When parents, busy over the kitchen table with their children, glance at the television flickering across the room and see their smiling president beneath a "Mission Accomplished" banner, they assume the worst is over. Image trumps truth. The stage is more important than the facts. The polls go up.

Democracy, to Karl Rove, is like a very large board game. The winner is whoever gets the most money and controls the message and dominates the game in perpetuity. The challenge of the game is to create sufficient doubt about opposing ideas and candidates that voters are drawn to their historical default positions. Maybe John Kerry was not the lousy, embellishing soldier the Swift Boat Veterans for Truth claimed him to be. Maybe he was a medal-winning patriot. But a barrage of critical ads moved Republican moderates and independents to reconsider whether they might stick with President Bush. Many did; enough to reelect him.

We're not suggesting that Rove is the first political operative to lie, nor that deception is the only ax he swings. Rove works with the truth, if and when it's an advantage. We are insisting, however, that he is American politics' most talented, prolific, and successful dissembler. When his policies and their merits, supported by his candidates' rhetoric, are not enough to succeed, Rove will do whatever is necessary to win.

His history is to attack opponents by working through cutouts, surrogate organizations, and various third-party operatives. When Rove's fellow campaigners such as Mark McKinnon insist there is not a detail of any contest or policy that goes untouched by Rove, they are, as a result, indicting him in the long history of undignified acts by surrogate groups and operatives that always seem to accompany Rove's campaigns. Are we to suppose that the Swift Boat Veterans for Truth spontaneously arose to attack the characteristic strength of John Kerry and that Rove had nothing to do with the development? Do we think that all of the untruths spread in South Carolina in 2000, meant to portray John McCain as a mentally unstable, biracial adulterer, rose up from the grass roots without any guidance and became the stuff of push polls and busy citizens placing flyers on windshields in church parking lots? Of course not. If Karl Rove is master of all, then he is master of both the artful political strategies of victory and the ignominious slurs used against those who oppose him and his candidates.

But what is the proof? In politics, the evidence tends to turn on the consequences. No one ever found Richard Nixon's fingerprints in the Watergate apartments, and no one is likely to discover "Karl's Been Here" signs on the smash-mouth politics directed at his political enemies. Rove is cautious about being interviewed and going on the record unless in controlled conditions such as when giving a speech. He is, after all, the best, and like Newton's example of God as divine mechanic, the best political expert sets operations into motion and creates environments that produce specific results. His distinctive talent is marshaling the most effective attacks against his political enemies without leaving fingerprints. Over the years, Rove's political campaigns have followed a pattern: bad things happen to his opponents, often by anonymous leak or third-party attack. For his part, Rove has always managed to maintain several degrees of separation between himself and the bad actors carrying out his plans. Catching Karl doing anything, as special prosecutor Patrick Fitzgerald has learned, is not easy. Deniability is a perfected skill. In Rove's practice of it, even incontrovertible proof can be insufficient to compel admissions. Up until the moment that it appeared Matthew Cooper of *Time* was going to testify before the federal grand jury investigating the leak of Valerie Plame's identity, Karl Rove was insisting he had had no communication with Cooper until after the secret agent's name was already published. When he was finally confronted with his e-mail to the deputy national security adviser, which gave the lie to his assertion about Cooper, Rove conceded the communication must have occurred. If the e-mail had not existed, Rove would have persisted in his denial. Rove has been manufacturing alternative realities to fit political needs for so long, one has to wonder whether he, at least on occasion, confuses the real world with the alternative one his political imagination insists exists.

Ultimately, Karl Rove will be measured not just by the tactics and strategies he uses to achieve his goals but by whether he reaches his distant visionary finish line. Rove wants nothing less than Republican dominance of American politics, a GOP realignment so powerful it creates a virtual one-party nation. Rove's plan was to guide George W. Bush to the White House, but his larger mission was to establish an enduring Republican majority, not just for eight years but for a generation.

He may soon achieve his great goal. And the evidence that follows will show that Rove is willing to do just about anything to get the job done. The construction of a Republican castle on the Potomac, however, will require the sacrifice of much that is already shining and valuable in the American way of life. Karl Rove is not *asking* us to give up anything, though; as he has done in the vigorous pursuit of political victories, he will *take* it. And then he expects America to follow his party toward a far horizon. But before we take another step, let's look closely at where our country is heading and how Karl Rove became our guide.

ONE

AMERICAN DREAMER

Big Plans and Powerful Friends

All roads lead to Karl.
—Kenneth J. Duberstein, Republican lobbyist,
Ronald Reagan chief of staff, Rove adviser

When Marc Schwartz thinks back on the incident, he sees it as a kind of strutting by Washington lobbyist Jack Abramoff. Schwartz, who was consulting for the Tigua Indian tribe of El Paso, Texas, was involved in a political effort to help his client reopen the Speaking Rock Casino in Ysleta, the dusty province of the Tiguas on El Paso's southeast side. The casino had been shuttered when the state of Texas had pressed its antigaming laws in the federal court system. The Tiguas had eventually decided to spend millions of dollars with Abramoff's lobby firm in an attempt to save the tribe's only real source of income.

"I gotta meet Rove," Jack Abramoff told Schwartz one afternoon as they talked in the backseat of the lobbyist's car. Abramoff's driver, Joseph, was working his way through the crowded streets of Washington. The lobbyist gave Joseph a location for a rendezvous, and he set a course in the direction of the White House.

"Really?" Schwartz asked. "We're going to the White House?"

"No. No. We don't do that," Abramoff answered.

"Why not?" Schwartz joked. "I'm sure George would want to see me."

Schwartz was in the midst of one of several trips to Washington to get a sense of what the Tiguas were purchasing with the more than $4 million they were spending with Abramoff. Burdened with unrelenting poverty, tribal members had begun to receive respectable annual stipends from the casino's revenue stream before the state forced closure. They were acquiring educations, building modern homes, and taking jobs at Speaking Rock. Spending millions to save the tribe's financial security was an acceptable risk. Schwartz nonetheless wanted to take frequent measure of progress and met with Abramoff as often as was reasonable. Abramoff, in turn, felt compelled to display his influence to show Schwartz what the Tiguas were getting for their money.

He explained to Schwartz why they were not going to see Karl Rove at the White House.

"They've got movement logs over there and everything, and we like to keep things kind of quiet. So just watch. You'll really get a kick out of it."

A few minutes later, Abramoff pointed through the front windshield at an approaching street corner and turned to smile at Schwartz.

"You recognize him?" the lobbyist asked his client.

"Son of a bitch," Schwartz muttered. "He's just out in the middle of the street."

"Uh-huh."

As the car came to a stop, Abramoff stepped out, and Schwartz lowered his window. The first part of the conversation between Abramoff and Karl Rove was easily heard.

"We've got a problem, Jack." Rove mentioned a member of the House who was not cooperating on a piece of legislation. Schwartz was unable to hear the congressperson's name. "And this is getting really out of hand. We need to clamp down. We need this to stop. Can you put the fireman [Tom DeLay] on this and let Tom know we need this ended? This is not good for us."

"You bet," Abramoff told the presidential adviser. "Taken care of. Not a problem. On it."

This was how Rove and Abramoff conducted their business. Rove tried to avoid any record of meetings. Although President Bush and Tom DeLay were both from Texas, there was no great warmth between the White House and the majority leader. So Rove used Abramoff to deliver messages to House leadership, allowing the überlobbyist to brag frequently within the concentric circles of Washington politics about his connections to the White House.

Because the conversation Marc Schwartz had just heard had sounded private, he raised his window and thought about the political process he was witnessing. Karl Rove was out on the street, a few blocks from the White House, delivering detailed instructions to a Republican lobbyist. Is this the way it is done? If there were nothing to hide, why would they not be sitting down in Rove's office? Schwartz had seen this kind of hookup on previous trips to Washington, but he had to concede he was still impressed. It was a vivid vision, riding around the city with Abramoff when the lobbyist's cell phone rang and Rove asked to meet on a street corner. Schwartz had watched as Rove "bebopped" into view and Abramoff got out for a brief conversation.

Schwartz later explained, "Jack just told me they did that because of the movement logs in the White House. If Rove called him, there'd be a phone log. If Abramoff showed up [at the White House], there'd be a log of that. But if Rove signed out and said, 'I'm going to get a haircut,' and left, you'd have no earthly idea who he just met with."

"That, to me, is a stud deal," Schwartz said to Abramoff the first time he'd witnessed such a clandestine rendezvous.

"We're not stupid," Abramoff bragged.

"And the bottom line is," Schwartz conceded in retrospect, "that's exactly how they did it. They *weren't* stupid."

When his latest sidewalk strategy session with Karl Rove had concluded, Jack Abramoff settled into the backseat of his chauffeur-driven car at the window on the opposite side of where Schwartz was sitting.

"That's the weirdest thing I've ever seen. The guy's a heartbeat away from the president's office, and he's out here on a street corner."

"Yeah, it's just easier," Abramoff said, shrugging. "Like I said, everything that comes out of the White House is logged in. The phone calls he makes. The phone calls he receives. So this is just easier. It keeps things a lot cleaner. And he's a fat fuck, and he can use the exercise. If the weather's nice, we meet in a couple of spots, and if not, he'll drive over and come in through Signatures [Abramoff's restaurant] or one of the other spots."

Abramoff's relationship with the Tiguas later was proved to be more performance art than accomplishment after e-mails between him and an associate were made public. The exchanges gave the impression he was more interested in the tribe's money than its political issues. The FBI, a federal grand jury, and five different federal agencies began to investigate Abramoff and what one senator called "a cesspool of greed." Senator John McCain launched a government investigation into Abramoff and his partners for allegedly defrauding various tribes of about $82 million,

$4.2 million of which came from the Tiguas. By early 2006, Abramoff and associates had pleaded guilty in perhaps the biggest government scandal in Washington in a generation.

At the time Schwartz was with Abramoff, what he and the Tigua tribal leadership didn't know was that the lobbyist, according to disclosures from the Senate investigation, had been paid millions in consulting fees by the Alabama Coushatta and the Choctaw tribes of Louisiana to keep the Tigua casinos in Texas from ever doing business. Investigators also discovered that Jack Abramoff had been using money from those same tribal gaming interests to pay the firm of former Christian Coalition leader Ralph Reed, who used the money to fight gambling, especially in Texas, where the Tiguas were trying to restart their casino. Eventually, the government's evidence indicates, Abramoff appeared to become comfortable with the concept of taking money from both sides of a legislative fight, and he decided to go after Tigua cash. In an e-mail to Reed, Abramoff wrote, "I wish those moronic Tiguas were smarter in their political contributions. I'd love us to get our mitts on that moolah."

Abramoff ultimately convinced the tribe's leadership he was the guy to help them change the law and open their shuttered Speaking Rock Casino. The El Paso tribe's legal problems, however, didn't disappear as a result of Abramoff's work. Marc Schwartz implied that about all the tribe got for its money was the exhibition of Abramoff's consorting with Rove in a public thoroughfare and a photo op at the White House with the president.

The story recalled by Schwartz is as revealing about Karl Rove as it is about Jack Abramoff. According to Schwartz, the meeting took place in the spring of 2002 as President Bush was busily making his case for the invasion of Iraq, which was to take place a year later. Rove was a chief strategist of that effort with a responsibility to develop the messaging and political support for the president's plans to depose Saddam Hussein. Also, because midterm congressional elections were only six months distant and Rove was charged with seeing that his party continued to increase its numeric strength, he was busily crafting a strategy that was to make the GOP the first political party since Franklin Roosevelt's Democrats to gain seats in an off-year midterm election.

Historically, no detail has ever been too small for Rove's attention, regardless of the size and complexity of the projects he's managing, and thus, he might have been distracted by a member of Congress who was wavering in support of the upcoming war. He wanted to bring it to the attention of the majority leader. Tom DeLay was certain to be responsive to Abramoff, who'd been a major fund-raiser for the Texan and a close counselor on Republican issues. Subsequent federal investigations of Abramoff focused on examining his relationship with DeLay and other key lawmakers and lavish overseas golfing and lobbying trips, including one to Saint Andrews in Scotland. The junket was reportedly paid for with Tigua money and was used to cultivate the political kindness of Republican Bob Ney of Ohio. Ney, according to Abramoff, was a likely sponsor of legislative efforts to legalize gambling on the Tigua reservation. Unfortunately for the tribe's ambitions, everything fell apart in a haze of impropriety, subpoenas, and arrests, which had nothing to do with the Tiguas.

That late spring of 2002, however, power flowed mightily in Republican circles, and there were no GOP members of Congress who didn't owe a portion of their electoral success to Karl Rove and the president who was leading their party. The "Architect" was at the peak of his powers and determined to execute his vision of Republican dominance in American politics. Applying a template developed by Newt Gingrich and the Republicans who had created the Contract with America, Rove, Bush, and the Republican National Committee raised money for virtually every candidate their party ran for national office. In return, they demanded unfaltering loyalty from the officeholders, which meant they were always expected to vote with the party and the president. Independence wasn't tolerated. On the day Marc Schwartz watched the president's political adviser and Jack Abramoff commiserate on a D.C. sidewalk, Rove had obviously gotten word that a congressman had decided to think for himself, and the White House political guru wanted Abramoff to carry instructions to House Majority Leader Tom DeLay that this was to be immediately addressed.

Retaining an almost lockstep control of Congress is a small but essential part of a larger master political plan Karl Rove has been dreaming of implementing since early in his career. During interviews, speeches, and casual conversations over the course of many years, Rove has detailed his greater goal of a complete political realignment for America. By gaining majority control over U.S. political power and government institutions, he seeks to create a kind of dominance that risks turning America into a one-party nation.

The elements of his strategy involve numerous direct assaults on institutions serving the Democratic Party. While publicly Rove has indicated that a political party can only be destroyed by a lack of candidates and ideas, he's proceeded to assist the Democrats with facilitating their demise by trying to eliminate their party's traditional sources of funding—as well as social policies that sustain their ideology and federal agencies that have historically serviced mostly Democratic constituencies. His goal is nothing less than the eradication or dramatic reformation of the government programs created under Franklin Delano Roosevelt's "New Deal," Lyndon Baines Johnson's "Great Society," and subsequent progressive policy that might bolster the Republican opposition.

If he can accomplish these goals, Rove will realize his dream of surveying a political landscape where the Democrats are a party in name only and the federal government renders almost no services and is so small that, in the words of Rove confederate Grover Norquist, head of Americans for Tax Reform, "It can be drowned in a bathtub." There are political risks to running a government that cannot deliver essential services in critical times. Karl Rove, though, considered the odds and thought they were good. He was always capable of taking any risk necessary, regardless of ethics or legality, to achieve a win. He was even more determined when it came to doing whatever was needed to give Republicans long-term political control of America. The question always lingering over Rove's great talents was whether he would be tempted to go too far to achieve a specific end and might ever get caught doing one of the many things for which he has been blamed.

He never seemed to think about such questions, however. That was for others who lived in a different reality. All he wanted to do was win and control. To do that, obstacles to Rove's goal of fundamental realignment had to be marginalized. If plaintiffs' attorneys find it difficult to file and win cases in courts of law, they'll be less capable of making financial donations to Democratic candidates and causes. Legislatively restricting access to the civil justice system could have big consequences. Reducing citizen lawsuits against business interests could result in more dangerous products but also mean higher corporate profits, guaranteeing a larger stream of campaign cash to GOP politicians, who, in turn, reward business by further suppressing access to the courts. Trial lawyers, conversely, eventually find it doesn't pay to pursue most liability cases. It was a neat cycle, and one Rove had been working on since the late 1980s. For Rove, he never had an easier enemy to malign than lawyers.

"What's happening is that the Republicans are incredibly focused and serious because they want it all," says Linda Lipsen, president of the Association of Trial Lawyers of America. "The Democrats are very comfortable with a balanced government. Checks and balances? The Republicans, they want complete dominion over every aspect of government."

"Should we be afraid of this?" Lipsen was asked.

"I think it's extremely scary, and actually, I would say that if the Democrats were doing it. I don't think it's healthy to have one party in control of government and every branch. I think it produces corruption."

Corruption has indeed proliferated during the Bush administration. Even the president's most ardent supporters were forced to suspend all skepticism to believe that the CIA and the United Nations were fooled by a blustering Iraqi dictator on the matter of weapons of mass destruction. More likely was deception by the White House, guided by message-maker Karl Rove. There is a convincing case to be made that all of the Ph.D.'s and experienced bureaucrats and politicians within the administration knew that the Niger documents, the key piece of evidence against Iraq, were fake but decided to use the information anyway. The White House might even have been involved in channeling the bogus intelligence into the U.S. system.

If, as turned out to be the case, the pretext for war was fictitious, the consequence only fed a rising tide of questions about ethics and influence in Washington on a wide scale. It was against that darkening cloud of scandal that Republican influence peddler Jack Abramoff bilked Native Americans out of tens of millions of dollars and House Majority Leader Tom DeLay was indicted for helping to engineer a corporate donation scheme that circumvented Texas election regulations in order to finance Republican candidates.

Power, though, has to be acquired before it can be used for ill or good. Republicans are in control of all branches of government and are writing laws and making rules that, if unchecked, will have profound impact on everything from the environment to the economy, foreign relations, health care, and every aspect of American life. It's precisely the kind of monopoly power Karl Rove has been dreaming of almost since the day he hung a "Wake Up, America" poster on his bedroom wall as a teenager.

The labor movement turns out to be as crucial a target for Rove's plans as trial lawyers. Although the number of people identifying themselves as members of unions has dropped dramatically over the course of the past few decades, labor continues to raise vast amounts of money for Democratic candidates. In the 2004 contest between President Bush and John Kerry, unions and their members contributed more than $200 million to the effort to elect the Massachusetts senator. Additionally, union members voted, as they have traditionally, in disproportionate numbers for the Democratic candidate for president. Unions also provided formidable resources to Democrats at the state level and in efforts to get out the vote nationally.

Rove's desire is to render the labor movement too weak to sustain viable opposition to Republican policies and candidates. Rulings by the National Labor Relations Board, which under the Bush administration has sharply restricted efforts to organize workers, as well as legislation and policies favoring corporate and business interests at the expense of employees, have weakened the foundation of an already struggling U.S. labor movement. One AFL-CIO official described it as an "all-out attack on the working men and women of this country."

David Swanson, formerly of the AFL-CIO's International Labor Communications Association, believes that historic union political behavior has made organized labor into a target for extinction by Rove.

"Do you really think he [Rove] wants to destroy the union movement?" Swanson was asked on a snowy spring day in Washington. "You actually think that he doesn't want a sort of viable opposition to corporate interests?"

"Absolutely, I do. They take every step one would take if their goal was to obliterate the labor movement. And Karl Rove knows his politics and knows his groups and knows that being a labor union member is one of the most likely factors to make you a Democratic voter. The only major group of white males in this country that votes Democratic is union members. Latin[a] women, African American men, white women, whatever. You're more likely to vote Democratic if you're a union member. And not only that, but union members are twice as likely to turn out and vote."

While Rove and the GOP have conducted a broad policy assault on unions, their immediate focus has been on government workers, the labor movement's only real area of growth and increasing political strength. As an example, language was inserted into the Homeland Security Bill to restrict the organizational capabilities of the overwhelmingly Democratic public-employee unions of the federal government. Using such a policy strategically is a considerably more effective method of diminishing Democratic opposition than is a purely political confrontation. It is, in fact, what Rove has always done best: he defeats his enemies before they are conscious of even being in a fight.

Eliminating government institutions or programs that are widely viewed as products of Democratic success is an essential element in Rove's plan and as critical as the debilitation of the party's funding sources. The public education system in the United States is generally perceived as being refined and enabled by Democrats, who have historically argued for better teacher salaries, improved curriculum standards, and tax policies that pay for these community goals. Although the "Leave No Child Behind" act promoted by the president and Karl Rove has been vilified by educators at the state level, Republicans have sought to use it to position the party as advocates of education.

At the same time, critics say GOP support for school vouchers, a concept championed by Rove to help rally the party's conservative base, has undermined public education. Democrats insist that providing a child with a voucher to take tax money and pay for attending a private school is a recipe for destroying public education because it erodes the tax base, and the only children left behind in public schools will be those from low-income families who don't have private transportation and support systems to make the transition.

The unspoken political dynamic in the voucher movement, which accounts for much of Rove's enthusiasm for the plan, is that it animates the Christian Right. Vouchers are viewed as an instrument for using tax money to get their children into a religious educational setting, and it is one more motivation for evangelicals, homeschoolers, and other antigovernment conservatives to stampede to the polls in record numbers and vote for Republicans such as George W. Bush.

Privatization of Social Security is another key plank of Karl Rove's career aspiration of decimating the Democratic Party and building an enduring Republican majority. As with many of Rove's ideas, reform of Social Security, in terms of both politics and policy, works for the GOP on a number of different levels. The government pension plan is the product of a Democratic administration and a mainstay of its ideology. Rove cannot destroy Social Security, nor does he want to, but sees long-term political advantage to giving workers the option of investing their government contributions in private accounts. The consequence, of course, would be that Wall Street brokerages and funds managers would eventually get their hands on hundreds of millions of new dollars. Already predominantly Republican, these financiers would have even more motivation to donate to the GOP's candidates as an act of gratitude for expanding their businesses. Possibly even more important, Rove believes he can expand the investor class, which has traditionally voted Republican.

Karl Rove's plans are ambitious on a grand scale, but they're achievable and therefore dangerous to the U.S. government and the country's political processes. Without the checks and balances designed to assure that political power is dispersed and decentralized, a monopoly government can veer to the extreme. That's why Rove hasn't publicly discussed in any detail his overall strategy. It's been necessary to piece together its basic tenets through more than two decades of interviews and observation of his work.

The president's chief political counselor does, however, have rare moments of hubris, which have provided limited clues to his plan. As a strategist and an operative, Karl Rove lives and works in a political universe where his client wins the glory and the architect of victory sits mostly in the back room earning acclaim limited largely to his professional peers. In Rove's case, however, he's often motivated by the same impulse that sends an arsonist back to the curb to watch the burning of a house he's set aflame. He revels in the attention. Consequently, Rove has consented to a handful of profiles written for glossy magazines and nationally distributed newspapers.

In one article, Rove offered a rare glimpse of the machine he was constructing. During two lengthy interviews with the *New Yorker* magazine, Rove dropped his guard momentarily with writer Nicholas Lemann. After deconstructing many of Rove's steps during the course of his remarkable political ascension, Lemann had concluded that Rove was in fact seeking to transform the Democratic Party into little more than a symbolic shell of a political organization.

And Rove conceded the point.

"Well, I think it's a plausible explanation," Rove said. "I don't think you ever kill any political party. Political parties kill themselves, or are killed, not by the other political party but by their failure to adapt to new circumstances. But do you weaken a political party, either by turning what they see as assets into liabilities, and/or by taking issues they consider to be theirs, and raiding them? Absolutely!"

Rove's comment undoubtedly chilled Democrats, whose candidates had been consistently defeated by the Republican's talents. His was an image of political dominion that reflects a self-confidence acquired from recurring successes against Democrats. He was determined to continue adding to that string of victories, no matter what rule, regulation, or law had to be skirted. And his focus was equally on protecting what he'd already built for the GOP with George W. Bush and what he intended to construct beyond 2008. Realigning the American political landscape for decades of absolute Republican control required that Rove think in broader terms and develop political tools to further befuddle and incapacitate the opposing party. Not surprisingly, Rove had been contemplating the GOP takeover of American politics for many years.

Rove once told a colleague that he had no religious affiliation and was "not a Christian." Nevertheless, in his systematic pursuit of Republican hegemony, he turned to a higher power for political strength. He discovered that his most powerful weapon in battle was going to be religion, and with extraordinary effectiveness, he deployed the armies of God. To make his political warriors even more ferocious, he filled their hearts and heads with questions about sex.

In the published profiles that attended his political ascent, Rove brimmed with confidence and ideas. On the verge of fulfilling his sweetest political dreams, he appeared to his opponents as unstoppable. And Rove undoubtedly felt that way.

He was very, very close to having it all.

GOD IN THE MACHINE

How Jesus Became a Republican

*The clergy, by getting themselves established by law and ingrafted
into the machine of government, have been a very formidable engine
against the civil and religious rights of man.*
—Thomas Jefferson, 1800

Karl Rove and Ralph Reed were unlikely partners. Rove was a private agnostic and Reed a very public Christian. If they seemed a political odd couple, they nonetheless shared the bond of a keen instinct for the gamesmanship of politics and an appreciation for its higher strategies. Rove was never out looking for friends, though. He was always too busy. And friends tended to be distractions from his greater political goals. People were largely assets to Rove. Those who shared his exuberance for political history and the arcana of campaign strategy were a bonus. But he considered few people close friends. What was more important was how they fit into his plan and what someone might contribute to the construction of a Republican dynasty. Karl Rove saw great value in Ralph Reed's intellect, his faith, and his commitment to a cause. Reed was an asset first and then a friend.

As executive director of the Christian Coalition in the 1990s, Reed nudged Pat Robertson toward combining grassroots political organizing with the new techniques of microtargeting and list management. From his operations center in a modest office park in the old navy town of Chesapeake, Virginia, between Virginia Beach and the Great Dismal Swamp, Reed built a better religious machine. And eventually, Rove would use the

Robertson-Reed apparatus to fulfill his dream of Republican realignment in American politics.

At the same time Reed was building his coalition in Virginia in the early 1990s, Karl Rove was creating his own version of an ascendant Republican machine in Texas. The instrument of Rove's success was to be George W. Bush, and Bush's occupation of public office in Texas hinged on winning over a constituency that his father never really earned. He needed the conservative Christian evangelicals.

Rove had worked for George Herbert Walker Bush at the Republican National Committee and as an aide to the elder Bush's exploratory bid for the party's 1980 presidential nomination, trailing the candidate across the country with a briefcase jammed with position papers, itinerary details, and the names of golden GOP moneymen from the high plains in Texas to the corn-fed regions of the Midwest. Rove was in constant search of campaign cash.

After Bush joined the Reagan ticket as vice president, Rove moved to Texas and opened a political-consulting business in a building set on the limestone bluffs above Shoal Creek, west of downtown Austin. The jewel of his company was Praxis Lists, a subsidiary in which Rove systematically collected names of Republican campaign contributors. They became the foundation for the Republican realignment in Texas and gave Rove his first notion that the resources might be found to create a similar GOP dominion on a national scale. Even the name of his list operation underscored Rove's no-nonsense approach: he called it Praxis, as in hardened by real-world practice, not theory.

Rove was, by his own admission, a classic geek, skinny with huge spectacles. He wore plaid sport coats and had thin blond hair, which he combed in a flat swath across his forehead. He had a jangling enthusiasm and a visible confidence that, whatever the setting, he was just about the smartest person in the room. In high school, he was considered the best debater in Utah. In college, he was attracted to politics so strongly that he never graduated, instead throwing himself into one political campaign after the other, first as a College Republican, then with the elder George Bush, and finally in Texas with his own direct-mail firm. Politics consumed his passions and his time, ending a brief first marriage to a Houston socialite who did not like his sustained absences from home. His second marriage has lasted. Darby Rove was a graphic artist, a political liberal with sandy blond hair who worked at Rove's direct-mail business. She was as steady and quiet as he was exuberant.

When they married, Darby said she understood her husband's strong competitive streak, although she had to temper his instinct to treat a game of chess with his son as if it were the final days of a presidential campaign.

"He's learned to lay back a little bit when he and Andrew play chess," she once told a reporter. "But even in croquet he'd be hitting my ball so far I was crying on vacation."

As Rove was beginning his long slog to Republican power in Texas, his first important state political client was Governor Bill Clements. It was while working for Clements in the 1980s that he kept bumping into Richard Land, a professor at Criswell College in Dallas. Criswell is a conservative Baptist college, named for an icon of the faith, W. A. Criswell, who preached that the Bible is the literal word of God, Darwin is the mouthpiece of Satan, and conservatives were preordained to dominate the Southern Baptist church.

Land was a huge man with a high pompadour and booming voice, a scholar of early church history who had studied at Oxford before coming to Texas. Eventually, he would become the Southern Baptists' most influential man in Washington, but in the 1980s, he was a young religion professor who discovered that he and Rove had something in common. Land was interested in applying matters of religious faith, especially limits on abortion, in public policy. Rove was looking for assets, resources he needed to build his dream machine for a Republican America. Land had a bloc of voters who wanted politicians to reflect their values; Rove had the politicians who needed the votes.

"I got very much involved in the Texas pro-life movement," Land said. "The pro-life movement was trying to get pro-life legislators elected at every level. And Karl Rove was a struggling young consultant in Austin trying to get Republican legislators elected."

Rove's political plans for Texas and beyond also found early purchase with Bill Clements. Clements, a Texas oilman and the state's first Republican governor since reconstruction, was a Rove client. Clements was a free-market conservative who saw the party's social-conservative wing as a gaudy appendage—a source of votes but largely irrelevant to the GOP's more serious mission of lowering taxes, cutting regulations, and shrinking government. He hired Land as his ethics adviser and emissary to the Christian Right.

Karl Rove and Richard Land saw each other frequently in Austin. Over

lunch, Land and Rove talked about history and the nexus between politics and religion. Land expounded on Aquinas and Tertullian; Rove held
forth on Madison and McKinley. It was obvious to Land that Rove was
not an ideologue but a tactician.

Sitting across from each other at a local eatery one day, Land and Rove
exchanged notes on the political potential of religious voters as an ener-
gized force. Land was talking about advancing an issue, one election at a
time. But Rove was onto something larger.

"I think that Karl understood in the same way that Newt Gingrich understood that this was an absolutely essential element to any Republican
governing coalition," said Land.

If Karl Rove had a god, it was victory. He worshipped success. His faith
was in his ability to learn and win elections and create powerful constituencies. Neither Rove's intellect nor his background allowed him to
jump the great divide between pragmatic realism and religious conviction. Rove had no interest in making the leap of faith. That just was not
who he was.

High school friend Mark Dangerfield told a reporter that it seemed to
bother Rove that "he was raised in a completely non-religious home."
And Bill Israel, who taught a government and politics course with Rove
at the University of Texas in the 1990s and considers him a friend, recalls
engaging Rove once in a discussion about religion shortly after their students had left the classroom. "I asked him what his religion was, and he
said he considered himself to be agnostic. He said he wished he could be
otherwise but he could not."

Religion was never important to him, but using religious people, tap-
ping their fervor over moral issues, was something that Richard Land
helped him to understand could elect candidates. His political instincts ran
naturally toward assembling different groups with the solitary goal of winning. And Karl Rove was never satisfied just to win; he needed to crush the
opposition, to dominate the landscape so that his enemies might never
again pick themselves back up to fight another day. And to build a machine
capable of crushing the opposition, Rove would need the evangelicals.

The man who'd benefit the most from Karl Rove's insights into the
power available by merging faith and politics was George W. Bush. The
future president got his religion in Maine, but his epiphany really took
root on the anvil-flat plains of West Texas.

Bush was living in Midland at the time, working in the oil business, and in the fall of 1985, he accepted an invitation from a couple of businessmen buddies to join a community Bible-study program. The men met every Tuesday after work in a classroom at the local Presbyterian church. Midland was the heart of the Texas oil business, a place given to high rollers and conspicuous consumption, but by 1983, the bottom had fallen out of the oil business. The First National Bank, a gleaming citadel with its grand collection of Norman Rockwells, went under in the bust. The Rolls-Royce dealership, which once offered Rolls-helicopter packages, closed its doors. Despair seemed to wring the sense of certitude from the place, and for the newly humbled businessmen of Midland's go-go years, the community Bible study became a kind of refuge.

When his father sought the presidency in 1988, Bush became a campaign liaison to Christian conservatives. He was perfect for the role. He spoke their language and was not shy about recounting his own conversion experience with evangelical leaders who loved Ronald Reagan but had doubts about his successor. Delivering those voters was crucial if George H. W. Bush was to win the White House in 1988. To facilitate that end, the campaign brought aboard Doug Wead, a former Assemblies of God minister and motivational speaker, whose task was to introduce George W. to leaders of the religious conservative network.

"He [George W.] was just on the cusp of his own religious awakening, without understanding the culture or the demographics or the numbers of the evangelical world," said Wead.

But that changed during the course of the campaign—so much so that, by the end, Wead was startled to see Bush evaluating campaign memos on ways to woo evangelical voters in terms of his own political future in Texas.

"He would look at those memos and just salivate about Texas," said Wead. "He'd say, 'God, I can do this in Texas.' It was like the missing piece for him."

Wead said he saw in Bush something he hadn't expected. Bush wasn't simply a man comfortable in the company of fellow evangelicals but a politico fully aware of how he would use them in a future race for governor. Rove, who'd met George W. more than fifteen years earlier and had maintained involvement in the Bush family's political fortunes, had to have seen the same thing.

"He's got the stuff in his blood," said Wead. "People miss how calculated, how sophisticated and nuanced, his approach to evangelicals really is. You think it's all spontaneous, that he's operating totally by instinct on matters of faith in public, but that's not true. He is a calculated animal from top to bottom."

In the 1994 governor's race, Bush triumphed where his father had not. The elder Bush was forever plagued by lukewarm support from Christian conservatives, who voted for him because he was a Republican but without the passion they'd shown Ronald Reagan. The younger Bush won wide support from conservative evangelicals in beating incumbent Ann Richards. According to exit polls, one in four Texas voters said they considered themselves part of the "religious right political movement." And of those, most had backed Bush.

Under the bright skies of victory in the governor's race, Karl Rove gave credit to the Christian Coalition and, by extension, to his political comrade-in-arms Ralph Reed.

"Christian conservatives helped tremendously in the suburbs where many of these churches are located," Rove said.

The Christian Coalition in Texas had swelled to 63,000 members and had actively targeted Richards for defeat. Bush was the right choice on abortion: he opposed it. And Bush allies launched a whisper campaign across East Texas, a staunchly conservative and historically Democratic region, raising questions about Richards's tolerance for gays and lesbians in her administration, a tactic Rove would use with disturbing efficiency in presidential politics more than a decade later. It was a red-meat issue for "values voters" of East Texas, a heavily Baptist region where political pollsters didn't even call on Wednesday nights because so many people were at church.

The Christian Coalition was not the only reason Bush was elected governor, but it was an important part of the equation. The group identified church coordinators and distributed 2 million voter guides in churches, conducted phone banks, voter-identification drives, and get-out-the-vote efforts on Election Day.

The Sunday before the November 1994 election, campaign media consultant Don Sipple visited Bush at his home in Dallas. Sipple found him in his backyard, sitting in a lawn chair, throwing tennis balls into the pool for his dog to retrieve. Bush was smoking a stogie and radiating confidence.

"I gotta tell you, as a first-time candidate at this level, I'm telling you I'm in awe of your performance over the course of the campaign," said Sipple. "How you grew stronger and more confident and exuded it."

Bush smiled. He had gone into the governor's race with assurances from Rove that he would win. Even as Bush's mother predicted he could not beat the popular incumbent, Rove made the case. The political team produced a picture-perfect campaign, avoiding direct attacks on Richards that might appear personal, challenging her record on crime and education, sticking to a clear-cut agenda of Rove's design. Team Bush did a lot of things right in the race, but nothing was more important than cultivating the state's Christian conservatives. Bush sought out evangelical leaders in Texas and won them over in a way his father never did. In the decade to come, Bush became the most overtly religious president in memory, and, unlike his father, Christians became the foundation of his political success.

Karl Rove made certain that the failures of the father informed the strategies of the son.

Bush tossed another tennis ball into the pool. "Sip, my man," he told Sipple, gazing casually at the water, "don't underestimate what you can learn from a failed presidency."

With the Christians, all things were possible.

From Ralph Reed's window at Century Strategies, he could see the Lexus dealership. The November sky was a clear blue outside the window of Reed's consulting firm, and the sun exploded off the cars in a million bursts of light. Reed's office was on the fifth floor of one of several gleaming glass buildings rising like citadels above suburban Atlanta. The interior walls were beige of a particular hue that exudes understatement and money. Reed's office location offered a view of the shopping mall along Satellite Boulevard, the upscale shops and car dealerships, and, beyond, the spacious sprawl of orderly neighborhoods built on the red dirt of Georgia. And in his meticulous preparations in November 2003 for the upcoming presidential reelection race, all that he surveyed was Bush country.

"My precinct, my neighborhood did not exist in 1996. And now, it probably has twelve hundred to thirteen hundred registered voters," said Reed. "This is a classic suburban bedroom community precinct, heavily Republican, strongly Bush."

Reed rearranged himself in his chair, impeccable in jacket and tie.

"We know that if we take a neighborhood directory," he said, explaining the Bush campaign plan to turn out the vote in the 2004 reelection race, "and we match it against the voter files—and there's 150 unregistered voters in that neighborhood—and we hit them with a mail piece and a phone call and a personal visit to get them registered to vote, we know we're going to get seven or eight of every ten people we register."

That November afternoon in 2003, as he explained the machinations of the Bush campaign, Ralph Reed was hard into the president's reelection, much as he had been four years earlier when Bush first ran for president and Reed's job, then and now, was to deliver the vote—especially the Christian vote, the true believers who were looking for a candidate who was guided by the same spiritual inspiration that led them. And a big part of the Bush plan, overseen by Rove and Reed, was to microtarget white evangelical Christians by radio, mail, and telephone with the message that George W. Bush shared their values, especially opposition to abortion and gay marriage.

"It's really not rocket science," Reed said.

Reed's path to national political prominence began in 1988, when he had what he calls "an epiphany" while attending a Republican precinct caucus in his suburban Atlanta neighborhood. He had earned a Ph.D. at Emory, writing his dissertation on the history of evangelical higher education, and seemed directed toward a career in teaching and writing. But politics had always had the stronger allure. And in January, he and his wife attended the GOP caucus as Jack Kemp delegates. Kemp was the economic conservative in the race, the choice of young pragmatists such as Reed. He expected the usual crowd: bow-tied young propeller-heads who saw themselves on the ramparts waving the gospel of supply-side economics. But when Reed and his wife stepped into the hall, they found the place packed with charismatic Christians organized to deliver the caucus for somebody else: Pat Robertson, who won handily.

The epiphany struck him with all the power of divine revelation, but it was a political one, not religious. He saw in this group a long line of Christian conservatives, millions of like-minded evangelicals receding into the distant horizon but marvelously disciplined and marching inexorably in a single direction. All they needed, he thought, was guidance and command. Walking back to the car after the meeting, Reed tried to make sense of what he had just witnessed.

"My candidate had been trounced, but I was nevertheless euphoric about the outcome. Why?" he wrote later. "Because my own dream of bringing religious values and conservative principles back into the political arena after two generations of liberal dominance seemed possible for the first time. I had seen the beginning of a new political era."

A few months later, at President George H. W. Bush's inaugural in 1989, Reed found himself at a table with Pat Robertson, who was struck by the young politico with the choirboy's face and earnest demeanor. Robertson said he wanted to take advantage of the grassroots groundswell he had created by starting a new organization. The Reverend Jerry Falwell's Moral Majority had fallen into disarray, and Robertson saw an opportunity for a more focused and efficient Christian-based political machine. Reed and Robertson immediately realized how they might help each other with their common goals. Reed was quickly engaged in refining the tools and messages of an operation that was destined to lead to profound changes in the American democratic process.

At the Christian Coalition, he built an efficient religious organizing force that operated leadership schools for thousands of Christian activists and formed rapid-response networks—connected by phone, fax, and modem—across the country. The Christian Coalition succeeded where Jerry Falwell's Moral Majority had failed. Reed led winning political efforts by emphasizing grassroots organizing at the precinct level. The Christian Coalition ran candidates for school boards and sent delegates to state GOP conventions, seizing control of the apparatus of entire state Republican parties.

Every third Tuesday, the Christian Coalition delivered to hundreds of churches satellite downlinks of "Christian Coalition Live," an hour of political instruction with Reed as host. What Reed understood was that, politically, conservative Christian evangelicals were the best constituency group in the nation. They were easy to organize. They felt themselves to be a beleaguered minority, under assault by a hostile secular culture. And they already belonged to churches that served as organizing centers.

"The advantage we enjoy is that liberals and feminists don't generally go to church," Reed said. "They don't gather in one place three days before the election. We can print 25 million voter guides and insert them in the bulletins of 10,000 churches across the country. We can mobilize the people; we can send the message."

Pat Robertson defined the terms of engagement when he told a private gathering of about one hundred members of the Christian Coalition's statewide branches in 1997 that they had to step up their activity if they hoped to select "the next president of the United States." He pointed with admiration to the Tammany Hall political machine and the Chicago of Mayor Daley.

"They have identified cores of people who have bought into the values, whatever they were, and they worked the election and brought people out to vote," Robertson said at a closed breakfast of the coalition's annual meeting in Atlanta.

That was the model the Christian Coalition needed to emulate. The televangelist then invoked not Scripture but Sun-tzu, the Chinese warrior who wrote *The Art of War*.

"This is going to be more sensitive, but I think you ought to hear me; this is family," Robertson said, looking around the room. "The principle of warfare that has been used forever by those who wish to beat another enemy is, you know, divide and conquer."

In April 1997, Reed left the Christian Coalition to set up his own political-consulting firm in suburban Atlanta. It was immediately successful. Candidates vied for his business. Corporations sought out his advice. At the coalition, Reed had overseen two thousand local chapters with 1.7 million members who were often mobilized on a moment's notice. And now that boy wonder of Christian politics had turned from God to mammon; he was a hot property on the political scene, and Rove wanted him on Team Bush for the 2000 presidential run. Rove could learn from Reed, use him and his coalition, and build something even greater and longer-lasting than a two-term presidency.

Rove had been thinking about taking Bush to the White House since 1990, when a GOP colleague recalls a meeting in Austin in which Rove, a largely unknown young political operative in Texas, already had a startlingly specific blueprint to make George W. Bush governor, then president. At the time, Bush had never held public office and was part owner of the Texas Rangers baseball team. Rove had no doubt that he could make Bush governor of Texas, but for his larger plans, he needed to forge much stronger relationships with people such as Ralph Reed and organizations such as the Christian Coalition.

Rove and Reed had crossed paths over the years. Both had been active in College Republicans and had worked on behalf of the same candidates. As the 2000 presidential race approached, Reed was being courted by several candidates and spoke in glowing terms publicly about John Ashcroft of Missouri. Rove needed Reed, though, and he wanted to freeze him in a political place until his skills would be called upon to serve the Bush campaign. At the same time, Rove did not want to signal too early that Bush was assembling the machinery of a presidential race or make it appear that a Bush candidacy would be a captive of the religious Right.

According to Marshall Wittman, a director at the Christian Coalition, Rove approached Reed with a deal that was to make them the best of friends.

"Ralph was very, very, very close to Rove," Wittman explained. "Ralph asked me in 1997 if I wanted to work on the Bush campaign. Rove was operating everything. Rove parked Ralph at Enron. Ralph told me before the New Hampshire primary that he would do what it took to eliminate McCain as an opponent if he posed a challenge to Bush. He would do whatever it took, that means below the radar, paint his face. Ralph has a dual personality, Dr. Jekyll and Mr. Hyde, charming in public and then ruthless and vicious."

Karl Rove turned to Ken Lay, an old friend of the Bush family, and Ralph Reed found himself signing a high-dollar consulting contract with Enron. For $380,000, Reed helped the Houston-based energy company spread its message on Capitol Hill and build grassroots support for energy deregulation. Reed prepared a memo for Enron executives saying he had a history of harnessing "the faith community" on behalf of issues. The arrangement kept Century Strategies off the Bush campaign payroll until 1999, and then only in small amounts that belied Reed's major role.

Ralph Reed knew how to use the culture war dividing America as few other people in politics. He understood that conservative evangelicals were anchored in the notion of the absolute. Either you were with us or you were against us. In every inference, every arc of judgment, the implication was clear: the world was divided between the secularists and the people of faith. Good versus bad. Believers against skeptics. This was a perfect battlefield for Rove, who had always fought his political campaigns as a war against enemies not only to be beaten but crushed, destroyed, annihilated. Voters were drawn to simplicity. It was not such a long step from the low plains of smash-mouth politics to the eschatology of the Children of Darkness against the Children of Light.

From a distance, the divisions of the old culture war seemed to separate people of faith and the godless. Ralph Reed knew better, though. In fact, the true religious divide was not between denominations but through them. It was not Protestants on one side and Catholics on the other, not Baptists in one party and nonbelievers in another party. The key political calculus that Reed and savvy supporters such as Richard Land brought to the Rove and Bush camp was an important insight into faith that had never figured in politics. The more fundamental divide, they realized, was within religious America. And any successful political machine needed to exploit that division.

"It depends on which side of this sort of great divide in American life you're on. Whether you're on the traditional side or whether you're on the postmodernist side," said Land. "That's how you explain that I, a Southern Baptist, have more in common with Pope John Paul II than I do with Jimmy Carter or Al Gore or Bill Clinton. Because it's less important whether we're Roman Catholics or Baptists as it is which side of that divide we're on. Do we believe in absolutes? Do we believe in a traditional values system where some things are always right and some things are always wrong?"

Most Americans are religious, and they are overwhelmingly Christian. Their faith informs every choice they make. These were the people Ralph Reed and Karl Rove wanted to reach and inspire. A family that gets to church one Sunday a month was not the demographic with which George Bush hoped to communicate in his presidential campaign. In fact, Bush already had many of those households on his side, and the remainder was not a significant enough number to pursue. Instead, Rove had to reach the ardent souls who were looking for a leader who was inspired by God and who was dedicated to making America more moral, more Christian, more conservative.

This was a new politics of division, and Ralph Reed and Karl Rove understood the political instruments needed to identify different types of believers. These computer-age tools were microtargeting, detailed voter identification, and sophisticated get-out-the-vote programs. The true believers were poised to cross battle lines pitting conservative Protestants, traditional Catholics, and Orthodox Jews against moderate Protestants, Catholics, and Jews. My team, your team. The same ferocious certitude that was to eventually darken the president's claim that the nations of the world were either "with us or with the terrorists."

As Rove launched Bush's first campaign for president, Reed arranged for his network of conservative pastors and evangelical leaders to send word ahead to people in Iowa, New Hampshire, and elsewhere that Bush was their kind of candidate. In the summer of 1999, many of the Republican faithful knew little about George W. Bush except that he was the son of President Bush, not exactly a credential to evoke passionate support.

So Reed set out to build Bush's evangelical résumé. Seemingly out of the blue one day in 1997, the Reverend John Hagee, a Texas preacher with a national television audience, called Bobbie Gobel, an Iowa Republican influential in Christian circles.

"I'm supporting George Bush," said Hagee. "He's a godly brother." And Gobel was impressed.

Hagee preaches biblical prophesy from his megachurch in San Antonio. He proselytizes the end of the world and that Christians will be instantly swept up into the sky during the Rapture while billions of nonbelievers are left behind in a hellish seven years of torment known as the Tribulation. To many conservative Christians in Iowa, that vision is the unvarnished truth, and Hagee was a pastor of uncompromising character. And now here he was on the phone, endorsing George W. Bush.

"I was, like, wow!" said Gobel. "Pastor Hagee is a man of God, so when I heard that come from him, it did make me turn my head."

A number of calls reaching out to religious leaders were made from Texas and orchestrated by Rove and Reed. The people who made those calls considered themselves "the Texas missionaries." They telephoned religious activists in Iowa and New Hampshire and South Carolina to vouch for Bush. Richard Land called, as did TV evangelist James Robison. David Barton of WallBuilders, a conservative Christian group that challenges the separation of church and state, did Christian radio talk shows. Jerry Falwell and, most notably among Reed's galaxy of high-powered preachers, Pat Robertson sent word to the faithful that they were backing Bush.

In June, when the Bush camp held its open house in Iowa, it was raining, but the place was packed. More than two hundred people, an overflow crowd, jammed the campaign office and the parking lot. There was competition in the GOP primary for the support of the religious Right. Christian activist Gary Bauer postured for attention against the streaming rhetoric of conservative Pat Buchanan and radio host Alan Keyes. But Reed and Rove had laid the groundwork early with an astonishingly effective preemptive strike that went completely unnoticed outside the fraternal confines of the Christian Right.

"It was absolutely amazing," said Gobel. "The man hasn't even stepped into the state of Iowa, and he has brought so many people who are excited that he's going to run."

The public Bush embraced the religious Right. Privately, he was less comfortable with some of his evangelical allies, especially the more garish TV preachers with their powder pink sets and theatrically mawkish appeals for money. At heart, Bush was a country-club Republican, the son and grandson of a family that knew its way around the walnut-paneled corridors of Wall Street. But the Christians were his base. And so Rove, the agnostic who saw religion as a political tool, built a God machine guided by the sword of righteousness and George W. Bush. The born-again Methodist Bush understood the value in using Rove and Reed's invention to build his political power.

Bush's embrace of the Christian Right might easily have been viewed as cynical pandering given the fact that his own religious beliefs were not as sharply defined. During the 2000 campaign, Bush traveled to the West Coast for an event at a Boeing plant in Washington, where he stood before a wide-body airplane bound for China and said he favored free trade with the communist nation. The message was music to Boeing employees, but a Texas reporter joked on the way back that his embrace of free trade with the communists might cost him among the church crowd back home. Bush knew that the reporter lived north of Austin in a politically conservative county known for an abundance of churches and Christian activism.

"Oh yeah?" Bush said, grinning as he pressed his face close to the reporter's. "You only think that because you live around all those wackos."

As it turned out, the wackos did not turn out in the numbers Rove had hoped for in 2000. George W. Bush lost the popular vote but gained the presidency in a squeaker after Florida and the Supreme Court. In the aftermath of the campaign, Rove did the arithmetic and made a disturbing discovery. He concluded that at least 3 million conservative evangelicals did not go to the polls. *Bush voters and they stayed home?* Clearly, the old formulas of dropping campaign literature at churches and having allies spread the word that Bush was right on abortion were no longer sufficient methods of winning. Rove decided he'd have to do more next time. He had to expand the base of religious voters with a sharper, harder, more direct message to invigorate the faithful. Maybe throw a little sex and fear into the mixture. Bush needed to win reelection, and Karl Rove did not care who had to suffer on the road to victory. Victims were a part of the process.

And homosexuals, he concluded, were the perfect enemy.

THREE

THE GOSPELS OF KARL

Gay Ain't Good

When I was in the military they gave me a medal for killing two
men and a discharge for loving one.
—Epitaph of Leonard P. Matlovich

Patrick Guerriero spotted Karl Rove across the room, just past the chamber ensemble, next to one of the elaborately decorated Christmas trees that gleamed in various rooms of the White House. Then he saw the president. Guerriero was a Republican, but also gay and concerned that President Bush might use same-sex marriage as a political issue in his 2004 reelection campaign.

Guerriero was sensitive to the fact that it was the holiday season and this was a festive night at the White House, so as he approached Bush and shook his hand, he made a few gracious comments thanking the president and first lady for their service. Bush knew that Guerriero was executive director of Log Cabin Republicans, an organization of gay Republicans. The group had endorsed Bush in 2000, touting his record as a compassionate conservative. During that campaign, Bush talked in inclusive language and met with a group of gay Republicans in Austin, after which he declared himself "a better man" for having done so.

But the political environment approaching the 2004 race was different. In April 2003, Republican senator Rick Santorum of Pennsylvania compared homosexuality to bigamy, polygamy, incest, and adultery. In June, the U.S. Supreme Court struck down the antisodomy law in Texas, and by

November, the Massachusetts Supreme Judicial Court declared the state's ban on same-sex marriage unconstitutional. The religious Right, Bush's base, was clamoring for him to endorse a federal ban on gay marriage.

And so on this night, in the convivial glow of holiday celebration, Bush had an uneasy look.

"Mr. President," said Guerriero, "I don't think we need to divide the country by amending the Constitution."

Bush nodded, not in assent but in a gesture that suggested he had heard his guest. Guerriero walked away with the clear impression that gay marriage might very well be part of the reelection equation.

He buttonholed Rove.

"Karl, you're the smartest political brain on the planet. I think you can win without using gays to do it."

What Guerriero got back from Rove, he said, was hardly reassurance. "From Karl, it was, This is the Christmas season, and wink, wink, this stuff is going to unfold, and it isn't going to be easy, but that people push too hard and too fast, and this is kind of a no-brainer."

Guerriero sought out White House chief of staff Andy Card and White House political director Matt Schlapp, pleading his case that, certainly, the Bush team could engineer a reelection without alienating the 1 million gays and lesbians who had voted for Bush over Al Gore. But all the conversations led Guerriero to conclude that the 2004 race was going to be about mobilizing the base, and the base did not like gay marriage.

"The only thing that could have stopped it," Guerriero suggested, "was the president marching into Karl Rove's office and saying, 'Hey, I don't have the stomach for this. I think we're going to win based on these other issues, and I don't want to go this far.' And he didn't do it."

In fact, Rove had already privately reassured the most important group of religious conservatives on his political radar screen, the Arlington Group. In early December, a year before the 2004 election, members of the Arlington Group met in Washington at the headquarters of the Family Research Council, a group affiliated with James Dobson's influential radio ministry. Membership included the most significant figures on the religious Right; Rove was getting advice and consent from the Reverend Jerry Falwell, the Southern Baptists' Richard Land, conservative activist Gary Bauer, Paul Weyrich of the Free Congress Foundation, Don Wildmon of the American Family Association, and Dobson, perhaps the nation's premier arbiter of political conservatism. Together, they represented a huge swath of Bush's political base, the key to mobilizing the additional 4 million evangelical voters that Rove knew he needed in 2004.

Meetings of the Arlington Group are confidential. There is an agreement among members not to talk publicly about what goes on around the table in Dobson's conference room, not even to confirm who attends. The idea was to encourage frank discussion, and in early December 2003, the conversation was heated. The Massachusetts ruling on same-sex marriage threatened to open the floodgates of homosexuality across the country, court by court, state by state, and the big guns on the religious Right wanted the White House out front by endorsing a constitutional ban on marriage of two people of the same gender.

The meeting was important enough that Rove got on the speakerphone from his office at the White House. He had already gotten the word that Christians were restless. Everybody wanted Bush to step out and take the lead and say that he's firmly behind the gay-marriage ban and that he would not rest until it was passed.

"If the president leads on it and there's a real focused discussion, it will definitely have a huge difference in emerging the base," said Kelly Shackelford of the Liberty Legal Institute. "There really isn't another issue out there of the type to bring out the 4 million who weren't there four years ago."

So where was the president? When would he announce support for the ban? The White House had twisted the arms of enough conservatives to ram through the House a bill restructuring Medicare and providing a prescription-drug benefit, so what about gay marriage?

Rove assured them that Bush was on their side. Members sat around the table, looking at one another as Rove's disembodied voice, straining more through his sinuses than his mouth, filled the room, offering assurance. Finally, Land, who had known Rove the longest, demanded a commitment.

"Will you commit as much support and effort by the president and staff to support the marriage amendment as you did with prescription drugs?" Land asked.

"Yes," Rove said.

The room was satisfied. The president was on board, not simply in word but in deed. Two months later, Rove called Dobson personally to give him the news that Bush would announce publicly his support for amending the U.S. Constitution to ban same-sex marriage.

Guerriero got word on his cell phone from the political director of Log Cabin Republicans and headed to the office in a second-story walk-up in Dupont Circle, where he watched Bush make the statement on TV.

"It felt like someone kicking me in the stomach," he said.

Guerriero was disappointed that an administration whose vice president had a gay daughter and whose principles embraced the idea of less-intrusive government, whose president once ran as a "compassionate conservative," would capitulate so completely to the Pat Buchanan wing of the Republican Party. He had seen Buchanan on the *Today* show declare the fight over gay marriage to be "the blazing social issue of the campaign of 2004." Ted Haggard, president of the National Association of Evangelicals, declared, "The federal marriage amendment should be at the center of this election."

And Karl Rove was determined to put it there.

Back at the offices of the Log Cabin Republicans, in the swirl of bad news, political director Mark Mead understood exactly what was happening. "This is a move to start a culture war."

Making the political case to the president wasn't hard, but Rove had to overcome Bush's natural instinct against intolerance. For one thing, Bush didn't share the zealotry against homosexuality that guided some of his more garish religious allies. His conservatism was economic, not cultural, and unlike the Gary Bauers and Jerry Falwells of the Christian Right, Bush never lost any sleep over fears that a voracious, pastel army of homosexual insurgents was about to overtake the nation. Moreover, the pure politics of gay bashing was dicey. Embracing the amendment could undercut Bush's "compassionate conservative" image and alienate suburban moderates. But the presidential campaign of 2004, and the architecture of the Rove Republican machine, was not based on unifying people toward the middle but energizing them at the edges. The 2004 race was about mobilizing the base and ginning up their numbers. The country was divided over Iraq, and what Rove needed was a wedge issue to rally the troops, something that would excite evangelicals to boost the president's numbers and attract a few newfound voters. In Rove's campaign arithmetic, antihomosexuality was a winner.

Besides, he'd already used the issue before. And it had worked very well in Texas politics. Rove had gotten results without taking the blame.

The evidence against him was only whispered words and printed flyers that nobody was able to connect to Karl Rove.

The flyers would have been offensive almost anywhere in Texas, but especially in conservative East Texas, home to vast thickets of loblolly pine, southern sensibilities, and old-time religion. Of all the institutions that define East Texas, the church is the most influential, especially the Baptist church, with its white steeples triumphant over the landscape and sermons crackling on local radio. Across the brick wall of one downtown building, painted in huge letters, are the words "Jesus Is Lord over Lufkin." It's a sentiment widely held in the region. So when the flyers picturing homosexuals appeared one Sunday under the windshield wipers of cars at church, they had the effect of a political atomic bomb.

Two men, stripped from the waist, kissing, were prominent on the front of the printout. One of them was black; the other was white. Under the picture were the words "This Is What Ann Richards Wants to Teach Your Children in Public Schools."

The flyers were inflammatory enough for their blunt sexual messages, but they were made significantly more incendiary by the racial component. They also followed a virulent whisper campaign that bubbled for months across the region from coffee shops to barbershops to church basements. In the summer of 1994, when George Bush challenged Ann Richards for the governorship of Texas, it was virtually impossible to go anywhere in East Texas without hearing about Ann Richards and the lesbians.

"I thought it was a joke," Richards later explained. "I never took that seriously. I have dealt with that in every race I've ever run. When I ran for county commissioner, I told [ex-husband] David, you know that before this is over, they're going to have me sleeping with every man in this county. Little did I realize it was going to be every woman."

As governor, Richards had built a record of inclusion, opening Texas government to unprecedented numbers of women and minorities and, in the process, appointing a half dozen gays and lesbians to positions of authority, including a high-profile appointment to the state agency regulating utilities.

And very quietly, Karl Rove decided to play on voter fears that their governor was a lesbian and convince them she was quite different from the average Texan. The diversity that Ann Richards and the Democrats saw as a strength of her administration was, in Rove's view, an electoral opportunity. His particular political genius has always been to attack not the weakness of an opponent, as most consultants do, but the strength. Destroy an opponent's strong point; ruin that aspect of personality or performance most attractive to voters and you've destroyed your political opposition.

In this case, Rove knew that Ann Richards's strongest asset was her reputation for opening government to those excluded in the past, including gays. Hammer her for that, make it a defect in her judgment, and you win. The criticism, however, could not come directly from the campaign because the new GOP was trying to change the perception that it was self-righteous and intolerant. The new Republicanism of the Bush/Rove regime was to be conservative but also compassionate. What was needed for electoral victory was a formula to attract moderate suburbanites. Hence, it was crucial that Bush maintain deniability in any use of homosexuality as a wedge issue. The attack must come independently from values voters who could be counted on to drive the conversation about Richards and the lesbians and her dubious relationships.

Years later, Rove recalled with a measure of pride the campaign's success. In an interview with *Texas Monthly*, he said Richards's record of promoting gays was fair game.

"When she touted 'I'm appointing this person to the funeral commission because they're gay,' that offended some people. It was not the fact that the gay person was on there. It was that she was touting the fact that being gay somehow qualified them to be on the funeral commission. I think the gun issue and generally her lack of cultural connection with East Texas, she didn't connect well with them, were problems of her own creation, not ours."

In fact, Richards had not touted promotion of homosexuals. In a conservative state such as Texas, it did not take much sense to know that emphasizing an appointee's sexuality was bad politics, especially in a conservative Democratic stronghold such as East Texas, a region she needed to win. When the Lesbian/Gay Rights Lobby of Texas issued a press release celebrating her selection of "an 'out' lesbian" to the state's utility commission, it was to the consternation of the Richards political camp. Richards emphasized the professional credentials of her appointees. The Bush side, however, pressed the case for her possible lesbianism through surrogates who spread the word from church parlors to town squares in a remarkably efficient rumor campaign. The story line was that Ann Richards had appointed militant homosexuals to positions of authority in her administration and surrounded herself with a staff of suspiciously single women, and who knows, she might even be a lesbian herself.

Inside the Bush camp, the political team marveled at the effectiveness of the whisper campaign. "It worked," said Don Sipple, Bush's chief media strategist. "It was always talked about. It was a subterranean text of the campaign."

Rove was careful to distance the official machinery of the Bush campaign from the issue, fearing alienation of moderate suburban voters Bush needed to win. Two months before the election, when a state senator who served as Bush's East Texas campaign chairman announced that Richards's appointment of homosexuals could cost her support in the region, the Bush team moved quickly to erase any fingerprints. The campaign issued a news release praising the senator as "a person of great integrity and strong convictions" but said he was speaking for himself. Bush, campaigning east of Dallas, allowed that some of his rival's appointees apparently "had agendas that were personal in nature" but said someone's sexual orientation was a private matter.

"That's not an issue to me," he said.

The Richards camp was not persuaded. "There was clearly an organized Republican movement to keep a couple of issues, gays and guns, in the forefront," said Chuck McDonald, Richards's campaign spokesman. "And I don't think it's any secret that the person who really set the Republican agenda was Karl Rove. He drove it."

Karl Rove denied any association with the whisper campaign, much as he has denied involvement in a pattern of political dirty tricks and hardball tactics that have consistently accompanied his campaigns over the years. Sipple, a GOP consultant on the Bush campaign, said plausible deniability is part of Rove's considerable political skill.

"If I had a nickel for all the things that Karl said he had nothing to do with, I'd be a wealthy man."

As for the flyers in East Texas, Rove did not need to deny anything. They happened late, the Sunday before the election. There were thousands of anonymous pieces of paper stuck on car windshields in church parking lots reinforcing a theme that Rove, in the privacy of the campaign office, was only too happy to advance. The flyers informed East Texas churchgoers two days before they voted that Democrat Ann Richards favored homosexual rights and George W. Bush did not. Richards didn't see the flyers until after the election was over, but she had seen the strategy used effectively when she was a young woman.

"Fear is a tremendous organizer," Ann Richards said during a conversation looking back on her career and the rise of the conservative movement. "Fear will engender loyalty; it will engender commitment. We have seen that with the religious Right. You have to keep people worried and afraid, or they aren't going to pay their dues."

Richards said she paid little attention to the whisper campaign until it was too late and she'd lost and George W. Bush had become the first Republican running for governor to win East Texas in more than a century. It was only after the election that she understood the power of homosexuality as a wedge issue when, as the Bush side showed, the opposition is skilled at using implication and innuendo. And because the tactic was so effective, Karl Rove was to use the gay-marriage flyers against Senator John McCain in 2000 and Senator John Kerry in the 2004 Bush reelection campaign. Homophobia, in fact, turbocharged the evangelical Christian turnout and was essential to reelecting President Bush.

Just like Ann Richards, Mark Kennedy never saw the whisper campaign coming in his direction, either. Kennedy was a Democratic incumbent seeking reelection to the Alabama Supreme Court in 1994, the same year Richards was trying to win a second term in Texas. Kennedy was a smallish, tweedy man, fastidious and impeccably dressed. His image was anything but the archetypal Alabama good old boy. But he was George Wallace's son-in-law, and that credential, coupled with his financial support from Alabama trial lawyers, made him a strong political candidate for a second term.

In the early 1980s, Kennedy had helped start the Children's Trust Fund of Alabama, and later, he founded a private, nonprofit foundation that assisted abused and neglected children. Joe Perkins, his political consultant, shot a television commercial of the judge holding hands with children to underscore his work on behalf of juveniles. Down-ballot races such as supreme court tend to get lost among the flurry of statewide campaigns in election years, which prompts strategists to look for anything that might raise a candidate's name identification among voters. Kennedy's work on behalf of abused and neglected children was the differentiator to separate Perkins's client from the field. He had no idea such public service might become a liability. But he had never been in an election campaign against Karl Rove.

Kennedy's opponent was Harold See, a University of Alabama Law School professor. See was recruited by business interests and bankrolled by the Business Council of Alabama. More critically, though, his political consultant was Karl Rove.

The public campaign was all about tort reform. The legislature had passed a package of bills in 1987 capping jury awards against business, but the Alabama Supreme Court struck down the laws in 1993. The situation in Alabama caught the attention of a Washington public relations expert named Neal Cohen, a Rove associate, who created a national network of local "lawsuit-abuse" groups that seemed to spring up spontaneously to fight rising jury awards. The enemy was always the trial lawyers. And the solution to end problems caused by the lawsuit-happy trial lawyers was to urge voters to support business-minded Republicans.

The lawsuit-abuse groups did not endorse candidates or make campaign contributions, but they worked closely with interests that did. So in 1994, Alabama Voters against Lawsuit Abuse sounded the alarm about rising jury awards, and the See campaign, under Rove's direction, targeted Kennedy as a friend of greedy trial lawyers, whose million-dollar judgments were harming local business and forcing insurance companies out of the state.

A much darker issue was swimming just beneath the surface of the campaign, however. Kennedy's volunteer work with children was breaking through with voters. The See campaign had to do something to blunt his advantage. Perkins said that after he started airing the TV commercial of Kennedy holding hands with children, word began to spread along the loose network of University of Alabama Law School faculty and students that Kennedy was a pedophile. The whisper campaign moved with a kind of ruthless efficiency from the hallways of the law school to folks back home, to big cities and small Alabama communities, everywhere students lived. Perkins said he heard about the whisper campaign directly from friends inside the law school, and as he studied polling data, he saw that it was working. But what to do about it? Call a news conference and announce you're not gay? Perkins was in a box, and he knew it.

"Mark is not your typical Alabama macho, beer-drinkin', tobacco-chewin', pickup-drivin' kind of guy. He is a small, well-groomed, well-educated family man, and what they tried to do was make him look like a homosexual pedophile. That was really, really hard to take."

After Karl Rove had become a figure of historical importance in presidential politics, one of his former staffers from that campaign told *Atlantic Monthly* writer Joshua Green about the effort to smear Kennedy.

"We were trying to counter the positives from that ad," the staffer said. "It was our standard practice to use the University of Alabama Law School to disseminate whisper-campaign information. That was a major device we used for the transmission of this stuff. The students at the law school are from all over the state, and that's one of the ways that Karl got the information out; he knew that the law students would take it back to their hometowns and it would get out."

Kennedy survived his race, although he was terribly bruised in the process. He described himself as "collateral damage," and eventually, he left the court. Although Kennedy and Ann Richards never met, they had lived parallel lives: they were both Democrats and had faced the same virulent whisper campaign in the same year against opponents guided by the same consultant.

There was another similarity, however. Each was part of a larger blueprint for Republican ascendancy. Karl Rove represented most GOP candidates in Alabama's high court races from 1994 through 2000, a period in which the court went from all-Democratic to virtually all-Republican. In Texas, where Democrats had long dominated politics, Rove's reach was broader. By the end of the 1990s, Republicans had won every statewide office from the courts to the governor's office, and Rove was the consultant in every case. Texas became the template for his plans for a national Republican realignment, and in the Richards race, as in the supreme court contests in Alabama, gay baiting was not just the random, marginal noise of the religious Right. Homosexuality was a wedge issue of choice in the Republican machine Rove was building.

Through much of the politics in recent decades, especially in the South, race was most reliably used to divide the electorate. Democrats dominated, but there were two factions within the party. Conservative Democrats and progressive Democrats struggled to find common ground on ideology and policy. In the mid-1950s in Texas, Governor Allan Shivers and the Dixiecrats, the segregationist wing of the Democratic Party, dominated the state's politics. The major thrust of his 1954 campaign was to label his opponent the candidate of minorities, and the best way to discredit a progressive candidate was to label him a "nigger lover." By the 1960s, a familiar billboard along Texas highways, including the desert landscape of Midland, where George W. Bush grew up, pictured Dr. Martin Luther King at a civil-rights meeting under an alarmist headline announcing it was a gathering of the Communist Party.

"The core of it was about race," said Ann Richards. "But the question in my mind is whether race was just the thing used to hold together their troops. If they could scare people about blacks coming into public schools with their children, if they could make people feel uneasy about what blacks might do if they had the rights the liberals on the Left want them to have, then they could control the power. They used race as an organizing and mobilizing tool. And I think we are seeing exactly the same thing today with gays and lesbians, homosexuals."

It was also a weapon, an instrument of intimidation. The subject of homosexuality was so potent in the service of Rove's larger political aims that he used it at will, almost capriciously, to advance his cause. Rove once threatened to smear a journalist whose reporting he did not like. In 1994, the Bush team had been pressing the media to write about supposed wrongdoing in Ann Richards's administration. Rove got telephone records that showed a number of calls from a top official, who happened to be a lesbian, to Anne Marie Kilday, a reporter with the *Dallas Morning News*. Rove complained to Kilday's boss, questioning the reporter's objectivity because she and the official were acquaintances, but Rove got nowhere.

The next morning, Rove called Kilday herself at home. Rove said he does not recall the conversation, but Kilday does. She said Rove told her he had been poring over the telephone records and noted that several calls had been placed at night, to the reporter's home. Kilday is not gay, but it did not seem to matter to Rove. She heard a warning from the other end of the phone.

"You've just got to be careful about your reputation," he said, "and what people might think."

Rove was hardly the first operative to use homosexuality as a tool for both intimidation and political edge. But in the White House political infrastructure he had been building since his days in Texas, the impulse to use gay bashing was not only allowed but expected. In the Bush reelection effort in 2004, Rove went back to the scare tactic of distributing gay-marriage flyers, just as he had in the governor's race against Ann Richards a decade earlier. Two months before Election Day, the mailings began reaching voters in West Virginia and Arkansas, important states in

Rove's 2004 reelection plan. A picture of one man on his knee in front of another, a typical visual cue for a marriage proposal between a male and female, was captioned with the word "Allowed," while a photo of the Bible bore the text "Banned." Readers were informed that both actions would occur if they voted for Democrats. The Republican National Committee later admitted to distributing the controversial leaflets.

The resemblance to the flyer used in Texas a decade earlier to smear Ann Richards was remarkable. In each, the photo of two homosexual men was intended as a warning against the menace of gay rights and an appeal to vote Republican. And the result both in Texas and in the presidential campaign was a Bush victory. The ban-the-Bible mailing in 2004 came from the Republican National Committee, whose director, Ken Mehlman, was handpicked by Rove. There was effectively no difference between the campaign and the committee. They were both part of the larger architecture of the reelection effort, which Rove commanded with a kind of manic energy and attention to detail.

The gay and Bible mail-outs did not happen without Rove's involvement.

"There's not a part of this campaign that Karl didn't touch in some way significantly. And what's remarkable about Karl is, there's no detail too small," said Mark McKinnon, the Bush campaign media director. "I'd get a call from Karl, often from Air Force One, saying, 'The television script is eighty-seven words; it only needs to be eighty-five. And by the way, you don't need that second comma.' And I'd think, Are you kidding me?"

Rove and his protégé Ken Mehlman at the RNC talked constantly, plotting the campaign's various turns. When cable television needed someone to go on the air, sometimes it was McKinnon, sometimes Mehlman. But always, the talking points were Rove's. When the ban-the-Bible flyers blanketed mailboxes in West Virginia and Arkansas, they carried a return address of the RNC, but the message was pure Rove: homosexuality was fair game in the wedge politics of 2004.

Nowhere was that more true than in Ohio. The Buckeye State was a key battleground in 2000 and crucial to victory in 2004. Bush won the state in 2000, beating Al Gore by 160,000 votes, but Ohio was hardly a reliable red state, and Rove knew that if he hoped to capture the state's twenty electoral votes, he had to stimulate the Republicans' culturally conservative base, and that took more than just some flyers in the mailbox. And he found what the president and his party needed in Issue One.

Ohio was one of eleven states with referenda on the ballot to ban gay marriage, even though much of the party hierarchy opposed the amendment. Republican senators Mike DeWine and George Voinovich and Governor Bob Taft considered Issue One too harsh, too sweeping. The state already had a law on the books affirming marriage as between a man and a woman. Officially, the word from Rove and the Bush campaign was that they were keeping their hands off, saying such matters should be left to the state. In fact, Rove actively exploited the issue by sending campaign operatives to Ohio to facilitate turnout and support Issue One.

Secretary of State Kenneth Blackwell, who fueled his ambitions for governor by closely courting the religious Right, took the lead among elected officials supporting passage of Issue One on the November ballot. He became a familiar figure in church pulpits, warning against the onrushing scourge of same-sex marriage and urging the faithful to register and vote. In Blackwell, Rove saw an instrument of his greater design.

"It's a great organizing tool," said University of Akron political science professor John Green. "A lot of these folks would have been targeted anyway, but Issue One just made it easier, because whatever doubts people may have had about George Bush were overcome. The pastors and activists really wanted to turn out the vote to pass it. And they didn't just want to win, they wanted to win big. Even if Karl Rove wasn't directing that huge army, the organization that Rove created at the grass roots in combination with the Ohio Republican Party picked up these people. Issue One in Ohio reinforced the master plan."

Rove and the Bush campaign were involved, though, in spite of their public claims that they were keeping a distance from the issue because it was state politics. Ken Mehlman of the Republican National Committee contacted Blackwell directly to press the case in Ohio.

"All things flow from there," Blackwell told the *Cincinnati Enquirer.*

And Mehlman made it clear that a strong turnout for the gay-marriage ban was important in "determining where Ohio's electoral votes will go," a message the secretary of state sent to supporters in a letter.

"The president's campaign has asked me to help with [Issue One] and I have agreed," he wrote. "I am working closely with state and national leaders to protect and defend the sanctity of marriage. No one is spending more time communicating with the key elements of the GOP base on behalf of the president than I am."

Meanwhile, the RNC also dispatched David Barton, vice-chairman of the Texas Republican Party and a figure well known in evangelical circles, to help organize church congregations in Ohio around opposition to gay marriage. Barton was a lean, youngish-looking Republican ideologue with a penchant for cowboy hats and crisp red, white, and blue shirts in the motif of the Texas flag. He founded WallBuilders, an organization that produces books and tapes debunking the separation of church and state. The group's name was from an Old Testament reference to Israel's rebuilding the walls of Jerusalem, which Barton compares to rebuilding America's moral foundation. The RNC paid Barton to drop directly into churches and preach the message of Issue One.

"I was a paid surrogate for the RNC, but of course, at that point, it's the president's campaign because Karl's got the party," said Barton. "The Bush campaign, obviously, did help. The Republican leadership in Ohio, short of Ken Blackwell, was a hindrance, but Bush was a real help. He was in several states, actually."

As Karl Rove had envisioned, gay marriage became the wedge issue of choice across the country. In South Dakota, Senate Minority Leader Tom Daschle was targeted for defeat in TV spots that portrayed him as supporting gay marriage. In Wisconsin and other states, robo-calls pretending to be from the John Kerry campaign told swing voters, "A vote for Kerry is a vote for gay marriage; it's our time." In Kentucky, incumbent Republican senator Jim Bunning attacked his opponent, a forty-four-year-old bachelor, as "limp-wristed" and a "switch-hitter," forcing the Democrat into the unenviable position of publicly announcing that he was not gay.

Ohio, though, would pay the biggest dividends. Phil Burris of the Cincinnati-based Citizens for Community Values, understood the equation. "Bush would not have won without Ohio, and he would not have won Ohio without Issue One."

The beauty of the issue, from Rove's point of view, was that when Pastor Dallas Billington of the Akron Baptist Temple declared from the pulpit "Vote your Bible!" everybody knew what he meant. Vote Republican. Vote Bush. The same when televangelist Rod Parsley of the World Harvest Church exhorted five hundred "Patriot Pastors" to register voters with the warning that gay marriage represented "the most horrific untested social experiment in human history." And at Columbus Christian Center, the Reverend David Forbes told his largely African American congregation that God favored the party of George W. Bush. One African American pastor in Ohio went so far as to warn his congregation, "Don't you dare vote against God."

In Rove's political arithmetic, division equaled addition. Making gay marriage an issue not only boosted turnout among white evangelicals but also attracted new Hispanic and African American voters who shared the party's cultural views.

Dan Trevas, a spokesman for the Ohio Democratic Party, knew there was a problem a few days before the election when he went to Cincinnati for a Bush rally at the Great American Ball Park. On street corners were young African American men with signs that said, "One Man, One Woman." The gay-marriage message had penetrated the most reliable constituency in the Democratic Party. Trevas knew that most black voters would still support Kerry, but Republicans clearly were making inroads. Exit polls confirmed the Democrats' fears. Nationally, 88 percent of African Americans voted for Kerry, 11 percent for Bush. But in Ohio, where Team Bush beat the drum for the marriage ban, the president got 16 percent of the African American ballots. Latinos, whom the Bush campaign targeted with Spanish-language radio ads emphasizing family values, also voted Republican in greater numbers in 2004. The only two methods for building a sustainable majority for the GOP were to boost the base and expand the field. And Rove was doing both.

He had studied his history.

Richard Nixon's "southern strategy" in the 1960s and the party's appeal to working-class "Reagan Democrats" in the 1980s used racially coded messages. There was, however, no place for that in Karl Rove's "national strategy." Willie Horton, the menacing undertow of the 1988 presidential campaign of the first George Bush, had become a wheezy, slightly discomfiting vestige of the politics of the past. The new maxim was to grow or die. And to do it, Rove needed to exploit the cultural divide. Success required a powerful new wedge issue. And he found it in the debate over gay rights.

To win with gay marriage as a lead issue, though, Karl Rove had to keep a few secrets. He was always good at that. But this time, it was not going to be easy to hide the fact that some of the leadership of the Republican Party was gay. He also had to ignore the fact that there was homosexuality in his immediate family. And it had created a profound effect on his own life.

FOUR

DEVILISH DETAILS

It's the Israelis, Stupid

*When religion and politics travel in the same cart, the riders believe
nothing can stand in their way.*
—Frank Herbert

When the decision had been made for George W. Bush to run for
governor of Texas, a key part of launching the endeavor was to
sit down with the state's political reporters. Karl Rove, who was
already putting a shine on his candidate's public persona in 1993 by taking him around the state to speak with small groups of supporters, was
confident Bush had the charm and rhetorical finesse necessary to handle
the interviews. One by one, reporters from the major daily newspapers
and the big-city television stations filed into Bush's Dallas office to ask the
requisite questions on his background and issues. And things were going
quite well.

Until Bush started talking about religion.

Ken Herman, who was the Austin bureau chief for the *Houston Post* at
the time of the 1993 interview, was trying to cover a number of topics
with Bush in order to give his profile story the appropriate depth and
color. Bush's candidacy had not yet been formalized, but he was interested in communicating with Christian voters, who were emerging as a
profoundly important political force in the United States and especially in
Texas. Bush knew the importance of Christian voters as intimately as did
his strategist Karl Rove. And when his conversation with reporter Ken
Herman turned to religion, Bush volunteered an anecdote about his faith

and a debate he'd once had with his mother over salvation. Herman, who is Jewish, betrayed no reaction to what the future president was saying.

According to Bush, he was talking with his mother about redemption and going to heaven. He was raised Episcopalian but had converted to Methodism after getting married, and the denominational differences sometimes prompted religious discussions in the family. Bush suggested to his mother that the only way for people to gain entrance to heaven was through the personal acceptance of Jesus Christ as their savior. His mother, however, had suggested there might be some exceptions. To resolve their modest dispute, Bush told Herman, his mother called the Reverend Billy Graham for clarification. Nothing Bush heard altered his perspective. Herman wrote, "One doctrine of which Bush is certain is that heaven is open only to those who accept Jesus Christ."

Herman had no idea whether Bush knew he was Jewish, but he did know that he had acquired a significant political story when he was anticipating nothing more than a standard political profile. After its publication, Bush was criticized by the Anti-Defamation League and various Jewish leaders, but he did not publicly step back from what he'd told the newspaper. Although it may have been a misstep to share his Christian convictions with the reporter, there was pure political calculation by Karl Rove in Bush's refusal to address the controversy publicly with the Jewish community. There were 18 million people living in Texas, and only 100,000 of them were Jews. The Muslim population was even more minuscule. Christians comprised the overwhelming portion of the electorate, and Christian fundamentalists had emerged as a significant political force. The last thing Karl Rove wanted was for this emerging constituency to see Bush go wobbly on religion. Nonnegotiable tenets of the religious Right in Texas were a belief in Jesus and opposition to abortion, and that is the spot Rove wanted occupied by Bush. Any backpedaling with Jewish or Muslim or any other non-Christian voters jeopardized the base. And Bush's comments never became a major campaign issue in his run to the governor's mansion in Texas.

Bush's position on Jesus and the Jews was, however, untenable in the long run and presented his political adviser with a troubling conundrum. Karl Rove's plan for winning the White House and asserting overwhelming Republican control of American democracy involved acquiring significant Jewish support. He intended to do that by tilting his candidate and the GOP more toward Israel, thereby attracting both Jewish voters and conservative evangelicals who're convinced that the nation of Israel is vital to the fulfillment of biblical prophecy. But that was no strategy to win Texas in 1994. Rove decided to keep the Christian Right Texans happy by having Bush quietly endure criticisms of the ADL, the American Jewish Congress, and the influential American Israel Public Affairs Committee. The strategy changed years later when Bush set out to win the White House and he needed to strike a different tone with Jewish critics.

Abraham Foxman, who was director of the Anti-Defamation League when Bush made his remarks about accepting Jesus Christ as the only route to heaven, discovered that talking with the Texas governor about Jewish beliefs was unproductive. "We had exchanges a number of years ago, which went nowhere," Foxman told reporter Ken Herman, who had gone to work for the *Austin American-Statesman.*

Only six months before he boarded a chartered 727 in Austin in June of 1999 to begin his first presidential campaign trip, Bush began to clarify his Christian faith. Reporters were informed that in the phone call with Billy Graham, the evangelist had told Bush and his mother that he "generally agreed" with the Bible that the acceptance of Jesus as savior was essential for spiritual entry into heaven. According to Bush, Graham had added, "I want to remind both of you to never play God." The governor said that the lesson he took from that conversation was "Listen to the New Testament but don't be harshly judgmental of others."

In 1998—five years after he had excluded Jews, Muslims, and other non-Christians from eternal bliss—Bush was suddenly, and quite publicly, "troubled if people misinterpreted his comments to indicate anything other than his great respect for people of different faiths." A year earlier, as Rove was quietly crafting the White House run, Abe Foxman of the ADL had returned to Austin, where Bush told him, "Listen, I have this problem." Regardless of the fact that the Jewish community had considered Bush's remarks a "problem" when he first made them in 1993, Bush and Rove did not view them as much of a liability in Texas, and they did not matter politically until the governor's reelection appeared almost certain and the race for the presidency was increasing in probability. Bush had acknowledged his "problem" to Foxman less than a year before he was reelected in 1998, and the ADL leader had responded by telling the governor, "You need to deal with it."

Karl Rove and George Bush began to mitigate Bush's difficulties with the Jewish community as soon as the votes were counted in Texas and the governor had earned his second term in 1998. Although no written statement was issued, Karen Hughes, Bush's spokesperson, was quite willing to explain what the governor really meant to say during his session with reporter Ken Herman.

"As a Christian, he believes that Jesus Christ is his personal savior," Hughes said. "He tells the Billy Graham story to remind people he is very mindful of Reverend Graham's admonition that he should not play God. Judgments about heaven and hell do not belong to the realm of politics or of this world. They belong to a higher authority, and he recognizes that."

Foxman advised Bush to "put this behind him" and "say how he feels," which the governor was quite willing to do, but not publicly. Going public might have the effect of diminishing the enthusiasm the Christian Right had expressed for the Texas governor. Bush acknowledged to Foxman that he "regrets having said it" and "regrets even more the way it was interpreted." Instead of making a public statement, however, Bush wrote a personal letter to Foxman and the ADL in a tactic that generally kept the story out of the newspapers but allowed the message to get directly to Jewish voters. Rove remained worried about Christian voters and did not want the issue of Jews in heaven back in the headlines. In his communication with Foxman and the ADL, Bush said he was "troubled that some people were hurt" by his statement that only people who accept Christ as their savior can get into heaven.

Not all Jewish organizations and leaders were willing to unconditionally accept Bush's apology, but Rove and the governor considered the matter closed and began to make plans to raise the governor's profile on Israel and Jews in preparation for the presidential run. During a Republican governors' conference in New Orleans a few weeks after Bush was reelected as governor of Texas, he invited reporters to his room to inform them he intended to make a trip to Israel. The announcement caught reporters and political analysts by surprise. During most of his adult life, both privately and as governor, Bush had been almost completely incurious about international affairs and as governor had limited his interest to cultivating relations with Mexican leaders who shared concerns over economic issues along the border. Even after Bush's stumble in the interview with Herman, Israel was not a question expected to occupy the governor's attention. Bush had, however, been overwhelmingly reelected in November, and he had a maximum of two years to improve his status with the Jewish community and add to his political portfolio, and that was the purpose of his trip to Israel.

Unfortunately for Karl Rove, Bush goofed up again in another exchange with Ken Herman. As the closed-door session with Texas journalists concluded, Herman lingered and moved toward the elevator with the governor. Outside of their professional exchanges, the reporter and the politician had shared a chummy, fraternity-brother sort of relationship and were comfortable joking with each other and offering irreverent asides on news of the day and political personalities. Herman's wit is unique and relentless and flows with such abundance, he often appears to be channeling comedian Robin Williams, though Herman is often funnier. Both before and after news conferences and other public events, Bush and Herman were frequently seen sharing jokes and laughing, and yet there was never any indication in Herman's journalism that this level of friendliness might have compromised his objectivity.

As the doors to the hotel elevator opened and the governor stared out the window at the New Orleans Superdome, he smiled at Herman and offered a joke at his own expense. "You know what I'm gonna tell those Jews when I get to Israel, don't you, Herman?" Bush asked.

"No, what?"

"I'm tellin' 'em they're all going to hell."

Herman laughed. Bush had always shown good judgment when using his sense of humor and was very adept at self-deprecating jokes. Clearly, this was one of them. Nonetheless, Ken Herman was a journalist, and his job was to report public statements by the governor of Texas. Bush's wiseacre comment was not off the record, but it was made in an unguarded moment, which often reflects a truer indication of an individual's beliefs. Herman knew, though, that Bush was simply cracking wise. Just as certainly, he understood he had an ethical question to confront.

"You know what he just said to me?" Herman quickly approached another journalist in the governor's entourage. "You're not gonna believe this."

"No. What is it?"

"He was joking," Herman quickly explained. "But he said he was going to tell the Jews in Israel that they were all going to hell."

"Well, you can't write that. You know he was just kidding."

"I don't know what to do," Herman conceded.

Herman did not immediately write about Bush's joke. Before publication, he and his editors debated how to handle the situation, and when he finally used Bush's comment in the piece he filed for the *Austin American-Statesman*, the quote was buried deep in a larger story about the Israel trip and the governors' conference. Before too long, he was contacted by Bush's communications director, Karen Hughes, who, more than anything, conveyed to Herman the governor's personal disappointment. A private moment had been made public.

"So, what, am I in trouble here?" Herman asked lightheartedly.

"No, but maybe you should stop over to the mansion for a visit."

When Herman arrived, Governor Bush had just returned from a run. He was not angry with the reporter, just a bit confused. He had obviously defined the boundaries of their relationship slightly differently than had Herman.

"You know, I could have kept you from writing that, Herman," Bush said.

"How's that?"

"I could have just not said it."

"I understand."

Bush was telling Herman, in a political fashion, that the nature of their relationship, both professional and personal, had changed with the publication of his remark. The governor was under the mistaken impression that he could comfortably share off-color jokes with certain members of the Texas capitol press corps.

The story had also again complicated Bush's emerging connections to the Jewish community, which he was going to need for a presidential campaign. Herman had contacted Abe Foxman of the Anti-Defamation League, who was traveling in Saudi Arabia, and had asked him for a comment on Bush's joke. Foxman was, not surprisingly, bothered by the clunky humor, which had occurred not that long after his having received the apologetic letter from Bush explaining his 1993 analysis of who does or does not get into heaven.

"Religion is serious," Foxman told Herman's newspaper. "This is a religious country. People take their beliefs seriously. Comedians can joke about it. I think serious people, people in leadership positions, people who set a role model for behavior and values cannot. That's something not to joke about."

Karl Rove again had to set about fixing more fences, which had been knocked down by Bush's political ineptitude. The trip to Israel, two years before kicking off the presidential run, was designed to soften criticism that the Texas governor was too close to the Christian Right and neither understood nor cared about the Jewish electorate. Even the most cynical of Rove and Bush's critics, however, doubt that the then gubernatorial candidate's original comments to reporter Ken Herman were intended to motivate the Texas Christian Right. Nonetheless, that was the result, and Bush made no significant overt public moves to retract his assertions about heaven's being the exclusive province of Christians.

Rove's influence, though, is visible in the time line for soothing the political wound with the Jewish community and the measured manner in which communications were handled. After the original 1993 faux pas, there was virtually no public discourse on the matter, and discussions with Jewish leaders were private. Rove did not have Bush reach out and offer a serious apologia until reelection as governor appeared inevitable and a presidential race a logical consequence of that vote.

In Israel, Bush was photographed at the Western Wall in Jerusalem's Old City, one of the holiest sites in all of Judaism. The governor wore a traditional Jewish yarmulke. Joined by three other Republican governors, Bush took a helicopter tour over the West Bank, which was led by Ariel Sharon, the Israeli foreign minister who later became prime minister. Bush had intended to visit a Jewish settlement on the West Bank, but those plans were "abruptly cancelled," a display of restraint that kept Bush from being accused of prompting any backlash that might have occurred from Palestinians. Regardless, Bush maintained a high profile during his time in Israel, visiting the Holocaust Museum and laying a wreath at the grave of the late Israeli prime minister Yitzhak Rabin. Journalists and political analysts in the United States and Israel viewed Bush's visit as the first stop on his unannounced campaign for president, in spite of the Texas governor's protestations and insistence that he hadn't yet made up his mind.

Upon Bush's return from Israel, the Texas governor wrote another letter to Foxman at the Anti-Defamation League backing away from his 1993 statement that only Christians can go to heaven. "I regret the concern caused by my statement and reassure you and the Jewish community that you have my deepest respect," Bush wrote. Foxman quickly responded in a helpful fashion. "The matter of his 1993 statement is now behind us," he told reporters.

The Israeli photo ops were necessary to undo Bush's rhetorical stumbles and to continue closing the daunting political divide between Jews and Christians. Karl Rove, who'd been dreaming of a George W. Bush presidential candidacy for years, had already been hard at work on this challenge with his friend Ralph Reed. Bush's comment about Jews turned out to be a strategically positive mistake because it had increased turnout of Christian fundamentalist voters in Texas.

Rove had to fashion an improbable coalition of Jews and Christians, if he were to cause long-term damage to the Democratic Party and get Bush elected president in 2000. That was not an easy task, however, when Christians such as Bailey Smith, one of the founders of Robertson's Christian Coalition, were making denigrating remarks about Jews. During a religious roundtable in Dallas, Smith had once told fifteen thousand people in attendance that "God Almighty does not hear the prayer of a Jew."

The Christian Coalition—in part, because of Robertson's 1991 *New York Times* bestseller *The New World Order*—was frequently accused of anti-Semitism. Robertson's book was distributed to every member of the Christian Coalition and exhibited unabashedly anti-Semitic and anti-Muslim themes. Only seventeen pages into his narrative, Robertson quoted Pat Buchanan, who accused Jewish and German intellectuals of conspiring to create communism. As disturbing as the charges were in Robertson's writing, they were consistent with the statements he'd been making on his television program *The 700 Club* for many years. In his interpreting the U.S. Constitution as a Christian document, Robertson implied that the people who didn't agree with him were a danger to America because they didn't understand what the founders had intended.

"[But] the minute you turn the document into the hands of non-Christian and atheistic people," he said during a 1981 broadcast, "they can use it to destroy the very foundation of our society."

Robertson's Christian Broadcasting Network, a surprisingly effective presidential campaign in 1988, and then a bestselling book gave him an inevitable cultural impact. The Anti-Defamation League decided to take a close look at messages Robertson was sending to American religious constituencies. Just as candidate George W. Bush as governor was making his intemperate remarks about Jews and heaven, ADL executive director Abe Foxman had already commissioned David Cantor to conduct an extensive examination of Robertson's rhetoric and the messaging in

The New World Order. Cantor ultimately published a book-length report entitled *The Religious Right and the Assault on Tolerance and Pluralism in America.* According to Cantor, "Robertson's repeated references to America as a 'Christian nation' and to American governance as a 'Christian order' insults not merely Jews but all who value religious freedom."

Critics on the Christian Right accused the Anti-Defamation League of defamation for the findings in Cantor's writings. Writing in the *Washington Times,* Patrick Buchanan characterized the ADL's report as a "bellicose barrage of Christian bashing" and said that Cantor was wrongly equating Christianity with bigotry. Buchanan also said that Jewish voters were guilty of hypocrisy, and he quoted a fund-raising letter from the American Jewish Congress, which "describes the rise of the Christian Right in scare terms once used to alert us of the presence of communists."

The text of the AJC letter referred to by Buchanan said, "In my neighborhood and yours, the Christian Coalition is hard at work building a machine to 'Christianize' America. . . . [I]f we permit them to set the political agenda . . . you and I could be in for some nasty surprises." According to the columnist-candidate-broadcaster, a friend of his received the mailing and wrote Buchanan that "if a Christian group were to send out an equivalent letter designed to arouse and rally Christians to combat the sinister program of Jewish political activists, it would be loudly denounced as shameful 'hate literature.' Apologies would be demanded and heads would roll."

Mainstream writers also vilified the report by Cantor. Don Feder, a columnist for the *Boston Herald,* considered the 193-page document to be an attempted "political assassination," and he argued that "instead of debating the issues like a gentleman, it stoops to implications of anti-Semitism to discredit a legitimate voice in the values debate." Some Jewish groups also took exception to Cantor's findings. The Jewish Action Alliance portrayed the ADL's research and conclusions as "a plainly partisan smear campaign against traditional Christians who energetically and quite legitimately advocate what they believe are important moral and social values."

This kind of distance between Jews and Christians was a problem for Karl Rove. Crucial to the success of his effort to build an enduring Republican political machine was the ability to manage the support of Christian conservatives while making entreaties to the Jewish vote. Marrying conservative Christians and Jews in a political alliance was a critical element in Rove's long-range planning. And key to that alliance was a mutual interest in the security of Israel. For Christian evangelicals, the establishment of the state of Israel in 1948 was hugely significant, since it was viewed as a manifestation of biblical prophesies. The relationship between American evangelicals and Israel deepened considerably with the success of popular broadcast ministries that preached an "end-times" theology and prompted conservative Protestant leaders to take a newfound interest in Middle East politics.

If, however, their interest in the establishment of a secure Israel was the same, their belief in the eventual outcome was not. For Christian evangelicals through much of the twentieth century, the guiding principle was premillennialism, the belief that reforming the world was impossible until Christ returned in the Second Coming. Although the details differ among evangelical groups, the essential story line is that Jesus' return will inaugurate a one thousand–year rule on earth and that all the saved Christians, both dead and alive, will be swept up into the clouds with Christ prior to, during, or after (depending on the school of theology) in an event known as the Rapture. Both Jews and Christian evangelicals saw the creation of Israel as an essential moment in the divine narrative, but each anticipated a different end. One side predicted the restoration of Jewish influence and power on earth, and the other anticipated the end of the world.

Max Blumenthal, an author and a researcher who has closely studied both the interrelationships and the conflicts between Judaism and Christianity, has become convinced that evangelical Christians are determined to create the dominion necessary for Christ's return, and they are helping to elect leaders who will, in turn, assist them with implementing the Bible's plan. All Karl Rove wants to do is win elections.

"I think what we are seeing is a subculture that is producing America's political hierarchy," he said. "And it is coming out of the Dominionist Right. And they believe that America is a Christian nation and everybody else is going to have to step aside and be silent, and if they try and speak up for themselves, then they are persecuting Christians."

As Rove was asserting his control over the Texas GOP in the 1990s, Reed was busily laying the foundation for just such an alliance. Shortly after George W. Bush took office as Texas governor, Reed appeared before a national meeting of the Anti-Defamation League. Reed's employer, Pat Robertson, had been widely quoted as describing America as a "Christian nation" and frequently blamed problems in the United States on non-Christians in government. Rove and Reed understood that a more nuanced approach was necessary if Jewish voters were truly to be brought under the Republican tent. Jewish voters accounted for only about 2 percent of the U.S. population but were an important source of campaign money to Democrats—funds Rove envisioned diverting to the GOP. There was time to deal with Bush's Jewish problem after he'd solidified his political base in Texas, but in the interim, Reed's overture to national Jewish groups was an important political maneuver for the longer term.

In a speech entitled "From Confrontation to Cooperation," Reed acknowledged that many religious conservatives have been "insensitive and have lacked a full understanding of the horrors experienced by the Jewish people." A few minutes into his address to the ADL, Reed very carefully cast Christians in the same oppressed category as Jews and then very explicitly said, "Let me be clear: the Christian Coalition believes in a nation that is not officially Christian, Jewish, or Muslim. A nation where the separation of church and state is inviolable." He reminded his Jewish audience of the words of William O. Douglas, that America was made up of a "religious people whose system of government presupposes a Supreme Being," but sought to cast the fight in mutual terms as a fight that "requires all the hands it can find." This common struggle Reed characterized as an effort to maintain the influence of morality and religion on government.

Reed's speech was broadcast on C-Span rather than a major network news program. Nonetheless, it marked a signal moment in the evolution of the evangelical Christian movement and the nascent political ascension of George W. Bush to national office.

"It was an extraordinary moment," said author and researcher Frederick Clarkson, who's studied the Christian Right for many years. "The media was asleep on that one. A détente was struck. And you can't really overstate its importance."

A few years later, Karl Rove had his candidate make a similar overture to the national Jewish community. His challenge was to motivate the Christian Right without alienating the Jews, no simple task. But it was critical to the future of the Republican Party and the presidential aspirations of George W. Bush. Rove was engaged in refining and launching the most effective political and religious movement in modern American politics, and if he got it right, Republicans had a chance to run the country for decades.

When the first goal of that vision had been accomplished and George W. Bush took office as president, he was already unabashedly pro-Israel and only marginally concerned about the Palestinian and Arab perspective on the Middle East. Prior to 9/11, Karl Rove had kept the president at a measured distance from the intractable conflict between Palestinians and Israelis. After a fractious campaign in which he was awarded the White House in a U.S. Supreme Court ruling, Bush needed to comfort the electorate and not generate further unease with geopolitical moves. He was, however, decidedly more comfortable with Israel's issues and politics than he was with those of Arab interests across the Middle East. Bush knew the role Jewish money had played in getting him elected, and as a result of Rove's ministrations and relationships with Jewish political leaders in the United States, he'd also grown to see Israel's destiny as inevitably connected to America's. His Bible, he believed, also told him as much. The attacks of 9/11 seemed to confirm for Bush that he'd chosen the right side in an ancient conflict.

The president was, in fact, so certain of his policies regarding Israel that he was able to joke about a crisis that has never had a sufficient political solution to end the dying of Jews and Palestinian Arabs. During his initial meeting with Israeli prime minister Ariel Sharon, the president clarified whose side he was on during the first five minutes of their conversation.

Sharon had come to the White House to speak with the new president about Israel's challenges. As they sat in the Oval Office, Sharon already knew from the campaign that Bush was probably a stronger friend of Israel than any modern-era U.S. president. While they talked, the subject quickly turned to Yasser Arafat, the leader of the Palestine Liberation Organization. One of the first questions President Bush asked the Israeli prime minister was astonishing.

"Are you going to kill him?" The president gave the Israeli leader a level stare indicating the question was intended to be serious.

Ariel Sharon was unquestionably surprised. The leader of the free world, a man whose election had spread discontent across his own country and uncertainty around the globe, was suddenly suggesting a dramatic move that promised a dangerous political outcome.

"Mr. President?" Sharon said, pausing, uncertain he had heard the question correctly. "We're ready—"

Bush did not let Sharon complete his thought.

"No, you can't do that," the president interjected. "If you do, you make an enemy of the United States, immediately, for the rest of your life. I'm telling you, you can't do that."

Sharon waited, uncertain how to respond to a president who'd just suggested an idea rarely spoken aloud in Israel.

"No," Bush continued. "If he needs killing, I'll do it."

The wisecracking fraternity boy was now president of the United States of America. His intemperate remarks about the leader of the PLO, however, offered a glimpse of something beyond Bush's discomforting sense of humor. A president who'd famously bragged that he didn't read newspapers or deeply study policy had surrounded himself with advisers whose interest in Israel's sovereignty and safety might have outweighed their concern for the United States. The president and the vice president took daily briefings, analysis, and advice from senior staffers and think-tank analysts whose perspective had long been influenced by assumptions about Israel's importance. Many of these administration counselors had been involved in the Project for the New American Century (PNAC), a proposal drafted by neoconservatives who'd been arguing for more than a decade for a U.S. military presence in the Middle East and an invasion of Iraq. The White House sought little input from those articulating the Arab point of view. The vice president's office acquired even less.

The default position for all of President Bush's Middle East decisions was always to favor Israel. This was what Karl Rove had planned. He wanted the president to be aggressively pro-Israel to prompt money and votes to flow from American Jewish voters and to show his solidarity with the beliefs of the Christian Right. This fit nicely with the broader policies outlined by the PNAC to project American force into the Mideast with the unspoken goal of protecting Israel while also promoting democracies in the Arab world. It was a dangerous, provocative approach to shoring up domestic political support for the president.

And it was to lead to a crisis that threatened the very existence of the Bush administration.

FIVE

NOT AS I SAY

Gay in the GOP

Hypocrisy: prejudice with a halo.
—Ambrose Bierce

K arl Rove began working with Ken Mehlman in 1997 while Mehlman was chief of staff for Kay Granger, a Republican congresswoman from Texas. Rove, whose reputation had already been firmly established in Texas, was acting as the congresswoman's political consultant. Mehlman might have become friends and initially connected with Rove by telling stories of knocking on doors for Ronald Reagan in Baltimore County, Maryland, during the 1980 campaign. Regardless, they grew close as political associates, with Rove playing the role of mentor.

Mehlman's political career has been in ascension from the time he met Rove. A graduate of Harvard Law School, Mehlman went from running the office of an inconsequential member of Congress from Fort Worth in 1999 to national field director of the Bush for president campaign in 2000. Subsequently, he was named White House political director before taking over the 2004 Bush campaign as manager and eventually ending up with the chairmanship of the Republican National Committee. Mehlman's allies and adversaries describe him as focused and capable, but he would not be running the RNC without Rove's tutelage. Ken Mehlman's career is another creation of Karl Rove.

In the 2004 presidential election, Mehlman played the senior role in promoting anti–gay marriage amendments in eleven states. In Ohio,

Mehlman worked closely with Ohio secretary of state Kenneth Blackwell on passage of Issue One. Gays in Ohio, and the ten other states where pro-marriage referenda were on the ballot, considered the terms *values* and *pro-marriage* code for antihomosexual.

"I think the best way of phrasing it is they have decided to use sex as a weapon in the family values war," said John Aravosis, a gay political consultant and lawyer in Georgetown. "When Bush made his announcement [that] he was going to push for the marriage amendment, something snapped in the gay community. Watching the president in the White House talking about this was unbelievable. And I got involved by saying that if you want to live by the family values issue, we can also make you die by them."

Aravosis had run successful Internet publicity campaigns in the past to protect the rights of a gay U.S. serviceman and to maintain awareness of issues in the Matthew Shepard murder case. When radio doctor Laura Schlessinger said that gays were "biological errors" and were "sexually predatory on young boys," Aravosis used a website and e-mail to lead a successful advertiser boycott of her newly syndicated television program, which was eventually canceled because of the controversies. Those experiences led John Aravosis to begin asking questions about Ken Mehlman.

To Aravosis's ear, the new chair of the RNC had remained suspiciously quiet on gay-rights issues and rarely went beyond the bounds of repeating that "the president believes a marriage is between a man and a woman, and there are appropriate structures in place for legal arrangements between gay couples." Mehlman was thirty-eight in the heat of the presidential campaign, unmarried, and in speeches around the country, he insisted the federal marriage amendment and the state proposals were neither divisive nor antigay. Regardless of whether he was straight or gay, Mehlman's rhetoric was animating gay activists with the same powerful effect that the marriage amendment was having on the Christian Right.

"We don't know if the chairman of the Republican National Committee is gay or straight," said Aravosis. "I mean, he's reached the peak of his profession and has all this power and influence. Why wouldn't he just denounce all these people who suggest he is a hypocritical gay man promoting antigay measures? He has to be the most unique case of heterosexual I've ever met. He's a closeted heterosexual."

Under the unwritten rules of engagement, mainstream journalism generally ignores a politician's private life unless that private life interferes with official duties or conflicts with public action. A philanderer who wraps himself at election time in the flag of moral values or a reformer who cheats his employees in private business is fair game. The same consideration applies to a private homosexual who publicly presses an antigay agenda, a standard known as the Barney Frank rule, which was named for the gay congressman who promised not to confront homosexual public servants unless their policies were harming other gays and lesbians.

Hypocrisy reflects character, obviously, and character is something voters have a right to know. To the mainstream media, though, the rules are clear. Just refusing to say you are not gay does not mean you are. But in the blogosphere and among various gay and lesbian political interest groups, Mehlman's reluctance to publicly say he was heterosexual was enough to catch the attention of gay-rights advocates. On his website, Americablog, John Aravosis said it only made sense that the RNC chairman would want to dispense with the question in order to reassure the GOP's most ardent constituencies. Mike Rogers, a gay activist who'd launched his own site, named Blogactive, aggressively pursued information about Mehlman's sexual orientation.

"You just don't get to act the way he is acting," said Rogers. "He's working for a party that is full of homophobes, and they are pushing laws that harm and oppress gay people. And if he is gay, which I am confident he is, he's one of the biggest hypocrites I have ever seen. He's just opened himself up to all of this by promoting this hateful garbage of President Bush."

If speculation about Mehlman did not meet the standards of the mainstream media, gay-rights blogs and liberal radio were under no such constraint. Their obsession with the matter became a kind of cultural phenomenon. Shortly after Mehlman was named as chairman of the RNC by President Bush, an Air America radio host asserted that Mehlman was gay. "We're a big tent," said Randi Rhodes. "And apparently it's gonna be fabulously decorated 'cause Ken Mehlman is the head of the Republican National Committee. And he's gay." A fiery radio personality, Rhodes punctured her bristling critique of the GOP's use of wedge issues with the cry "Gay! Gay!"

Fair or not, the issue began making its way around the Web. Rogers posted the assertion on his website. Another radio broadcaster and columnist, Michelangelo Signorile, argued that questions about Mehlman's sexual orientation were fair because the GOP itself typecast people in what Bush strategist Matthew Dowd called the "voter matrix" for distinguishing Republican from Democratic supporters.

A few weeks after President Bush had won reelection, Mehlman told a group of GOP governors in a speech that "if you drive a Volvo and you do yoga, you are pretty much a Democrat. If you drive a Lincoln or a BMW and you own a gun, you're voting for George W. Bush." Signorile, a talk show host on the Sirius radio network, was put off by such external typecasting. He inveighed against Mehlman's effort to create what the RNC chairman called the "exact kind of consumer model that corporate America does every day to predict how people vote—not based on where they live but how they live."

"Since he's so confident labeling people based on outward characteristics," Signorile wrote in the *New York Press*, "Mehlman must understand why his being a 38-year-old 'bachelor' who refuses to answer questions about his sexual orientation is a tip-off to many that he's a pathetic closet case, and a pretty vile one at that, having used antigay hatred—aka 'moral values'—to help elect Bush."

John Aravosis and Mike Rogers used their blogs to foment criticism of Mehlman's refusal to acknowledge his sexual orientation. In response, the White House began a quiet initiative to head off the rumors. Rogers said he got a phone call from a deputy White House press spokesman who told him off the record that Mehlman was straight. Rogers said he was baffled by the fact that the Bush administration official refused to say anything for attribution. According to Aravosis and Rogers, mainstream reporters were being told that Mehlman was not gay, but on "background only." The GOP found itself in exactly the predicament in which Rove and his political allies had long put Democratic opponents in the past: they were forced to announce publicly they were not gay or to remain silent and be ravaged in the rumor mill. Damned if they did, damaged if they didn't.

Regardless of efforts by the White House, the noise from the Internet played against the escalating public debate over gay marriage. When Mehlman appeared on NBC's *Meet the Press*, host Tim Russert asked whether the president was going to continue his pursuit of a constitutional ban on same-sex marriage. The RNC chairman delivered his standard boilerplate about Bush's believing that marriage is between a man and a woman. Asked by the interviewer if he thought homosexuality was a choice, Mehlman told Russert he did not know the answer to that question. The discussion briefly centered on the use of gay marriage as a wedge issue, and Mehlman denied that the Defense of Marriage Amendment was about oppressing gays. He insisted that the gay GOP organization Log Cabin Republicans was wrong to make that claim.

Russert said, "But the Log Cabin Republicans will say if you're born gay, it's a biological determination, not a matter of choice."

"And that's—that may be," Mehlman countered. "But the fact is, that's irrelevant to the question of the public definition of marriage. They're two totally different issues."

While Russert had, for the most part, limited his discussion to policy, Rogers's approach was more personal, earning him the attention of *GQ* magazine and an article that referred to the Mehlman controversy. In the profile, Rogers said that if Ken Mehlman, as campaign manager for President Bush, "is going to use my private life to elect a president, I have every right to ask about his private life. What I'm amazed at is that Ken Mehlman won't say he's straight."

The publication of the *GQ* story was the first time the White House offered any type of official response about Mehlman. Steve Schmidt, an aide to Vice President Dick Cheney and "friend of Ken Mehlman," was quoted by author Jake Tapper as saying, "Ken Mehlman is not gay."

"What Mike Rogers is doing to people is despicable," Schmidt added. "And Ken understands that his answering that question at the insistence of Mike Rogers legitimizes the question and compels every 22-year-old staff assistant on Capitol Hill to answer the question should Mike Rogers turn his sights on them."

Rogers had been unsuccessful getting Schmidt to go on the record prior to the president's reelection, so he called Mehlman directly and was surprised when Mehlman answered his own phone. Rogers said he identified himself and described the story he was writing. Mehlman refused to answer questions and hung up.

Rogers's aggressive effort underscored a deep division within the gay community over the practice of "outing" public figures. Although many activists saw no problem targeting public figures or their aides who work against gay rights and condemn homosexuality, others questioned whether the practice was counterproductive or even fair. Within the newsroom of the *Washington Blade*, owned by the nation's largest chain of gay newspapers, an editorial war broke out over whether to run a story outing Ken Mehlman during the reelection campaign. Ultimately, chief editor Chris Crain decided not to publish the report. A number of staffers, quoted anonymously by Raw Story, claimed the Mehlman piece never went to print because the RNC chair had been a good friend of Crain's during their years together at Harvard Law School. Crain had been the editor of the *Harvard Journal of Law and Public Policy*, and Ken Mehlman had worked for him on the publication. When Mehlman was named to lead the RNC, Crain wrote in the *Blade* that it gave him "mixed emotions" but that he had "no personal knowledge" about Mehlman's sexual orientation. Nonetheless, he added, Mehlman "has ridden to success on the coattails of a candidate who betrayed the core principles that we both stood for as young political activists."

According to unnamed reporters at the *Blade* who were quoted by Raw Story, Chris Crain told them that he had verified that Ken Mehlman was gay but he would not provide his sources to other reporters at his newspaper. "Chris would confirm it," one of them said. "But he wouldn't give out any names." Crain denied that he was hiding anything but said that the story did not meet the standard he set in terms of editorial policy. "I don't think you can report someone is gay—unless someone says it to you," he explained.

Mike Rogers had a considerably different standard. "It's not the gay thing that's the problem; it's the hypocrisy," he said. When public officials are overly vocal about gay issues, Rogers says he sets out to see whether their behavior comports with their rhetoric. Often, it does not, which was the case with a conservative Republican from Virginia.

Congressman Ed Schrock, a navy veteran of the Vietnam War, had served Virginia's conservative Second District for two terms. His constituency included Virginia Beach, the home of Regent University, founded by Pat Robertson, who had also been the creative force behind the Christian Coalition. Schrock was expected to articulate conservative and Christian ideals and was one of the original twelve cosponsors of the Federal Marriage Amendment (also known as the Marriage Protection Act), which was more restrictive than the state versions of the Defense of Marriage Act because it was designed to legally eliminate homosexual marriages. For his work in Washington, the Christian Coalition had given Schrock a 92 percent voting record, and various pro-life organizations rated his performance at 100 percent. The *National Journal* ranked Schrock as the second most conservative member of Congress, behind only Speaker Dennis Hastert. The Human Rights Campaign gave him a zero.

Shortly after being elected, Schrock undertook a personal project to repeal the Clinton administration's policy on gays in the military, known as "Don't ask. Don't tell." Politically, he was making a gesture toward the 300,000 military men and women in the nine bases located in his district. The congressman, who had spent twenty-four years in the U.S. military and retired as an officer, told the *Virginia-Pilot* newspaper that servicemen ought not to have to work and live with homosexuals.

"You're in the showers with them, you're in the bunk room with them, and you're in staterooms with them. You just hope no harm would come by folks who are of that persuasion. It's a discipline thing."

A number of gay publications had already accused Schrock of running his own outing campaign against other members of Congress. U.S. senator Barbara Mikulski of Maryland reportedly announced her opposition to the Federal Marriage Amendment after Schrock made insinuations about her sexuality. Schrock was accused by the *Washington Blade* of repeatedly calling the offices and cell phone numbers of members of Congress who he thought were gay and demanding that they answer his charges of hypocrisy for supporting antigay legislation.

Mike Rogers was watching.

Ed Schrock seemed "a little too aggressive" to Rogers, who believed the congressman's bluster was a cover for something going on in his personal life. Through his website, Blogactive, and his contacts in Washington, the gay activist sent out word that he was interested in any information about Schrock's own sexual habits. Rogers was provided with audio recordings from a free online dating service for gay and straight people called MegaMates. Congressman Schrock, or someone who sounded distinctly like Schrock, left several messages on the site hoping to have a strictly sexual rendezvous with a particular type of man.

"Uh, hi, I weigh 200 pounds, I'm 6'4" [inaudible] blond hair . . . very muscular, very buffed up, uh, very tanned, uh, I just like to get together with a guy from time to time, just to, just to play. I'd like him to be in very good shape, flat stomach, good chest, good arms, well hung, cut, uh, just get naked, play, and see what happens, nothing real heavy duty, but just, fun time, go down on him, he can go down on me, and just take it from there . . . hope to hear from you. Bye."

Rogers posted links to the audio recordings on Blogactive, and the story was eventually picked up by some mainstream journalists. Although the text of what Schrock had said in a half dozen calls to the dating service was not printed in traditional publications, the political pressure was too great for Congressman Ed Schrock to continue to serve. He resigned, saying the allegations made it impossible for him to concentrate on the issues "facing the nation and our region."

John Aravosis, who'd used his Americablog website to help disseminate Rogers's findings about Schrock, said the Schrock episode points up the internal conflict of public officials who find their private lives incompatible with their political agenda and, indeed, their very political survival.

"Schrock is the archetypal story of what we are trying to figure out," Aravosis explained. "He's in the military more than twenty years, married, has a kid, and he's involved in gay sex on the side. But he's busy gay bashing. Then he calls phone sex lines? The thing he asks for on the line? He wants the perfect guy. A group of us were listening to those tapes. I could only wish to meet the kind of guy he was describing. He wants perfection, and that's what's so sad."

For many homosexuals, coming out is a difficult decision. For politicians who depend on conservative values voters for election, it is impossible. Openly gay members of the Republican Party believe that using sexual orientation as a wedge issue will fade in future presidential campaigns. Patrick Guerriero of the Log Cabin Republicans is confident gay questions will die off as social attitudes change and more closeted Republicans go public. Until they do, however, gay Republicans will contribute to the success of Karl Rove and Ken Mehlman's use of sexual orientation as an effective political weapon.

"I think, at this point, gay and lesbian Americans and their families are feeling a little bit under siege," Guerriero said. "And I don't know how much longer there's going to be a stomach for so many gay Republicans in so many prominent positions being part of a party that chooses to go any further than it already has. I actually think this issue is going to turn around fairly fast, but it's probably going to take one more presidential cycle to get through."

Meanwhile, Mike Rogers and John Aravosis say they will continue pursuing people they believe are closeted gay Republicans. And Matt Drudge, who has one of the most popular news sites on the Internet, is one of their primary targets. Drudge's notoriety as a cybersnoop grew to national proportions when he was the first person to write the Monica

Lewinsky blue dress story. With millions of visitors daily to his Drudge Report, he has acquired an enormous influence on political thinking for conservatives. The stories he posts are carefully selected to further culti-vate GOP ideology and often include reports that advance the use of gay marriage as a wedge issue, a political strategy that Karl Rove has used un-abashedly to facilitate the implementation of his larger Republican politi-cal plans.

Drudge's website is a critical element of the right-wing infrastructure Rove and his operatives use so effectively to harm their opponents. When ABC News correspondent Jeffrey Kofman broadcast a report from Iraq on plummeting morale among American soldiers, he found his sexual orientation making headlines on the Drudge Report. Kofman's broadcast story caused the White House headaches when one of the soldiers said on live network television from Iraq that "if [Secretary of Defense Donald] Rumsfeld was here I'd ask for his resignation." Other soldiers interviewed by Kofman also accused President Bush of sending them into a hopeless situation. The headline on the Drudge Report announced, "ABC News Reporter Who Filed Troops Complaint Story—Openly Gay Canadian." Visitors to Drudge's website were provided a link to *The Advocate,* a gay and lesbian magazine that had published a profile of Kofman in which he described how he thought it was important to live openly as a gay man and try to be a role model.

Asked about it, Drudge said he did not know about the ABC story until "someone from the White House communications shop tipped me to it" along with the profile in the gay magazine. Although the term *gay* was removed from the Drudge Report text after only eight minutes on the site, the message was sent. Rove is hardly the first operative to use homosexuality as a political tool. But in the White House he built, the impulse to use it was not only allowed but expected.

Drudge has frequently headlined stories using homophobia to moti-vate the Right. During the 2004 presidential campaign, Drudge ran a se-ries of photos of Democrats John Kerry and John Edwards, claiming, "Hugs, kisses to the cheek, affectionate touching of the face, caressing of the back, grabbing of the arm, fingers to the neck, rubbing of the knees. John Kerry and John Edwards can't keep their hands off each other! In the past 48 hours, 'candidate handling' has become the top buzz on the trail."

Drudge's editorial cant might have been dismissed as standard liberal bashing were it not for the fact that he has found himself snagged in the superheated journalistic environment he helped create. In two separate books, Drudge had been identified as gay by authors claiming to have incontrovertible proof. The first was Jeanette Walls, who included the allegation in her book *Dish: How Gossip Became the News and the News Became Just Another Show* (Harper Paperbacks, 2000). David Brock's *Blinded by the Right: The Conscience of an Ex-Conservative* (Crown, 2002), however, had to be the most disturbing to Drudge, who depends on conservatives' supporting his website. Brock published an e-mail Drudge had sent him that indicated the GOP Web gossiper found the author to be attractive.

"Drudge picked me up at a friend's house in the Hollywood Hills in his red Geo Metro," Brock wrote, "arriving with an impressive bouquet of yellow roses. Jesus, I thought, Drudge thinks we're going on a date. After dinner at the famed West Hollywood restaurant Dan Tana's, he suggested we go bar hopping along the gay strip on Santa Monica Boulevard, which Drudge navigated like a pro. . . . (Six months hence, I received the following e-mail message from Drudge, under the subject heading 'XXX.' Drudge wrote: 'Laura [Ingraham] spreading stuff about you and me being fuck buddies. I should only be so lucky.')"

Drudge insists he is not gay but was clearly uncomfortable talking about the issue during an appearance on the Alan Colmes radio show when confronted by fellow guest Mike Rogers.

"What does Drudge do when he is not plugged into cyberspace?" he was asked.

"That's a very good question and I am not going to discuss it."

Rogers, unlike mainstream reporters who have steered clear of the question, saw a contradiction in Drudge's public politics and his personal behavior. "Hold on, Matt, you're always exposing the private lives of public figures. You can't go all coy now."

"I'm not very social," Drudge answered. "I live on an island in Miami, Florida, and I do my own shopping and pay my taxes. And I'm not mean."

"So, are you a gay, right-wing Republican?" Rogers asked.

"No, I'm not gay. I was nearly married a few years ago. And no I'm not a right-wing Republican. I'm a conservative and want to pay less taxes. And I did vote Republican at the last election. But I'm more of a populist."

Drudge is not the only high-profile person working within the conservative infrastructure who's endured allegations he's a homosexual harming other homosexuals. Shepherd Smith, FOX network news television anchor, was attacked for his hypocrisy in an editorial by Kevin Naff, managing editor of the *Washington Blade* gay newspaper. *FOX News* is generally viewed by gays and lesbians as facilitating the homophobia that leads to oppressive antigay legislation, and Smith is one of the network's most widely recognized faces.

According to Naff, he had a personal experience with Shepherd Smith. "Smith once chatted me up in a New York City gay piano bar, bought me drinks, and invited me back to his place. When I declined, he asked me to dinner the next night, another invitation I politely refused. We sat at the bar chatting and drinking martinis until 3 a.m., our conversation interrupted only when he paused to belt out the lyrics to whatever show tune was being performed."

To the insiders, operatives, and journalists who occupy the cloistered precincts of Washington politics, it's well known that some Republican operatives involved in promoting the party's conservative, antigay policies are themselves gay, both closeted and living openly. During the height of his political career, U.S. senator Jesse Helms of North Carolina was fervently antigay, and his campaigns were being guided by GOP consultant Arthur Finkelstein, who eventually publicly married his male partner of forty years during a civil ceremony in Massachusetts. The fifty-nine-year-old Republican strategist had been involved in directing a series of high-profile conservative political campaigns that succeeded, in part, because of homophobic rhetoric and strategies.

Mike Rogers has used his Blogactive site to target Dan Gurley, the national field director of the Republican National Committee during the 2004 election. Gurley worked closely with then Bush campaign manager Ken Mehlman in executing political maneuvers to help Republican candidates. His work included driving passage, in eleven states, of the pro-marriage amendments, which gays and lesbians considered to be oppressive and frightening. Rogers reported on Blogactive that Gurley had a profile posted in a gay chat room at America Online that included his physical dimensions as well as the information that he preferred "bareback" sex, a euphemism for anal intercourse without a condom.

Pushing Bush administration "family values" by day during the election, Gurley was apparently in pursuit of gay sex with strangers during his off-hours. His AOL profile said he was "just looking for good sex, whether with one or several. Always versatile and love to fool around." Under the heading "Things I'm into:" Gurley had written, "Anal sex, Body contact, Groups, Kissing, One-on-one, Oral sex, Porn." Gurley, who used DGCapitol as his screen name, also mentioned to chat room visitors that he was in an "open relationship," which meant he was looking for sex with men other than his partner.

According to Mike Rogers, Gurley subsequently acknowledged to Raw Story that DGCapitol was his screen name but claimed it had been stolen by another AOL member. Rogers spoke with AOL officials and was told that screen names are always retired after members leave the service. In any case, Rogers had already downloaded Gurley's profile from the gay chat room, and it included a number of pictures of the man who was to become deputy political director of the RNC and field director for Ken Mehlman when he took over the Republican National Committee.

Georgetown political consultant John Aravosis, who had led a campaign to send thirty thousand letters to Vice President Dick Cheney's lesbian daughter, Mary, wonders about the psychology of gay Republicans. Overt, unvarnished homophobia is easier for Aravosis to understand than the actions of those who harm their own community.

"In some ways, we are a community in collusion with these guys," Aravosis explained. "They are members of our community, but we don't want to tell anybody. They want the privileges of membership but without doing anything in return. They become gay when in defense of themselves, but attacking us, they are Republicans."

An example of that dichotomy is the 2004 election and the "Ban the Bible" mailer, which surfaced in Arkansas and West Virginia. Warnings on the flyer told the reader that "if you don't vote . . . liberal activists and their hand-picked judges" will work for an agenda "allowing same sex marriage" and they will ban the Bible. The admonitions are accompanied by a photo of one man proposing marriage to another, a scare tactic Rove had deployed originally in Texas.

RNC spokesperson Christine Iverson confirmed that the party was responsible for the mailer, ironic given that field director Dan Gurley and chief financial officer and director of administration of the party organization Jay Banning had both been outed by Mike Rogers as gay.

In telephone conversations with Rogers, both men claimed that their sexual orientation was no secret at the RNC and that fellow workers were supportive.

"Are you out at work?" Rogers reports asking Gurley over the phone. "Um hmm," he replied.

"You are?"

"I mean, I don't go around telling people about myself, but my supervisors know, the people I work with and work for know," Gurley said. "So it's not like I'm being outed."

Rogers asked Gurley about the RNC's antigay "Ban the Bible" flyers in West Virginia and Arkansas, and Gurley declined to comment.

"I'm not going to discuss those," he said.

"Are they something you agree with, by your silence?"

"No, I don't discuss my work," said Gurley. "I work for the committee. That's all I'm going to say."

"So you have no crisis of conscience at all about what they are doing to gay people like you and me in the campaign?"

"I, like anyone else, have policy disagreements with any number of elected officials," Gurley added. "I don't expect to agree with everything, with everybody."

A ravosis finds these rationalizations predictable. "You can come up with a top-ten list of gay Republican cop-outs: Being gay is a part of me; it's not all of me. We don't agree on every issue, but no one agrees on every issue with their party. How do you expect someone to agree with every aspect of their boss or their party? But I have to ask them if they would say that about a black person working for David Duke."

The social strictures and political realities of Republican politics assure that however many homosexuals there are working within the GOP, few can go public. Even the president's personal assistant from the time he was governor of Texas, Israel Hernandez, waited until the president's second term to tell him he was gay. Hernandez has since been named by Bush as an undersecretary at the Department of Commerce.

Inevitably, tensions boil up. George Allen of Virginia, a U.S. senator many in the GOP hope will become their presidential candidate in 2008, was targeted by the religious Right after blogs raised questions about members of his senatorial staff. Allen's chief of staff, Jay Timmons, who was instrumental in the senator's 2000 election, was promoted to executive director of the National Republican Senatorial Committee, headed by Allen. Suddenly, Timmons found himself a subject on Rogers's and Aravosis's websites. Additionally, Rogers outed two other Allen staffers and declared the senatorial office "the gayest place on Capitol Hill."

Even though Allen voted for the Federal Marriage Amendment, the idea of having gay people on his Senate payroll was more than the Virginia-based Family Policy Network could abide. The organization issued a statement saying, "Pro-family conservatives throughout Virginia have been largely unaware of George Allen's affinity for selecting homosexuals to serve on his Senate staff. They don't know about his support for the Log Cabin Homosexual club, and they are ignorant about his vote to give special status to some crimes simply because of the victims' private sexual misconduct."

Joe Glover, president of the Family Policy Network, was particularly incensed by the appointment of Timmons to run the National Republican Senatorial Campaign. "If someone is going to run the day-to-day operations for the Republican apparatus to elect U.S. senators across the country, then dog-gone-it, it better not be somebody who practices a lifestyle that is dramatically opposed to the evangelical Christian base that delivered George W. Bush and the Republicans in the Senate the victory they saw in November [2004]."

Both the Left and the Right shared consternation over the hypocrisy of homosexuals engaged in pressing an antihomosexual agenda, but they came to the debate from very different places. The Right did not want homosexuals in its politics, period. For the Left, and a gay and lesbian community uniquely sensitive to the conflict between politics and personal behavior, there was a deeper sense of betrayal. Complications regarding gays loomed larger, however, for Republicans. Homosexuality and gay marriage, a wedge issue that had helped elect President Bush, was slowly turning into a problem for the GOP.

SIX

TIN SOLDIERS AND NIXON'S COMING

Turning On the Turnout Machine in Ohio

Political technology determines political success.
—Morton C. Blackwell, Karl Rove mentor

The odd thing about Karl Rove's phone call was not its breezy familiarity, as if he and Mayor Janet Creighton were longtime friends, which they were not. What struck Creighton after a few minutes on the phone with Rove was a sudden revelation, like the twist in a movie where you suddenly realize that everything you've been watching is not what you thought. That was the effect, anyway. The longer they talked, the more Creighton realized that her victory as the first woman mayor of Canton, Ohio, was not altogether of her own making.

"Congratulations," Rove declared. "A great victory. We needed you to win."

Creighton was surprised to get a call from the White House. Like so many local Republicans around the country, she knew Rove by reputation as the president's political guru, "Bush's Brain," the strategic genius who had guided the trajectory of George W. Bush's political rise. She had met Rove in the spring of 2003 when President Bush came to Canton to preach economic growth and job creation at the Timken ball-bearing plant. At the time, Creighton was a candidate for mayor and part of the local GOP delegation when the presidential entourage swept in and out with all the noise and electricity that such campaign events bring to a community. But now here Rove was on the phone a week after her election victory in November 2003 explaining how the party had been closely tracking the progress of her campaign at a level unknown to her and how happy everyone was that she'd won.

She had no idea she was just a piece of a political jigsaw puzzle. In retrospect, Creighton discovered that her small campaign was a part of a much bigger plan. "I'm the only Republican mayor of a major city in Ohio. It was very important to them that they not lose the one foothold they had," she explained.

Canton is a swing city in a swing state. Since 1960, Stark County has picked the winning presidential candidate with near-perfect accuracy. More critically for Karl Rove, Canton is the burial place of William McKinley, a historical icon of Rove's realignment ambitions for the GOP. He saw in McKinley's 1896 presidential election the beginning of thirty years of GOP dominance of American politics, a model he hoped to duplicate. From her window at city hall, Creighton can see the McKinley memorial, a pink granite rotunda at the top of a hill overlooking downtown and a bronze statue of the former president, thirteen feet high. Rove told her he had a special affection for Canton and for McKinley, the last president to inaugurate an enduring Republican majority.

After Creighton had announced plans to run for mayor, two men from Republican Party headquarters in Columbus showed up at her campaign office. They had a plan: an ambitious get-out-the-vote program featuring a seventy-two-hour finale that assured no targeted voter would be left behind.

"We have done phone calls before, and we've walked door-to-door, but when I saw this—I mean you had names and addresses and phone numbers, and you may go to Sixteenth Street and knock on Fred's door but then drive two blocks over and knock on Sally's door," Creighton said. "This was really pinpointing. This was like taking little pins on a map and saying this is where your guys are going. This was finite. This was amazing. We'd never done this before."

What the pros from Columbus were offering was a dry run of the party's seventy-two-hour program that targeted GOP voters in a final election-eve blitz. The original 72-Hour Task Force was designed by Karl Rove to boost turnout in the 2000 presidential race through an unprecedented campaign of last-minute phone calls, leafleting, and rides to the polls. It was, however, a limited run. For the 2002 midterm contests, the party assigned seventy-two-hour directors to all fifty states, often with good results. With the president's reelection looming, the Canton mayor's race offered the opportunity to further fine-tune the program in a state that everybody knew would be a crucial battleground.

"They laid their plan. They worked their plan. They executed and thought it through to the very end. And it made the difference in this election," said Creighton.

What Creighton had not known was how far up the planning went.

"We've been watching you," Rove said. "We've watched this race, and we're happy you won."

Not just happy, she thought, but instrumental. While she was running for mayor, they were test-driving the reelection of a president.

"I was a guinea pig to see how well it works," she said.

It worked, and well. Creighton won by 311 votes, and in the process, Rove got his fire drill for 2004.

After the presidential squeaker of 2000, Rove and company were hailed as political geniuses, but the joke inside the Bush camp was how the brainiacs would have been seen as idiots had the vote tallies been slightly different. Victory offered redemption for a host of sins. Regardless of the vigorous celebration, Rove was troubled by what he saw in the aftermath of the presidential race. In Arizona, Rove had expected Bush to win by ten points, but he only had a margin of six. The polling promised a victory in Florida by two points. Instead, Rove thought, "We won by a chad." Internal party polls predicted Bush winning Ohio by eleven, but he finished beating Al Gore with less than four percentage points. In state after state, the margins that Rove had expected did not hold up. As he assayed the architecture of his most important political victory, Rove could not help but ask himself an unsettling question. "Why," he wondered, "did we come so close to losing?"

A year later, in 2001, Rove appeared before the American Enterprise Institute and offered an assessment that forecast his plans to retune the machine.

"We failed to marshal support among the base as well as we should have. The big discrepancy is among self-identified, white, evangelical Protestants, Pentecostals and fundamentalists."

Rather than 19 million, he said, only 15 million "politically involved religious conservatives" went to the polls for Bush. The rest sat on the sidelines. "I hope it's temporary."

Hope was not the preferred currency of a Rove campaign. Planning—

detailed, comprehensive, and exhaustive—began for the president's re-election even before Bush moved into the Oval Office in 2001. Under Rove's direction, White House political director Ken Mehlman, pollster Matthew Dowd, and campaign media chief Mark McKinnon began meeting to develop a strategy for 2004, including improved techniques for targeting voters. Rove dispatched Dowd to presidential libraries to study second terms and reelection strategies. Dowd was ordered to go deeply into the numbers and examine vote totals, exit-poll results, demographic shifts, focus-group opinions, census data, and the blunt mathematics of an increasingly polarized America.

Dowd was the perfect guy for the job. Dispassionate and cerebral, he had a gift for statistics and was the campaign's resident pessimist. When the big-money boys were pumping Bush's sky-high poll numbers in advance of the reelection campaign, Dowd issued an e-mail dryly predicting Bush's numbers would soon go down. (He was right.) Around campaign headquarters, Dowd could be a cold splash of realism at moments of ill-founded exuberance. Balding and serene, he had the look of a Catholic priest from the black-and-white *Bells of St. Mary's* era. On the door of his campaign office, he taped a favorite quote from Yeats: "Being Irish, he had an abiding sense of tragedy which sustained him through temporary periods of joy."

The 2000 race was barely over, and Dowd was already preparing for round two. "It was, like, two years before the election that we started doing all this—getting ready, designing the media, designing the buy, deciding what we were going to do and how we were going to do it," said Dowd. "There was a lot of thought and effort and resources going into this, all based on certain premises that turned out to be right."

The fundamental premise, based on Dowd's assessment, had daunting implications. Rove was convinced that long before Election Day 2004, most voters had already made up their mind. America was so polarized, so divided, that Team Bush concluded only a sliver of the electorate, maybe 7–8 percent of voters, was up for grabs. As a result, the reelection strategy was to abandon the "compassionate conservatism" of 2000, in which Bush emphasized his softer, more moderate side. The reelection race was to be about rallying the base.

Bob Klaffky, who runs Ohio's most influential Republican campaign consulting firm with Franklin County GOP chair Doug Preisse, believes

Rove designed and launched a precise election unprecedented in American politics.

"We were talking to people who we know if we get them to vote, they're going to vote for us," he explained. "And I think the weakness of the other guy's plan was they were going to people to get them to vote, period. But they weren't certain they were going to vote for them."

Karl Rove knew precisely who his audience was. In his briefcase, he carried a laminated card, a kind of talisman that was equal parts history and prediction. The card had five bar graphs for each presidential election since 1988 and the 2002 midterm elections. Republicans were in red and Democrats in blue. Between them, in green, were independents, in a line steadily dwindling from election to election.

This was the germ of a big idea.

All campaigns are about persuading new voters and motivating true believers. "In 2000, we spent 75 percent of our resources on persuasion," said Dowd. "In 2004, we spent 75 percent of all resources on motivation."

And to do it, Rove had ordered the creation of an expensive, elaborate, and technically ingenious political machinery for the 2000 race. Karl Rove dreamed of an operation that would not only elect Bush once but deliver a second term and give the Republican Party political dominance for a generation.

First things first, though, and Ohio was at the top of Rove's long list of things to do. Word had reached Washington that Bob Bennett, longtime chairman of the Ohio Republican Party, had accepted a job with a large law firm and was planning to leave his position of political leadership. In December 2000, a couple of weeks before the first Bush inauguration, Rove and Ken Mehlman invited Bennett to Washington for a Christmas reception and breakfast at the White House to talk about his plans.

"The deal was, they wanted me to stay as full-time state chair," said Bennett. "The message was, we'd like you to stay around, we'd like to see some stability in Ohio. We're going to have to make some tough decisions. Karl said the race was going to come down to Ohio, and we don't want a change in leadership. It was a lot of puffery, lots of patting me on the back, you're family, that kind of thing."

Bennett, a good party soldier, agreed to stay. Not long after that, he ran into Rove at a national party meeting. Rove reminded him of how close the 2000 vote was in Ohio.

"You guys really dodged a bullet on us," the president's adviser said.

"I'm aware of that. We're finishing up the precinct analysis," said Bennett, who was still awaiting the secretary of state's detailed report.

Rove, though, already had it. Bennett was astonished. Rove was in possession of a precinct-by-precinct analysis of Ohio voter turnout in 2000 even before the state's GOP chairman was, he'd crunched the numbers, and he had absorbed its myriad lessons as he looked forward to 2004. Most disturbing, Rove felt, was the significant drop-off in turnout in many heavily Republican precincts.

"With the heavy turnout against us, we had to make sure that didn't happen again. So we had to fire up our base county organizations." Bennett understood that, next time, there would be a very different kind of campaign, a red-meat war aimed at rousing the party's most reliable constituencies, the rich and the religious.

In Karl Rove's portfolio of political achievements, none was more important than his success aligning religious and economic conservatives. The two wings of the party had different, sometimes conflicting, agendas. The party's social conservatives wanted more religious expression in public life and, by extension, had no problem with an activist government to stop abortion, ban homosexual marriage, authorize prayer in school, and allow the installation of Judeo-Christian monuments on public property.

Business conservatives, by contrast, wanted less government, which meant lower taxes, fewer regulations, and more policies to help business. At best, the interests of the two groups were mutually exclusive. And inevitably, they were bound to sometimes clash. Part of the fallout of the religious Right's opposition to gay marriage was over domestic-partner benefits, something that many businesses used as a benefit to attract employees. Rove's genius was the ability to work both sides, promising each its separate agenda while reassuring both that the best hope of success was forging a unified front to keep Republicans in control at the White House and in Congress. He melded Christian conservatives, the U.S. Chamber of Commerce, the National Rifle Association, small-business tax-cutters, opponents of gay marriage, and megachurch congregations, turning conservatives of every species into a solid political base.

"Karl Rove is the guy who kept all those factions together," said Marshall Wittman, a former Christian Coalition lobbyist.

A key battleground, Rove already knew, would be Ohio. The state's twenty electoral votes were crucial to Bush. And without reelection, Rove's larger blueprint was nothing more than an unrealized dream. In many ways, Ohio was a microcosm of the nation, and the themes and machinery that Rove brought to bear in the Buckeye State reflected the national campaign in high definition.

Even though Republicans dominated state politics in Ohio, they were a party battered by corruption investigations and an economy on the decline during the watch of GOP officeholders. Ohio State University political scientist Herb Asher thought the dynamics in Ohio ought to make election probable for Democrats.

"Just looking at this," he said, "Ohio should just throw Republicans out of office en masse. They've controlled everything. Things have gone downhill. We are worse off than the rest of the nation. There's no Democrats to blame for anything."

Asher's analysis, however, did not count on Rove's considerable capabilities. No Republican has ever won the White House without Ohio, a political factoid Rove knew well. To win, a candidate must navigate five distinct territories, each with its own social, economic, and cultural identity. Northeastern Ohio is part of the urban rust belt, heavily unionized and staunchly Democratic. The center is home to rapidly growing suburbs around Columbus, and it is politically balanced. The southwest is dominated by Cincinnati and is strongly Republican; the northwest is largely farm country, and the southeast is an extension of Appalachia, economically depressed, culturally conservative, and inclined to vote against incumbents whatever their political stripe.

Victory in Ohio was going to require more of Rove than just a mastery of its geography and demographics. The president's policies had stirred discontent among some conservative Republicans in the state. They may not have viewed Democrats or John Kerry as preferable, but many Ohioans did not like what President Bush was doing in the name of their party. Rocky Saxbe, a Columbus attorney whose father was a Republican U.S. senator and ambassador to India, was not enthusiastic about his party's presidential candidate.

"Here we are a party that has been traditionally for less government and less interfering with personal choices—a party with no deficits and with responsible economic policies," Saxbe said. "And now we're still saying those things but doing the opposite, and that's what's hard for me as a lifelong Republican. And it certainly seems to me that we are just scaring people. And clearly, this administration has used it masterfully with terrorism and keeping people scared and reinforcing this need for vigilance and this kind of xenophobic approach to anyone who disagrees with us. And at the same time, they're cutting funding for safety and emergency forces. It's all smoke and mirrors. Whatever it takes to get elected."

Getting around Ohio's economic problems was probably going to be Rove's greatest challenge if he was to get his president reelected. Ohio was hard hit by recession. The state had lost a quarter million jobs during the Bush presidency, which was the steepest decline since the Great Depression. Bush's reelection pitch was that his tax-cut plan would make things better. Rove chose Timken, the largest employer in Stark County, where Janet Creighton was to become mayor, as the backdrop for Bush's big tax-cut speech in April 2003. The company's chairman, W. R. Timken, was a Bush "Ranger," one of an elite tier of campaign supporters who had each raised at least $200,000. Bush declared the company a powerful symbol of economic resilience and revival.

"It's a roll-up-your-sleeves company," Bush said. "The future of this company is bright, and therefore, the future of employment is bright for the families that work here."

A year later, Timken closed three plants in the area and laid off thirteen hundred people.

While the economy was working against Bush's reelection, there was something else in Ohio *favoring* the president. The constitutional amendment to ban gay marriage would clearly inflame the religious Right and generate turnout, but the Bush camp knew the issue had to be handled gingerly so as not to alienate moderates and country-club Republicans. The solution was microtargeting and a confederacy of allies. Neither was new to Rove, and both became part of a larger strategy to sell the president to voters on two separate tracks. He was to be promoted as the commander in chief in time of war and as a protector of religious values. What few understood at the time was that Rove, chastened by the realization he'd almost lost in 2000, set about creating something he hoped would assure Republicans would never lose again.

The machine that Rove was designing and piecing together depended on a massive e-mail list, a disciplined cadre of campaign volunteers, an innovative set of techniques to target voters, and the use of allied groups that would slip seamlessly after the election into promoting the president and Republican policies. Subsequent to the election, Rove wanted a machine in place that would take up the task of advancing the GOP agenda. No one had ever combined politics and policy in quite the same way.

"We spent a lot of money and a lot of resources on this microtargeting stuff, building a list of phone banks, direct mail," said Bush pollster and strategist Matthew Dowd. "We took voter files and marketing files and combined them. Then we did these huge polls in individual states, and we modeled each state. Who was a likely Republican but wouldn't turn out? Where did they live? What did they read? These were models that we'd never done before.

"Then, in advertising, we approached it differently because we had information and data that could tell you Republicans and independents in a market [were] watching this TV show or that show. They watch *CSI* and *Law and Order* in Cleveland or Cincinnati. Or there are more people on this cable channel or that cable channel, which is why we bought all this sports, FOX News, CNN, the Learning Channel, the History Channel."

In 2000, the Bush campaign didn't buy TV ads on cable. In 2004, it spent $25 million on cable, which allowed it to reach specific target audiences.

The channels with the highest percentage of Republicans were Speedvision and the Golf Channel. For Democrats, it was Court TV and the Game Show Network. Coors beer and bourbon drinkers tended to be Republicans; brandy and cognac drinkers were more likely Democrats. College football audiences were more Republican; professional football audiences more Democratic. Republicans tended to watch Jay Leno, and Democrats stayed up for David Letterman.

Dowd's data showed that Republicans, especially Republican women aged eighteen to thirty-four, liked *Will & Grace,* a program featuring a pair of gay characters. Many were "security moms," a group particularly susceptible to a political pitch about terrorism. The Bush campaign broadcast nearly five hundred commercials on *Will & Grace* during the presidential campaign in markets across the country, according to one survey. The irony was not lost inside the campaign. While the president was reaching out to social conservatives by supporting a constitutional amendment to ban same-sex marriage, his ad team was buying commercials on a sitcom celebrating gay life.

Using a firm called TargetPoint to conduct surveys and collate information, the Bush campaign created a massive database in which nearly three dozen characteristics were overlaid to identify millions of potential voters, including what magazines they read, what TV shows they watch, where they live, what activities they prefer, what they buy, and how they vote. Surveys identified consumer "anger points," such as trial-lawyer fees, estate taxes, same-sex marriage. Dowd said the information allowed the Bush campaign to quadruple the number of Republican voters who could be reached with specific messages through phone calls, direct mail, and door-to-door appeals.

Meanwhile, Bush's conservative allies spent nearly $8 million on TV advertising in Ohio. The biggest groups in the air war were Swift Boat Veterans for Truth and Progress for America Voter Fund. Both were 527 organizations, named for the section of the Internal Revenue Code under which they operate. Under the rules, 527s cannot coordinate with campaigns or advocate for a specific candidate. Like their counterpart Democratic organizations in the 2004 presidential race, though, there was no doubt whose side the 527s were on. And there was evidence everywhere of coordination and cooperation between the campaigns and 527s.

In September, Ohio voters saw their first windsurfer ad, which was a thirty-second spot using film footage of John Kerry windsurfing, his board twisting back and forth on the calm waters off Nantucket. Mark McKinnon, the Bush campaign's media chief, said the visual was perfect for their message that Kerry is a flip-flopper. "Kerry voted for the Iraq war, opposed it, supported it, and now opposes it again," a narrator says. "He bragged about voting for the $87 billion to support our troops before he voted against it."

The ad concludes: "John Kerry. Whichever way the wind blows."

A day later, Progress for America began airing a remarkably similar ad. Dubbed "Surfer Dude," the commercial featured a cartoon Kerry negotiating the waves on a neon-colored board. "Whichever way the wind blows," an announcer says, "Kerry rides the wave. And Kerry surfs every direction on Iraq."

By law, the Bush campaign and Progress for America could not coordinate their activities, and both sides denied doing so. Nonetheless, there were clear ties between the two. Many of the contributors were the same, notably premier Bush fund-raiser Alex Spanos of California and Texas financial backers Bob Perry and oilman T. Boone Pickens. Moreover, Progress for America lawyer Ben Ginsberg was also counsel to the Bush-Cheney campaign. Progress for America was founded by Tony Feather, a pharmaceutical lobbyist and longtime Rove associate who was political director for the Bush-Cheney 2000 campaign.

But if the two organizations seemed to share personnel, it was nevertheless the message of the ads—the same theme with some identical wording—that suggested a remarkable coincidence. The term *flip-flopped* that appeared on-screen in the independent group's "Surfer Dude" commercial fit neatly with the Bush campaign mantra that Kerry was too unsteady and inconsistent to be president.

Inside the Bush campaign, the polling and focus groups made it clear that Americans were still shell-shocked over the 9/11 terrorist attacks and wanted a leader who was firm and resolute. The Bush political camp knew it was going to be difficult to paper over the problems in Iraq, but it also understood there was a visceral fear among voters about the threat of terrorism on American soil. Stoke that fear, they figured, and then market Bush as the Texas Ranger guarding the door with a .357 and a commitment to blow away anybody who dared step on the porch.

"I'm telling you," Bush pollster Dowd explained, "the number one thing motivating folks broadly was [that] they thought, 'I know this guy. I know where he stands. He's true to himself. He's going to protect me. I believe this guy wakes up every day and thinks, We will kill terrorists.'"

By moving early to portray Bush as firm and decisive, the campaign's goal was to frame Kerry implicitly as just the opposite. The Bush camp, strategically, had to make 2004 a national-security election. It could not be a referendum on the president but instead a choice between two candidates: one you could depend on, one you could not.

"If it were just a referendum on the president, we knew we would lose. But if we made it a choice between Kerry and Bush, we could win that proposition," said Bush media manager Mark McKinnon.

The effort to label the Democratic nominee as a flip-flopper started early, before Kerry became the Democratic nominee. The first target was Howard Dean, whose upstart campaign convinced Rove that he'd be Bush's opponent. The reelection team assembled a thick file on Dean titled "Howard Dean Unsealed: Second Edition, Wrong for America." On the cover were a dozen pictures of Dean in various unflattering poses. McKinnon's media team had cut a spot called "When Angry Democrats Attack!" featuring an animated Dean in fulsome attack, and posted it on the Bush-Cheney website.

More than a year before the 2004 election, the crew met for eggs-and-brainstorming sessions on Saturday mornings at Rove's house in northwest Washington, a brick colonial that during the uncertainty of the CIA leak investigation was to become a familiar stakeout for TV crews filming Rove as he climbed into his blue Jaguar and headed to the White House. Rove called his Saturday-morning sessions "the Breakfast Club." He made eggs and bacon and peppered the conversation with a rat-a-tat zeal.

At the stove, with bacon frying, Rove would wave a spatula to summon campaign ideas as if they were flights arriving on a busy runway. "Fabuloso!" he yelled at a particularly good suggestion. "Boring! Boring!" he hooted at something that failed to meet the standards of the team. In this circle of political equals, Rove was clearly numero uno, the president's guru, and he presided over the affairs of his Breakfast Club with a wild exuberance. Rove's breakfast of choice was doughnuts, which he brought to staff meetings in the White House, and which, Bush noted pointedly on occasion, had added pounds to his increasingly round physique. But here on Breakfast Club mornings, the menu was eggs, bacon, venison sausage, fruit, and coffee. Decaffeinated coffee. Rove drank decaf, so the rest of the team would have to bring their own.

"Karl on caffeinated coffee would be one of the more interesting sights," said pollster and strategist Matthew Dowd.

Rove's speciality was his scrambled eggs—eggies, he called them—which he announced with great fanfare were prepared with a special ingredient, most likely cream. As in everything, Rove pursued his cooking with manic, relentless attention. Dowd or GOP Chairman Ed Gillespie, who typically arrived first, might help fry bacon or set the dining room table, but it was Rove's show. Usually, about a half dozen people attended, half from the White House and half from the Republican National Committee. For the hour of brainstorming, people typically put their BlackBerries away. Only a call from the president, which came on occasion, had priority over the meeting.

According to those who attended, the sessions were mostly about message—how to respond in the event the opponent did something, what someone should say in an upcoming TV appearance, what themes the next round of commercials should emphasize. Many of the initial decisions regarding how the campaign wanted to frame the look of the Republican National Convention were decided at Rove's dining room table.

His wife, Darby, had applied her skills as an interior designer to creating a colorful, inviting interior. She'd arranged the rooms with light and color, aquas and light greens, giving the house an open and peaceful feel that sometimes stood in contrast to vigorous disagreements around the table—and to Karl's combustible personality, which could careen between manic optimism and distrustful silence. Rove felt comfortable here, although he spent less time at home than he did at the White House and on the road.

No one worked harder than Rove. He left for the White House before dawn every day, and he returned well after dark. At work, he might see President Bush a half dozen times a day, usually in the Oval Office. And sometimes, Bush would send instructions through Rove or counselor Dan Bartlett to resolve a pending campaign issue during the weekend Breakfast Club.

It was there during December 2003 that Rove and company prepared various attacks on Dean portraying him as irresolute and emotionally unsteady. By January, though, the Dean boomlet was losing steam, and Kerry emerged as the likely Democratic nominee. When Kerry won in the New Hampshire primary, the Bush team revised its talking points to frame Kerry as the flip-flopper, and within forty-eight hours of the primary, Republican allies on talk radio and cable TV were advancing the theme.

"We see John Kerry, who understood that Iraq had weapons of mass destruction, supported it [the war]; now he is against it. Who understood the need for the Patriot Act, and now is against it. John Kerry, who once supported No Child Left Behind, now is against it," said Sean Hannity on *FOX News.*

Rich Lowry, an editor with *National Review,* delivered the money shot: "He's got the flip-flopping down."

"He's got the flip-flopping down. That's good," Hannity declared.

Lowry repeated the talking point: "Flip-flop, flip-flopping down."

After that, the deluge. "You can't trust this guy," said Fred Barnes on *FOX News.* "He flip-flops like crazy," said Brit Hume on *FOX News Sunday.* Radio commentator Hugh Hewitt wrote in the conservative *Weekly Standard,* "Kerry's indecision combines with his well-documented flip-flops to make him the Hamlet of the Senate."

Rush Limbaugh followed, along with fellow radio talkers Laura Ingraham and Ann Coulter. By the time Kerry had won the California primary in March, Bush himself took up the script from Rove's kitchen.

"He spent two decades in Congress. He built up quite a record," the president told an audience of financial backers in Los Angeles. "In fact, Sen. Kerry has been in Washington long enough to take both sides on just about every issue."

The attacks by Swift Boat Veterans for Truth followed, exploiting the caricature of Kerry as flip-flopper. The power of the Swift Boat Veterans assault was that it undercut Kerry's central credential that he was a strong and resolute military hero.

"The whole thing of the Bush campaign and its shell group, Swift Boat Veterans for Truth, was that this is somebody you can't count on, who is squishy, who we can't afford to have sitting in that chair in the Oval Office," said Kerry campaign adviser Chad Clanton.

Swift Boat Veterans was bankrolled by three Texas billionaires with long ties to Bush and Rove. The notion that the organization rose up spontaneously with neither coordination nor assistance from Rove is incredible, considering the strategist's long history of managing every aspect of every campaign. In the case of the Swift Boat Veterans, Houston homebuilder Bob Perry, Dallas oilman T. Boone Pickens, and Dallas corporate raider Harold Simmons put $10.5 million into the group, about 70 percent of its total contributions. All three were among a handful of wealthy businessmen Rove began cultivating in the late 1980s to finance the GOP takeover of Texas politics. The group's lawyer was Bush campaign counsel Ben Ginsberg, also counsel to the other major pro-Bush independent group, Progress for America. The chief strategist of Swift Boat Veterans was Chris LaCivita, a veteran Republican Party operative and onetime executive director of Progress for America.

In spite of its insistent claims of independence, Swift Boat Veterans was part of an incestuous network of GOP operatives who switched back and forth between the Bush/Rove camp and allied groups. The ties binding the presidential campaign and its support organizations prompted critics to cry foul. But there was more to the 527s than just the campaign. The genius of groups such as Progress for America was not that they boosted Bush's reelection but that they did not go away. Rove envisioned them as part of his permanent apparatus that elects candidates, and then promotes their agenda and reelects them. The organizations were crucial to the self-perpetuating machine, a perfect blending of politics and policy, which was at the heart of the success of a permanent majority. Instead of dissolving after a campaign, the groups or their principals lived on as adjuncts of the GOP.

Progress for America, working closely with the White House, became an active cheerleader on the administration's premier issues: Supreme Court nominations, tax cuts, terrorism, and changes to Social Security. When Bush named Samuel Alito as his Supreme Court pick, it took Progress for America just thirty-nine minutes to introduce a slick website and begin lobbying for his confirmation. And on the day the Senate opened its confirmation hearings in January 2006, the group launched a nine-day, $500,000 advertising buy in support of the nominee. On its website, Progress for America rallied supporters, who received frequent e-mail updates urging them to action. Bush-Cheney campaign operative Gary Marx, a key liaison to Christian conservatives during the election, moved afterward to the Judicial Confirmation Network to push the nominations of Alito and John Roberts. Also joining the Judicial Confirmation Network was a Virginia-based public relations firm for Bush-Cheney. Swift Boat Veterans' political guru Chris LaCivita moved to USA Next, a conservative group that targeted critics of Bush's second-term call for private investment accounts. Until summoned to work in the next election, these "independent," grassroots groups likely will remain in place as assets in Rove's promotion of Republican causes and issues.

Ultimately, in Rove's mind, there was no difference between politics and governance. One flowed efficiently into the other. Election allies became policy advocates. Political operatives took over the levers of statecraft. Everything was a campaign, the permanent campaign building the ultimate machine for Republican political domination.

Once in the White House, Rove and company blurred the line between politics and policy in myriad ways, but none as important to Bush's reelection as the war in Iraq. In the run-up to 2004, Rove was a leader of the White House Iraq Group (WHIG), which was created to market the war. Rove had always treated Iraq and terrorism as a political opportunity, telling Republicans in advance of the 2002 off-year elections that they could "go to the country with this issue" by reinforcing voter perceptions that the GOP was strong on defense. The WHIG, whose members also included Vice President Dick Cheney's chief of staff Lewis "Scooter" Libby, pressed Congress for a war resolution in September 2002, two months before voters went to the polls. The election was a smashing success for the GOP, the first time since Theodore Roosevelt one hundred years earlier that a Republican president saw midterm gains in both chambers. Team Bush and the GOP were very much in charge.

In Rove's design, the central theme of the 2004 campaign was to portray Bush as the war president, strong and resolute despite the difficulty of the task, and there was no place to better represent the campaign's many moving parts than Ohio. Win Ohio and you win the country. Ohio's voters were reliably moderate to conservative, susceptible to a strong patriotic pitch, which Rove intended to deliver in the form of the president aboard Marine One accompanied by a flurry of choppers, striding into campaign events in a khaki jacket with the White House seal. The key to delivering the message and getting out the vote was an immense, disciplined organization with clear lines of authority. Rove prepared a three-inch-thick campaign manual. The team's test run of the seventy-two-hour campaign in the Canton mayor's race refined the effort for November. The campaign cultivated twenty-one coalitions, from gun owners to church groups, and prepared a massive media blitz, which would be reinforced by its independent allies Progress for America and Swift Boat Veterans for Truth. Proposition One, the gay-marriage ban, would gin up the conservative Christian vote. Tax cuts would motivate country-club Republicans, and everything would be wrapped around the central theme of fighting terrorism.

If campaigns are designed to inform voters, Rove's might just have fooled them. Tom Erney, who teaches at Columbus State College and is a former Democratic candidate for Congress, believes that too many people are bamboozled by Republican appeals on social issues into voting against their own economic self-interest.

"You think the electorate is dumb?" he was asked.

"Yeah, I do. Especially these rural voters who don't have a nickel in their pocket or a pot to piss in and can't go to college but they are embracing the Republicans because they are talking to them about God, guns, and being antigay. God, guns, and antigay is a great thing to be, especially in Appalachian Ohio."

They were nonetheless the people who voted and watched the television ads from the campaigns, and Karl Rove knew how to speak their language. Social issues lured them into the tent; the threat of terrorism would keep them there. An early Bush campaign TV ad, never seen publicly, was an extended shot of the president's chair in the Oval Office. As the camera slowly closed in on the empty chair, an announcer asked whether Americans would feel comfortable with Howard Dean sitting there in such dangerous times.

"It was a powerful spot, and it worked great when we thought Dean was going to be the nominee," said media adviser Mark McKinnon. "But when it appeared Kerry was the nominee, we tested it that way and people said, no, we *can* see him as president."

McKinnon prepared two other spots. And in late February, Rove and the campaign's inner circle gathered upstairs at the White House residence for a screening. Matthew Dowd had tested both commercials in a focus group, with good results. Now, it was time to show the president.

With Bush, his wife, Laura, Rove, and adviser Dan Bartlett looking on, McKinnon fumbled with the DVD machine, first bringing up the wrong spot and then struggling to shut off incorrect background music. Eventually, he played the first commercial, "Safer, Stronger," which featured a series of grim images, including a one-second shot of firefighters carrying out the flag-draped remains of a victim found in the rubble of 9/11. The president sat stoically, watching the flickering screen. McKinnon started the second ad, "Tested," which ended with a shot of the charred World Trade Center.

Bush looked perplexed. He questioned whether the spots were too pessimistic. His idea was to open the advertising with something more positive, more upbeat. The problem was, though, things were not particularly good. The economy was bad, and the war was certainly not going well. Rove had decided that what voters wanted was a president who was forceful and unyielding in the face of the bad guys. The theme would be "steady leadership in times of change."

"September 11 is the most important part of this campaign because it drives everything," McKinnon said.

Moreover, the spots would be controversial. Somebody was bound to complain that Bush was exploiting the tragedy, which would guarantee that another 40 million voters would see them replayed for free on the cable news shows. They were hoping to generate that discussion, not avoid it.

The president nodded. "Let's go," he said. "This is the strategy we're going with."

Within a week, voters in Ohio and the other battleground states got their first look at the Bush campaign commercials. Predictably, the media was harshly critical, calling them exploitive. Democrats denounced them. Rove was pleased. In the first blustery days of March, the focus of the campaign was exactly where he wanted it to be. Voters were having their beliefs reinforced that the world is a dangerous place; don't change commanders in the middle of a war.

From his early days as a Texas political operative, Rove liked to say that winning was a process, not an event. It had taken years to move Texas from a Democratic to a Republican state, and it was going to require years of relentless work to transform the nation's politics. Rove's blueprint envisioned starving the Democratic Party of its money and its most reliable network of workers by damaging trial lawyers and weakening organized labor and aligning the interests of business and religious conservatives.

And now it also meant using the war.

In Rove's campaign plan, the war was not policy; it was politics. Everything—including gay marriage, tax cuts, Swift Boat Veterans, the seventy-two-hour plan, TV ads, the battle for Ohio, and the war in Iraq—was useful in the service of Republican success until the party in power became a permanent majority.

The other side was not going to go away quietly, though. The Democrats still had money, a few ideas, and determination and considered themselves a worthy opposition party. What they didn't anticipate was that Karl Rove intended to use the power of the federal government to ruin anyone who stood in the way of his party, his president, or his dream of partisan domination in America.

SEVEN

LAPSED VOTERS

All God's Children Are Republicans

Difference of religion breeds more quarrels
than difference of politics.
—Wendell Phillips, abolitionist

D eal Hudson brought the blessing, priest and all. He also brought the code.

Karl Rove's new office was on the second floor of the West Wing, a space previously occupied by Hillary Clinton. In the bookcase, Rove discovered her hidden vanity mirror, which he liked to show off to guests. "I kept the vanity mirror because I'm so vain," the balding, portly presidential aide told visitors.

The office was not spacious by the standards of corporate America, but the address had the appropriate amount of prestige. Karl had finally arrived at 1600 Pennsylvania Avenue, the West Wing of the White House. A long line of people close to the president had worked out of his office. A general who served as Dwight Eisenhower's congressional liaison once performed his duties within the very same square footage, as had onetime Rove mentor Anne Armstrong of Texas, a Gerald Ford adviser who was cochair of the Republican National Committee. And, most recently, Hillary, which, Rove joked, was a reason the place needed to be purged of evil spirits. That's why he'd invited Hudson, his right-hand man for Catholic outreach in the 2000 presidential campaign, to arrange a Catholic blessing.

Hudson was publisher of the conservative Catholic magazine *Crisis*. He was a Southern Baptist turned Catholic, an intellectual with dark eyes, high forehead, and the easy manner of a Jesuit who knows his way around the best golf courses in Washington. For the blessing, Hudson arrived at Rove's office in the White House in early 2001 with Father John Cregan of Blessed Sacrament Church in Alexandria and Carl Anderson, the head of the Knights of Columbus.

"We kidded a little bit about it being Hillary's office," Hudson recalls. And then, in what must have seemed an odd moment even by the standards of a White House where Bible study would become the norm, three Catholics sat around Rove's table and prayed with the administration's premier agnostic, whose patron saint, Teddy Roosevelt, looked down from his portrait on the wall. Karl Rove, a man who'd been raised in a completely irreligious home and eventually acknowledged he had no real faith, was about to take part in a deeply spiritual ceremony. For Rove, though, the ritual was more about politics than faith.

"It was an actual liturgical ceremony," said Hudson. "We sat at the table; we prayed. A priest said a series of prayers, including a blessing. It was about five minutes long, but it was substantial."

Rove had discovered Hudson in 1998 while preparing for Bush to run for president. At the time, Bush was seeking reelection as governor of Texas and publicly dismissing questions about a potential bid for the White House. Rove was quietly building the campaign. Hudson was a magazine editor, not a political pro. He sensed, nonetheless, that the migration of traditional Catholic voters toward the Republican Party, largely because of abortion, had stalled in 1996. And he wondered why so many Catholics, who should have supported Bob Dole, instead backed a candidate with a weaker position on abortion and family issues. Hudson commissioned polling and, based on the results, assigned articles for *Crisis,* which were published in November 1998 under the headline "The Mind of the Catholic Voter." The series opened with an analysis that melded the spiritual with the political.

"Catholics—at 50 million strong and growing—have emerged as the Holy Grail of coalition politics, and they have the distinction of clustering in states rich in electoral votes, like Florida, Texas, California, New York, Ohio, and Illinois. Everyone agrees that their political allegiance is now up for grabs after decades of being a lock for the Democrats, but they are also surprisingly finicky, refusing to become solid party voters."

That made them prospects for Karl Rove.

Catholics had voted for Ronald Reagan, but also for Michael Dukakis and Bill Clinton. There seemed to be no driving principle guiding their choice. Ralph Reed had been preaching political collaboration between conservative Protestants and Catholics, and the *Crisis* report provided a road map for constructing a religious coalition. *Crisis* explained that there were two Catholic votes. There were active Catholics and inactive Catholics, those who went to Mass regularly and those who did not. The best indicator for assigning Catholic voters to the Republican Party was regular church attendance. Hudson commissioned conservative columnist Robert Novak, a frequent Rove source and, in turn, someone whose stuff the presidential adviser regularly read, to write one of the articles.

"The reality of two increasingly distinct Catholic votes should provide clear lessons for Republican politicians," Novak wrote. "Inactive Catholics are an amorphous blob, undetectable from the rest of the electorate and certainly not classifiable as a voting bloc to be courted. Active Catholics certainly do not constitute a monolithic bloc in the nature of African-Americans or even pious white Protestants. But they do have distinctive characteristics—including an anti-abortion position that belies claims by pro-choice Catholics."

When Rove read the piece, it was like a thunderclap. Catholics who attend Mass weekly were the target audience. They were more likely than nominal Catholics to be sympathetic to Bush's "compassionate conservative" pitch, and they could be identified and cultivated on the basis of traditional themes such as opposition to abortion and the demise of cultural values, which Bush would promote. This was the missing piece in Rove's bid to build the enduring Republican machine. Years later, a Pew Research Center poll offered strong statistical evidence that the more frequently Americans went to church, the more likely they were to be Republican, especially white Protestants, but here was evidence that Mass-attending Catholics fit the same mold.

Rove was on the phone immediately to Hudson.

"You going to be in Austin anytime soon? I'd like you to meet the governor," Rove asked.

"I can be," Hudson said.

He hopped a plane to Austin in January. At the Governor's Mansion, a white-pillared antebellum estate near the capitol, Hudson summarized for Bush the findings of his Catholic project. The task was to identify

Mass-attending Catholics, call them, pitch a message about moral decline, get them to the polls, and they'd be overwhelmingly yours.

Fish in a barrel, Rove thought.

"Deal, when I saw your article, I realized that the Catholic vote is the key to this election," Rove said, most likely overstating the case. But Rove had a machine to build, and Deal Hudson and his Catholics were to be one of its gears.

After a full day of meetings at the Governor's Mansion, the pair retreated to Rove's office overlooking the limestone outcroppings of Shoal Creek, where he asked Hudson to handle Catholic outreach for the fledgling Bush presidential campaign. Hudson agreed. Rove knew that Catholics—especially in battleground states such as Ohio, Michigan, and Pennsylvania—would account for a quarter of the vote, maybe more. They were part of the new wave of Reagan Democrats that marked the end of Democratic political dominance in the South and in the working-class neighborhoods of the Midwest. They'd returned to Clinton, and Rove was determined to win them back. Rove and Hudson talked about the importance of abortion as a binding issue for voters, of the message of moral decline and the values vote. Hudson cautioned that appealing to Catholic voters involved more than just sending the right social-conservative message. There was the matter of language.

"What the gang in Austin didn't know was the importance of how to speak differently to Catholic groups," he said. "It's partly a diction issue, partly a style issue."

For one thing, many Catholics were turned off by the strutting Baptistspeak of many southern white evangelicals and suspicious of politicians who sounded as if they had experience preaching from those pulpits. Having been raised a Southern Baptist in Texas before converting to Catholicism as an adult, Hudson had a good sense of respective differences in tonality and word choice. He told Rove that to communicate effectively with Catholics, Bush must guard against self-righteous or haughty language. In other words, do not sound too evangelical. The trick was building an alliance between Catholics and Protestants that would override their inconvenient history. It was undeniable, after all, that many Southern Baptists still called the papacy the "mark of the beast." Rove quickly realized that candidates needed to talk to different audiences in different ways, and he was delighted that Hudson instinctively understood that the strategy within the Bush camp was speaking in code.

Bush's chief speechwriter was Michael Gerson, a graduate of evangelical Wheaton College, who had a gift for informing the messages and language of his boss's speeches with the sound of the pulpit. Hudson read the speeches and then listened to Bush on the stump. Too Protestant, he thought, at least for audiences with large numbers of Catholics. Early on, Hudson would temper Bush's speeches for Catholic sensibilities, striking through some phrases, penciling in others. He struck out "Bible" and wrote in "Scripture." He changed "moral decline" to "social renewal." Hudson pressed the Bush team to use the phrase "culture of life," which worked fine for evangelical Protestants but had a special meaning to Catholics. Pope John Paul II introduced the term in his 1995 encyclical, "Evangelium vitae," and often repeated its most critical phrase:

"In our present social context, marked by a dramatic struggle between the culture of life and the culture of death . . ."

So it was no accident that during one of his debates with Democrat Al Gore, Bush told a national television audience that, as president, he would discourage abortion. "Surely, we can work together to create a culture of life," Bush said. To active Catholics who heard the pope's words week after week at Sunday Mass, it had a familiar sound. This was a man who talked their language. And he had learned it from Deal Hudson and Karl Rove.

In fact, the process of Bush's speaking to separate audiences at the same time—in effect, speaking code—was a much more calculated political strategy than was known at the time. For example, in seeking the presidency, Bush ran television ads prominently talking up phonics. To most people watching, the ads were about a candidate promoting education. Conservative evangelicals saw something else, however: cultural identity. Phonics was a hot topic on Christian radio, a key battlefield in the culture war. For many social conservatives, promoting phonics as a teaching tool was a rejection of moral relativism, of secularism and the infections of John Dewey and his philosophy of progressive education that encouraged children to follow their feelings and accept arbitrary opinions as fact. It was, fundamentally, about reasserting the Absolute.

Phonics taught children by letters and sounds. The competing "whole language" approach emphasized the meaning of the words. One method was clear and rigid; the other invited interpretation. Educators were split on which method was better but not conservative Christians, who believed that phonics was a bulwark against the creeping secularization of an educational system robbed of school prayer and moral values. They took their message to churches, school boards, and religious radio.

As governor, Bush promoted a literacy initiative that featured phonics and peppered his speeches with the term. When the state initiated a curriculum rewrite in 1997, Bush declared, "We now have phonics in our curriculum for the first time in a long period of time." Most Texans were oblivious to the deeper meaning, but not the religious Right. They knew the code. Karl Rove had his man speaking the correct religious language in plenty of time to become fluent before he ran for president.

In his inaugural address in January 2001, Bush opened with praise for his defeated adversary, thanking Al Gore "for a contest conducted with spirit and ended with grace." In purely secular terms, the presidential race was spirited, and Gore, in deciding not to contest Florida, did end the matter graciously. But to social conservatives, the words *spirit* and *grace* resonated with higher meaning, which is exactly what speechwriter Michael Gerson meant to suggest. He wanted the correct audience to understand they were listening to a man who was comfortable with the vocabulary of evangelicals. It was hardly even code anymore by Bush's 2003 State of the Union address, in which he said, "There is power, wonder-working power, in the goodness and idealism and faith of the American people," an allusion to the old Christian gospel hymn, "There is power, power, wonder-working power in the precious blood of the Lamb."

Rove had been an instrument in all this, of course, prompting Bush in his appeal to the religious base. By the 2004 reelection, Rove, Ralph Reed, and Deal Hudson had assembled the most effective religious political machine ever in presidential politics. The Christians were the foundation of the enduring Republican majority. And Bush was the perfect messenger to communicate with them.

Bush was a profoundly spiritual man, and he knew his convictions had political value. The making of Bush as the nation's most openly religious president took time. As governor, Bush promoted an agenda appealing to Christian conservatives, but he did not wear his religion on his sleeve. He did not need to in Texas as governor. It was only when he opened his campaign for president that Bush projected a larger religious persona as part of a political calculation to attract a broader national audience. In

April 1999, two months before launching his White House bid, Bush began the rollout with two Dallas reporters who'd sought an interview. He'd agreed to the discussion but still seemed uncomfortable.

"I view my religion as very personal," he said, sitting in his capitol office. "I want people to judge me on my deeds, not how I try to define myself as a religious person of words."

He fidgeted in a chair in his high-ceilinged office, speaking in a slow, calculated tone, as if to control every word. The expression on his face took turns, sometimes tetchy, sometimes not. Karen Hughes sat against the wall, looking on.

"I'm comfortable talking with evangelicals," he said. "And I think one reason I'm comfortable is because I'm comfortable with myself, because I'm comfortable with my religion."

Clearly, though, he was not yet comfortable talking openly to a wider audience through the mainstream press. The Bush camp wanted to introduce a candidate to Republican primary states attractive to Christian conservative voters but without sounding preachy or politically opportunistic. Two months from liftoff, Bush was still calibrating the delivery.

In February, Bush appeared on evangelist James Robison's television program *Life Today*, where he suggested that he was part of a divine drama, an instrument in a battle between good and evil, right and wrong. "People walk up and say, 'Governor, I'm praying for you.' It matters a lot to me. It's a reminder to me that I'm not it, I'm just part of a larger scheme."

The public rollout of his religion came later in the year in the mainstream press. By the fall, the candidate was talking publicly with greater confidence on matters of personal faith. And in so doing, he assured himself a loyal base of supporters that his father had never won.

But even Karl Rove made miscalculations.

On paper, the stop at Bob Jones University looked like a good idea. The Rove blueprint called for invigorating the faithful in South Carolina, where Team Bush needed to stop the insurgent John McCain campaign in the 2000 GOP primaries, so an appearance at the state's premier evangelical campus seemed like a no-brainer. The problem, which Bush and Rove did not anticipate, was the public backlash over Bob Jones's policy banning interracial dating and its anti-Catholic bias. The school's founder, articulating the fundamentalist boilerplate of an earlier era, called Catholicism a "Satanic cult." So after Bush won the primary in a savage battle in which Bush allies smeared McCain, the McCain forces went to work in Michigan, the next primary stop, with an offensive labeling Bush an anti-Catholic bigot.

A group called "Catholic Voter Alert" phoned thousands of Michigan voters with a script saying Bush was silent on the anti-Catholic bigotry at Bob Jones. Inside the Bush camp, Rove, Reed, and Hudson were worried. Bush had to do something to atone for his sins in South Carolina or risk losing the conservative Catholic voters the campaign had sought to woo. The answer was a contrite letter to New York Cardinal John O'Connor, which Bush solemnly read before a battery of TV cameras.

"On reflection, I should have been more clear in disassociating myself from anti-Catholic sentiment and racial prejudice. It was a missed opportunity causing needless offense, which I deeply regret." In both sentiment and language, Bush had delivered an apologia similar to the letter he'd written to the Anti-Defamation League when his remarks about heaven had offended Jews. He was developing a sort of pathology for offending and then enticing religious groups.

Michigan and New York lay ahead, both with sizable Catholic populations. After reading the letter, Bush boarded the campaign plane, still miffed by the McCain insurgency in Michigan.

"I can't believe anybody would think I'm an anti-Catholic bigot," Bush said aboard the campaign plane.

A couple of reporters questioned whether the letter to the cardinal was sufficient, considering the campaign's hopes of targeting traditional Catholics in richly ethnic regions of the Midwest. Bush looked exasperated. In a startling gesture, Bush pulled out a penknife, opened the blade, and put it to his throat.

"What do you want? I just ate crow on national TV!"

"Jim Crow, I believe," one reporter fired back, and everybody laughed.

The thing about the Catholics is that they were integral to Rove's plan for an enduring Republican majority. The GOP had long had the support of fundamentalist Protestants, but Catholic voters remained an elusive voter bloc. There were 65 million Catholics in the United States, and 45 percent of them were registered voters. Politically, they were divided. About one-third of Catholics described themselves as strongly Democratic and about one-third strongly Republican. In part, Bush's theme of "compassionate conservatism" was an effort to lure more Catholics into the Republican tent.

Karl Rove's Republican realignment machine would require more than the narrow constituencies of the past—self-interested business, Protestant evangelicals, and the "leave me alone" crowd. Job one was electing Bush, but Rove's reach was longer than that, longer than simply one or two terms in the White House, longer even than winning a period of Republican dominance in Congress. Rove wanted a fundamental partisan realignment of American politics, and he had known that since he first stepped into Lewis Gould's class at the University of Texas.

Rove never graduated from college. The lure of politics always interrupted. But once his political direct-mail business was firmly established in Austin by the 1980s, Rove toyed with the idea of returning to school for a few classes to earn his bachelor's degree. He enrolled in Gould's class on the American presidency. Gould was a renowned scholar, author of several books, including *From Canton to the White House: The Presidency of William McKinley.*

Gould prefaced his study of McKinley by recalling the off-year congressional elections of 1894, two years before McKinley was elected president. The year marked the largest turnover of House seats from one party to another in American history. Republicans picked up 117 seats and controlled the House for the next sixteen years. Voters had a distinct choice between Democrats, with their backward-looking agrarian policies, or the Republicans, who embraced a new cultural pluralism. They chose the GOP.

Rove opened Gould's book and began reading, and there on page 5 was a paragraph that would stay with him for years:

"The election of 1894 remade national politics. It terminated the years of even balance, opened a generation of Republican dominance, and condemned the Democrats to a minority status, with the exception of the accident of Woodrow Wilson's presidency, until the Great Depression and the New Deal."

There it was in black and white: *a fundamental realignment of government, not just for years but decades.*

America had undergone two political realignments in the last century. The first was a sustained period of Republican dominance beginning with McKinley and then four decades of Democratic dominance starting with Franklin Roosevelt. Rove was curious to understand exactly how this had happened. What had the McKinley forces done to inaugurate an enduring majority? How do you build a permanent Republican machine?

McKinley recognized that the economy was changing and a new urban workforce would be needed to operate it. The key, McKinley knew, was to make it comfortable for urban ethnic working people to identify with the Republican Party. So while his political guru, Mark Hanna, engineered a staged procession of prominent visitors to McKinley's home in Canton (dubbed "the front-porch campaign") and pioneered the most successful fund-raising effort in history, McKinley went about pitching his candidacy to the new urban workforce.

As Rove prepared to launch Bush's 2000 race for the White House, he sat with a reporter and recalled with bubbling enthusiasm the lessons he had learned about the McKinley model.

"He knew his party, the Republican Party, was ill equipped to make the shift from the Civil War generation to a newer, younger generation," Rove said. "And he says, 'We've got to find out how we do something different.'

"He reaches out to Catholics, which, after 'rum, Romanism, and rebellion,' is absolutely anathema. He realizes that immigrants are a strength; they are the new rising class, part of the new economy. They are of value to the new America he sees coming, so he reaches out to them. McKinley visits the archbishop of Minneapolis. He talks about reform with Teddy Roosevelt.

"He sends fourteen pieces of mail and publications to every voter who voted in the 1896 election. Croatian American literature, the first mass-produced political publication in Yiddish. It was a pretty amazing campaign under the surface."

Rove gave Bush his own "front-porch" campaign with numerous political leaders traveling to Austin to implore the governor to consider running for president. This was the beginning of a McKinley-like money-raising machine that was to break all records in presidential races. Rove, though, had a considerably more detailed and comprehensive plan for Bush and his party. To build his own new Republican machine, Rove had to completely duplicate the McKinley model in modern terms. Part of that meant expanding the base beyond business and white Protestant evangelicals to include more Catholics and minorities and other often-overlooked demographic groups.

In 2000, Al Gore beat Bush among Catholics, 49 percent to 47 percent. But Rove saw something promising in the numbers because Bush had won 55 percent of practicing Catholics, those most likely to attend Mass once a week. It was just as Ralph Reed and Deal Hudson had said: the important divides were not between denominations but through them. And the weapon to exploit that division was moral values. And the values issue that worked best with Catholics was abortion.

Many in the church hierarchy liked Bush because of his opposition to abortion. Hudson's job included introducing Bush to the bishops and building support. One day in 2000, Hudson was in Cardinal O'Connor's rectory in New York setting up a meeting, and for a moment, he wondered aloud whether he was making a mistake linking church and state at Rove's behest.

"Should I be doing this?" Hudson asked. "I'm the publisher of a nonprofit magazine."

"Deal, you should do it, and you should win," the cardinal said. "You have to."

Rove, Hudson, and Reed were grooming one of history's most overtly religious presidents.

Early in his first term, Bush made plans to visit the pope. Care and feeding of the Catholic vote, according to the Rove blueprint. Bush and his entourage, including Hudson, flew to Rome for the private audience with John Paul II at his elaborate summer residence, Castel Gandolfo. The pope took Bush out on the balcony of the residence to view the clear blue lake below and then moved inside, where they sat under a painting of the Virgin Mary and baby Jesus.

The issue on the pope's mind was stem cells, and he spoke forcefully on the subject. John Paul called research using stem cells taken from human embryos "an evil on the level of infanticide." Bush sat stiffly and respectfully at the pontiff's side. He promised to consider the Holy Father's words. Afterward, members of the entourage, including Rove, went up to the pope and received a gift of a paper medallion. Bush looked somber as the entourage left the retreat for the U.S. embassy at the Vatican. Inside the embassy, Bush was back to his boyish self.

"Hudson," he said with a bouncy grin, "I love your pope. You can really tell this guy is holy. What a great pope."

And that pope's influence was eventually to guide the president's policies regarding important stem cell research.

The question of federal funding for stem cell research was pressing on the Bush policy team, Karl Rove as much as anybody. The stem-cell decision would be big in the antiabortion community, and Rove knew it. Long before the Vatican visit, he began studying the issue. On the day that Hudson and the Catholics came to bless Rove's office at the White House, an aide arrived with a stack of papers two feet high. It was an exhaustive exploration of the issue Rove had requested from Richard Doerflinger, the Catholic bishops' point man on bioethics and abortion. Hudson looked at the imposing stack of paper and asked if Rove wanted him to read it and prepare a synopsis. Rove shook his head. "No, I want to read it myself," he said.

It was typical of Rove to immerse himself in an issue, even something as complex as stem-cell research, to understand the competing arguments of science and religion before advising Bush on the politics involved in their awkward confluence. The subject was fraught with politics. An absolute ban would be popular among evangelicals and Catholics but would leave Bush open to charges of intolerance, which might alienate the BMW exurbanites he also needed to build the party. Acquiescence, however, would kill Bush with the base.

Along the way, Rove sent signals to Hudson. "We're going to get it right," he assured. "You're going to be happy."

In the end, Bush divided the question. He announced that he would support federal funding for research, but only on existing lines of embryonic stem cells. Initially, some Roman Catholic and Protestant leaders did not like his policy, but eventually, as they came to understand the decision, most grew to accept it, even praise it, which was just as Rove had predicted.

By the 2004 reelection, Bush actually won a majority of the Catholic vote. He raised his share from 47 percent to 52 percent, which was remarkable considering that challenger John Kerry was a Roman Catholic. In the crucial battleground state of Ohio, where the Bush camp sent droves of field-workers to Catholic churches preaching antiabortion and support of the state's gay-marriage ban, the president got 55 percent of the Catholic vote. Bush boosted his numbers among white Protestants, too. The Protestants were the core; Catholics expanded the base—each drawn into a political alliance around the larger theme of moral values. A permanent Republican machine required a lot of alliances, but the Christians were a start.

As Bush's reelection campaign approached November, Rove heard about the Christians in camouflage. Every summer, Jersey Baptist Church, east of Columbus, Ohio, hosts its Wild Game Extravaganza for the community. On a sun-splashed Saturday in August 2004, hundreds of people gathered in a park across from the church for an annual high holy day in honor of the great outdoors.

Jersey Baptist is located in the exurbs, prime GOP country, and has a politically conservative congregation. It is an article of faith at Jersey Baptist that the Bible is the literal word of God, evolution is the theory of the devil, and Jesus is the only way to Heaven. A few years ago, Pastor John Hayes organized the first game expo as an outreach ministry, and the annual event has become wildly successful. There are booths for free antler scoring, tips on fly casting, a fishing contest for kids, and the 3-D bow shoot for adults. The evening buffet features buffalo, bear, elk, and pheasant, and a closing program is a gospel presentation by a big-game hunter. There is also a booth for voter registration.

A few days before the election, a reporter asked Rove about the voter-registration drive by Jersey Baptist. What better demographic for Bush, hunting and fishing Christians?

"No! No! No!" Rove said, vigorously shaking his head.

"Christians first. Then hunters and fishermen."

Rove and company built the most successful confederation of religious voters in history during that summer of 2004. Not just white Protestants, but African Americans moved by opposition to gay marriage. And Catholics, which meant more Hispanics, a dream demographic in Rove's political calculus. It was McKinley all over again, building a new Republican majority one piece at a time. The architecture of Rove's realignment would include corporate interests, small-government types, low-taxers, security moms, inroads among minorities, appeals to the exurbs.

But the family values vote was the foundation, and Rove knew it. Christians first. He had them. And after professing a faith he did not possess and seducing Catholics to vote for George W. Bush, Karl Rove had other important work to complete.

He had to get back to the business of shutting down the opposition.

EIGHT

FOR DADDY IN OHIO

Making McKinley Proud

*God is on everyone's side . . . and in the last analysis, he is on the
side with plenty of money and large armies.*
—Jean Anouilh

From the doorway near the loading dock, Doug Preisse heard the roar
from twenty thousand people jammed inside the hockey arena in
downtown Columbus for a big event at the close of the 2004 presidential campaign. He felt the thrum of the place, the exuberant sense
that the president of the United States was about to arrive. And not just
the president but also . . . *Arnold*!

The Terminator was coming, Arnold Schwarzenegger, who'd agreed
to make only one out-of-state campaign stop for the president, and this
was it, here at Nationwide Arena on the final weekend of a race that
might be decided right here in Ohio, maybe Columbus, maybe here in
this stadium filled to the nosebleed section with Bush and Schwarzenegger fans. And so Preisse, who was the county GOP chairman and the
evening's master of ceremonies, was a little nervous as he stood by the
door waiting for the dark line of the motorcade. He'd never spoken to a
crowd this large, which was enough to make anyone anxious, but what
really worried Preisse was the prospect that the president on the final
weekend of his reelection campaign might ask how things were going.
And things weren't exactly going well.

The motorcade arrived. Bush jumped out, flashing a jaunty smile.
Schwarzenegger emerged, along with Karl Rove and the rest of the

entourage, which headed inside. Bush shook Preisse's hand, and they walked through an unadorned area toward the sound of the crowd.

"How we doin'?" Bush asked.

"Well, I think it's very close," Preisse said. "I think we might be down a few points in central Ohio. Why, I don't know, but I'm nervous."

Bush barely blinked. "Karl tells me we have a little bit better numbers than that."

Preisse did not dispute him. "You're supposed to have better information, and I'm glad to hear that."

By then, Rove had come up next to Preisse and the president and, catching a sense of the conversation, nodded affirmatively as if everything was on target. Preisse sensed that Bush was not so sure. The president, moving ahead with the brisk pace of a gladiator entering the arena, looked back.

"Well," he said with finality, "Karl has better information."

A moment later, Bush and Schwarzenegger stepped onstage to a thunderous reception that ebbed and swelled for ten minutes. The rally was great TV. The president and the Terminator were shoulder to shoulder.

Bush used the event to strike back at John Kerry with a new twist. Earlier, news had broken of a new videotape from Osama bin Laden. Instantly, the chattering class on the cable shows was debating who would benefit from Osama's October surprise. Kerry used the news to remind voters that Bush had allowed the terrorist kingpin to get away. Rove knew, however, the tape was a boon that was certain to rekindle voter fears of the terrorist threat while also focusing the campaign's final days on exactly what Rove wanted to talk about: steady leadership in a time of change.

From the stage in Columbus, Bush denounced Kerry's critique as "the worst kind of Monday-morning quarterbacking. It is especially shameful in the light of a new tape from America's enemy." The crowd screamed in affirmation.

By now, the tape was all over television, and it was playing in the war room at Kerry headquarters in Washington. Kerry pollster Mark Mellman noticed that when the spectral figure of bin Laden came on-screen, the room grew quiet, and some members of the team had blanched, showing the poleaxed look of victims on the way to the abattoir. This could be a problem for the Kerry side. If the race came down to a referendum on Osama bin Laden versus George W. Bush, there was no doubt who was going to benefit. Rove was certain of that much. Back in Ohio, he was sanguine about the prospects for Tuesday.

"I'm not sure if I was sitting in the cockpit of the other campaign, I'd want this to come down to the war on terror," he said.

As it turned out, Franklin County in central Ohio went for Kerry, just as Preisse had feared. But the bellwether state of Ohio went for Bush, just as Rove had predicted.

The battle for Ohio showcased the considerable strengths of the GOP organization Rove had assembled, but it also signaled weaknesses that could bedevil Bush's second term and undercut the goal of Republican ascendancy. By emphasizing the base, Rove and the GOP infrastructure committed themselves to a politics of division. Outside the base, it created fierce enemies against the war. Inside, it gave birth to coalitions with outsize expectations. Religious conservatives expected judges to be appointed who were determined to overturn *Roe v. Wade.* Economic conservatives wanted smaller government. Wealthy donors envisioned lower taxes. Evangelicals anticipated a constitutional amendment to ban gay marriage. Businesses offering same-sex benefits did not expect government interference. The promises piled up: more religion in government, less government regulation, expanded markets, secure borders, a smaller deficit, a bigger round of pork for Republican districts.

"Coalitions that get created are often made up of people who hate each other only slightly less than they hate the opposition," said Walter Dean Burnham, University of Texas political historian. "A slight change in the payoff schedule or circumstances and they're likely to defect. The fact that you have large coalitions that are not completely monolithic is important. You can have infighting. And what happens when you get a superlarge coalition is that too many people out there are demanding payoffs and you can't possibly realize them all. You have to figure out which ones to slight."

Rove understood the perils of creating a superlarge coalition of disparate parts, but the task at hand in 2004 was winning reelection. And the lever for victory was the most elaborate, disciplined, and well-financed political machine in history.

Jo Ann Davidson, the former Ohio House speaker, knew something was different when Ohio Republicans were asked in the middle of summer to show up and walk door-to-door and make phone calls at a time when nobody was paying attention to the election. Davidson was a veteran of Republican politics, but she'd never seen a campaign start so early and prepare so thoroughly. Rove's three-inch-thick planning manual had state-specific time lines, recruitment goals, and periodic tests of the system. Rove was obsessed with the "metrics" of the campaign, precise measurements of how it was doing at any given moment. Sitting in Washington or aboard Air Force One, he could type a date into his computer and chart the campaign's "metric mileposts."

"They had reports every day, reports from volunteer people and from staff people. They tracked it across the country, and they tracked it across Ohio," Davidson said. "We'd know exactly where we were, what percentage of our goals we were meeting—recruiting precinct leaders, what percentage of county chairs, what percentage of recruiting Bush volunteers."

All political campaigns operate at the edge of chaos. They are huge, dysfunctional enterprises that burst into being and careen toward a preordained end, spewing millions of dollars and making an enormous amount of noise marketing a candidate who either wins or loses. And then, they disappear. Davidson, though, sensed something more permanent in the plan Rove and company delivered, in terms of both its preparation and its potential as an instrument to sustain Republican success. Two things were different from every campaign she'd seen in the past. There was absolute seriousness about accountability and a near obsession with early testing to verify that the organization was working. Davidson's responsibility was Ohio, West Virginia, Kentucky, and Indiana, which were all red states the president needed to hold. Ohio was crucial, and Davidson spent most of her time there.

"Twice we did a rollout," she said. "For maybe three weeks in a row, we'd have people turn out to target door-to-door. Or we'd ask people to show up Monday through Thursday night to volunteer. And we could see exactly what was happening, whether people were responding, where they weren't responding. The organization was tested all the way through, so by the time you got to the very last key time, the seventy-two-hour program, you knew by that time your people were going to respond. And you knew you could do this never-done-before number of volunteer phone calls. Our total voter contact was over 4 million—and about 2.3 million of those were made in that last push right before Election Day."

Ohio organizers had hoped early on to have two people handle one hundred homes, going door-to-door. Instead, the Rove plan had one per-son for every twenty-five homes. If the longtime local Republican captain complained in the spring it was too early to begin, the Bush team found somebody else for the job. By the end, there were ninety-nine people on the payroll at the state GOP, twelve thousand active local party officials, and eighty-seven thousand volunteers statewide.

"I've never seen anything like it before," Davidson said.

Neither had Lee Leonard, who was covering his last presidential cam-paign after decades as a political reporter for the *Columbus Post-Dispatch.* Over a bowl of chili at a restaurant across from the Ohio capitol building, Leonard's years of experience didn't diminish his wonderment at the Rove achievement. He looked up from his lunch with a serious look as if to reinforce that his guest completely understood the importance of what the Republicans had done.

"There's no way that Bush would have carried Ohio without what they did," Leonard said. "And I heard about it way ahead of time, in 2003 or early 2004, about this ground game they were going to do. And that he [Rove] told them at the Republican State Committee meeting what they were going to have to do. It was the seventy-two-hour program. And they did it in a way that, I mean, the Democrats around here are still marveling at."

Democrats have long dominated the grassroots game. With a huge voter pool and an army of organizers supplied by labor unions, Demo-crats have been better able to target communities of common interest such as working-class neighborhoods and the inner city by using rented vans and walking-around money and a team of volunteers willing to knock on their neighbors' doors in search of voters. Republicans were less adept at reaching their communities of interest, especially the emerging exurbs.

Democrats knew the best contact was neighbor-to-neighbor. Geogra-phy was destiny. But Matthew Dowd believed that demography was des-tiny. In the inner sanctum of the Bush-Cheney campaign headquarters in suburban Virginia, Dowd explained that although neighborhoods were important, the new model for identifying voters would be based on lifestyle, not precinct. How did voters live? What lifestyle traits did they share? What institutions reflected or shaped their identity? And one im-portant institution, he concluded, was the church.

"What churches were to us is a vehicle to communicate with potential voters," said Dowd. "And that's the future, how to find these new groupings of folks that didn't exist 20 years ago and figure out ways to communicate to them."

Democrats were slow to figure out how the Bush camp was using suburban churches, especially the new megachurches, to communicate on subjects beyond abortion and conservative values. They were perfect institutions to pitch George W. Bush as the war president. There was not an evangelical pulpit in suburbia that did not mix its religion and patriotism, sometimes with large-screen displays of Old Glory and stirring music celebrating America's military heritage. Add Issue One to the mix and it was a prescription for motivating the base. Eleven states had a same-sex marriage ban on the ballot in 2004, and for Republicans, none was more important than Ohio.

"All the Issue One folks, they had volunteers," said Bob Bennett, the state GOP chairman. "They came out of the churches. We were asking them to work their area."

The Bush-Cheney church campaign was an elemental part of an intricate plan. An e-mail went out seeking thousands of "friendly congregations" in which Bush supporters "might gather on a regular basis." Team leaders were named in individual congregations. Allied groups outside the campaign were encouraged to buffet pastors with a flurry of calls to set up voter-registration drives in their sanctuaries. The Southern Baptists distributed thousands of "I Vote Values" kits instructing church leaders how to set up voter-registration drives and providing pastors with legal guidance on avoiding jeopardizing their tax-exempt status. The Baptists, the Christian Coalition, and other allied groups printed millions of voter guides comparing candidates on the basis of "biblical principles."

In keeping with the campaign's insistence on discipline and accountability, it distributed to religious volunteers a list of twenty-two duties to be performed by specific dates. For example, by July 31, volunteers were to talk with their pastors about holding a Citizenship Sunday to register voters. By August 15, they were to talk with specific Sunday school classes about the Bush-Cheney campaign and recruit five people within their congregation. By September 17, they were to host at least two campaign-related potluck dinners with church members. The results were reported to campaign headquarters locally, then to Columbus, then nationally, where Rove accessed the results in his voracious review of "metric mileposts." In effect, churches became wholly owned subsidiaries of the campaign.

"The Bush campaign's innovation has been to move their church liaisons in-house," said John Green, the University of Akron expert on church-state issues. "It's difficult to maintain the fiction that churches are religious institutions and campaigns are political institutions when you have a campaign organizing a direct outreach to churches."

Much of the activity remained under the radar, largely missed by the media until an e-mail seeking church directories found its way into national newspapers. A story in the *Washington Post* disclosed that the Bush camp had asked volunteers to "send your church directory to your state Bush/Cheney '04 headquarters." Names, addresses, phone numbers, and church affiliations were fed into Matthew Dowd's massive database, and church coordinators got back lists of "all non-registered church members and pro-Bush conservatives." The request set off a firestorm. Democrats denounced it as a violation of church-state separation, and Christian pastors were upset that their church directories were being used for political ends.

Ralph Reed, the Bush campaign's southeastern regional chairman, saw the story and picked up the phone.

"What happened?" he asked Deal Hudson at the Republican National Committee.

"It was your guy," Hudson fired back.

The e-mail had come from a young political operative named Gary Marx, a Reed protégé who worked for the Bush campaign.

"We had a rule, and everybody knew it," said Hudson. "You couldn't steal it, you couldn't lift it. But if someone wanted to give it to you, you take it. You don't publicly ask for this to be done. You do what you've always done privately. You just don't get out there and look like you're stealing lists."

After the story appeared, the Reverend Jerry Falwell went on television and was asked by an interviewer about the propriety of a campaign's soliciting church directories.

"Well, first of all," said Falwell, "I called the White House about the directory thing. An underling wrote that memo. He did not have the blessing of anybody at the top. It's long since been negated."

None of which was true. Marx said the solicitation of church directories in seventeen battleground states was an important element in building the campaign's voter file, and it continued despite the public dustup.

"It was astounding how successful we were," he said. "For instance, in Ohio, we expanded our voter file in the neighborhood of hundreds of thousands, not just thousands. We achieved what we wanted to in terms of building a much better data profile to make sure they're all registered to vote and those who aren't, to send them information about getting registered."

Marx's mistake was not that he solicited church directories but that he allowed the effort to go public. After Bush won reelection, Marx had a place in the permanent campaign. He launched the Judicial Confirmation Network, recruiting religious conservatives in support of the president's Supreme Court nominees.

He'd done his job well.

"They stole God," said Tom Erney, a frustrated Democratic candidate in Ohio. "They stole God. It was masterful how they did it. They went to the churches and said, 'Who's got values that match yours?' Gay unions, the abortion issue itself—those were core issues, and people who take the Bible literally believe they have justification to hate both of those acts. And what's more important than God when you are talking to the church? I think they were co-opted."

And it's likely that would not have happened without Karl Rove and Ralph Reed's combining their considerable skills and ambitions. Early in their friendship, Rove and Reed shared the goal of having the Christian Right actively involved in the GOP, but to different ends. In Reed's approach, the Christian Coalition was an instrument to broaden religious influence in government and public policy. Rove viewed the Christian Coalition and allied groups as a giant, continually growing delivery system of voters for his Republican Party candidates and policies. He would use them. But he didn't want them at the gears and levers of government.

"Religion is all a political utility to Karl, not a personal utility," said GOP strategist and Rove colleague Don Sipple.

Reed was as religious as Rove was agnostic. Like his boss, Pat Robertson, Reed hoped to take over the Republican Party with an army of Christian evangelicals whose agenda could not be denied. Early in his tenure at the Christian Coalition, Reed was planning a stealth invasion of the GOP, which he characterized as nothing less than a guerrilla war.

"I want to be invisible," he told a Norfolk, Virginia, reporter. "I do guerilla warfare. I paint my face and travel at night. You don't know it's over until you're in a body bag."

In Texas, even as he was preparing George W. Bush to make his initial run for governor, Rove learned what it was like to be on the wrong side of the Christians, whose Pat Robertson–inspired stealth campaign effectively took control of the state GOP, starting at the local precinct level. Tom Pauken, a Goldwater conservative and former Reagan administration official, quietly enlisted the support of religious activists and was elected chairman of the Texas Republican Party at a tumultuous 1994 state party convention where his GOP opponent was booed when she told delegates, "The Republican Party is not a church."

Pauken and the new grassroots majority, however, saw in themselves a higher political calling, something more than simply a gear in Rove's machine to elect Bush. Rove was directing Bush's campaign for governor and wanted the party to take orders from the campaign, but Pauken would have none of it. His fidelity was to the party's conservative wing, not all of whom were enamored with George Bush 41 and had questions about the son. Pauken's first action as state chairman was to cancel Rove's contract to handle the GOP's direct-mail account, and with that, the struggle for control of the state party was joined.

Even before the 1994 election, Rove knew that Pauken had the votes to gain leadership of the state's Republican Party and the associated Victory '94 committee, which was set up to assist GOP candidates. Rove began asking big-money donors to redirect their money to the Bush campaign, not the party or Victory '94. Pauken and the evangelicals retained control of the party, in spite of the reduced budget, through the 1996 presidential election cycle. But not without a confrontation.

"That's when I was invited to the [governor's] mansion," Pauken recalled. "Served salmon. Bush must have known I don't like salmon. Rove was there, and they had it wired for Ernie Angelo to be head of Victory '96. They hard-core pressed me to turn it over to them. I said no."

Rove and Bush's resentment toward Pauken intensified when Texas delegates to the 1996 state convention elected Pauken, not the sitting governor, to head the delegation to the Republican National Convention in San Diego. This was to be Bush's first stroll across the national political stage, and that he was not the chair of the Texas Republican delegation was an embarrassment. Rove, who'd long cultivated the state's affluent political givers, went to the state's biggest Republican donors and finally and completely cut off the Texas GOP's money supply. Pauken was doomed to failure.

"It was Karl turning the spigot off," Pauken explained. "He could turn it on. He could turn it off. If you don't play ball, he's going to make life difficult. And that's the way it was."

Pauken was dispensable, but the Christians were not. To deliver important voter groups, Rove needed predictable leaders. "Karl tries to get key evangelical leaders to deliver the religious Right vote—whether it's Ralph Reed or [state Christian Coalition chief] Dick Weinhold or Pat Robertson. Falwell on down. That's the way they work. Karl's thinking is how he can control a group," Pauken explained.

Ultimately, in Rove's view, the value of religious conservatives was not that their beliefs enrich public policy but that their cohesion enabled his politics. Former White House speechwriter David Frum said Rove sees the American electorate as "an enormous box of toy magnets. Some of the magnets were white, and some were black or brown; some were rural, some were urban; some married, others single. . . . The job of a political strategist was to gather together the maximum feasible number of magnets."

In Ohio, the Bush campaign had twenty-one coalitions.

"We had religious coalitions, pro-life, sportsmen, gun owners. We recruited state coalition chairs, regional coalition chairs, and county coalition chairs," said Jo Ann Davidson, who oversaw the effort.

They were the magnets of Rove's political design, each attracted by something different, all sharing a place in the campaign's conservative base. Doug Preisse got nervous midway through the campaign because he was hearing a mounting chorus of complaints about how bad Bush was—wrong on the war, on gay marriage, on abortion. Preisse worried that Bush might be losing votes on several fronts. Or, he wondered, was the equation just the opposite? Might a highly charged campaign that inflames its opponents have the effect of provoking its various allies and producing even more votes for the president?

"And a light went off," he said. "And I'm thinking, somewhere in the recesses of the White House or somewhere, Rove is going to move the issue agenda to the Right and turn people out on a set of issues, not one. You probably do gay marriage on the ballot, and it worked. Essentially, it's all the same plan: go figure out who's for you, just like Lincoln laid out in the 1850s. Find out who's for you, and on Election Day, you turn them out at the polls. Instead of using horse carts and whiskey, we used direct mail and phones and e-mail."

Preisse, a partner in Ohio's best-known Republican political consulting firm, was a perfect example of how Rove's menu approach worked. As a gay man, Preisse could be expected to resent potential legal intrusions into his personal life, which were represented by the Issue One amendment. Preisse, however, as the consummate political professional, understood how the gay-marriage amendment was both motivating and expanding the party's religious base. Many gay Republicans put aside their resentment over the anti–gay marriage referenda because they knew these amendments would help to advance other issues they viewed as being of greater importance. More than any other U.S. presidential election in memory, turnout was the answer for both Bush and Kerry in 2004, and gay-marriage amendments were certain to bring voters to the polls.

To win the turnout war, Rove also turned to an unlikely source. He looked very closely at Hillary Clinton and her 2000 New York Senate race. In Clinton's success, Rove saw the prototype for the kind of grassroots campaign that Republicans needed to adopt. He concluded that all his campaign's whiz-bang technology was for naught unless it closed the sale at election time with person-to-person contact. It was not enough to tout the president on TV; supporters would have to go block to block, door-to-door. In an internal presentation entitled "The 72-Hour Task Force," Rove wrote that Republicans must fundamentally rethink how the party motivates its voters. "Perhaps the president's leadership will lead to a realignment of the electorate, but we would be foolish to plan on it," the presentation said.

Democrats such as Clinton had the advantage of labor unions canvassing neighborhoods on behalf of candidates. Republicans would have to build an apparatus that did the same thing. A change of mind-set was required, though. Having the town's local bank president or a Federation of Republican Women veteran in a Chanel suit going door-to-door with campaign literature was hardly a GOP tradition. But Rove was convinced the reason Janet Creighton was elected mayor of Canton in 2003 was because of the party's seventy-two-hour program, in which teams of volunteers combined phone calls with direct voter contact in the final days of a campaign. The Creighton race was one of several trial runs around the country in which Rove's strategists compared the traditional emphasis on

TV and phone banks versus person-to-person politicking. Personal contact always won.

In Florida, Pennsylvania, Ohio, and other battleground states, both Republicans and Democrats had a sizable turnout machine. But the models were different. Democrats largely outsourced the operations of their 527s, groups such as Americans Coming Together and MoveOn.org. Unlike the Bush-Cheney effort, which relied on 1.4 million volunteers, the Democratic 527s depended on large numbers of paid operatives, many from outside the states where they were working. Rove's rule was that volunteers be indigenous to the city, if not the neighborhood.

"What's interesting here in Ohio with the Republicans is that their get-out-the-vote effort was really native and indigenous, and the Democrats had so many people coming in from out of state. The rest were underutilized, misutilized, or misplaced," said Herb Asher, professor emeritus of political science at Ohio State University. "What's worrisome for the Democratic Party is that the Republican effort and the Republican infrastructure is already in place for 2006. It may need to be updated, but a lot of people who worked for the Democrats are out of date."

The task for both sides was registering voters, then getting them to vote early and, finally, turning them out at the polls on Election Day. But in each case, Rove had better numbers, in his computer and in his head.

Rove was consumed by numbers—poll numbers, registration numbers, early-voting numbers. Bush had a rule through much of the campaign that Rove could only give him poll numbers once a week. When, on one occasion, Rove sought to break the rule by bringing him particularly positive poll numbers, Bush snapped, "Once a week!" As Rove walked away, the president turned to a campaign ally and smiled. "I don't need him to tell me. I could tell by the look on his face."

Out on the trail, though, with fellow campaign operatives or journalists, Rove faced no such restriction. His ability to juggle a dozen sets of numbers and spout them at will was his most distinctive trait. In late October, as Bush stood on the fifty-yard line of a football field delivering his third campaign speech of the day to thousands of cheering supporters in the stands, a reporter asked Rove if he had paid enough attention to Ohio, where, according to media reports, Democrats were doing a better job at voter registration. It was as if someone had opened a fire hydrant.

"We've been to Moreland Hills, Ashtabula, Cleveland, Cambridge"—

he spouted cities like a manic travelogue—"Canton twice, Akron, Cambridge, Portsmouth, Marietta, Troy, Lima, Columbus several times."

As for voter registration, he glanced at his BlackBerry and delivered a real-time accounting: fifty-seven Ohio counties that voted Republican in the past four presidential races had added about 20,000 likely Bush voters to the rolls. And the state's eleven biggest Democratic counties? "There are 106,000 fewer registered voters today than there were four years ago—106,000 fewer!" he declared.

Reports from the field were fed with rigorous precision into the campaign's computer database and, it seemed, in the process, through Rove's brain. In the final seventy-two hours, the campaign turned its data into bound, updated walking lists complete with names and addresses, voter issue interests, and a map of the neighborhood on the back. The day before the election, Doug Preisse was out knocking on doors with a very specific list in his hand.

"We went to every third or every sixth house. This was the final distillation of the available information from the technology we have now," Preisse said.

As the campaign came to a conclusion, the event with Schwarzenegger was fine theater, but it was machinery and science that were making the difference out in Ohio's neighborhoods. Even in the campaign's showy stagecraft, there were indications that Rove's operation was more effective. The Republicans brought the Terminator to Ohio; the Democrats imported the Boss. MoveOn organized a thirty-three-city "Vote for Change" tour that included stops in Ohio featuring Bruce Springsteen and his E Street Band. The money went to America Coming Together's considerable registration and get-out-the-vote effort for John Kerry. When Springsteen took the stage in Cleveland, he shouted to the audience, "We're all here tonight to work for a more progressive government," and the crowd cheered.

But Dan Trevas wasn't so sure.

Trevas worked for the Ohio Democratic Party and had traveled to Cleveland for the concert. The Democratic 527s had spent enormous energy assembling the concert tour amid great noise and fanfare, and . . . for what? This crowd was twenty thousand screaming rock and rollers, not targeted Democratic voters.

"I'm in a row with some guys who came to hear Springsteen," he said.

"They're voting Republican. They were very vocal about it. Just play the music! No more speeches!" Trevas started having doubts about the efficiency of his allies. "Just because a 527 got them involved in politics doesn't mean they got Democrats."

By contrast, Rove's Republican machine was more efficient, more precise. Because he did not outsource so much of the operation, Rove remained in control. He had worked nearly four years building a database, targeting voters, implementing a hierarchy of responsibility, cultivating churches, road testing campaign operations, and perfecting a seventy-two-hour program that in the final three days of the campaign made 1.8 million telephone calls and knocked on 761,000 doors in Ohio alone.

During the last weekend of the campaign, both sides finished with a flurry of activity, hitting all the state's major media markets. Kerry rallied in Cleveland on Sunday before the election. Bush was in Columbus on Election Day visiting a phone bank, a gambit that was not altogether reassuring.

"Karl Rove was by no means confident of what was going to happen in Ohio," said a Republican political veteran close to the campaign. "The president came here and looked like a dork on Election Day. This guy came to Columbus and hung out at a phone bank. It was pathetic. He looked like a candidate for Ohio treasurer." He shook his head. "They were coming in here on Election Day, hanging out at the only place they could think of going. They were down to that."

Ultimately, it had come down to Ohio. Motivate the base and get them out in massive numbers. And after that, according to Rove's blueprint, incorporate them into the permanent campaign that was designed to assure GOP realignment. Kerry and his allies succeeded in turning out more than 550,000 new voters in Ohio, but it was not enough to offset the Republican gains in the new town houses and McMansions of the state's growing exurban counties. Bush won with 50.7 percent of the vote and, with it, retained the presidency. Nationally, Republicans not only kept the White House but also expanded control of Congress, winning an additional four seats in the Senate and three in the House.

In January, after the reelection, Rove's key contact in Ohio, Jo Ann Davidson, was elevated to cochair of the Republican National Committee. Her job was to engage grassroots activists in a national program aimed at building an enduring majority.

"Time will tell if this is a realignment," Davidson said. "Can we take this huge number of people who became involved in the Bush-Cheney campaign, and can we keep them involved? That's the key. Our ability to do that is the key to making this a permanent realignment."

A generation of Republican dominance was Karl Rove's goal. And he was close after winning two presidential elections with George W. Bush. The second victory prompted the president to cite the political capital he'd earned and intended to use to accomplish great things. Rove had helped deliver to Bush the keys to an operation capable of great political and policy achievement.

As was always the case in his campaigns, Rove had toyed around the edges of ethics and law to protect what he had created, and it was hard to change his behavior in the White House. Political decisions made at the highest levels of the Bush administration were suddenly threatening to destroy Rove's dream of realignment and disassemble his great victory machine.

And for the first time in his career, Karl Rove was not in control of what came next.

NINE

A FEW SIMPLE QUESTIONS

What's in Karl's Closet?

Truth is not determined by majority vote.
—Doug Gwyn

E ric Resnick did not want to ask the question. He felt an obligation, though, because other reporters were avoiding the subject. They ought to have long ago confronted Ken Mehlman about the contradictions between his politics and his personal life. Resnick thought the question had needed to be asked during the 2004 reelection campaign. Mehlman, the chairman of the Republican National Committee, was constantly around reporters from the *New York Times*, *Washington Post*, *Time*, *Newsweek*, CNN, ABC, NBC, and all of the major media outlets. None of them, however, had dared to question the RNC chairman about what Eric Resnick considered a blatant, obvious hypocrisy. The president had begun his second term and the GOP was expanding its power base, and Resnick was angry over harm done to gays by Republicans during the campaign.

Mehlman, Karl Rove's general for handling issues and elections across the country as President Bush's campaign manager, had been closely involved with the Issue One referendum in Resnick's home state of Ohio. Republicans there referred to the ballot item as the pro-marriage amendment and the Defense of Marriage Act. People such as Eric Resnick, a gay man who was a reporter for the *Gay People's Chronicle* in Cleveland, considered Issue One to be an antihomosexuality law designed to make

their lives miserable. He resented being used as a political device to motivate a hate vote against homosexuals.

"For our community, it was absolutely incredible," he explained.
"Every single debate and discussion had something gay in it, and we've
never seen anything like that before. At that point, it is part of the public
policy discussion, and those guys revved up their base and used our community as an issue to win votes in that election, and at that point, it does
become a public matter."

Resnick and most of the gay, lesbian, bisexual, and transgender community of Ohio were incensed at Republican efforts, led by master strategist Karl Rove, to use a political wedge issue to drive a huge turnout of
Christian Right voters. Even more than that, though, gay political organizations had begun actively questioning whether RNC chairman Ken
Mehlman was gay, making it difficult to believe that he was complicit in
the antigay part of Rove's Master Plan. A gay bashing gays? Resnick had
trouble believing in such a concept. Nobody in the mainstream media
had considered Mehlman's apparent hypocrisy that important. But
Resnick did. He thought that he had a right to know, that the GOP had
made gay Republicans an issue by advancing an anti–gay-rights agenda in
its bid to win the presidency.

Coincidentally, Resnick was being presented with a chance to confront
the hypocrisy in person during a trip to Ohio by Mehlman. And he was
not going to pass it up. Resnick intended to be the first reporter to ask Ken
Mehlman if he was gay. So when an invitation came from the Log Cabin
Republicans to a fund-raising banquet in Akron, Resnick knew he was
going to attend. Ken Mehlman, the target of a relentless Internet outing
campaign and the new chairman of the Republican National Committee,
was the featured speaker for the post–2004 election thank-you dinner for
Summit County Republicans. Even better, Resnick thought, the event was
being hosted by the county party chair, fifty-year-old Alex Arshinkoff, a
married father and closeted gay man who'd been at the wheel of the Issue
One campaign in that part of the Ohio River Valley.

In Resnick's estimation, here were two of the biggest hypocrites in all
of the Republican political power structure. Most of the people gathering that night either were unaware of the controversy or didn't care. But
Eric Resnick did. And as a good journalist, he knew that the dinner and
speech in Akron was exactly where he needed to be. As a result, on

March 19, 2005, Resnick was making the quick run between Cleveland and Akron to attend the Summit County Lincoln Day Dinner.

Out the window of his car, the mercurial weather of late winter offered the possibility of warm days ahead in the Great Lakes basin or the unexpected dump of new snow. Resnick had purchased a forty-dollar ticket from the Log Cabin Republicans to attend the fund-raiser at the Quaker Station convention hall in Akron. He had no intention of presenting reporter's credentials, but neither was he making the trip as a participant in Summit County's Republican Party politics.

"I knew Ken Mehlman would be there," Resnick explained. "And I knew I'd have access to him afterwards just because of the way people are when they line up to talk to the head table. I knew what I was doing when I went in, and I knew the question I wanted to ask him."

The question, of course, was aimed at learning Mehlman's true sexual orientation and, if he was gay, reconciling that with his championing of Issue One. In the 2004 presidential election, there'd been no way for Resnick or any other Ohio resident to avoid Issue One. It was all over television and radio, on phone messages, and in sermons at church. It was impossible for Ohio voters to miss the message about the sanctity of marriage and the need to protect all those "years of human history" by defining the institution of marriage as a union between a man and a woman.

Even Secretary of State Kenneth Blackwell, the Ohio officeholder whose constitutional mandate calls for nonpartisan supervision of the state's elections, recorded "robo-calls" promoting Issue One. Blackwell, a Republican with designs on the Ohio governor's office, is a conservative African American. His association with Issue One helped broaden the appeal of the measure to conservative black churches and increased the turnout for President Bush among minorities sympathetic to a gay-marriage ban.

Herb Asher, a political scientist at Ohio State University, abandoned his academic detachment in describing the Ohio secretary of state's active involvement in promoting the change of law in his state.

"I actually came home one night, and there on my answering machine was a message: 'Hi. This is Secretary of State Ken Blackwell urging you to vote yes on Issue One, an issue that will uphold the sanctity of marriage. It's a simple little amendment.' You fucker. I mean where are the ethics from the National Association of Secretaries of State to say he shouldn't be involved?"

During the 2004 race, Eric Resnick had aggressively sought out political candidates and campaign operatives. When the vice presidential debate came to Case Western Reserve University in Cleveland, Resnick pursued Ken Mehlman, who was then running the Bush campaign, and asked him how closely Blackwell was working with the president's re-election team on Issue One and why such a divisive subject was being used as a tactic. Mehlman denied that Issue One was antigay or divisive, but he acknowledged that Bush officials were coordinating with the Ohio secretary of state on Issue One. Officially, Karl Rove's position was that the marriage amendments had arisen organically within eleven states and the Bush campaign was not connected to those efforts. In fact, it was part of Rove's active strategy to divide and conquer by microtargeting religious conservatives and motivating the base.

It struck Resnick that Mehlman's answers at the vice presidential debate were evasive and mostly inconclusive, and so in the wake of Bush's reelection and the smashing success of Issue One in galvanizing GOP voters, the gay journalist decided to make the trip to Akron.

In addition to Mehlman, there was another attraction for Eric Resnick. Summit County's Republicans were led by Alex Arshinkoff, the longest-serving county chair for the GOP in the United States. A powerful and controversial figure in Ohio Republican politics, Arshinkoff was enduring publicity about his own sexual orientation after a profile of him was published in *Cleveland Scene,* a weekly newspaper. According to an article entitled "The Godfather in the Closet," the Summit County Republican Party chairman was stopped by police in Akron after he'd picked up a twenty-one-year-old male Kent State college student and solicited sex. The story was based on an Akron police report, which has been widely circulated in Ohio political circles. According to the police record, the student jumped from Alex Arshinkoff's car and ran off. An officer driving behind Arshinkoff witnessed the incident and stopped him for questioning. The unidentified student, who was interviewed by the Cleveland paper, said Arshinkoff rubbed his thigh and asked him if he were gay or bisexual and if he wanted to make some money.

Arshinkoff, who is married, was not arrested and the student declined to file charges against the influential Summit County GOP chairman. The story of that encounter, though, was no surprise to many people in

Akron politics. A former member of the Republican central and executive committees in Akron, Chris Bleuenstein, says, "Most people are aware of it. Stupid him; he just keeps getting caught."

Michael Curry, a Democrat who works on the Summit County Board of Elections, said he ran into Arshinkoff at a gay bar called the Leather Stallion in Cleveland. Thirty minutes after he'd said hello to the Republican leader, according to Curry, Arshinkoff said, "If there's anything I can do for you, I'd be happy to do it." Curry told the Cleveland paper that he joked about not wanting two of his Democratic judge friends to face an opponent in the general election, and Arshinkoff reportedly responded, "I can do that."

Curry said he ran into Arshinkoff several months later in 2001, more than a year before the incident involving the college student and Arshinkoff, and the GOP leader offered to "live up to his end of the bargain." The encounter reportedly occurred at another gay dance club in Cleveland called The Grid. After that, Curry decided he needed to talk.

"I've just decided he's a hypocrite about it," he said. "He's gone out and recruited candidates who are homophobic and anti-gay. If he ever openly admitted he was gay, I think a lot of money would dry up."

During his work for *Gay People's Chronicle*, Eric Resnick said he had been introduced to Alex Arshinkoff by a gay friend. The idea that any Republican leader might be gay, coupled with the GOP's saturation advertising campaign on Issue One targeting gays and lesbians in the 2004 election, struck a nerve with Resnick.

Alex Arshinkoff and Ken Mehlman were in the same room for the Lincoln Day Dinner; Mehlman was the keynote speaker, and Arshinkoff, the event's host. But the reporter was not interested in the Ohio Republican. Eric Resnick ignored Alex Arshinkoff but lingered near the head table after Ken Mehlman concluded his speech. Mehlman had thanked Summit County because it had "increased its votes for George W. Bush from 2000 to 2004 more than any other county." A line had formed in front of Mehlman near the dais, and Resnick waited until it had shortened before approaching the chairman of the Republican National Committee. He was not carrying a recorder or wearing reporter's credentials.

"I shook his hand and introduced myself as a reporter for the *Gay People's Chronicle*," Resnick said. "And I began asking him innocuous questions about things he had said in his speech. But I prefaced each one by saying, 'Since the bloggers have outed you,' or 'Since you were outed on

national radio, is that going to change how the party treats gay people?'
He just ignored my premise and gave me canned, standard answers."

A new line of Mehlman well-wishers had gathered behind Resnick,
but he ignored them and kept peppering the GOP chair with questions.
Eventually, Mehlman's patience ran out, and he denied that he had been
outed.

"That's inaccurate," Mehlman said.

"What do you mean?" Resnick thought *inaccurate* was an odd word to
use in that context.

"What they are saying in the blogs," Mehlman answered, attempting a
delicate political clarification.

"You mean you are not gay?" Resnick was hoping for some clarity of his
own, and he did not expect to get another chance to pose such a question.

"You have asked a question people shouldn't have to answer," Ken
Mehlman said, before slowly backing away from the reporter.

It was the first time a journalist had publicly asked the chairman of the
Republican National Committee about his sexual orientation. Resnick's
story for his paper, headlined "GOP National Chair Avoids Questions
about His Sexuality," created a brief phenomenon in the gay and lesbian
community that came to be known as "Mehlmania." There was more
blogging on the Web and talking on the radio, but Mehlman's ambigu-
ous reply did not meet the standards of news for mainstream journalists,
who neither noticed nor wrote about it.

"I just went in there believing if reporters started asking the question
multiple times, it would start to have an effect on him," Resnick said.

But nothing changed. Ken Mehlman still ran the Republican Party.
Powerful gay members of the GOP continued to exercise their influence
in a manner that many considered both contradictory and hypocritical.
To Eric Resnick, it appeared that hardly anyone seemed to notice or care.
"I am extremely angry about it all. I still am. And sometimes it's hard for
me to do this job as a reporter and put that all aside effectively and appro-
priately and truly get the story. And I am not sure I will ever get over the
anger. Sixty-two percent of the people who voted in Ohio basically told
us to go to hell. And that is not an easily reconcilable thing."

It was, however, a key to victory for Rove and the Bush reelection.
When he reviewed the numbers immediately after the 2004 election,
Rove saw that the machine had worked in Ohio. He'd increased turnout

of the conservative base significantly, more than offsetting the Kerry team's efforts to energize labor, urban voters, and traditional Democrats. The large message in 2004 was Bush the leader in time of war, but in the battleground of Ohio with a crucial cache of electoral votes, Rove needed something more to vanquish the enemy. And he found it in a legal attack on gay marriage, a wedge idea with profound electoral effect in eleven critical swing states.

Karl Rove was getting closer to realizing his dream.

Karl Rove remembers the end of his parents' marriage very clearly. If he recalls the causes of its dissolution, he is less forthcoming about those facts. His father, Louis Rove, had received an offer from Getty Oil in Los Angeles to be the chief geologist in the mineral department. After working for many years at Vitro Chemical in Salt Lake City, Louis Rove figured this was the type of opportunity he ought not to decline.

"This was a great job," Karl Rove remembered during a breakfast conversation one bright morning in Austin. The tone of the political operative's energetic voice softened as he spoke of his father, a man he clearly loved.

"He's my stepfather," Rove explained. "He's my adoptive father."

"When did that happen?" he was asked.

"Oh, I have no idea; very early in life. I did not know he was my adoptive father until I was twenty. But he's my father, my adoptive father. I don't refer to him as Louis Rove."

In spite of his deep and obvious affection for the man who raised him, there was a problem in Karl Rove's household when he was coming of age. His four siblings might have missed the undercurrent of tension, but it seems unlikely that an astute and intuitive observer such as Karl, even as a teenager, wouldn't have realized the disturbing complications in his parents' relationship. Louis Rove was commuting frequently between Los Angeles and Salt Lake to be with his family beginning in the spring of 1969, Karl's senior year in high school. As he was preparing to enter college, Karl was adjusting to the idea that his mother and father, possibly his brother, and his three sisters would be leaving Salt Lake to resettle in L.A.

"The theory was that, after I graduated from high school, the family would then move to Los Angeles," Rove explained as he pulled apart a bagel and looked out a hotel's broad windows at Austin's Town Lake. "And murkily, that didn't happen, for reasons that were not really clear or explained."

On Christmas Eve of 1969, Louis Rove came home to be with his family for the holidays. Karl's birthday was the next day, and he was pleased to have his father back in town. Whatever that unnamed thing was, though, that had been moving through the house when his parents were together, it took on a form and an importance that made it impossible for Louis Rove to ignore it any longer. Karl watched as his mother and father began to argue at a time when the family was supposed to be gathering for celebration. When the squabble had ended, Louis Rove walked out and returned to a hotel where he had already registered before going to see his wife and children. He had obviously intended to deal with an important matter and stop pretending it did not exist. The family was not going to be reunited by moving to Los Angeles with Louis.

"My mother, who was great in sort of explaining things in her way, said there were reasons that couldn't happen," he said. "They fought. So there were obviously difficulties between the two of them that caused him to do that. But he left, went back and got on the airplane, and flew back to Los Angeles."

Louis Rove filed for divorce and began life as a single man in Southern California. At the conclusion of his career as a geologist, he moved eastward to the desert and retired in Palm Springs, California. A large man, whom one friend estimated to weigh about three hundred pounds, Louis Rove met retired insurance executive Joseph Koons through a neighbor, and they became best friends over the course of the next thirteen years.

"I thought of him as my brother," Koons said. "He was more than my best friend. We saw each other just about every day and always talked every day. Louie was very much a wonderful, wonderful person, very warm and accommodating. He was just a tremendous man and a good father to Karl."

Joseph Koons had been living openly as a gay man throughout his adult life, but Louis Rove had only come out after he'd left his family in Salt Lake City and moved to Southern California. Koons said the two of them were never romantically involved and were simply looking to socialize with older gay men who'd retired to Palm Springs, in part, to join its large gay and lesbian community.

"Louie didn't hide the fact that he was gay," said Koons. "But he didn't play it up either. We had lots of gay and straight friends. I was never the effeminate type, and neither was Louie. We didn't play it up that way, either. But he was gay. And so am I."

Perhaps because of his size or the fact that he'd begun to live openly as a gay man relatively late in life, Louis Rove appeared to be uncomfortable in social settings. His friend Joe Koons began to take Rove to an informal gathering of retired gay men referred to by its members as the Old Farts Club.

"We are just an innocuous, inane group of older gay men that gets together to just eat and make fun of each other," one of the participants explained. "Back at the time Louie came around with Joe, there were only about eight of us involved. We've limited it to twenty-four now because of the limitations of the restaurants around here. We do things like creating coloring books teaching kids how to wage peace."

The men met every Friday, usually at the Rainbow Cactus Restaurant (jokingly referred to by the group as the "Rainbow Casket") or the Martini Burger, to eat, drink, and socialize.

"These were very public, openly gay restaurants," Joe Koons explained. "That's why we all went there."

Although Koons convinced Louis Rove to attend some of these lunches and dinners, Rove never settled into the lighthearted conversations and conviviality and tended to stay home.

One of the regular members of the Old Farts Club tried to befriend Louis Rove but without much success. "He was a sad and lonely man who didn't open up to people readily," according to the gay man, who'd retired to Palm Springs from the Pacific Northwest. "I suppose he was gregarious, but not beyond a certain point. Joe only brought Louie around three or four times, and then they didn't come anymore."

Joe Koons and Louis Rove began spending most of their time together in Rove's home in an upscale Palm Springs neighborhood. Their habit of nightly drinking, and what Koons described as Rove's "prolific smoking," caused significant deterioration in Louis's health. During the last part of Louis's life, however, Koons said Karl Rove was a fairly frequent visitor to his father's home, and, when Louis's health permitted, they traveled together. Koons saw no indication that Louis's sexual orientation caused any complications between father and son.

"No," Koons explained. "I don't recall that there was any great tension over it. I don't know how much impact that plays in the family and when they did find out about it. Karl is certainly not dumb. I am sure he knows more than anyone about his father's position. The times I spent with Karl and Louie were wonderful, and Karl was always just very, very nice. I didn't notice any problems. Louie was very proud of his son, and rightly so. I wish I could have had a son like him."

Neighbors of Louis Rove first introduced him to his friend Joe Koons. A mutual friend of the neighbors and Koons, who looked in on Rove during the time when he was housebound and receiving oxygen therapy, described a picture of Karl Rove on a wall near the kitchen and another on the mantel. This was years earlier during evening cocktails at Louis Rove's before his health had begun to fail. The friend asked Louis about the photographs of Karl.

"That's my son," he was told. "He's in politics down in Texas. I think he might be something big someday."

"This was well before George W. had even run for governor," the friend said. "I think the elder Bush was president back then."

The man, who remains friends with Louis Rove's neighbors, went with them on occasion to check in on Rove as his vitality declined further and he became confined to a wheelchair. The friend said he has socialized with Karl Rove during his visits to Palm Springs and finds it incomprehensible that the political strategist plays innocent when talking about the end of his parents' marriage.

"He [Karl] obviously was hurt by the divorce," Louis Rove's friend said. "It's just absurd when he says, 'I had no idea what the problems were with my parents and their marriage.' He knew damned good and well what was going on. His father had decided to come out of the closet."

Any mild estrangement that might have existed between Louis Rove and his adoptive son was eventually resolved. Karl began seeing his father on a regular basis in the 1980s and vacationed with him in Santa Fe, New Mexico, almost every summer. During that time, Karl and his older brother, Eric, found their biological father and met with him, but no relationship developed and they never saw him again.

Rove has always seemed to honor Louis Rove as his father and was especially moved when he learned Louis was depriving himself to send money to Reba Wood Rove's two oldest children, who weren't Louis's biological offspring. Karl, however, has never publicly acknowledged the context his father's homosexuality might have offered for all that has transpired in the Rove family life, including the possibility that it may have been a contributing factor to his mother's 1981 suicide more than a decade after the divorce.

"Again, it's hard to figure out," Rove said. "You can speculate on what demons she just wasn't able to overcome, but she couldn't. And it's very sad for my sisters, who were very close to her."

A man of almost startling intelligence, Rove is not likely to have ignored the possibility that his father's homosexuality might have figured in his mother's choice to end her own life. Nonetheless, such a causal connection had no impact on Rove's relationship with Louis. Rove took his father to Norway in 1998 for an exploration of Louis's ancestry, and when California was enduring the rolling electricity blackouts in 2001 as Enron's Ken Lay (a major Bush supporter) and his company gamed the electricity markets to drive up profits, Karl coordinated emergency efforts with his siblings to keep Louis's breathing machines functioning.

"I think they were reasonably close," Louis Rove's friend Joseph Koons said. "And I think Louie's sex orientation didn't affect that. I got along quite well with Karl. I think he was a devoted son, and I know his dad loved him."

When Louis Rove died, Karl was executor of his estate. No legal death notice or paid obituary was published in the Palm Springs paper. The seventy-six-year-old Rove was not buried in either of the two cemeteries in the Coachella River Valley on the southern edge of the Mojave Desert. A close friend said there was no funeral. The final disposition of his mortal remains is known only to Louis Rove's immediate family. The son, of whom Louis was so proud, has kept a photo of his smiling father in a star-shaped frame in his office in the West Wing of the White House, a few steps from the Oval Office. And Karl Rove is convinced his father was a happy, contented person.

"He lived life exactly the way he wanted to live it," Rove said.

Which was as a gay man.

Louis Rove passed away quietly at home on July 14, 2004.

His son was in the midst of launching the antigay issues campaign that was to lead to the reelection of George W. Bush.

TEN

LAWYERS, DUNS, AND MONEY

Closing Down the Courthouse

*Political language . . . is designed to make lies sound truthful
and murder respectable, and to give an appearance of
solidity to pure wind.*
—George Orwell

Ruby Calad assumed she was dreaming. Before she was admitted for her operation, Calad thought she'd been reassured she'd be able to stay in the Houston hospital for as much recovery time as was necessary. Instead, while the drugs from her anesthesia were still in her bloodstream, Calad heard through the haze the angry voice of her doctor telling her she had to be discharged and recuperate at home. Only a day had passed since Ruby Calad had undergone a hysterectomy operation as well as procedures to repair vaginal tearing and rectal and kidney problems. Her surgeon reached into drawers near her bed and began pulling out her clothes, throwing them around in anger.

"You have to leave," he said.

"Listen," Ruby tried to explain, "I'm in an extreme amount of pain. There's no way I can leave this hospital."

"If you don't leave," her doctor explained, "you're going to have to pay $1500."

"But I can't even walk." Calad said later that she was so overwhelmed by drugs and pain that she was unable at the time even to recall her own phone number.

Calad's doctor left the room and went down the hall to argue with her health care company's discharge nurse, but to no avail. He was informed that Calad's insurance company, CIGNA's HMO, refused to pay for additional days in her room. She'd been precertified for only one day of postoperative care and didn't meet CIGNA's medical-necessity criteria for more care.

Ruby Calad went home and developed complications. She was readmitted to the hospital a few days later and eventually faced further corrective surgery. Convinced that she'd been sent home by CIGNA's nurse for reasons of profit and not medicine, Calad was angry. She thought her life had been endangered because her HMO had made a medical decision instead of her surgeon. It all felt very wrong and unfair, and Ruby wanted justice. So she hired a lawyer, George Parker Young of Fort Worth.

Only months later, Calad's attorney paired her with an ally in her cause. Juan Davila, who also lived in Texas just north of Fort Worth, was a victim of polio who'd developed severe rheumatoid arthritis. Davila was in constant pain and asked his doctor for medication to ease his suffering. The appropriate prescription, according to his physician, was an expensive brand-name pain reliever. Unless he had potential allergies, it was the most promising form of pain relief for Davila's condition.

Davila's doctor was informed by the pharmacist of his health care company, Aetna, that a less-expensive generic drug had to be tried first. A prescription was written for that drug, which had a higher risk of causing internal bleeding. Within a few weeks, Juan Davila was rushed to an emergency room with extensive internal bleeding and was given seven units of blood during transfusions. Emergency room doctors told him he was just a few hours away from death. After five days in critical care, Davila was sent home but had to be readmitted for follow-up care. The crisis left him unable to take any pain medication that is absorbed through the wall of the stomach.

Juan Davila and Ruby Calad were certain that what had happened to them was simply that their health insurance companies were making economic decisions that preempted the better medical judgment of their doctors. They decided to sue Aetna and CIGNA for putting their lives unnecessarily at risk. Fortunately, they lived in Texas. Not known for progressive legislation, the state had nonetheless approved a Patients' Bill of Rights in 1997 during the administration of Governor George W. Bush. Although the key piece of the legislation became law without Bush's signature, the Managed Care Responsibility Act made Texas the first state to allow patients to sue their HMOs for medical malpractice.

Most of the Patients' Bill of Rights measures had been embraced by the conservative governor but not the provision allowing for lawsuits against HMOs. Regardless, during his first run for the White House, George W. Bush bragged about his involvement in the Texas law enabling patients to sue their HMOs. In the final presidential debate of 2000, Bush told the country that he was determined to take the Texas model to Congress and create federal regulations to protect people insured by HMOs.

"I do support a national patients' bill of rights," Bush said. "As a matter of fact, I brought Republicans and Democrats together to do just that in the state of Texas . . . to get a patients' bill of rights through. . . . We got one of the most advanced patients' bill of rights. But we did something else that was interesting. We're one of the first states that said you can sue your HMO for denying you proper coverage."

The future president either had strategically mischaracterized his lack of involvement or forgotten his own record. The original version of the law, which would have made Texas the national leader in HMO reform as early as 1995, was vetoed by Bush. Regulations in what was named the Patient Protection Act would have prevented HMOs from firing doctors without reason or failing to pay for emergency room visits. HMOs would also have been restricted from denying expensive procedures or needed treatments and would have had to allow patients to choose their own doctors. When Bush vetoed the measure during his first legislative session as governor, he told reporters, "It was the easy thing politically to sign the bill and the headline of your story ought to read, 'Governor shows political courage.'"

In spite of what he told voters watching the televised presidential debate from Saint Louis in October of 2000, the law that enabled Juan Davila and Ruby Calad to file lawsuits against their HMOs in Texas bore neither the signature nor any signs of the involvement of George W. Bush. It was passed two years after the veto and became law without Bush's signature. Politically, Texas business interests and conservatives had expected another veto from Bush, but he might have feared an override that would prove embarrassing in a presidential campaign. The chairman of the House Public Health Committee, Democratic state representative Hugo Berlanga, had warned Bush of potential political consequences of a veto the second time around.

"I said, 'You cannot afford to veto this legislation,'" Berlanga explained. "I pointed out the enormous coalition we had behind it, every medical provider group, every consumer group, the trial lawyers, organized labor. I laid out what it meant to him politically."

One of the sponsors of the 1997 bill in the Texas Senate was an old and steadfast Republican confederate of Governor Bush's. Senator David Sibley kept responding to veto threats from the governor's staff by attempting to draft changes to the measure that would make it more politically palatable for Bush. Eventually, he ran out of patience and political decorum and complained on the floor of the full Senate.

"I can't make them happy, no matter what I do, unless I completely gut the bill," Sibley said.

The bill Bush had wanted to gut but didn't have the political courage to veto was nonetheless promoted by his presidential campaign as a significant achievement by the governor. In Texas, he'd said the legislation had "the potential to drive up health care costs and increase the number of lawsuits," but on the national stage, the Bush-Cheney campaign issued a news release taking credit for the Patients' Bill of Rights with what can be graciously interpreted as inaccurate information and, more harshly, as a lie.

"In 1997, Bush *signed* [emphasis added] legislation providing patient protections that are considered a national model. The legislation, based on rules enacted by the state insurance commissioner at Governor Bush's direction, was considered by expert medical professionals as a model for the country."

Bush had, in fact, put his name on four out of five new laws governing review and regulation of HMOs and PPOs, which his political adviser Karl Rove had described to reporters and others as a Patients' Bill of Rights. The most critical measure of the package, however, was the law governing liability for HMOs, and Bush did not sign it. (If a sitting governor does not veto a particular piece of legislation in Texas, it becomes law without his or her approving signature.) The facts surrounding the right to sue HMOs were parsed to fit the politics. George W. Bush did not want his name attached to any law likely to anger the insurance companies and employers he expected to be major contributors to his future presidential campaign. And if he'd vetoed the measure, Bush would have faced the embarrassment of an override because it had passed the state Senate by a twenty-five to five margin.

Ruby Calad and Juan Davila thought the Texas law was pretty good, though. They saw it as a legal means to gain justice in their disputes with the HMOs that had denied them coverage. Oddly, their lawyer, George

Parker Young, was a lifelong Republican and had been one of George W. Bush's original fund-raisers in his first run for governor and a donor to the Florida fund to protect the Bush electoral lead in 2000. Additionally, Young had been intimately involved in the creation and passage of the Texas Patients' Bill of Rights law and had defended the measure in court for the state when Aetna Insurance sought to have it overturned in 1997.

George Parker Young believed in the Texas HMO liability law, and he took George W. Bush at his word when he said he wanted to pass a similar measure for the nation. He did not, therefore, expect to spend most of the first Bush presidential term fighting the White House to protect the Texas law on behalf of Ruby Calad and Juan Davila. Young wanted to test the law and prove its fairness and strength. And his determination was destined to get him and his clients into an argument with the president of the United States before the highest court in America.

Linda Lipsen sat at the head of a large oval table and looked at the thirty-five people who'd gathered in the room. The light was dim, and a late winter snow fell softly outside along the canal in Georgetown. An American flag hung in one corner. Attendees shuffled their feet across the gray carpet as they settled into chairs beneath tall shelves of law books.

The Association of Trial Lawyers of America (ATLA) was having another weekly strategy meeting. Lipsen, who led the organization, showed only traces of fatigue with a fight that had greatly intensified since George Bush and Karl Rove had begun their rise to political prominence. Rove's long campaign had effectively demonized attorneys. They were the bad guys. The thinking was, lawyers filed frivolous lawsuits that drove up the costs of medical care and made it expensive for businesses to operate. In fact, a study conducted by the Joint Economic Committee of the U.S. House claimed that between 1994 and 2001, the typical medical malpractice award, for example, had risen 176 percent to $1 million and that malpractice insurance topped $21 billion, twice what it had been ten years earlier, in 1991. Lawyers were not the only reason for that, but they were a part of the problem.

What Karl Rove never talked about, of course, was the primary source of his disdain for the legal profession. He hated trial lawyers because they were a primary source of funding for the Democratic Party.

Lipsen and ATLA had assembled a savvy group of political operatives.

Among them was a well-known Republican lobbyist who was compelled to work anonymously as a consultant to avoid becoming anathema to his own party. His job was to consistently inform ATLA of the latest strategic thinking of conservative members of Congress as they drew up legislation to change the country's civil justice system and reduce the income of plaintiffs' attorneys. John Weaver, a former business partner of Karl Rove and the once and future campaign manager of Senator John Mc-Cain's presidential bids, sat at the head of the table near Lipsen and offered GOP insights. Weaver was a retained consultant, but ATLA also had a Republican lobbyist on staff payroll.

For all the talk of million-dollar verdicts, the trial lawyers were no match financially for the pharmaceutical and insurance companies. Many personal injury lawyers were making a lot of money, but they didn't make up the majority of ATLA's membership. And on Capitol Hill, the pharma firms deploy more than three hundred lobbyists. Overall, the entire health care industry spends about $300 million on lobbying, whereas ATLA's members have been able to muster only about $5 million annually. While outgunned by business interests, trial lawyers remain a major source of funding for candidates. In the 2005 election cycle, they spent more than $112 million on campaign donations, with 80 percent of that amount going to Democrats. Regardless, the list of challenges confronting these members of the plaintiffs' bar seemed to grow each week.

Lipsen's agenda requires more time and commitment than is available in the two- to three-hour weekly gatherings. On this particular morning in 2005, she turned the discussion to a version of the antiterrorism bill that included provisions to protect big business and mitigate consumer claims.

"This is a very broad terrorism bill," Lipsen explained. "Look, this thing gives permission for drugs and devices that aren't even FDA [Food and Drug Administration] approved, including vaccines. If they are on the track for approval and could be approved in eight years, they can get approved almost immediately under this act. All liability protections and provisions kick in."

"God, this is just amazing shit," a voice from the far end of the table says.

"Don't we need to have some media attention on this?" Lipsen looks at Carlton Carl, who was then leading ATLA's messaging and media strategies. "I mean, it seems like reporters might be interested in the fact that the leadership is using terrorism to eliminate laws and liability for big corporations. This is really outrageous. We can't let ourselves be so immunized to all the nutty things that are being done that we don't pay attention. This is just amazing."

There was much that needed attention. Congress had just passed and the president had signed a law moving class-action suits from state courts to federal court. Conservatives had long railed against federal judges, arguing their preference for local control. But in this case, with business at stake, they espoused a different principle. It was a first order of business for President Bush at the beginning of 2005. Because of crowded federal dockets, most class-action cases under the new law were never going to make it to a courtroom even if a judge agreed to certification. For a state court to retain jurisdiction, it must meet a series of qualifying criteria that many lawyers consider impossible. Federal judges, already overburdened with work, opposed the legislation, but it was an essential piece of the Karl Rove plan to reduce sources of income for plaintiffs' attorneys. His task was made easier by the actions of "coupon lawyers," who had reputations for venue shopping in various states, winning huge class-action fees, and then leaving their clients with little more than a coupon for a modest cash refund.

One of Rove's most ambitious goals has always been to shut down the lucrative medical-malpractice litigators. As Bush campaigned, Rove made sure the president used the terms *meritless* and *frivolous* to describe suits brought by attorneys dealing in medical malpractice. The president's unwavering message was the same as Rove had written for him in Texas— that such claims were driving up the cost of health care to the average American through rising insurance premiums and more-expensive fees for medical procedures. Led by Rove, the Republican majority sought to put a federal limit of $250,000 on the damages that could be awarded for pain and suffering in those lawsuits while also capping contingency fees for lawyers. A court would still have the authority to award total coverage of any economic losses by the victim.

The debate over tort reform is based more on statistics than rhetoric, but discerning fact is nonetheless difficult. Figures cited by the trial lawyers' community are the opposite of those used by the administration. They cannot both be right. The situation, as described by Bush administration treasury secretary John Snow, is disturbing.

"We know that the current tort system is costing America well over $200 billion each year," he told the American Tort Reform Association's annual meeting in 2004. "That's a tort tax—paid in the form of lower wages, higher product prices, and reduced investments—of $809 for every individual and more than $3200 for a family of four. And this is a regressive tax, imposed indiscriminately across our economy. To make the situation even less fair, less than 50 cents of each dollar of those tort costs go to victims, and, of that, only 22 cents goes to compensate them for actual economic losses they have suffered. Meanwhile the personal injury lawyers profit enormously."

The American civil justice system Snow details is indeed in desperate need of reform, but it is not the same one plaintiffs' attorneys believe exists. They concede there are problems, though they are not as severe as the Bush administration argues. Mostly, they think there is a concerted political attack to shut down trial lawyers and close off the civil justice system to consumers who might harm corporations. And they blame that on Karl Rove.

After hobbling trial lawyers handling class-action lawsuits and medical-malpractice claims, Rove, the trial lawyers think, intends to go after asbestos attorneys and, eventually, no-fault auto insurance lawyers, effectively forcing most of ATLA's membership out of business, one practice area at a time.

"Go back and look at the Contract with America," said Carlton Carl, ATLA's communications chief. "When [Newt] Gingrich drew that up back in the early nineties, it was designed to take down the trial-lawyer industry completely with one or two laws. It was a comprehensive attack. The larger point now, though, is that the Republicans in the chamber got smart and realized you don't have to take it all down at once. You take it down a piece at a time. You don't need umbrella tort reform."

The "piece" Linda Lipsen and her ATLA team were most concerned about in early 2005 was medical-malpractice reform. A group of doctors from the American Medical Association was coming to Washington, D.C., for discussions on advocacy of their issues and the development of policies to protect them from the increasing cost of malpractice insurance. ATLA wanted to confront the doctors, who'd recently been turned into an active constituency by Karl Rove. Physicians, many of whom had once viewed insurance companies and their exorbitant premiums as the cause of their problems, were suddenly buying into the notion that lawyers were at fault for higher premiums.

This type of political jujitsu was a measure of Karl Rove's considerable genius.

"He now has the doctors," Linda Lipsen said. "They were never a force politically because they never give money. So what Rove does is he finds new constituents. That's just brilliant. So he went to the doctors and said, 'Leave your patients. Strike.' And people freak out. I mean, that is just an amazing thing that you could tell doctors to go on strike in thirteen states." Lipsen shook her head in wonderment, disgust, or admiration. "That one," she insisted, "definitely had his fingerprints on it."

As a strategy, an us-versus-them posture had worked exceedingly well for George Bush and Karl Rove in the war on terror. No reason it should not be as effective in the fight against trial lawyers. Great politics is simple politics. In the middle of the president's first term, Rove began pushing the idea of putting doctors on the side of the malpractice insurance companies. The move was certainly counterintuitive to the physicians, since they were convinced their insurance providers were overcharging them. Rove needed to have doctors' groups perceive their patients almost as enemies because they often turned to trial lawyers when they'd been harmed by a bad doctor or an unfair health care company decision. The "us" was doctors and their malpractice insurance companies, and the "them" were plaintiffs' attorneys and the patients they represented in their malpractice liability cases.

The president began forging this unlikely alliance at a speech and rally in High Point, North Carolina, in July of 2002, a gathering that was one of the kickoffs of a series of events that became another Karl Rove campaign. "Our badly broken medical liability system is responsible for higher costs for patients, for lower quality of care, and for decreased access, and I worry about it," the president explained to almost two thousand people. Democrats argued that the White House was taking up the fight of big insurance companies that did not want to pay out damage judgments. A Bush spokesman said the president was siding with "pregnant mothers, people who want to have access to their doctors."

During the same trip, the president and Rove met privately with a group of doctors and American Medical Association president Donald Palmisano at a nearby hospital and urged them to mobilize the grass roots. Bush believed he had a chance to get a medical-malpractice bill through Congress in 2003 that would limit noneconomic damages to $250,000 and cap punitive awards at the same amount without restricting economic damages. And doctors responded to the president's request for political support.

By going on strike and putting lives at risk.

At the heart of the organized effort to build support with this unprecedented action, Rove and Republicans generated a disciplined message that excessive litigation was the cause of the high number of uninsured Americans. The foundation for the campaign was a federal government report called "Confronting the New Health Care Crisis: Improving Health Care Quality and Lowering Costs by Fixing Our Medical Liability System," which appeared to be as much political document as dispassionate analysis. Just before the president's trip to North Carolina, the GOP-dominated House Energy and Commerce Subcommittee opened hearings, which were entitled "Harming Patient Access to Care: The Impact of Excessive Litigation."

The lead witness of the three doctors who testified was delivered to the House floor by Karl Rove's friend and Republican ally from West Virginia Republican Shelley Moore Capito. Congresswoman Capito clearly considered the story of Dr. Samuel Roberts a perfect example of why something had to be done about malpractice lawsuits because his insurance premiums were about to put him out of the business of bringing babies into the world.

"I will have to stop," Roberts told the subcommittee, "leaving seven counties around me with no family physician delivering prenatal or maternity care. I have families I have delivered eight, nine children for. It makes me sad to know that I'm not going to be able to be there for those families."

Roberts did have expensive insurance costs: his annual rate had gone from $17,000 to $59,000 in just three years. But his premium charges appeared to be unrelated to frivolous lawsuits. According to the *Charleston Gazette,* he'd pleaded guilty to five counts of cocaine possession in 1987 and was given three years of criminal probation. The GOP poster boy for the malpractice insurance problem gave no more detail than to say he had a "situation" fifteen years earlier when he was asked if there were any reasons outside of medicine that his insurance premium might have gone up. Roberts did not mention that the State Board of Medicine had suspended his license for one year, stayed the suspension, and then placed him on supervised probation for five years. Even without malpractice lawsuits, such professional punishments affect insurance rates.

The executive director of the Foundation for Taxpayer and Consumer Rights, Jamie Court, was astonished when Roberts refused to either clarify his testimony or apologize for the omission.

"This," Court said, "is the equivalent of a convicted drunk driver complaining to Congress that his auto insurance has gone up."

Dr. Roberts would become one of the key spokesmen in the Rove public relations attack against lawyers. The campaign's compelling media attraction was the organized doctor walkouts. They began with a strike in West Virginia in January of 2003, six months after the congressional report and testimony and the president's private plea to doctors that they get out the grass roots. As Rove had anticipated, media coverage by the television news networks and major publications was extensive. Eighteen doctors, mostly surgeons, walked out of a hospital in Wheeling, West Virginia, and prompted an immediate debate over the ethics of their decision. No one in the national media, however, looked too closely at their backgrounds.

One of the doctors with the highest profile was Robert Zaleski. Dr. Zaleski's photo was in *New York Times Magazine,* and he served as a de facto spokesperson for his colleagues on CNN and other news shows while constantly claiming he was "on the brink" of moving out of West Virginia because of excessive malpractice insurance costs. When President Bush spoke in nearby Scranton, Pennsylvania, to hammer on his theme that lawsuits without merit were threatening the health care system, Dr. Zaleski received a personal invitation to attend the event. Zaleski's record as an orthopedic surgeon, however, made him yet another flawed leader for the doctors' protests.

According to *Washington Monthly* magazine, Zaleski admitted in a lawsuit that he was addicted to prescription painkillers during the early 1980s while he was performing surgeries. The publication reported that he had a Percodan habit, which he maintained by writing prescriptions for local addicts and getting them to share their pills with him. *Washington Monthly* cited court documents that included depositions from some of the addicts and copies of the prescriptions. Although he has claimed full sobriety for twenty-one years, Zaleski was nonetheless sued fourteen times by his patients from 1987 to 2002. Records of the West Virginia Board of Medicine showed that eight of those cases resulted in total payments of $1.7 million. Zaleski told reporter Stephanie Mencimer of *Washington Monthly* that the figure misrepresented the claims against him because it included the fees he paid to his defense lawyers.

Half of the doctors striking in Wheeling had questionable records. They included a surgeon who had cut into the wall of his patient's stomach during an operation. The error led to a fatal infection. Another striker had left a clamp on an artery and had caused his patient to have a liver transplant. Settlements and judgments against those nine striking doctors cost their malpractice insurers more than $6 million. The protesters included physicians who'd suffered suspension of their professional licenses or were convicted felons or drug addicts.

They did, however, add an exclamation point to the president's State of the Union message that year when he mentioned the issue of medical malpractice and a lawsuit crisis and how it was beginning to prompt walkouts and work stoppages by frustrated doctors. Two dozen surgeons in four hospitals of the West Virginia panhandle began to get extensive media coverage of their January 2 protest, which appeared to be timed for maximum effect leading up to the State of the Union speech a few weeks later.

Largely unreported in the stories about the medical-malpractice insurance crisis was the manner in which doctors are assessed their premiums. Unlike, for example, an automobile owner, physicians are not experience-rated. Bad drivers pay higher auto insurance premiums, but incompetent doctors have some of their increasing fees absorbed by a pool of physicians in their city. Practice areas are banded together and assessed premiums as a group. A proficient and successful surgeon, therefore, might see a rise in insurance costs even if he or she has never been sued but is practicing in a community with a disproportionate number of doctors who are being sued for poor performance.

"If I sideswipe another car, my insurance company would know it before I got home," said ATLA's Linda Lipsen. "Not so with doctors. The same doctor who commits malpractice over and over again, it's not reflected in his rates. I don't know why insurance companies do it with doctors and they don't do it with anything else. You need to get these people out of practicing, or you have got to let the market do it and raise their rates so much that they are not gonna practice."

This policy does cause pricing problems for competent physicians but is not responsible for dramatic increases in malpractice premiums. Research by physicians and medical organizations, in fact, indicates there's no medical-malpractice crisis. According to the General Accounting Office, "Some reports of physicians relocating to other states, retiring, or closing practices were not accurate or involved relatively few physicians." In another section, the 2003 report said, "Many of the provider actions taken in response to malpractice pressures were not substantiated or did not widely affect access to health care."

As is the case in most professions, a small number of bad doctors accounts for most of the malpractice lawsuits. According to a report by the National Practitioner Data Bank of the Department of Health and Human Services, from 1990 to 2002, only 5 percent of the nation's doctor population accounted for 54 percent of malpractice payouts. In New Jersey, for instance, according to the watchdog group Public Citizen, during the 1990s, 6 percent of that state's doctors accounted for more than 60 percent of all malpractice suits filed.

The greater problem affecting insurance rates for doctors might be a lack of discipline by professional boards charged with monitoring medical errors. Of the thirty-five thousand doctors with two or more malpractice payouts from 1990 to 2002, only 8 percent were disciplined by various medical regulatory boards. In the March 3, 2003, edition of the *New York Times*, Dr. Sidney Wolfe wrote that the "major cause of the malpractice problem is ignored: the failure of state medical boards to discipline doctors.

"Amid the uproar about malpractice premium increases," Wolfe added, "there is a deadly silence from physicians' groups on the crisis of inadequate doctor discipline. The problem is not the compensation paid to injured patients, but an epidemic of medical errors."

In the reality Karl Rove has created, though, it is the fault of greedy lawyers. In spite of his assertions that caps on damage awards won by plaintiffs' attorneys will resolve the problem of high insurance premiums for doctors, there is a significant body of evidence to the contrary. California, which was the first state to confront malpractice insurance costs in 1975, passed the Medical Injury Compensation Reform Act (MICRA) and placed a $250,000 cap on noneconomic damages. Sliding scales were adopted for attorneys' fees, which meant that the larger the likely settlement, the lower the contingency percentage share. The net effect was that lawyers were discouraged from bringing malpractice suits.

MICRA, though, did nothing to control insurance costs for California doctors. Over the next twelve years, premiums rose a dramatic 450 percent. The situation helped to prompt the passage of Proposition 103 in 1988, a measure to control insurance costs instead of attorneys. In the three years after voters adopted Prop 103, malpractice premiums dropped 20 percent, and the industry refunded more than $135 million to doctors.

In the twenty-five states that have adopted limits on med-mal awards, the trade publication *Medical Liability Monitor* found that malpractice premiums have not declined, though they have risen a bit more slowly than in states without the caps.

A number of analysts have suggested that the stock market is the real reason for the rise in malpractice insurance rates. The companies providing the coverage make their money on the investment of premiums in the stock market. If the economy falters, the profit margins of the insurance companies are reduced, and that, more than a crisis in the medical profession, drives increases in doctors' premiums. The National Association of Insurance Commissioners insists that only about a quarter of malpractice companies' premiums are invested in the bond and equities markets. Nonetheless, when the yields from these investments have gone down during historic recessions, malpractice insurance rates have gone up.

An in-depth analysis of the malpractice insurance price problem, commissioned by ATLA and several consumer groups, appears to show that settlements and judgments against doctors have not increased. "Falling Claims and Rising Premiums in the Medical Malpractice Insurance Industry" was based on statements and data supplied under oath to various state insurance commissions by the country's top medical-malpractice insurers. Authored by Jay Angoff, former state of Missouri insurance commissioner and an acknowledged industry expert, the report concludes that the total value of payouts by malpractice insurers remained flat from 2000 to 2005 while insurance premiums for doctors more than doubled. In fact, the findings reveal that "the increase in the premiums collected by these companies was 14 times as great as the increase in their claims payments on a gross basis and 21 times as great as the increase in those payments on a net basis (after reinsurance)." In the area of incurred losses, which are claims an insurer projects it will pay based on policies it has in effect that year, the Angoff report found that many malpractice insurers were dramatically increasing premiums while both claims payments and projected future losses were decreasing.

The Angoff report suggests that, instead of being victims of out-of-control personal-injury lawyers, doctors might be the target of price-gouging by their insurance companies. Among the most egregious examples cited in the study was Health Care Indemnity Inc. (HCI). The company is an affiliate of Hospital Corporation of America, the largest for-profit hospital chain in America, which is owned by the family of Senate

Majority Leader Bill Frist. HCI is reported to have increased malpractice insurance premiums by 88 percent, for a total revenue increase of $174 million, at the same time its claims payments were falling $74 million, or about 32 percent.

J. Robert Hunter, a former Texas insurance commissioner and federal insurance administrator, said, "Doctors and consumers deserve to see the facts behind the *true* crisis, which is that insurance companies are price-gouging their doctors, not an explosion in claims." Hunter made his remarks as the director of insurance for the Consumer Federation of America, which was a cosponsor of the Angoff report.

Both sides produced reports and statistics bolstering their position, but this much was clear: total med-mal awards and litigation were rising, but so was the number of doctors. The total number of practicing physicians in the United States doubled to 750,000 from 1975 to 2001. And the rise in jury awards reflected climbing medical costs and inflation over the same period.

Integral to the Rove campaign against medical-malpractice suits and trial lawyers was the notion that doctors are ordering excessive, often unnecessary tests as a legal precaution, which also drives up overall costs. According to a detailed study conducted by the Congressional Office of Technology Assessment in the midnineties though, defensive medicine costs were "negligible" and had minimal or no impact on access to medical treatment.

The striking doctors disagreed.

The timing of their walkouts, which seemed designed to serve the president's fund-raising and reelection efforts, was not the only indication of White House assistance. Frank Galitski, a Bush campaign worker who runs a political front group called the Texas Alliance for Patient Access, met with doctors in Scranton, Pennsylvania, a few weeks after the walkout began in West Virginia and admitted "there is some coordination" between the protesting doctors and the White House. Also, as the West Virginia strike was under way, patient petitions began circulating in doctors' offices along with printed public relations collaterals, which delivered information on lawsuit abuse. According to *Washington Monthly,* the materials were produced by the West Virginia Care Coalition. The organization was formed by the Charleston-based PR firm Maple Creative, an agency whose principals reportedly have close ties to the Bush administration. To pay for Maple Creative's services, an HMO organization and a hospital association in West Virginia gave the coalition $200,000. More money came from chambers of commerce, the Business Roundtable, the West Virginia Oil and Gas Coalition, and the state's Building and Industry Coalition.

Although the West Virginia doctors refused to call their protest a strike, it had the effect of one. The state legislature very quickly passed a law restricting awards in malpractice lawsuits, even though only 1 percent of the state's doctors had five or more medical-malpractice payouts or settlements in the preceding decade. A computer analysis by the *Charleston Gazette* examined two thousand medical-malpractice cases reported to the West Virginia Board of Medicine. Between 1993 and 2001, verdicts against doctors and total dollar amounts declined to the point that West Virginia was ranked thirty-fifth in the United States for malpractice payouts.

Previous experience in other states also shows there will be no dramatic drop in the premiums doctors pay for malpractice coverage in the wake of West Virginia's legislative caps of med-mal awards. What will happen, however, is a reduction in the number of suits brought against doctors. With a conventional limit of $250,000 on noneconomic awards, most law firms cannot afford to take on med-mal cases. The hiring of experts, depositions, and an extensive discovery process needed to get to the heart of a question can often require an investment of $250,000 before a med-mal suit even makes it onto a court docket.

If court dockets in the United States are crowded, it is not the result of "frivolous" lawsuits in personal-injury cases. More than 80 percent of all litigation in America involves businesses suing businesses, a situation the Republican Party and Karl Rove have not sought to control.

"It's ridiculous," suggests ATLA's Lipsen. "Can you imagine telling Coca-Cola that they are going to be limited if they think that their patent has been violated? It's ridiculous. Or a small company wanting to pursue a larger company because of anticompetitive statutes and saying you can't do that? You can't do that because the courts are clogged? It's ridiculous. People would say that's ridiculous."

In Karl Rove's political calculations, tort reform is less about controlling the cost of doctors' insurance premiums and improving access to health care than, as Lipsen suggests, reducing access to the courts by the consumer. If people cannot bring suit against businesses, regardless of the merits, profits are protected, risks are reduced, and the Republican Party gets both the credit and the campaign contributions for this accomplishment. Combine obstacles to getting into court with the appointment and election of conservative, business-friendly judges, and the American civil justice system becomes completely "corporatized."

According to Carlton Carl, a communications executive at ATLA, Rove's objective regarding lawyers has been largely successful. "I don't care what you call this movement, and I refuse to call it tort reform because that's not what it is. It's a campaign to shut down the average person's ability to go into a courtroom and get justice. That's all it is. And it's working. If you get seriously harmed by the negligence of a business, you will soon find it nearly impossible to get a lawyer, much less get your case all the way to trial."

In packaging an antilawyer, anticonsumer campaign as reform, it was important to control the terms of the debate. Language has always been among Rove's most important tools. In 1994, a Rove colleague, Neal Cohen, instructed a gathering of corporate lobbyists and public relations executives on how to frame the fight. First, he said, call it reform. Second, hide the real beneficiaries behind front groups such as small-business owners and doctors. "Don't talk about the details of legislation," said Cohen, who teamed up with Rove in Texas on the issue in the early 1990s. "Talk about frivolous lawsuits, lawsuit abuse, trial lawyer greed. In a tort reform battle, if State Farm—and Nationwide—are the leaders of the coalition, you're not going to pass the bill. It's not credible, OK? Because it's so self-serving."

While trying to privatize Social Security, Rove would use much the same linguistic assault. First, there was a crisis; then, a call for reform. The idea of disassembling Social Security presented a partisan benefit but also intrigued the political historian in Rove with the delicious prospect of undermining the last great New Deal program. The idea promised to take Social Security away from Democrats who had created it and to stamp it with the imprimatur of the Republican Party. As for politics, if half of Social Security funds were given over to private accounts, billions of new dollars would end up in the hands of Republican Wall Street investors. Young people managing their own retirement funds might increasingly think of themselves as Republicans.

The campaign to change Social Security, like the campaign to curb lawsuits, began with the same dark warning that a crisis was looming that required reform. According to Democratic pollster Ed Lazarus, in both cases, there is a designed deception at work.

"You ask people if they want to get rid of frivolous lawsuits, and, of course, their answer is yes," Lazarus explained. "But they don't realize they are basically getting rid of all lawsuits. When you ask the follow-up question about whether they want the guy who lost his leg in an accident caused by his employer's negligence to be able to sue, they always answer yes. Tell them they are getting rid of his rights, too, and they go, 'You mean, the guy in the wheelchair with one leg, he can't sue, either?' and their opinion changes. People think they are getting rid of *only* frivolous lawsuits, and they aren't. They are getting rid of them all because caps means lawyers can't afford to take a case on a contingency fee."

After West Virginia, doctors' strikes spread to Nevada and New Jersey and beyond to thirteen states. A busy trauma center was shut down in Las Vegas when the specialists practicing there refused to operate on patients, citing malpractice insurance costs. State after state adopted restrictions on the amount of money to be lawfully awarded victims of incompetent doctors. The threat of a strike was all that was required to prompt passage of legislation. More than two dozen states approved the caps while Karl Rove was busily working the political levers of Congress for a comprehensive federal solution.

As the states engage on tort reform and med mal in particular, Rove uses his faux crisis to raise more money for the Republicans by going back to health insurance companies and doctors. Even without federal legislation on medical-malpractice caps, the controversy has the power to keep trial lawyers off-balance, constantly under attack, and spending money they might use more effectively on other programs.

The Association of Trial Lawyers of America, though, was stepping up its campaign to counter the Rove offensive. Linda Lipsen and her staff were raising money, sharpening their message, and girding for a long fight. They did not view this battle as being lost. Karl Rove was in the emperor's chair with more cash at his disposal than the lawyers, and he had hundreds of lobbyists to apply pressure where it was needed. He figured he could handle ATLA without using too much of his intellect and energy.

Rove was just running another campaign. And he was very good at that . . . as unions and the labor movement were also discovering.

ELEVEN

IT'S HARD WORK

The Sad State of the Unions

The labor movement means just this: It is the last noble protest of the American people against the power of incorporated wealth.
—Wendell Phillips

Ty Runyan heard the phone ringing in his office on Yeager Lane in North Austin. His company, Titus Electrical Contracting Inc., had recently landed a very nice deal to do the electrical work at the Town Lake (Palmer) Community Events Center, and he'd been very busy. There had been a few problems, though. Titus Electrical took over the project from Guy's Electrical, a union shop in nearby Marble Falls. The general contractor on the construction of the new facility, MW Builders, fired Guy's and offered the work to Titus Electrical. Fifty union electricians, who'd been working for Guy's, expected to keep their jobs. Ty Runyan, though, wanted to hire his own people, and all of Guy's union employees were released.

That's when the trouble started.

The call coming in to Ty Runyan's office was because, earlier in the day, he'd filed trespass charges against a union picketer. Local 520 of the International Brotherhood of Electrical Workers in Austin had been trying to unionize Titus Electrical Contracting after the union's members had lost their jobs when Guy's Electrical was fired. The workers had particularly resented being fired at a time when the construction business in Austin was slower than it had been in many years. Contract work for skilled tradesmen was very hard to find from 2001 to 2003.

IBEW accused the general contractor, MW Builders, of violating federal law by not requiring Titus to hire the union electricians. While that allegation was being considered by the National Labor Relations Board, Local 520 attempted to organize the workers who'd landed jobs with Titus. According to Shelly Runyan, vice president of Titus, a dispute began between Titus and the union on the first day Ty had arrived on the job site and was told by a Local 520 member, "This here's a union job and you'd best get on outta here. You don't know what you're getting into."

The voice on the other end of the phone was considerably more threatening.

"Hey, you motherfucker, if you're going to have one of our people arrested, you better start wearing a bulletproof vest because you're going to take a bullet. You motherfucker." Runyan had filed criminal trespass charges against a picketer he claimed was on his property near a retaining wall. (The charges were later dismissed for lack of evidence.)

In his confrontation with the IBEW, Ty Runyan found himself at the nexus of a clash between powerful economic and political forces. The argument Titus Electrical Contracting had with the IBEW in Austin transformed Ty Runyan into a political activist and became a microcosm of the problems facing the union movement. Both circumstance and choice made Runyan an asset of Karl Rove's in his scheme to destroy the finances and political strength of unions. Everything Rove needs to facilitate his campaign against organized labor is represented by Ty Runyan. Square-faced with red hair and a neatly trimmed beard, Runyan is a self-made millionaire who started out as a ditchdigger. He is a half-Hispanic minority and hates unions. He despises lawyers unless they are his own "great lawyers." And Ty Runyan passes the most critical test for Rove by believing so deeply in the Bush agenda that he is willing to write large checks for the cause.

He also delivers a message very well.

"This union mentality of strangling the chicken to increase egg production is from a time gone past," Runyan said. "We have to support business. Supporting business is going to create competition for workers, and that competition for workers will drive up pay rates and benefits."

Ty Runyan became political when his company became a target of a union tactic called "salting." The idea is to gain employment in nonunion businesses for workers who are either union organizers or sympathetic to efforts to create collective-bargaining agreements. The National Labor

Relations Act makes it illegal for employers to exclude applicants from the workforce simply because they intend to promote unionization. If they're qualified and hired, the law also offers equal protection to the "salts" and does not permit employers to discharge them with impunity.

After firing the 50 union workers from Guy's Electrical and refusing to recognize Local 520's collective-bargaining agreement already in place with the general contractor on the project, Titus Electrical Contracting hired new workers for the events center in Austin. After interviewing 530 technicians, the company hired 48, a few of them salts. According to Shelly Runyan, the business she and her husband had built from the back of a 1971 Dodge Satellite became a victim of vandalism by those salts.

"We have had a death threat, vandalism to employee and company property during pickets," she told a congressional subcommittee. "Trucks, tires, windows, beer bottles in [our] parking lot at night, anonymous, threatening phone calls to employees' homes at 1:00 a.m. and intentional damage and sabotage to our work by these salts." In one instance she outlined for federal investigators, Ryan said sabotaged wiring had caused an explosion.

The IBEW, not surprisingly, considered itself the victim and insisted that the behavior of Titus Electrical's management was outside the bounds of the law. Local 520 filed nearly two hundred unfair labor practices complaints with the NLRB, several Equal Employment Opportunity Commission charges, and various civil lawsuits. According to the allegations the IBEW made against Titus Electrical, workers sympathetic to the union were videotaped during picketing and under constant surveillance. Police were frequently called for no apparent reason to the scene of legal picketing on public property outside of Titus's offices. Workers were fired because of union activities or were refused employment for being either union members or sympathizers. Layoffs were threatened, and Titus changed company policy on clothing with logos after union members began showing up at job sites wearing shirts with Local 520 IBEW insignia.

Ty Runyan denied each of the assertions made in the unfair labor practice complaints. "These guys gloated about the fact that they had some eleven of those [unfair labor practice charges] stick. If you file enough of that crap, some of it is going to stick, particularly when you've got an administrative law judge who works for the National Labor Relations Board. These guys are wolves watching over sheep."

The administrative law judge who heard the case against Titus Electrical for the NLRB ruled in favor of the union on its main complaints. Reinstatement of employment and payment of back wages was ordered for four Local 520 IBEW employees who had been fired by Titus. The final order required Titus to post a notice in its workplaces informing employees of their right to organize for purposes of collective bargaining.

Shelly Runyan later responded by calling the NLRB a "government agency which is ostensibly an independent arbiter [that] has become a corrupt organization whose agents act with a hidden agenda, directed by the AFL-CIO."

The Titus management attitude toward the union, though, was not consistent throughout the conflict with Local 520. Testimony in the NLRB hearing indicated that Ty Runyan had once used a company meeting to describe two IBEW salts, Kevin Gustin and Alan Stockton, who he knew were union members, as two of his most productive employees. Lawsuits related to the clash between Titus and the union were amicably settled out of court in March of 2004, and a $10,000 donation was made to a community program to provide training for skilled construction trades.

But Ty Runyan, the 2003 Texas Hispanic Businessman of the Year, who built a multimillion-dollar company with only an eleventh-grade education, was still angry. "We were attacked by the international brotherhood of electrical thugs. And we spent a half million dollars in one year on legal fees. They wanted to put us out of business because we were a nonunion company."

Although Runyan views laws to protect unions as the work of an out-of-control government, he is appreciative of federal regulations to protect minorities and their businesses, but he has been inconsistent on that point. Runyan told *Fortune* magazine that minority set-asides create a "false economy" because the free market is not allowed to prevail and some qualified contractors are excluded. Nonetheless, Titus Electrical sought and was given minority certification in 2001 because, according to Runyan, he was tired of losing work where he was a low bidder but lacked minority representation.

"We look at the certification as a value-added service—if our clients need it, it's there. Are we a beneficiary? Yes. Has it gotten us work? You betcha. We've closed a couple of government projects in the past 12 months that stipulated minority participation. Together they are worth more than $2 million."

While Runyan has benefited from a minority set-aside program promoted by Democrats, he's been undeniably enriched by antiunion policies advanced by Republicans. Laws to facilitate his success are good. Laws to help unions are bad. So when a representative of the Republican Party in Austin called Ty Runyan, he was open to a conversation. GOP officials had undoubtedly picked up information in the news media regarding Titus's struggle to deal with the union. Runyan's information was forwarded from the GOP's Texas office to the Bush reelection campaign and a 2004 inaugural committee fund-raiser named Roger Williams. Ty Runyan then got a phone call that was much different from the one a few years earlier when he heard a disembodied voice that had threatened him for resisting unionization.

"I was talking with Roger Williams for donations for the inaugural," Runyan said.

"Really?" the reporter asked. "What were they looking for?"

"One hundred thousand dollars."

"What did you tell them?"

"I said I might be interested, and I started talking and I wrote a check. Prior to two years ago, I had no interest in politics. And then I had people start busting up my trucks, busting up my property."

President Bush is taking precisely the kinds of steps Ty Runyan wanted to see by creating a more probusiness NLRB and by issuing executive orders and new regulations that make it harder for unions to organize, function, and assert themselves politically. Runyan thinks his money was well spent.

"Now, having spent a half a million dollars in one year on legal fees, you think me spending $100,000 to support my president who represents American business . . . is a bad investment?" Runyan asked the reporter. "No, I think it's a fantastic investment."

Karl Rove had just enlisted another soldier in his war on American labor unions, long a nemesis of the GOP. In 2004, unions had spent about $200 million on behalf of Democrat John Kerry and issues supporting his candidacy. That had to be stopped or Rove might not be able to successfully execute his plan for Republican realignment and political control of America. He was not about to lose, though. From his perch inside the

White House, he'd already begun to implement a government and political strategy to ruin the labor movement. And squabbling unions appeared ready to help with their own demise.

The information, even though it was acquired inadvertently, had the potential to be devastating. The deputy secretary of labor, Stephen J. Law, was testifying at a hearing in the U.S. House of Representatives. He mentioned that the DOL was in the process of putting together new regulations regarding financial reporting procedures for unions. When a committee member said, "We assume you've consulted with the labor people who'll be most affected," Law had to concede he hadn't yet taken that step.

The AFL-CIO was subsequently invited to a meeting with the Department of Labor. The union representation included General Counsel Jon Hiatt. Across the table, Hiatt was looking at Don Todd, deputy assistant for the Employment Standards Administration at DOL.

"I assume you've done your homework and you know who I am," Todd said.

They knew. Don Todd was a former director of research for the Republican National Committee. And he was in charge of drawing up new requirements for financial reporting by unions.

"I know you guys aren't happy about this," Todd added. "I've spent a lot of my life analyzing record keeping and filings of my political enemies."

Hiatt, who'd spent much of *his* professional life fending off various federal and legal attacks on labor, was amazed by Todd's brazen admission.

"He was wearing his DOL hat," Hiatt said. "They didn't pretend for a minute this wasn't political. The smoother ones at least know how to pretend to be acting in the public interest."

The former RNC official in charge of digging up information on opposition candidates was now leading the federal government's effort to rewrite provisions of the Labor-Management Reporting and Disclosure Act of 1959. The idea behind the original legislation was to protect the democratic rights of union workers by mandating full disclosure of how union management was spending their dues. Business management was also required to disclose its expenditures under the reporting provisions of LMRDA. If union members disagreed with various decisions on how their organization was being managed—for example, with respect to using money for supporting political candidates instead of organizational or recruitment efforts—a democratic process for changing those expenditures was protected. Corporations, which had been reporting finances under various other federal disclosure laws to shareholders and others through SEC filings, viewed the LMRDA as essential to fairness because too much of their information was already in the public domain.

The Department of Labor's Don Todd, the former RNC researcher, was drafting alterations to LMRDA forms known as LM-2s. Unions were required to file them annually to tell the government and union members how money was being spent. A separate section in LM-2s for reporting by business executives and management does not require the level of detailed information that must be delivered by unions. Business interests have long argued, however, that the reporting categories for unions were far too vague and millions were hidden by unions under headings such as "other disbursements." Allegations were also made that dues were used to create nefarious trust funds for unrestrained political use by union leaders.

Mark Tapscott of *Capitalism Magazine* argued in favor of the new reporting requirements being written by Todd and DOL. "For years," he wrote, "unions have created trusts, which are little more than slush funds available only to selected officials who use the money to pay for campaign activities like fund-raisers, candidate literature and get-out-the-vote efforts. The trust arrangement has put the detailed expenditures out of public reach. The revised LM-2 ends that cozy arrangement."

The information in LM-2s is valuable, however, to more than just dues-paying members of unions. Companies often hire management consultants to advise them on how to remain nonunion, and more detail on union spending was certain to reveal strategies being used for organizing. And if forcing unions to increase the amount of information in LM-2s was an advantage to antiunion business consultants, it was even more important to the historic enemy of unions: the Republican Party.

Jon Hiatt of the AFL-CIO saw the hand of Karl Rove in it all. "This was done purely to harass us and force us to spend huge resources," he said. "This was all coming from their right-wing base, who wanted a road map to what we are doing, where we are spending, and what campaigns we are looking at. Management consultants for corporations were urging their clients to push for this, and they got Rove and the White House to do it."

Hiatt could not prove Rove's involvement, but there were connections. If Don Todd came from the Republican National Committee, he

worked for Ken Mehlman, and Mehlman, who ran the RNC, took his orders from Karl Rove.

The idea of using the LM-2s and the Department of Labor for political
attack on the Republican opposition was at least as old as February 19,
1992, the last year of George H. W. Bush's administration. Congressman
Newt Gingrich sent a memo to the labor secretary on that date urging
that the LM-2s be modified because it "will weaken our opponents and
encourage our allies." Republican Gingrich asked Secretary Lynn Martin
to "order the Office of Labor-Management Standards to institute changes
in the LM-2 union reporting and disclosure form. . . ."

Although the unions delayed implementation of the reforms by filing
a lawsuit challenging the government software to handle the reporting,
the end result was still onerous for the labor movement. Every receipt of
each expense must be retained. If an outside attorney is hired to write a
brief, the portion of time spent on political issues must be recorded along
with separate records for time billed for legislative, government, administrative, and collective bargaining. A ream of printer paper has to be
tracked for how much is used in each of the same categories. When a
union spends more than $5,000 with a vendor, every receipt must be
kept, categorized, and reported.

"When they [DOL] told us they were going to change the regulations
of LM-2s," Jon Hiatt explained, "they also said they were going to post
them online to make the information public and for members to get access. We asked if they were going to do that for employers, too. The answer was 'not initially.' They said, 'We may get to it.' But they have not.
This is blatantly one-sided. The DOL has virtually stopped enforcing requirements for employers but stepped up those for labor."

Unions have a reasonable amount of latitude for spending dues on political activities. The law allows them to inform members about the voting records of candidates and to fund programs such as voter-education
projects and get-out-the-vote efforts. Even advocacy of specific candidates is allowed if the dues money is used to communicate directly with
union members and not the general public. With the first reporting period concluded in September 2005, LM-2 regulatory changes put this information on expenditures into the hands of the public and the unions'
political enemies. For the more than five thousand unions ordered to report on the LM-2s, the annual cost could approach a billion dollars. Only

about 120 of those unions covered under the regulations are considered national organizations. The rest are small local shops.

Conceptually, the goal is to reduce government and privatize most of its services, and making a move against unions is an element of that design. Democrats are weakened, in Karl Rove's long-held view, when the public relies not on unions or government but on markets. In order to reach that point, however, government needs a little nudge in the right direction.

The Bush administration's business-friendly, antiworker sentiment within the Department of Labor has gone to such extremes that the DOL's own inspector general has criticized the agency's policies. Gordon S. Heddell accused DOL's Wage and Hour Division of violating its own handbook by making significant concessions to Wal-Mart stores. DOL granted the giant retailer a fifteen-day notice before it would conduct any child labor law inspections of one of its stores, and it agreed to allow the company to "jointly develop news releases" regarding any findings. In January of 2005, Wal-Mart had been found guilty of eighty-five child labor law violations for allowing employees under age eighteen to operate dangerous machinery such as chain saws and cardboard balers. According to Heddell, DOL's agreement with Wal-Mart will hurt the agency's authority to assess penalties and issue violations; he also argued that the precedent was likely to restrict the flow of information from DOL to the public.

Politically, this assault on unions makes sense in pursuit of an enduring Republican majority. To achieve his goal, Rove and the Bush administration have a three-pronged strategy: executive orders that undercut union-organization efforts, a more business-friendly National Labor Relations Board, and increased privatization of government activities. It is focused, Rove's program. And the administration's priorities were never clearer than in its changes at the Department of Labor.

The number of people enforcing laws governing employer standards on minimum wages, occupational safety, rights to organize, child labor, and overtime have all been dramatically reduced. The office of DOL that audits and investigates unions, however, is enjoying a jump in staffing levels. A 15 percent budget increase was approved in 2005 for the Office of Labor-Management Standards, and forty-eight new people were hired. The first five years of the Bush administration saw a 60 percent increase in spending on resources to monitor union activities, and ninety-four jobs were added. About forty of those new bureaucrats are auditors and accountants, and they were immediately dispatched to begin DOL's first investigation of the AFL-CIO under the new LM-2 reporting standards. According to Jon Hiatt, the union was informed that the investigators needed to be in their offices "for months."

David Bonior, former Democratic member of Congress who became chairman of American Rights at Work, said there is nothing secret about what Karl Rove, the Bush administration, and their allies are trying to do to the American labor movement.

"There's been a strategy," he said. "It's not a conspiracy. They're very open. [Conservative Republican strategist] Grover Norquist says they want to get rid of unions, to break the labor movement."

The scheme most troublesome for unions is a change in the rules governing how unions are organized. Voluntary recognition agreements are the most widely used method for determining whether workers want to form a union. Also known as card check, the process involves laborers' signing cards and checking yes or no on union representation. If a majority approves, collective bargaining begins when the employer acknowledges the vote. Unions prefer this approach to organizing because an election on a specific day provides more opportunities for employers to distort the outcome by intimidating workers who show up to vote.

The Bush administration, though, has begun to end participation of the federal government in the card-check recognition process by eliminating federal mediators used to verify elections, which means many employers may be more willing to resist unionization.

"My God, Karl Rove is all over this," said John Ryan of the AFL-CIO local in Cleveland, Ohio. "There is a straight-out attack on unions. What Rove and Bush have told mediators is that you are not allowed to participate in the card-check process to let workers join unions even though workers want that and employers want it. This is a multilayered attempt to fight unions and workers, and it's unprecedented and stronger than we have ever seen before even under Reagan or the first Bush administration."

While unions view it as critical to sustaining significant membership, the Bush-majority NLRB has begun to assert a political strategy disguised as policy that claims that card check actually takes away a worker's rights because it has replaced elections on specified dates. The five-member NLRB is made up of presidential appointees, who, historically, have tended to be supporters of party politics. In one ruling, for example, the NLRB offered what unions considered a chilling summary that was a political attack on union organizing. "We have some concerns as to whether an employer can waive the employees' fundamental right to vote. . . ."

Card check, of course, is a vote. It's just not a vote on a specified election day.

"The current board," Jon Hiatt said in testimony before Congress, "appears intent on narrowing even further the means through which workers can enter the increasingly distant land of representation. To do so based on an expressed concern for employee free choice would be a dishonest distortion of that [National Labor Relations Act] statutory policy."

Another critical decision from the NLRB is whether a union's vote for collective bargaining should remain protected for the first year to give the union a chance to organize and begin wage and benefit talks with the employer. Removing that protected one-year period turns organizing efforts into an endless fight between the workers and their employers.

"It's kind of funny," said Per Bernstein of the International Labor Communications Association. "Bush and Rove are trumpeting democracy all over the world, and they are preventing democracy in the workplace. Maybe eight years of these kinds of attacks is what the union movement needs to wake up. Let them take away our health care. Let them take away our rights to negotiate. Maybe people will wake up and do something."

There is certainly no shortage of evidence that the Bush administration wants to bring down the house of labor. Less than a month after he took his first oath of office, the president issued a series of four executive orders designed to limit union strength. These decisions, in fact, were his first administrative actions as president of the United States.

According to then White House press secretary Ari Fleischer, "The four executive orders signed by the president are based on the principles of fair and open competition, neutrality in government contracting, effective and efficient use of tax dollars and the legal right of workers to be notified of how their dues may be used."

They were also interpreted by union leadership as shots to the heart of the labor movement. Executive Order 13201 was posted on February 22, 2001, and reminds workers that, under federal law, "employees cannot be required to join a union or maintain membership in a union in order to retain their jobs." Nothing in the text informs employees, however, of their collective-bargaining rights and their legal rights not to get fired or be intimidated if they choose to join a union. The president also let laborers know that they do not have to pay the portion of their union dues that is used for political or organizational activities and they are entitled to a refund of any monies not spent on "collective bargaining, contract administration, or grievance adjustment."

Less than a week after he had become president, Bush also circulated a draft of an order to dissolve the National Labor-Management Partnership Council, which had been formed under the Clinton administration. The council had required managers of federal agencies to engage laborers and staff on management issues and to resolve various disputes in the government workplace. The council and the American Federation of Government Employees (AFGE) said the record proved that the council increased government efficiency and savings while also improving the working environment.

"Bush was so intent on punishing labor unions," wrote Joe Henderson of AFGE, "that he did not care a whit for the real good that partnership brought to the government and the country. Incredibly, the first order of business for his presidency was not protecting our country from terrorist attack or adding jobs to the economy; it was eliminating labor-management partnerships from the government."

The president disposed of the National Labor-Management Partnership Council on the same day that he rescinded another Clinton order that had protected union workers on federal jobs even if the contractor that had provided them was replaced. Under the Clinton regulation, a new contractor had to hire the union workers from the previous employer or, as a minimum, give those workers a first right of refusal. These positions tended to be predominantly janitors and cafeteria workers brought to a job site at a federal building by a contractor. Bush also overturned a Clinton order that had mandated the hiring of union contractors on all federally financed projects.

The four sweeping executive orders in the beginning days of the first Bush administration left labor leaders convinced they were facing an aggressive assault. Initial meetings, though, between union officials and Labor Secretary Elaine Chao were relatively friendly. As a former president of United Way of America, she had dealt with board members from international unions. Shortly after Bush took office, Chao met with the AFL-CIO's executive council and said the White House would not take action on the four executive orders without direct communication with union leadership.

"We want to work with you," Chao said. "We want to have a dialogue. Before we do anything, we will come and discuss them with you."

Two days later, Bush issued the presidential orders.

Chao showed up at another meeting to discuss the onerous LM-2 reporting requirements. She brought with her a book listing what she and the administration considered egregious transgressions by unions. The unmistakable message was that unions were bad and they were out of line by opposing increased regulation of union spending.

Labor communicator Per Bernstein found the meeting offensive. "It was real insulting. The things she had on unions were minor, and this was right at the time Enron and WorldCom were getting away with ridiculous crimes, and the Bush people are concentrating on us? Everybody in labor was just super–pissed-off about it. That was a turning point."

Moments of cooperation between the Bush White House and unions were rare, but Jon Hiatt, general counsel for the AFL-CIO, was briefly optimistic when he was contacted by the director of the Wage and Hour Division of the Department of Labor. Although Tammy McCutcheon had been general counsel for Hershey Foods, she was not considered virulently antiunion. According to Hiatt, McCutcheon reached out to him and they met over lunch, and she acknowledged that making changes in overtime regulations under the Fair Labor Standards Act was at the top of her agenda. As their meal concluded, Hiatt said he asked McCutcheon if she knew other union people to talk to about wage issues. When she said no, Hiatt offered to arrange conferences with general counsels of the major unions and all of their attorneys who were experts on wage and hour questions.

"I told her we would all be happy to meet with her and provide her with our perspective," Hiatt explained. "She said that would be wonderful. We set dates, and I invited her to meet with two groups of our lawyers. The day before that initial meeting was scheduled, my office got a call and she canceled. A week later, she had somebody call and cancel the other meeting."

Hiatt finally reached McCutcheon on her private line, and she admitted that it was not her decision to cancel the lunches. "This is what I was told to do," he heard her say. Hiatt assumed the orders came from the White House and Karl Rove, though he had no proof.

"I ran into her a month later," Hiatt said, "and she sheepishly apologized. They've just got a corporate agenda."

The labor movement was suffering a decline in membership well before George W. Bush moved into the White House. More than 90 percent of private-sector workers in the United States do not have union representation. Unions had thrived as recently as the decade of the sixties. Wages increased, and productivity rose in the manufacturing sector. Both labor and management were comforted by a lack of significant overseas competition. As international market forces increased and manufacturing jobs went overseas, however, unions began to organize in the public sector. It was not until the Reagan administration broke the back of the air traffic controllers' union that increasingly hostile attitudes between workers and management began seeping into government. Republicans began to use the regulatory and rule-making authority of the federal government to affect the ability of unions to organize, recruit, and raise money. Even the Clinton White House angered its labor allies with an unflinching support for free-trade agreements. Jobs were outsourced overseas, and unions lost membership. Service employees organized in greater numbers, but their financial power was limited by wages. Combining those historic trends with an eight-year Bush regulatory assault and their own internecine squabbles and unions faced the possibility they might not survive.

"It's a cause for considerable worry," according to John Judis, a union expert and author. "I don't know how the labor movement will recover or even if it will. What it will take is a combination of a revival of the Democrats and a good economy—not a bad one, because a good economy puts unions in a better bargaining position. But I think again that Bush and Rove have accomplished their goals by doing things where initially they didn't even have the votes. They just did what they thought was necessary."

In effect, Karl Rove was tracking a wounded animal. The labor movement, after decades of declining membership, was easy prey. Although the union movement was weakened by falling numbers, Rove knew it remained a reliable source of money and political participants during elections. In 2004, labor activists knocked on an estimated 6 million doors and made more than 100 million phone calls by deploying approximately

225,000 volunteers. Those resources were expended largely on Democrats, and when results proved disappointing, a lingering philosophical conflict erupted among union leadership.

The AFL-CIO broke apart in a dispute over whether to spend more money organizing and growing membership or continuing to funnel resources into political campaigns. A third of the membership, which included about 13 million workers and fifty-seven unions, left the AFL-CIO in a disagreement over strategies for dealing with labor's decline in numbers and influence. Renegade unions believe they can only be saved by increased organizational and recruitment efforts. The split was led by the Service Employees International Union and the Teamsters. They were joined by the textile and hotel workers union, known as UNITE HERE, and the United Food and Commercial Workers. The labor divide threatens to expedite a goal Karl Rove has long expressed: limiting the ability of unions to raise money and support Democrats.

"Things are grim," said David Swanson, a former labor communicator who became a Democratic activist. "The worst-case scenario is that we lose the labor movement. The best case is that people wake up and they become active and aggressive in the way that they did in the thirties and forties and we have a labor movement that becomes a real cultural force."

As labor cracks and separates from within and argues over how to survive, the Bush White House continues to propose legislation and issue rulings that harm unions. Overtime regulations were altered to exempt tens of millions of American workers from being paid additional wages for tasks beyond a normal forty-hour workweek. The Economic Policy Institute estimated that 53 million workers lost their rights to overtime pay under the Bush law. In a case involving graduate students at Brown University, the National Labor Relations Board ruled that graduate students were not employees, even though they were working as researchers and teaching assistants, and were therefore not entitled to form a union under federal labor law. A group of disabled janitors who'd been cleaning Cape Canaveral Air Station tried to join the Transportation Workers Union and were denied labor rights by the NLRB because their relationship with their contract employer, the Brevard Achievement Center, was ruled to be "primarily rehabilitative." The board overlooked the fact that the disabled workers were doing the same tasks as the nondisabled members of the TWU janitorial staff.

The tally of procedures and political moves against unions by the Bush administration is long and has been effective. But a few illustrate Karl Rove's relentless focus on crippling the labor movement. The White House attempted to take away collective-bargaining rights from 160,000 employees of the Department of Homeland Security until a U.S. district judge overruled the president. Nonetheless, the administration has continued efforts to exempt from collective bargaining another 700,000 federal workers in the Defense Department, and the Transit Safety Administration (TSA), which handles all airport security in the country.

The administration's pursuit of privatization could prove the most effective tool yet in curbing organized labor. The president issued Executive Order 13180 to proclaim that air traffic control is not "an inherently governmental function," a move that will open the jobs to nonunion private contractors. The same approach is being considered for the TSA. The president has also used executive authority to investigate the International Longshore Workers Union on the West Coast, the flight attendants of American Airlines, United Airlines' mechanics, and even the unionized workers of the Southeastern Pennsylvania Transit Authority (SEPTA).

John Ryan is the executive secretary of the AFL-CIO in Cleveland, one of America's historic union cities. When his activist parents boycotted lettuce to help farmworkers, it inspired Ryan to get involved in the labor movement. As a leader in the Communications Workers of America and the AFL-CIO, Ryan has been involved in a series of grassroots campaigns to create a viable political climate for unions in northern Ohio. Instead of strength and growth, however, Ryan and union members have had to settle for survival. Industrial manufacturing along the shores of Lake Erie is dying, and jobs are being outsourced to other countries with lower wages, with the result that the AFL-CIO is shrinking in northern Ohio.

Ryan has no doubt that much of what is happening in his hometown and the rest of the country is an endgame pursued with a kind of ruthless vigor by Karl Rove and the Republicans. And he acknowledges a begrudging respect for his enemy and what Rove has done to achieve his political goals.

"I'll be honest with you that I wish we had a Rove on our side. It's real clear that he is smart. He put together a plan to win. It's been clear to me that he pushes harder than we do. He understands the stakes, and he knows how to win. And he has a long-term strategy he talks about through his candidates. He talks about their programs in ways that people understand. He understands that labor unions and trial lawyers are his major opponents. It is a sad, terrible situation."

Down in Texas, however, a kind of political sun is shining on Ty Runyan and his business, Titus Electrical. The National Labor Relations Board (NLRB), which he blamed for many of his union problems, has been given a Republican majority by President Bush, and subsequent rulings have weakened unions. Runyan's $100,000 donation to the Bush second inaugural was money spent in pursuit of an agenda.

Ty Runyan could not be happier.

"The NLRB had been big proponents of the IBEW's [International Brotherhood of Electrical Workers'] attack on us, and Bush has taken that pit bull and put a choke hold on it and jerked a knot in its tail."

There has been at least one other benefit to the Bush presidency for Ty Runyan. As he prepared for the second inaugural, he contemplated how a man who began his work life swinging a pickax and pushing a shovel to dig ditches now makes frequent trips to Republican and presidential functions at the invitation of Bush. Moving among the power brokers and monied interests driving American politics, Ty Runyan is a great geographic and cultural distance from his beginning in the South Texas brush country. He believes democracy is working. And he is being properly rewarded.

"We have tickets for every major event up there," he said.

TWELVE

A GREAT GRIEVANCE

How to Manufacture a Crisis

This is a court of law, young man, not a court of justice.
—Oliver Wendell Holmes

As the doctors' strike in West Virginia was beginning to gain national attention, President Bush jumped aboard Air Force One and went west to Collinsville, Illinois. The public relations campaign on lawsuit reform was being accelerated by political guru Karl Rove in advance of the president's upcoming 2005 State of the Union speech before Congress. Just across the Mississippi River from Saint Louis, the American Tort Reform Association had dubbed Collinsville and Madison County as a "judicial hellhole" for giving big awards to malpractice lawyers.

No journalists traveling with the president reported the fact that the county's bad name was largely a product of the political work of the Illinois Civil Justice League (ICJL), an ideological heir of Karl Rove's Texas Civil Justice League, which had begun the takeover of the Texas judicial system by business-friendly judges.

ICJL produced a report in 2002 that claimed trial lawyers were generously donating to judicial candidates in Madison County. Entitled "Justice for Sale: The Judges of Madison County," the study analyzed about $800,000 of campaign contributions over a twenty-three-year period for that one Illinois county and concluded that most of the money, not surprisingly, came from lawyers. One example was of a plaintiff's attorney giving money to a judge who had ruled on an asbestos case for the donor's law firm. When Rove had found the same thing occurring in Texas as a young consultant, he got businesses to find candidates and donate. Justice was still for sale; it was just going to a higher bidder. And that was a part of the purpose of the president's appearance in southern Illinois.

President Bush met with an obstetrician, a gynecologist, a pregnant woman, and a neurosurgeon and then claimed that malpractice awards had driven up the cost of insurance so dramatically that doctors were closing doors or cutting services.

Illinois trial lawyers accused the White House of demonizing the county, where large malpractice judgments had been scarce. Congressional Democrats insisted that the number of doctors in Illinois had been growing and the increase in malpractice insurance premiums was connected to poor regulation of insurers in the state.

To coincide with the president's trip to Illinois, lawyers spent $250,000 on a television ad in Washington, D.C., and Saint Louis, which told the story of a woman victimized by a medical error. Linda McDougal's doctor had examined the wrong test results, and the mistaken data led to an unneeded double mastectomy.

"It wasn't lawyers who switched my tests, told me I had cancer, and amputated both of my breasts," McDougal said into the camera. "I will never be the same, nor will nearly 100,000 people who die every year because of medical errors. Politicians and big corporations blame the lawyers. I don't buy it and neither should you. I'm glad I live in a country where we can trust a jury to look out for people like me."

The charge that tort reformers were trying to prevent victims such as McDougal from getting justice from bad doctors and their insurance companies gained little traction. The master of messaging, Karl Rove, kept the president positioned as a man fighting to protect the little guy, even though objective analysis suggested the rising cost of malpractice insurance was a product of incompetent physicians and insurance companies seeking greater profit, not frivolous lawsuits. Though the situation was no doubt compounded by greedy lawyers seeking big judgments, they were only a contributing factor to insurance and health care problems. Rove, as always, had simplified the crisis and named the bad guy. And Linda McDougal, tragedy or not, was on the wrong side. The president was heard across the nation that day; McDougal's story got a few thirty-second runs in Saint Louis and Washington, D.C.

Even the Karlspeak of the president's spokesman carried further. "We don't want to have to see pregnant mothers having their OB/GYN doctor go out of business or move to another area because they can't afford to practice their medicine," said White House spokesman Scott McClellan. "We want them to be able to get the care they need when they need it."

In Washington, Linda Lipsen, chief lobbyist for the Association of Trial Lawyers of America (ATLA), was more determined than angry. Her organization was getting a new CEO, Jon Haber, a former public relations executive, and there was a fresh commitment to fight back against the image of greed branded on members of the plaintiffs' bar. Lipsen, who was constantly interrupted by phone calls while speaking in her corner office in Georgetown, intended to prove that frivolous lawsuits are not pushing doctors out of business.

"Medical malpractice?" she asked. "Eighty percent of those cases are won by defense counsels. These are the hardest cases. It's hard to get witnesses to testify against each other. People have an emotional relationship with their doctors. They don't want to hurt them—especially if they say 'I'm sorry' or 'I care about you.' And then there's the cost of experts and investigations to prove the claim. And so the defense lawyers don't see any frivolous cases. You can't find any frivolous cases. You just don't bring them unless they are serious and real."

A few months earlier, Lipsen had accepted defeat as the president signed the class-action reform bill into law, thereby putting such suits in federal jurisdiction, where they're less likely to make it to trial. The president had kept repeating his mantra that "malpractice suits are driving really fine, competent people out of the practice of medicine." That had happened, of course, and in some cases, frivolous lawsuits might even have contributed to a doctor's decision. But there was no trove of evidence indicating a crisis. And in the case of class-action attorneys, they do not make up a significant percentage of ATLA's membership, but the new legislation was nonetheless a setback. At the bill-signing ceremony, the president charged that lawsuit abuse was costing the economy $250 billion a year. The White House's unsupported claims were motivating ATLA's members to raise money for a public relations campaign. Originally, they'd considered $8 million as a reasonable goal, but Haber insisted they needed at least $14 million to begin countering the president's bully pulpit.

And there was much that needed countering.

Peter D. Hart Research Associates was commissioned by ATLA to conduct a national poll, focus groups in four representative cities, and in-depth, confidential conversations with Washington, D.C., opinion leaders to assess the reputation of trial lawyers. What they discovered was both disheartening and motivating. American voters believed that frivolous lawsuits were a problem for the civil justice system and that "persistent attacks by opponents, news coverage of controversial cases, marketing activities of trial lawyers, and the absence of a counter message have cre-ated a negative environment that puts the trial bar on the defensive at both the ballot box and in the jury box."

Before the results of Hart's research were delivered, ATLA's leadership had decided to go on the offensive. They knew that President Bush planned to push tort reform and talk about frivolous lawsuits in his 2005 State of the Union speech. An ally of the trial lawyers, USAction (which receives funding from ATLA and other organizations), broadcast another medical mistake victim ad to local Washington television viewers and national cable audiences as a prelude to the president's antilawyer message. The spot aired in a rotation right up until Bush stood before Congress.

The commercial was built around the story of Ian Malone. When his mother, Christine, was pregnant, she was given a drug to induce labor. The manufacturer had warned that the drug had the potential to cause brain damage in the newborn. Ian suffered severe injury to his brain and endured cerebral palsy. He lived four years being fed through a tube in his stomach while having secretions removed from his mouth by a machine. The family won $4 million in a lawsuit in the case, and Ian's father, Dylan, insisted in the TV ad that his son's life was not "frivolous." Because the message had clarity and power, USAction and ATLA decided to spend an additional $90,000 for thirty seconds on NBC's national broadcast net-work. They were turned down, however, for unspecified reasons by NBC's Standards and Practices office.

Although there was no discernible impact on Karl Rove and the White House's messaging strategy, the trial lawyers persisted with their proac-tive plans to take on their critics. Preparations began immediately to con-front doctors from the American Medical Association who were coming to Washington for a meeting to discuss the issues challenging their pro-fession. The Mayflower Hotel, where the doctors were gathering, was contacted about airing the Dylan Malone ad on the in-house television network. The hotel's management refused to carry a commercial that would offend its guests, so USAction purchased four days of broadcast rotation on Washington TV. A larger coalition of organizations placed a full-page print ad with Malone's picture and the story of his son in *USA Today.* The ad was also turned into a billboard and posted on the side of a couple of trucks, which drove in circles around the Mayflower for two days and then followed the doctors to Capitol Hill for their lobbying day.

The ATLA attempt to tell the other side of the malpractice story also included a news conference with victims of medical errors or their family members. The news conference was held at the hotel where the doctors were conducting their meetings. Dylan Malone was joined by five other people who either had been harmed by medical mistakes or had lost a loved one as a result of an error by a physician. A fifty-eight-year-old woman whose heart was damaged by use of the weight-loss stimulant fen-phen brought her story to Washington, along with the husband of a woman who died ten days before the birth of her first grandchild. She had been given a drug to counteract the effects of fen-phen. There was also a middle-aged male who had been prescribed VIOXX and had suffered a debilitating heart attack.

But no one in the media noticed.

ATLA had spent close to $400,000 on its outreach effort but did not get any news coverage. Neither did the doctors, even though Senate Majority Leader Bill Frist, who is a physician, met with them at their hotel. A few months later, about three hundred doctors showed up on Capitol Hill for a "White Coat Day" with stethoscopes draped around their necks while they lobbied members of Congress to protect them from greedy malpractice lawyers. One of ATLA's allies, the Center for Justice and Democracy, led a coalition of supporting organizations in a news conference across the street in an attempt to provide some balance to the strictly local coverage of the day's events. The lawyers were still struggling to get out meaningful information on their side of the malpractice story.

"It's pretty simple," said one of the people involved in the public relations campaign. "Emotion and language always trump facts. Karl's got the language and the emotion. People love their doctors. And everybody seems to enjoy bashing lawyers."

The plaintiffs' bar might have had the facts on their side. But their image had taken a considerable beating, the result of a long, focused public relations campaign to characterize trial lawyers as something considerably less than honest. Jon Haber, ATLA's new CEO, had decided to launch his own campaign to undo the abundance of misinformation. After bringing aboard former Al Gore strategists Chris Lehane and Jim Jordan, Haber hired Chris Mather as a full-time manager of the communications initiative. Mather set up a "war room" and lined the walls with poster paper marked up with various core messages and a hand-scrawled calendar of important moments confronting ATLA in the coming weeks. Mather was often seen in her corner office on the speakerphone participating in seemingly endless conference calls on strategy.

ATLA had finally arrived at a strategic decision, which promised as much risk as potential for positively changing its image. The trial lawyers would admit that there were, in fact, frivolous lawsuits even as they were also rolling out a plan for what they were describing as "Real Legal Reform." No concession was made in the group's twenty-point draft plan to the charge that meritless suits were out of control within the civil justice system. But ATLA was acknowledging publicly that there were unethical and incompetent plaintiffs' attorneys.

"In addition to protecting the legal rights of American families," the document said, "the Association of Trial Lawyers of America (ATLA) and its members will do everything in our power to assure that only meritorious lawsuits that cannot be efficiently, expeditiously, and fairly resolved beforehand go to trial."

The Real Legal Reform premise also made clear that theirs was not the only profession that suffered from incompetent and unethical practitioners. The document served as a platform for a speech by the association's new president, Kenneth Suggs, who was to address the idea that ATLA would "identify for consumers those attorneys and other licensed professionals who have been publicly disciplined by a state licensing agency." This was obviously an effort to elevate public awareness that state medical boards were doing very little about disciplining physicians guilty of medical errors. ATLA contended that the media took little notice that bad doctors are allowed to continue to practice medicine and force up insurance premium rates for other physicians.

Trial lawyers did not dispute that they are responsible for a portion of their poor image. The two developments that have harmed the legal profession the most were advertising and the multibillion-dollar settlements against the tobacco companies. Although the public overwhelmingly

wanted accountability for the deceptive business practices of the ciga-
rette manufacturers, it did not understand individual fees for each of the
lawyers that, in some of the settlements, reached into hundreds of millions of dollars.

"The tipping point was the tobacco case and the billion-dollar fees,"
Linda Lipsen said. "It's hard for the public to understand why that is okay.
The second thing is lawyer advertising, which can be extremely tasteless.
I mean it's not always, but a lot of it is. It looks like they are drumming
up business from tragedy, and that's unseemly. It runs counter to the
American spirit."

The tobacco lawsuit settlement was also important to Karl Rove and
his plans for tort reform. In Texas, the tobacco companies agreed to pay
the state $15.3 billion. Attorneys, who'd taken the case on a contingency
basis, divvied up billions in fees. Rove used that hammer to take his antilawyer campaign into the national arena when his client, George W. Bush,
ran for president.

Beginning in the mid-1980s, Rove had been trying to build a grassroots movement to change Texas tort laws and get more business-
friendly judges on the state's bench. It was the template he wanted to use
across America to change the civil justice system, which would facilitate
Republican realignment.

From the start, Rove saw the lawsuit fight as a money machine to elect
GOP candidates. His work as a direct-mail specialist with the Texas Civil
Justice League, the state's premier business group, helped him create an
unparalleled list of deep-pocket Republican donors. Texas business interests wanted to protect themselves from lawsuits; Rove wanted to defeat
Democrats. As political marriages go, business had the money and Rove
would produce the candidates. The big question was how to make litigation
against business a sexy campaign issue. In the 1980s, the Texas Supreme
Court was a particularly nettlesome problem for business. All nine members were Democrats who ruled with some regularity on the side of trial
lawyers representing people injured by defective products.

"We had to get some Republicans in there," said Ralph Wayne, executive director of the Civil Justice League. "The conventional wisdom was
that Republicans were more attuned to tort reform."

Business had been an unreliable source of campaign cash, in part because there was no efficient organizing principle around which to build a

political machine. Tort reform became that principle, and Rove, the organizer. The beginning of the end of the Democratic Party in Texas was a meeting in 1988 in the conference room of an Austin law firm where Rove and representatives of the Texas Medical Association and the Civil Justice League developed a plan to raise millions of dollars to elect a select group of supreme court candidates and bolster that effort with an aggressive public relations campaign to make the term *trial lawyer* an epithet. The group, dubbed the Judicial Education Alliance, published a tabloid newspaper—650,000 copies the first year—promoting its candidates and denouncing greedy plaintiffs' attorneys. The alliance solicited money from 125 political action committees and printed 1.2 million slate cards of favored candidates, which doctors distributed in their offices.

"We spent a lot of time with Karl, and he did a lot of mailings for us," said Wayne.

But it was in recruiting candidates with a promise of campaign cash—coupled with warnings to potential Republican challengers that they would have trouble getting money—that Rove became a power broker on the emerging GOP landscape. When Ralph Wayne, the Austin lobbyist who ran the Texas Civil Justice League for Rove, spotted a district judge from San Antonio named John Cornyn as a likely prospect for the high court in 1990, he had Rove call him. Cornyn ran and won and served a decade before running successfully for the U.S. Senate, again with Rove's help. When Priscilla Owen from Houston, a bright lawyer but a political nonentity, called Wayne saying she wanted to run for the Texas Supreme Court, he directed her to see Rove also. She did and she won.

"Everybody knew who Karl was," said Wayne. "If he put his hand on your shoulder, you were the anointed candidate for raising money. And the word got to every Republican grassroots organization in the state that this was the anointed person."

During George W. Bush's tenure as governor, Rove remained a highly paid private consultant but regularly attended senior-staff meetings at the capitol as if he were on the government payroll. No adviser had more influence on the judiciary, both the candidates who ran for office and the appointments Bush made. So that by the time he and the president-elect left for Washington in 2001, all nine members of the Texas Supreme Court were Republicans, and most had been Rove clients.

"Karl was the key. He was the Republican fighting the war and trying to change the state," said Wayne. "And if Karl said, 'This is the person I'm working for,' that was it. Having Karl Rove for you is like having Tommy Franks for you if you were a private in the U.S. Army. You get a battlefield commission right quick."

One of Rove's key financial allies was Philip Morris, which was looking for ways to protect itself from smoker lawsuits. One way was the election of sympathetic political candidates in the legislative, executive, and judicial branches of government. As it turned out, Rove had clients in all three. The tobacco giant hired Rove in 1991 and put him on a $3,000-a-month consulting retainer. In Washington, a public relations expert named Neal Cohen was also on the payroll through his client, the American Tort Reform Association. Cohen's assignment was "assisting the PM family on national and state tort coalitions and other tort reform advocates with political, communications and grassroots strategies," according to internal Philip Morris documents released in the federal tobacco lawsuit.

Rove's task was electing candidates to office who'd be sensitive to grassroots protests by business in local communities. Cohen's job was to provide the grassroots protests. The essence of Cohen's effort was that he remain invisible and that so-called Astroturf groups spring up to denounce trial lawyers and lament high-dollar jury verdicts. A tobacco industry memo explained, "In order to be totally effective, the grassroots effort must appear to be spontaneous rather than a coordinated effort."

The dustup in South Texas actually was spontaneous in the beginning. In September 1990, a jury awarded $2.5 million to two Mexican American men who had been illegally fired from a local sugar mill. The local chamber of commerce, looking to counter what it believed was a proconsumer judicial climate in the region, hired a marketing consultant named Jon Opelt to set up a Citizens against Lawsuit Abuse office. In short order, Opelt's group was erecting billboards and engaging local newspapers in the fight against "frivolous" lawsuits.

Cohen knew a good thing when he saw it. He called Rove and said the regional effort needed to be institutionalized and taken statewide, then nationwide. Rove agreed and instructed Cohen to hire two people: Rossanna Salazar, who had worked with Rove when she was press secretary to former Republican governor Bill Clements, and a fledgling Rove associate named Scott McClellan.

Shortly thereafter, Opelt got a call from Salazar. She said she and

McClellan had been hired by the American Tort Reform Association and were available to handle communications, organization, and the building of a statewide membership base.

"Is this going to cost us anything?" Opelt asked. "No," said Salazar. "You can use our resources, our communications, our expertise—however you choose."

It sounded pretty good to Opelt. He had a new field director, McClellan. And Salazar helped foster expansion of lawsuit-abuse groups across Texas, then took the model national as an instructor creating similar "grassroots" uprisings in other states, including West Virginia, where the doctors' strikes in 2003 would punctuate the national political debate. As for Rove, he convinced Bush to include lawsuit abuse as one of his four principal issues in the 1994 campaign for governor. "I sort of talked him into that one," Rove said. Business-friendly donors poured millions of dollars into Bush's successful effort to unseat Ann Richards, and Governor Bush reciprocated with an aggressive program to limit personal-injury lawsuits against business.

Only days after his January 1995 inauguration, Bush announced that ending "frivolous and junk lawsuits" was an emergency, thereby putting the issue on the legislative fast track. He made the announcement at a salsa factory near Austin surrounded by a horde of media and scores of local lawsuit-abuse officials brought in by bus—a smashing public relations success arranged by Salazar at the behest of Cohen and Rove. After that, the issue—and the lucrative money lists of business donors that Rove cultivated along the way—served Bush well all the way to the White House.

After almost a quarter century of raising money, electing judges with a business perspective, guiding Republican officeholders to appoint conservatives to the bench, and running a relentless message campaign to destroy the reputation of trial lawyers, Karl Rove and the corporate Right had become durable allies. And even with mounting controversies and legal troubles that beset the Bush administration, there was not the slightest hint that the assault against trial lawyers and their sources of income was abating. To ATLA and its members, it felt as if almost every week, there was a new initiative or piece of legislation designed to do them harm. Often those features were hidden inside of proposals dealing with more important issues.

In the paranoia and fear over the possibility of a bird flu pandemic, President Bush called on Congress to appropriate $7.1 billion for pharmaceutical companies to develop vaccines. The administration's proposal included provisions to stop liability lawsuits by anyone who might be injured by improper inoculations or poorly designed drugs. The draft version of the bill pushed by the White House shielded any companies that might act negligently by protecting them from lawsuits related to antiviral therapies and devices as well as vaccines. Distributors of those drugs would also be protected, along with hospitals where the shots were administered.

The Bush White House said the liability protections were necessary to build up the national inventory of critical medicines to prevent a flu pandemic. The general counsel of the American Tort Reform Association (ATRA) offered a more revealing comment on the politics of the proposal.

"What I've seen with liability is if you say 'terrorist' or 'pandemic,' you're much more likely to get the shield because you're saying there is this sort of flag: national interest," said ATRA's Victor Schwartz. "That moves Democratic senators away from the plaintiff lawyers' column."

Including a liability shield in the funding bill for flu vaccines was further evidence Karl Rove was staying on task. If he got his president to regain political balance in 2006, Rove intended to continue pressing his case for changes in tort laws. An asbestos bill designed to limit compensation for victims and medical-malpractice measures were likely to be reintroduced in Congress, if for no other reason than to raise more money for Republicans and to force Democrats to publicly defend the greedy, ambulance-chasing attorneys.

As usual, Karl Rove was master of the game.

George Parker Young spent a fair amount of time contemplating the hypocrisies and contradictions in one of the biggest legal cases of his career. A lifelong Republican who had been active in politics since working for Texas U.S. senator John Tower, Young had been one of the first people to raise money to help George W. Bush become governor and then had worked with the legislature to pass important insurance and medical laws during the six-year gubernatorial administration of the future president. A decade later, Young was preparing to go before the U.S. Supreme Court to argue against a president he'd helped elect.

"I was very disappointed after he became president," Young said. "I was certainly struck by how different Governor Bush was from President Bush."

Both as a governor who'd yielded to political expediency and allowed a Patients' Bill of Rights to become law and as a presidential candidate, Bush rhetorically defended the rights of states to pass laws that shouldn't be contravened by federal legislation. When he was elected president, however, both he and political adviser Karl Rove began to worry about claims against insurance companies after ten other states passed HMO liability laws similar to the one in Texas. George W. Bush decided he had to overturn state laws protecting patients against negligence by their HMOs as soon as his administration had a legal forum to argue that state legislation was superseded by the federal ERISA (Employee Retirement Income Security Act) regulations, precisely the opposite of what he'd promised as a presidential candidate.

The test case for the White House came from George Parker Young. Two of his clients, Ruby Calad and Juan Davila, had sued their HMOs under the Texas law when their managed care insurers had refused to extend a hospital stay for Calad and pay for a specific brand-name drug for Davila. The defendants, CIGNA and Aetna, filed motions to have the cases removed from the state courts and placed in the federal system by arguing that there was preemption under the ERISA statute. The case made its way to the Supreme Court.

Calad's suit against CIGNA accused the insurer of practicing medicine by sending her home after only one day of recovery from a hysterectomy. She claimed under the Texas HMO liability law, which Bush had touted during his campaign, that she'd been harmed because complications developed and she had to be readmitted. Davila, whose case was consolidated with Calad's, had been given a generic drug instead of a name brand and developed near-fatal internal bleeding. Their attorney, George Parker Young, argued that their claims did not fall under the regulation of benefits management included in ERISA. If he were to lose the case, every one of the eleven HMO liability statutes in various states would be rendered functionally meaningless. HMOs and other managed care providers would be given legal immunity and protected from claims of negligence or mismanagement by the federal law.

The lead attorney for the U.S. government in the case was Bush's solicitor general, Ted Olson, who had stood before the Supreme Court in 2000 to argue the evidence that the Bush-Cheney campaign had won the election in Florida. Olson, whose wife had been on board the jet that 9/11 terrorists crashed into the Pentagon, was a partner in one of the country's most powerful law firms, Gibson, Dunn, and Crutcher. Because his former law firm was representing both of the insurance companies, Olson recused himself a few days before the brief was filed by the solicitor general's office on behalf of the Bush administration. Arguing the case for the companies was a lawyer in the firm named Miguel Estrada, a failed Bush nominee to the U.S. Court of Appeals.

From the outset, questions posed to Estrada and Young indicated the Court was likely to rule against Calad, Davila, and the state of Texas. Justice Antonin Scalia suggested in open court that HMOs were not making medical decisions when they refused to pay for certain treatment. "They're not managing care," he insisted. "They're giving out money." Attorney George Parker Young contended that by deciding what they will or will not pay for in terms of care, an HMO or a PPO was, in effect, practicing medicine. Ted Cruz, solicitor general for President Bush's home state of Texas, defended the Texas HMO liability law against the man who'd claimed credit for it in his campaign for the White House.

"Were Aetna and CIGNA to prevail," Cruz said, "patients would be left with no meaningful remedy for negligent and wrongful decisions."

Aetna and CIGNA prevailed.

The Court unanimously rejected the pleadings of Calad and Davila. Justice Clarence Thomas, who wrote the opinion, said that the plaintiffs' injuries could not be blamed on their health care providers if, in fact, those companies "correctly concluded that, under the terms of the relevant plan, a particular treatment was not covered." The issue for the justices was how much coverage Calad's and Davila's employers had purchased. According to Thomas, "the failure of the plan itself to cover the requested treatment" was the cause of injuries. In short, Calad and Davila were told by the Court that they ought to have purchased a health care plan that would have provided greater benefits.

Critics pointed to the president's change of political position on a patients' bill of rights. His insistence in his first campaign that he did not want federal law to supersede Texas legislation and favored a national patients' bill of rights seemed fatuous after his solicitor general convinced the high court to preempt the HMO liability laws in Texas and ten other states.

"The big story is the flip-flop here," said M. Gregg Bloche, a Georgetown law professor specializing in health care issues.

A White House spokesman insisted there was no contradiction. The president "continued to support [the] Texas law," the spokesman said, but decisions by HMOs to "deny coverage have always been covered by federal law."

However various political interests spun the ruling, the ultimate effect was to deny patients the right to sue their health care providers under state laws that had given them that authority. David Casey, who was president of the Association of Trial Lawyers of America at the time of the 2004 decision, knew that his profession would be injured by the ruling. The states' rights president had defeated states' rights.

"This decision takes away the rights of states to protect their own citizens and it takes away any recourse patients have to hold their HMOs responsible for bad medical decisions," Casey said. "Medical decisions should be left to doctors, not insurance executives who make a buck every time they deny a legitimate claim."

Back in the president's home state of Texas, the Republican-majority legislature gave voters a chance to approve a proposition capping medical-malpractice awards. And they did in September of 2003. By October, some doctor-owned medical-malpractice insurance companies were announcing rate cuts of up to 12 percent in Texas. But access to the civil justice system was even more difficult for health care patients with legitimate claims against their providers. Personal-injury attorneys were no longer able to afford to take on clients, since the cost of bringing cases to trial often exceeded potential earnings of a court win.

George Parker Young went back to practicing business law. "They pretty much did away with med-mal claims against doctors," Young explained. "And that's where most of my cases came from. I closed up shop. I know a number of lawyers who have just shut down as a result of all that."

Before moving on, however, Young took a cue from justice Ruth Bader Ginsburg, whose concurring opinion in the landmark case acknowledged that "a regulatory vacuum exists." The Supreme Court's decision affected 140 million Americans and their health care plans, and Young urged Congress to seek a solution to the "very real problem of HMO accountability." Congress, though, was not likely to launch any HMO liability initiative. Both the House and Senate were overwhelmingly Republican.

And they got their strategic advice from Karl Rove.

THIRTEEN

ROVE'S BRAIN

A Secret Chef Cooks Up the Case for War

A lie never lives to be old.
—Sophocles

As they met in Rome, the debris pile from the 9/11 terrorist attacks was still smoldering in New York City. It was early December 2001, and sixteen of them were gathered around a large table. Although there were three representatives of the U.S. government, the meeting was not official business of the people of the United States. The names of the Americans in the room, however, offered insight into the topics of discussion.

The meeting had been arranged by Michael Ledeen, a neoconservative who holds the Freedom Chair at the conservative think tank the American Enterprise Institute (AEI) in Washington and whose prolific writings have advocated "creative destruction" of much of the Middle East. Ledeen has been variously described as an author, a scholar, a historian, and a politician, but his involvement in American foreign policy as an intelligence operative does not appear on his résumé. At the time of this secret Rome conference, Ledeen was engaged as a consultant for Douglas Feith, undersecretary of defense for policy, the third most powerful position in the Pentagon. (Ledeen denies this.)

Two employees from Feith's office, Harold Rhode and Larry Franklin, had accompanied Ledeen on the trip to Rome. Rhode considered himself a protégé of Ledeen's. Assigned to the Pentagon's Office of Net Assessment, an in-house think tank, Rhode took a desk within Feith's operation and prompted the consternation of civilian advisers and career military staffers. Rhode is fluent in Arabic, Hebrew, Turkish, and Farsi and was influential in spreading the anti-Iraq, pro-Israel policy within the halls of the Pentagon and Congress. His attitude and politics were reflected in a widely reported incident when he pressed his finger into the chest of a diminutive Arab diplomat and told him there'd be "no bartering in the bazaar anymore. You're going to have to sit up and pay attention when we say so."

Rhode's job, when he came to Feith's operation to work for the Office of Net Assessment and the Near East and South Asia (NESA) bureau, was to clear out nonbelievers and Pentagon employees who weren't sufficiently enthusiastic about the policies being developed to pursue war with Iraq and favor Israel's political perspective. The people Rhode hired, according to a senior staffer who worked with him, "were mostly from conservative think tanks and pro-Likud operations." Eventually, Rhode became the "handler" of Ahmad Chalabi, the defamed leader of the Iraqi National Congress whose intelligence sources, mostly Iraqi defectors, were completely wrong on weapons of mass destruction. A U.S. intelligence source said that Rhode almost lived out of Chalabi's Baghdad office after the Iraq invasion and that he was often heard talking on his cell phone sharing information with Israeli officials. The detail Rhode was offering on deployments, politics, and other sensitive matters was described by that agent as "mind-boggling." UPI reported that three former CIA agents confirmed that Rhode's security clearances had been suspended for sharing sensitive information with Israel, a claim Rhode denied in an e-mail to the wire service.

While he struck most observers as a "regular bureaucrat," Rhode nonetheless busily generated the information the White House wanted to enable the politics and policies that led to the invasion of Iraq. In a rare instance of a reporter's reaching him on the phone, Rhode refused to offer any information about his work in the Pentagon with Douglas Feith and Michael Ledeen by saying "Those who speak, pay."

The third American in that Rome meeting was Larry Franklin. A self-styled "James Bond," according to one of his colleagues, Franklin was an Iran specialist in the Defense Intelligence Agency and was on loan to NESA at the Pentagon. A close friend of Michael Ledeen's, Franklin was very well connected with the American Israel Public Affairs Committee

(AIPAC), one of Washington's most powerful lobby groups, which has historically reflected the expansionist, right-wing ideology of Israel's Likud Party. Franklin's zealotry for protecting Israel's preeminence in U.S. foreign policy was nearly equal to his friend Ledeen's.

Ledeen was not technically an intelligence operative for the Pentagon, though he'd acted in that capacity during his career. Ledeen, Rhode, and Franklin all reported to Douglas Feith, who was also a hard-liner on the question of Israel. A radical conservative, Feith was appointed undersecretary of policy at the Department of Defense by President Bush. Feith, too, was closely associated with the conservative policy wonks of the American Enterprise Institute and had produced a large body of work as a writer and speaker on issues related to U.S. foreign policy and particularly Israel. His hawkish perspective is revealed by his opposition to virtually every international peace treaty, which includes the Oslo Peace Accords and all of the Mideast agreements as well as the Anti-Ballistic Missile Treaty and the Chemical Weapons Convention.

At the direction of Secretary of Defense Donald Rumsfeld, Feith worked with Abram Shulsky to create the Office of Special Plans (OSP) at the Pentagon, a counterintelligence operation designed to circumvent the analyses and findings of the CIA on the topic of Iraq. A soft-spoken, grandfatherly figure, Shulsky had been working in policy and intelligence for more than three decades in and out of government and was involved in the neocons' visionary plan known as Project for the New American Century, which was a politically aggressive proposal for asserting U.S. military strength in the Mideast. The entire OSP operation was overseen by William Luti, one of the earliest voices advocating an invasion of Iraq. Luti is a former navy aviator and close personal adviser of Vice President Dick Cheney. Along with Shulsky and Feith, Luti managed OSP out of the Pentagon's fourth-floor D ring.

Michael Ledeen was functioning out of DOD as a Feith consultant within a few months of the Bush administration's taking office. After authoring more than ten books and writing frequently for the *National Review* and other nationally distributed publications, Ledeen's commitment to re-creating the Mideast in a conservative, right-wing American and Israeli image had been broadly disseminated. His intellectual bent is in the direction of overthrowing Arab regimes and stabilizing the Mideast through the use of American military strength. He insists that the U.S. invasion of Iraq makes Bush a great president, and his only quibble with the administration's policies is that America is not moving quickly enough to topple the governments of Iran, Syria, and Saudi Arabia. Ledeen concludes his political columns for *National Review* with an insistent "Faster, please." Ledeen's perspective on Iraq and the 9/11 attacks was already evident twenty-four minutes after a plane struck the south tower of the World Trade Center and nine minutes before the Pentagon was hit. At 9:26 a.m. EDT, Ledeen, who was a frequent poster on the conservative Free Republic website chat room, left the two-word message "Saddam's revenge."

In Rome, Ledeen had arranged for his Pentagon colleagues Rhode and Franklin to speak with Manucher Ghorbanifar, an Iranian arms dealer and businessman, who brought along several of his countrymen. During Iran-contra, Ghorbanifar had acted as a double agent for Israel's MOSSAD intelligence agency while also working for Iran's SAVAK, the Iranian version of the CIA, to arrange the arms-for-hostages transactions that were to sully the Reagan administration's reputation.

Washington Monthly magazine reported that Nicolo Pollari, the head of Italy's military intelligence agency, SISMI, was also in the room, along with Italy's minister of defense, Antonio Martino. The Iranian delegation reportedly included a former member of the country's Revolutionary Guard who was supposedly offering information on dissidents in his country.

Whatever Ledeen was doing in Rome, it was not diplomacy with peace as a goal. The events of 9/11 had given him a kind of rhetorical bloodlust. At the same time he was in Italy for his secret meeting, Ledeen was posting a venomous editorial on the *National Review*'s website, which might have been dismissed as a silly rant had it not been written by a man who was working in international politics and was getting checks from the taxpayers of the United States through his DOD consulting agreement.

"We need to sustain our game face," he wrote. "We must keep our fangs bared, we must remind them daily that we Americans are in a rage, and we will not rest until we have avenged our dead, we will not be sated until we have had the blood of every miserable little tyrant in the Middle East, until every leader of every cell of the terror network is dead or locked securely away, and every last drooling anti-Semitic and anti-American mullah, imam, sheikh, and ayatollah is either singing the praises of the United States of America, or pumping gasoline, for a dime a gallon, on an American military base near the Arctic Circle."

Referred to sometimes as (Karl) "Rove's brain" by political opponents and intelligence operatives who believe he is helping Rove guide White

House policies regarding the Mideast, Michael Ledeen appeared to be involved in a kind of reprise of a failed scheme from his years assisting the Reagan administration. Ledeen, who'd arranged the meetings between U.S. and Israeli operatives involved in Iran-contra and Manucher Ghorbanifar, had described the Iranian as "one of the most honest, educated, honorable men I have ever known." Ghorbanifar, however, had, in the past, been unable to pass lie-detector tests administered by U.S. authorities. The CIA issued an extremely rare "burn notice" on the genteel Ghorbanifar, which meant agents were not to deal with him because he was, in the agency's estimation, a "serial fabricator."

The purpose of the meeting between Ghorbanifar, Ledeen, Harold Rhode, Larry Franklin, and the chiefs of Italian intelligence and defense has never been clarified. Presumably, there were detailed conversations about Iranian politics and the strength of the mullah-controlled government, which Ledeen has been obsessed with deposing. None of the participants has ever detailed the topics of discussion. Asked via e-mail for an interview and how he might have characterized the event, Ledeen wrote back that he had "not only 'characterized' the Rome meetings, I have written about them and testified about them. So, you don't need to talk to me you only need to do your homework." The "wealth" of journalism related to the December 2001 meeting in Rome was dismissed by Ledeen as mostly "fool's gold."

His own writing, however, resolves nothing and is doggedly vague. America was still more than a year away from invading Iraq and toppling dictator Saddam Hussein at the time of the Rome meeting. Ledeen suggested in the *National Review* that it was nothing more than "midlevel Iran experts at DOD [talking] to private Iranians to enhance our understanding about what's going on inside Iran, and what the Iranian regime is going, or planning to do, to Americans and our friends and Allies." As a neocon insider and consultant to Undersecretary Feith in the DOD, Ledeen was certain to have known how intelligence, as revealed in the Downing Street Memo, was being "fixed" around an already developed policy of the Bush administration to invade Iraq. The preordained conclusion of that debate might have given him the freedom to pursue the next step in his grander dream of transforming the Mideast, which was to overthrow Iran's government.

Nothing Ledeen has said or written, however, has sufficiently explained the presence of Italian military and intelligence leaders at his meeting in

Rome. Since the Pentagon had not notified either the CIA station chief in Rome or the U.S. embassy about what Ledeen was doing, there was nothing official or sanctioned about the gathering. Private citizens and "midlevel bureaucrats" of Iran and America can certainly meet in a third country to discuss politics, but do they need senior intelligence and military officers from the host nation sitting with them at the same table? Ledeen's initial reaction to questions related to the Rome meeting revealed an attitude suggesting the arrangement was not that unusual or, if it was, it was of no consequence to anyone other than those in attendance. When *Newsday* originally broke the story about Ledeen and his Rome compatriots, his refusal to offer an explanation was indignant.

"I'm not going to comment on any private meetings with any private people," he said. "It's nobody's business."

But a week later, in a published opinion article he called "Iran-Contra Revisited?" Michael Ledeen began to portray all of the parties to the Rome gathering as a group of innocents convening to talk about the mutual interests of their respective countries. While also managing to promote his new book about terror, Ledeen turned around inquiries about his trip to Rome and transformed the controversy into a screed against journalism's failure to "ask our diplomats the obvious questions: is it not correct that al Qaeda terrorists have been operating out of Iran?"

For reasons of both logistics and timing, however, unrelenting suspicion has been cast upon whatever was the true purpose of the Rome meeting. Less than two months earlier, on October 15, 2001, the CIA was reported to have just received the first of three top-secret dossiers that attempted to show that Iraq may have tried to purchase "yellowcake" uranium from the African nation of Niger. The information—which was also shared with France, Germany, and England—came from Italy's SISMI, the country's intelligence operation. The French, who control Niger's uranium mines, considered the intelligence unreliable and dismissed the claims, while the British eventually rolled it into a dossier that would be referred to by President Bush in his State of the Union speech in early 2003.

Michael Ledeen's long relationship with SISMI and Israel, together with the timing of meetings between him and associates in Italy and France, made Ledeen the focus of a number of journalists and government investigators. In an e-mail, Ledeen denied a claim made by a CIA source that he was receiving payments from SISMI as late as 2004, and he insisted that he was not doing any work for the Italian government.

"Obviously, I don't know who you are talking to," Ledeen wrote. "But if they are alleging these things they are lying to you."

Nonetheless, when U.S. National Security Adviser Stephen Hadley was informed of the unofficial meetings being conducted by Ledeen and others within the DOD's Office of Special Plans, he ordered them to stop. As if he were not the least concerned with Hadley's admonition or that it might have been nothing more than pro forma, Ledeen informed the U.S. embassy in Rome of future meetings (a step he did not take for the December 2001 talk with Manucher Ghorbanifar and SISMI). Repeated warnings from Hadley to Ledeen were ignored and may have been issued simply to establish a political record and give the administration deniability regarding any involvement.

Whatever he was doing, Ledeen was determined. There was a presidential administration in Washington that felt the same way about Israel and the Mideast as he did, and he was working for a Department of Defense that was preparing to project American power into the Arab world. He had even publicly acknowledged that Karl Rove listened to his policy advice. Michael Ledeen and the neocons had been waiting for this moment for a long time. And even though they gathered little more intelligence than what turned out to be fake documents involving uranium mines in Niger on which to base arguments for an Iraq invasion, the neocons were not to be stopped.

Before he had even launched George W. Bush's first Texas gubernatorial campaign, Karl Rove was determined to change the political dynamics of Jewish voters and donors. Historically, they'd been a Democratic Party resource, and both their theology and progressive politics had been at odds with the Christian and conservative Republican Party. When Bush had let slip his awkward comment as Texas governor that Jews were not going to heaven, he had expressed a belief deeply held by fundamentalist Christians, and they were drawn to Bush's political potential and his faith. Whether Bush's analysis of Judaism and the hereafter was by design or a stumble of his famously awkward tongue, it had served to gain the notice of the GOP Christian base, which had been unenthused about his father's presidency.

Karl Rove, in the meantime, began quiet efforts to repair any damage to Bush within the Jewish community. Along with his friend Ralph Reed, Rove had already taken the initial steps to form an unlikely coalition of Christians and Jews to support GOP candidates, even though the faith of both religions foresaw contradictory outcomes for the Holy Land. As improbable as the political alliance might be between Jews and fundamentalist Christians, Rove appears to have been intimately involved in engineering its creation and has consequently given it great influence.

Irrespective of any eventuality beyond immediate political concerns, Rove had Bush send letters to American Jewish leadership, conduct meetings and phone calls, and deliver the consistent message that Israel would have no better friend than George W. Bush. This prepresidential campaign rose to broader public awareness when Bush took a trip to Israel as governor and visited a number of holy sites.

George Bush kept his promise to Israel, and Jews in the United States responded with an increase in votes and Republican campaign contributions. Private White House dinners with Karl Rove and about twenty of the country's prominent Jewish leaders prior to the reelection campaign secured a deep commitment to Israel by Bush. The president had already filled his administration with appointees whose political convictions regarding Israel were so strong that they were, as a minimum, accused of having "dual loyalties" and, in the worst case, were described as "Israel-firsters."

The most influential of the Bush choices were Paul Wolfowitz, Richard Perle, and Douglas Feith, while Vice President Dick Cheney turned to I. Lewis "Scooter" Libby, John Hannah, and David Wurmser, all of whom had exhibited a predisposition to favor Israel in policy and decision-making processes.

Wurmser, who became Mideast adviser to the vice president as the war was unfolding in 2003, might be the most ideologically aggressive in the group. Along with his wife, Meyrav, and Perle and Feith, Wurmser had coauthored a 1996 paper for Israeli prime minister Benjamin Netanyahu. "A Clean Break: A New Strategy for Securing the Realm" called upon Israel to attack Syria and Lebanon and overthrow Saddam Hussein as critical steps for redrawing the political power structure of the Mideast. The document appears to have served as a kind of template for the government of Prime Minister Ariel Sharon and, in almost every aspect, seems to inform Bush administration policy.

During the course of their careers in government and lobbying, Wolfowitz, Feith, and Perle had all been suspected of various actions taken to benefit Israel. Wolfowitz was once investigated for passing classified information to an Israeli official through the lobbying group AIPAC. The data was reportedly related to the sale of U.S. arms to an Arab nation. During Wolfowitz's tour of duty in the Pentagon for Defense Secretary Dick Cheney in 1990, Wolfowitz's office pushed for the export of American missile technology to Israel even though the Israelis were violating nontransfer agreements by selling the weapons to China.

Feith, too, had been suspected of passing classified material to an Israeli official after publicly expressing his belief in "technological cooperation" between the United States and Israel. Perle had once been picked up on an FBI wiretap discussing classified data from the National Security Council (NSC) with an Israeli embassy official. He was also involved in the leaking of a classified CIA report while working with the Senate Foreign Relations Committee.

"Nearly every one of the people we would identify as neo-cons has had problems with their security clearances," said seventeen-year Mideast CIA veteran Philip Giraldi, "because they've been giving information to Israel or they are suspected thereof."

In addition to their unflagging commitment to Israel, most of the neoconservatives promoting the Iraq invasion had a common connection to Michael Ledeen. A founding member of the board of advisers for the Jewish Institute for National Security Affairs (JINSA) (Vice President Dick Cheney was also an adviser before taking office) in Washington and the creator of the Center for Democracy in Iran (CDI), Ledeen has been considered by the CIA and the Italian government to be "an agent of influence for Israel." Ledeen insists he has never done any political work for Israel, "nor any other kind of work."

He does, though, appear to have some effect on the thinking of Karl Rove. Although published reports claim the two did not meet until after Bush's election, Ledeen was working out of the Pentagon as an adviser to Undersecretary Feith almost from the beginning of the president's term, months before Feith was even confirmed by the Senate. Nonetheless, Ledeen said Rove told him, "Anytime you have a good idea, tell me." According to Ledeen, he faxes Rove every four to six weeks with ideas that he (Rove) needs to be thinking about. Some of those ideas, Ledeen claims, have become either policy or rhetoric.

The two men also share a fondness for Italy's Machiavelli and often refer to his political tract *The Prince,* which associated him with the fascist leadership of his era. Ledeen, in fact, suggested in his 1972 book *Universal Fascism* that what happened in pre–World War II Italy under fascist dictator Benito Mussolini was not totalitarianism. In trying to understand the behavior of millions of Europeans seduced by fascist regimes, he argues that it's more "plausible" "to attempt to explain their enthusiasm by treating them as believers in the rightness of the fascist cause, which had a coherent ideological appeal to a great many people."

Ledeen's own career as an ideological adventurer may have been a byproduct of rejection. He was denied tenure as a professor at Washington University in Saint Louis in 1972 because of charges of plagiarism. Denying the allegation, Ledeen said, "Any suggestion that my scholarship was less than professional is nonsense." Ledeen told the *Washington Post* that the head of Washington University's history department, Rowland Berthoff, informed him that the plagiarism charge had nothing to do with his failure to be granted tenure. Berthoff was quoted in the paper, however, contradicting Ledeen. "He seemed to have used the work of somebody else without proper credit. There was no other reason to vote against him."

Ledeen has, in spite of that rocky beginning, succeeded spectacularly in gaining a forum for his views, which are, as a minimum, provocative when they are limited to the political salon. Taken into the arena of international diplomacy, however, they are worrisome. There is grave danger when U.S. government officials take seriously a man who's argued for "breaking the law from time to time." Ledeen has also insisted it may be necessary for the leader of a country to "enter into evil whenever the very existence of the nation is threatened." Not surprisingly, Ledeen has repeatedly asked for changes in legal restrictions "that prohibit American officials from working with murderers" and an end to the 1975 executive order "prohibiting any official of the American government to conduct, order, encourage or facilitate assassination."

Such ideology may account for why, as the Reagan administration was ending, journalists began to examine Michael Ledeen's background. Edward Herman and Gerry O'Sullivan wrote in *The Terrorism Industry* that court documents from the 1980 trial of SISMI agent Francesco Pazienza showed Ledeen to be involved in undercover work in Italy. Pazienza was convicted of forgery, political manipulation, and the protection of terrorists and criminals as a member of Italy's right-wing extremist Masonic lodge, P2 (Propaganda Due). Jonathan Kwitny of the *Wall Street Journal* interviewed Pazienza, who claimed that Ledeen was paid $120,000 by Italian military intelligence in 1980–1981 and that some of the funds were deposited in a bank account in Bermuda. Ledeen reportedly used the code name Z3.

After refusing to do an interview to answer questions about Kwitny's reporting, Ledeen said via e-mail that he did not verify what was written in the article. "I didn't confirm it," he wrote. "I only confirmed having once used a Bermuda bank account. I should be so lucky to have been paid $100,000." Kwitny's editors, however, were not likely to have let such allegations be published in the conservative *Wall Street Journal* were they not without great substance, and Ledeen never filed any libel claims against the journalist or his publication.

When the allegations about secret payments from the Italian government were first reported by the *WSJ* in 1985, Ledeen did acknowledge at that time a financial arrangement with his consulting firm ISI. He told Kwitny that payments for intelligence consulting for Italy "may well have been $100,000; I can't remember." He also confirmed the Bermuda banking arrangement. "I had, I think, for a period of a few months, a personal account in Bermuda." As for the code name, Ledeen said he was never called Z3 "that I can remember." According to Kwitny's report, "A Tale of Intrigue: Why an Italian Spy Got Closely Involved in the Billygate Affair," testimony before an Italian parliamentary commission by top intelligence officials of the country indicated that Ledeen was paid for "risk assessment" projects and training agents on dealing with terrorism. Ledeen denied teaching any courses or connections to the Billygate controversy, which was an effort to discredit then president Jimmy Carter by connecting his brother Billy's business interests to Libya's strongman leader.

As Iran-contra evidence initially began to surface in the mid-1980s, Ledeen also recanted what he had earlier told Kwitny and the *Wall Street Journal.* In the *Washington Post,* on February 2, 1987, Ledeen accused journalists who repeated the story of being "malicious." "I've said to every journalist who asks about this, 'Find the money and you can have 80 percent of it.' I could use it. I have three kids and a dog." Always an astute observer of the media, Ledeen may have assumed his previous on-the-record remarks would not likely be used to contradict him, and there's no evidence they resurfaced as he was calling reporters malicious for repeating his own words.

At the time Ledeen was working in Italy, intelligence operations of the

Italian government were said to be in almost total control of P2. The organization has been historically linked to the 1980 bombing of the Bologna train station, which killed eighty people. Barbara Honegger, a former Reagan administration official, said in her book *October Surprise* that Ledeen was authorized by Henry Kissinger and Alexander Haig to buy the list of 953 names on the P2 membership rolls when the home of the terrorist group's founder was raided by Italian police. Ledeen has also frequently denounced anyone who suggests he was in any way connected to these events.

Ledeen was nonetheless identified in convicted SISMI agent Francesco Pazienza's indictment for allegations related to the Billygate affair. The court document describes Ledeen as a "well-known American Italianist" who worked "in collaboration" with Pazienza and "succeeded in extorting, also using fraudulent means, information—then published—in the international press—on the Libyan business of Billy Carter, the brother of the then president of the United States." Pazienza claimed that information used against Billy Carter was gathered by the P2-controlled military intelligence operations in Italy and was given to Ledeen, who broke the "Billygate" story in the *New Republic*. (Ledeen's coauthor on the report was Arnaud de Borchgrave, who was to become the editor in chief of the conservative *Washington Times*.)

While Ledeen was reportedly on SISMI's payroll, the new head of the spy agency told Italy's parliament that he was an "intriguer" and no longer welcome in the country. Taken seriously by the Reagan administration, however, Ledeen was hired as a consultant on terrorism by Noel Koch at the Pentagon, who'd been pressured to do so by White House official Richard Perle. Ledeen's work product was later referred to by Koch as "transparent crap."

What Ledeen did or did not do in Italy prior to the Iraq war is considerably less transparent. His record of admissions and then denials indicates he's not beyond a calculated deceit. Deception in the service of ideology is hardly uncommon in American politics, which probably accounts for the political weight put behind the obvious forgeries related to Niger. Given the number of experts on Iraq and the Mideast recruited into the Bush administration, it's unlikely they were all unaware of the fraudulent nature of the Niger documents involving the sale of uranium to Saddam Hussein. Their collective experience only furthers the argument that the fraudulent Niger papers were purposefully handed off to U.S. intelligence operations to achieve a desired political end.

Meanwhile, if Karl Rove does, in fact, have a meaningful association with Michael Ledeen, as Ledeen has publicly claimed, it can be interpreted as evidence the Bush administration is more concerned about Israel's future than Ledeen's past, which has been focused on advocacy of Israel and, most recently, the overthrow of Iran. According to Dr. Stephen Green, a former United Nations official who is also a researcher and the author of two well-respected books on U.S.-Israeli relations, Ledeen first consulted on terrorism for the United States in 1983 after he'd gone to work for the Pentagon during the Reagan administration. When Ledeen and his supervisor Koch traveled to Italy, Koch learned that Italian intelligence carried Ledeen on its books as an "agent of influence for Israel." Exhibiting a habit of reading classified documents in Koch's outer office, Ledeen later asked his boss about acquiring two highly classified reports from the CIA. He reportedly requested them by writing down a series of alphanumeric designators, which, according to Green's investigation, were as classified as the reports themselves. Ledeen "just ceased coming to work" when his access to all classified materials was cut off.

Ledeen eventually moved over to the National Security Council, and his supervisor was marine colonel Oliver North. At the time, the United States was trying to gain the release of American hostages in Lebanon, and Ledeen suggested to North that "Israeli contacts might be useful." The NSC was apparently suspicious of Ledeen's motivations because it tried to limit the man's role to that of messenger and eventually downgraded his security clearance. Also, North recommended that his employee be required to take "periodic polygraph examinations." Eventually, North expressed in a memo that he suspected that Ledeen and operative Manucher Ghorbanifar were making money on the sale of arms to Iran through Israel, although the final Iran-contra report by independent prosecutor Lawrence Walsh said "no evidence exists" to show Ledeen profited from the deals.

By the December 2001 meeting in Rome, Ledeen and Ghorbanifar were back in business together. Exactly what they were doing, however, remains mysterious, in spite of Ledeen's efforts to portray the meeting as innocent politics. Adding to the mystery is that Ledeen had acquired a number of interesting associates from his years spent in Rome as a reporter for the *New Republic* and through his consulting work. Not only had Ledeen been a terrorism consultant for the Italian government, but he was also close friends with former Rome CIA station chief Duane Clarridge. Like Ledeen, Clarridge had been intimately involved in the Iran-contra operation and was subsequently indicted on seven counts of lying to Congress before he was pardoned by President George H. W. Bush. Eventually, after retiring from the intelligence agency, Clarridge became a consultant and close associate of Ahmad Chalabi and the CIA-funded Iraqi National Congress along with former agent Alan Wolf, who had succeeded Clarridge as station chief in Rome. Ledeen and Clarridge were close enough as friends that the former agent spoke at a book-launch presentation for Ledeen at the Mayflower Hotel in Washington.

"The connection to all of these people—Clarridge, Wolf, Chalabi, Ghorbanifar, and SISMI—everybody, is Ledeen," said Philip Giraldi, a retired seventeen-year veteran of the CIA who served in Europe and the Mideast while specializing in counterterrorism. "It's clear to me that he was one of the likely implementers of this case, this process. There are a number of ways those phony documents could have been fed back into the system."

The Niger forgeries appear to have begun their journey into the U.S. intelligence systems on New Year's Day 2001, the date of a break-in at an apartment in the Niger embassy in Rome. Although the incident was reported to police when the embassy opened for business the next day, nothing noticeable was missing. Eventually, it was learned the only items taken were some letterhead with "République du Niger" at the top, documents with signatures, and some official stamps of the embassy of Niger. By October 15 of that same year, 2001, Italy's prime minister Silvio Berlusconi and the director of SISMI, Nicolo Pollari, were in Washington presenting the White House with a dossier on Iraq and Niger's purported uranium deal. The text of those materials was apparently based on the forged documents, which did not surface in the public debate until a year later.

Although the Italian government of Berlusconi has denied any involvement in the creation of the Niger forgeries, former CIA agent Giraldi and Rome's *La Repubblica* newspaper have insisted the prime minister was anxious to improve his country's stature as a U.S. ally by helping the new American president make his case for war. SISMI chief Pollari provided the dossier to the CIA at the same time it was delivered to MI6 in Britain.

Giraldi believes it is possible Michael Ledeen, working to help his neocon friends gather significant evidence for war with Iraq, may have used his SISMI relationships to move the bad intelligence into the American bureaucracy. Ledeen categorically denies any such involvement and says he has filed suit against *La Repubblica.*

"Ledeen goes way back into SISMI," Giraldi said. "And don't believe anything the Italians are saying officially. Just don't believe any of that crap about them not being involved. They are up to their eyeballs in this."

The Italian dossier was dismissed within a few days by the State Department's Bureau of Intelligence and Research (INR) because there was no corroborative evidence for the narrative report. INR said the information was "lacking in detail" and "limited in scope." The central criticism was that the French, who controlled the uranium industry in Niger, would have been aware of any alleged deal to buy five hundred tons of uranium. Additionally, one of the two mines cited as the source of the uranium was flooded, and Iraq was known by both the United States and the United Nations to already have a large stock of uranium oxide in its inventory.

The CIA, the Department of Energy, and the Defense Intelligence Agency (DIA), however, reported back that such a deal was "possible." The French and the Germans, who were also receiving the dossier, did not consider the data credible and doubted that Saddam Hussein would risk the consequences of violating U.N. sanctions against his country. Only the British and the Italians, allies and proponents of the Bush administration's Iraq war plans, were moving the information into their intelligence channels.

With the Niger story in the U.S. system (but not the forgeries on which it was based), Michael Ledeen convened his meeting in Rome with the heads of Italian defense and intelligence. He had not, however, informed either the CIA station chief in the city or the U.S. ambassador to Italy, Mel Sembler, an old Republican Party friend of Ledeen's with whom he had dinner the next evening. Ledeen was only a consultant to defense undersecretary Feith—and Larry Franklin, an Iran specialist in the Pentagon, and Harold Rhode, the linguist and a central figure in DOD's independent intelligence-gathering operation OSP, were just "midlevel" bureaucrats. By meeting with Iranian arms dealer Manucher Ghorbanifar and Italian defense and intelligence chiefs, Ledeen and his associates were nonetheless in clear violation of U.S. protocols requiring the CIA to facilitate and oversee official contacts with foreign governments. The U.S. ambassador was sufficiently embarrassed that he and the CIA station chief in Rome brought the meeting to the attention of the State Department.

In early 2002, about two months after Ledeen was in Rome, SISMI sent another report to Washington on the Niger story with what former CIA agent Giraldi describes as "embellishments." Those turned out to be the verbatim text of an agreement between Iraq and Niger (but not a copy of the agreement itself) for the sale of five hundred tons of yellow-cake ore, which had supposedly been signed July 5–6, 2000. Although no one in U.S. intelligence or the government bureaucracy had yet seen the documents on which the SISMI claims were based, the Defense Intelligence Agency nonetheless issued an analysis saying, "Iraq is probably searching abroad for natural uranium to assist in its nuclear weapons program." This conclusion was reached a week after the CIA's clandestine Directorate of Operations, on February 5, 2002, had issued a document with the complete text of the Iraq-Niger agreement.

Vice President Dick Cheney was given the DIA's report on Niger and Iraq and decided he wanted more information. Exactly a week later, a former U.S. diplomat who had served in Iraq and Africa under Republican and Democratic presidents was in a meeting with the CIA and the State Department. Both agencies had been made aware of Ambassador Joseph Wilson's background (which included the fluent French needed in Niger) by his wife, Valerie Plame Wilson, who was an undercover operative for the CIA. He was tasked with traveling to Africa to assess the credibility of the uranium story. His wife had not promoted him for the trip but had simply forwarded his list of qualifications to her supervisors. In spite of allegations that the choice of Wilson was made by his friends and political allies who wanted to circumvent President Bush's intentions of going to war with Iraq, Wilson said he was looking at a roomful of strangers and his wife left as soon as he was introduced.

"[My wife] was in no way political any more than I was before this all took place," he explained. "In the meeting where the decision was taken to send me to Iraq, there was nobody there that I knew or could identify then or now."

Just before Wilson was dispatched, both the State Department and the CIA expressed concern to NSC deputy Stephen Hadley about Michael Ledeen's meetings in Rome. *Washington Monthly* reported that CIA director George Tenet spoke directly with Hadley to ask that the unauthorized back channel between the governments be closed down. Hadley called DOD undersecretary Feith, who'd hired Ledeen as a consultant, to deliver the message. He also informed the U.S. ambassador in Rome, Ledeen's GOP friend, to let him know that Ledeen and the DOD's rogue operation were out of business. Ledeen might have already served his purpose for the administration by using his SISMI contacts to move the fake intelligence into the U.S. system, and his further engagement might have risked exposing the scheme, as would his personal obsession with widening the war to Iran.

In the Pentagon, where arguments and data were being marshaled to set up a war, the fake intel of the Niger forgeries was essential for building political support. Ledeen's companion in Rome, Harold Rhode, had worked with Undersecretary Feith to transfer or fire employees who were not enthused about making the case against Iraq. One of those analysts, quoted in *Mother Jones* magazine, said, "They wanted nothing to do with the professional staff. And they wanted us the fuck out of there."

Included among the individuals brought over to the Pentagon before he went to work for the vice president's office as Cheney's Mideast adviser was David Wurmser, a neoconservative from the American Enterprise Institute. Wurmser helped to finish the process of building the rogue intelligence operation that was to become known as the Office of Special Plans (OSP). His position on the question of Iraq was summarized in an op-ed he published in the *Wall Street Journal*, which was headlined "Iraq Needs a Revolution." Wurmser had also cosigned a letter with Richard Perle calling for American support of Amhad Chalabi, the Iraqi National Congress, and an Iraqi insurgency. As previously mentioned, he'd also been a coauthor with his wife, Perle, and Feith of the "Securing the Realm" analysis for Israel's prime minister.

The purpose of the intelligence operation that was to become OSP was to find evidence incriminating Iraq on weapons of mass destruction and connections to Al-Qaeda. The fact that no such data had ever been uncovered didn't seem to prove a deterrent to the group's work. The former director of the National Security Council, David Benjamin, said there was nothing new to discover about Iraq.

"In 1998, we went through every piece of intelligence we could find to see if there was a link between al Qaeda and Iraq," he said. "We came to the conclusion that our intelligence agencies had it right: There was no noteworthy relationship between al Qaeda and Iraq. I know that for a fact."

Facts were apparently not what OSP was seeking. As Wurmser was leaving for his position as Mideast adviser to the vice president, the appointment of a former navy aviator from Dick Cheney's office, William Luti, formalized the functions of OSP. A colleague at DOD said Luti "makes Ollie North look like a moderate."

Not much was known about OSP until the retirement of Lieutenant Colonel Karen Kwiatkowski. A twenty-year career officer in the air force, Kwiatkowski spent the final year of her service in the Pentagon at the Near East South Asia bureau, where she closely observed the war plans office and OSP. Kwiatkowski was amazed at how people without military experience—mostly academics, civilians, and private contractors—were brought in to work up war planning with OSP. According to Kwiatkowski, Luti was a direct conduit from OSP into the vice president's office. Those connections between a Pentagon intelligence operation and the VP's office were considered without precedent.

"Luti was permanently locked into the idea that he was an aide to Cheney," she said. "He came over from active duty on Cheney's staff, and it seems clear he was playing that role, just closely coordinating things. He was a very imperious, insecure, weird guy who was constantly publicly degrading staff people at meetings."

Kwiatkowski offers the only available window into the operations of the Pentagon's rogue intel operation. She described relationships and functions within OSP as unorthodox and troubling. She said the organization was constantly vetting intelligence and developing talking points based on information that had previously been cast aside. The intelligence, according to Kwiatkowski, was completely without context and was not considered credible by the military professionals on staff. Because the CIA was not producing any new intelligence, OSP was going through old data on Iraq, WMD, and Al-Qaeda and resurrecting reports that had never been verified. Kwiatkowski confesses to being astonished that such material went directly to the vice president's office and ended up in speeches by Cheney and President Bush.

"Yes, they were cherry-picking," she said. "But it's not like they were picking the good cherries. They were picking the rotten cherries, the absolutely rotten stuff that the CIA had pulled out and thrown away. I mean these were the nasty cherries that were down on the floor, and they picked them up and used them because they fit what they wanted to hear."

As an air force officer, Kwiatkowski had years of experience in the Pentagon hierarchy and bureaucratic functions. What she witnessed with OSP was profoundly disturbing. Civilian ideologues such as Michael Ledeen, who had a desk in Undersecretary Feith's operation, were using the military to promote a narrow political agenda against Iraq in spite of an overwhelming body of material that proved the neoconservative claims about WMD and Al-Qaeda were wrong. Intelligence was obviously being "cooked" by people such as Harold Rhode to fit the aggressive Mideast posture being pursued by the Bush administration.

Although she understood the corruption of the processes she was witnessing, Kwiatkowski was initially unaware of how easily the distorted intelligence was being inserted into the national political discourse over the impending war. In a meeting with William Luti, which was to discuss talking points, Kwiatkowski first heard the nickname "Scooter."

"I had never heard of Scooter Libby," she explained. "And Luti said, 'I've gotta get this over to Scooter,' and, 'He needs this by 3:00 p.m.' I just didn't pay attention to civilian personnel. I worked for the secretary of defense. And I was amazed that these guys were talking about directly providing stuff into Cheney's staff. I asked somebody later, 'Who's this Scooter? He must be an important guy.' I thought he was a general or something. They were giving him propaganda, though, not intelligence."

A significant portion of that information was built around allegations that Iraq was trying to get uranium oxide or "yellowcake" ore from Niger. When former ambassador Joseph Wilson returned from the country, however, he briefed two CIA officers at his home and told them there was no evidence to corroborate such a claim. A report on his findings was sent through routine channels. His information was given a grade of "good" by the agents who debriefed him, but the summary of his findings did not make its way to the vice president's office or to the national security adviser, who later suggested it may have gotten lost in the "bowels" of the bureaucracy.

Unofficial back-channel efforts continued to operate, circumventing U.S. government institutions not serving the war cause. Harold Rhode in OSP exchanged a number of faxes with the Iranian arms dealer Manucher Ghorbanifar. By June 2002, Ghorbanifar had arranged another meeting for an unnamed "high-level" U.S. government official, an Iraqi, and an Iranian. The U.S. embassy was again not informed of the fact that someone from

Washington was being briefed on Iraq in Rome. However, a month later, Michael Ledeen got in touch with Ambassador Sembler and told him he was returning to resume working with the Iranians. Sembler, again surprised that this was happening, contacted Washington, and NSC deputy Hadley gave Ledeen unmistakable instructions to cancel his plans. The ambassador, too, might have feared disclosure of a broader plan to deceive the American public with the forgeries because they were ultimately cabled a few weeks later from his office in Rome to Washington.

Regardless of denials that Italy and Washington were cooperating in a great international deception, a secret meeting between Italian SISMI head Pollari and NSC deputy Hadley was arranged. A spokesman later characterized it as nothing more than a "courtesy call," and Hadley did not remember discussing Niger or uranium ore. The September 9, 2002, meeting came only a few weeks after Italian reporter Elisabetta Burba had been delivered what were supposed to be the documents on which all of the Niger claims had been based. Burba works for *Panorama,* a glossy weekly tabloid owned by Italian prime minister Silvio Berlusconi, who was an ardent supporter in 2002 of President Bush's Iraq scenario.

The general public and Congress were unaware that the Niger uranium story, which was the primary basis for the war chants from the White House, was based on documents delivered to the United States and the United Kingdom by a disgraced former SISMI agent. Rocco Martino, who originally handed the forgeries over to reporter Burba, had been fired for unethical behavior, arrested in Germany for possession of stolen checks, and charged with extortion in Italy. Nonetheless, Martino was still receiving a stipend from SISMI, and he was telling a story the Bush administration wanted Americans to hear, regardless of its truthfulness.

Although Burba trusted Martino because he'd proved honest in previous dealings with her, she didn't write a story about what the dossier appeared to prove, which was that Iraq and Niger had a deal on the sale of five hundred tons of yellowcake ore. Her editor, a friend of Italy's prime minister and Bush ally Berlusconi, eventually told her to deliver the file to the U.S. embassy. According to former CIA agent Giraldi, the material appeared to be "expected" at the embassy. This has prompted suspicion that the meeting between Hadley and Pollari a month earlier in Washington might have been to plan delivery of the forgeries to the U.S. embassy. Normal procedure would have been to deliver them to the CIA station in Rome. Reporter Burba did not know that Rocco Martino had already taken the forged documents to the CIA officer in charge there, and he had kicked Martino out after he immediately "saw that they were fakes."

Burba and her editors had been in possession of the documents for exactly a month before they handed them off to the U.S. embassy on October 9, 2001. In spite of the fact that neither the vice president nor the national security adviser ever saw Ambassador Wilson's report from Niger refuting the yellowcake story, the poorly forged WMD dossier from a reporter at a tabloid newspaper owned by a Bush supporter went directly to Washington via cable, bypassed the CIA, and landed quickly on the desks of National Security Adviser Condoleezza Rice in the U.S. State Department and Vice President Dick Cheney. It did not get lost in the "bowels" of government. A State Department analyst, nonetheless, immediately became suspicious and wrote a note that the documents had a "funky Emb. of Niger stamp (to make it look official, I guess)."

The international political campaign to legitimize the dubious information was, however, well under way. A few weeks before the dossier had made it to Washington, the office of British prime minister Tony Blair issued a public dossier asserting that there "is intelligence that Iraq has sought the supply of significant quantities of uranium from Africa." The White House at that time was also energetically trying to convince Congress that Saddam Hussein was reconstituting a nuclear weapons program. A hastily written National Intelligence Estimate concluded, "A foreign government service reported that as of early 2001, Niger planned to send several tons of 'pure uranium' (probably yellowcake) to Iraq."

In America, political momentum and public support for invading Iraq were dramatically increasing as a result of the forgeries. The White House Iraq Group (WHIG), made up of Bush cabinet members and staffers, had already begun promoting the idea that there was a great risk of a "mushroom cloud" over America if the president didn't move against Iraq. Messaging, managed by Karl Rove and Karen Hughes, was designed to raise anxiety levels as it was delivered across global time zones. Although it's possible there wasn't a coordinated plan to use false information to sell the war, it couldn't be denied that events were conveniently unfolding for the administration as if orchestrated.

The only political danger was that the strongest case for war, the nuclear threat, was based on cooked intelligence and forged documents. Either the Bush White House was just learning about the Niger forgeries in the fall of 2002 or it had been complicit in the fraud all along, which would make that kind of deception one of history's greatest crimes. Any necessary risk would be taken to protect such a secret. The facts about Niger and Iraq had to be suppressed, and anyone who might have access to the truth and an inclination to share it with Americans had to be intimidated into silence or discredited.

And Karl Rove had some experience with that process.

FOURTEEN

THE UNRAVELING

Karl Losing Control

Pride goeth before destruction, and an haughty spirit before a fall.
—Proverbs 16:18

K arl Rove stepped into the deli and, spotting his friend Jack Abramoff, smiled broadly and approached with the jaunty assurance that comes to those in Washington who know their way around.

"Jack!" he declared, and grabbed a chair. Also at the table was Marc Schwartz, a representative of one of the Indian tribes that Abramoff was in the process of bilking out of millions of dollars through lobby fees. Rove and Abramoff chatted amiably for a while about people and politics of mutual interest. Abramoff eventually turned the conversation to a new subject. He was interested in the possibility of controlling the news media.

"Hey, Karl," Abramoff said, "you've got to tell them about your deal."

Rove proudly offered up a lesson on sources and access in Washington. As an example, he used a hypothetical candidate for office.

"You know, what if the candidate didn't respond to the media?" he asked. "If the media wants to write about his arrest in 1954 for having one too many beers at a fraternity party, you just tell your guy, We're just not going to talk."

Schwartz wasn't certain where Rove was going with this. Rove, though, loved these moments when he was with a friendly group and had the chance to strut the stuff that had taken him to the pinnacle of American politics.

"Yeah, you can tell them to do that," said Schwartz, "but it's not going to get the story killed."

Rove pressed on. "Now, what if everybody else didn't talk?"

"What do you mean, 'everybody else'?" Schwartz asked.

"What if every Republican member just stopped talking to that reporter? Eventually, that reporter is going to get the message that he has a job to do. His job is to write stories. And in order to write stories, he's got to have sources. And if he's not friendly, none of us talk to him."

Rove grinned, his face round and pink like a porcelain plate. Schwartz thought the idea was interesting, but unworkable. To succeed, you would have to control the entire apparatus of government—not just the White House but Congress and K Street and the political networks that drive so much of politics and policy.

Rove was two years into his job as the president's chief political strategist and Abramoff a master of the universe among lobbyists, but Schwartz doubted that these two men, as powerful as they were, actually thought they could impose such denial of access that they could control the news. Only later, when the Abramoff lobby scandals began to unravel and Rove's role in the CIA leak case emerged, did Schwartz come to realize that was *exactly* what they thought. To keep reporters in line, you had to control access to information that was the lifeblood of their work as journalists.

Rove's goal was larger than that of Abramoff, who wanted to make money, and Bush, who wanted to be reelected and establish himself as a consequential president. Rove would help Abramoff get richer, but only if the lobbyist reciprocated by moving Majority Leader Tom DeLay and other Republicans on Capitol Hill on issues the White House cared about. The political guru desperately wanted George W. Bush reelected, both out of a long-standing sense of loyalty to the Bush family and because the reelection was crucial to the long-term goal of Republican hegemony.

With Bush's reelection, everything, it seemed, had fallen into place. Rove had the agenda, the alliances, and the means of sustained Republican expansion. While the disputed victory in 2000 had caused critics to quibble, the victory in 2004 answered any question of legitimacy. Bush won not only the electoral vote but also a popular-vote margin of 3 million at the ballot box. The grand machine Karl Rove had nurtured for two decades was now positioned for a very long run.

There were distant signs of trouble, but nothing a master strategist couldn't control. Nobody seemed to be worried in the bright chill of February following Bush's second inaugural when the conservative elite gathered at the Ronald Reagan Building in Washington, filling the hall to capacity to hear Karl Rove issue a trumpet call of conquest. Rove arrived on a wave of applause.

"Four decades ago," he said, "the Republican Party and our movement were relegated to the political wilderness. And today, Republicans and conservatives control the White House, the Senate, the House, the majority of governorships and more state legislative seats than we've had in the last 80 years. That's a pretty remarkable rise."

Rove promised "the future realignment of American politics," but it was clear that this cheering crowd felt the realignment had already come. And Rove was more than just the standard-bearer: he was the architect. That's what George W. Bush had called him a few weeks earlier—*the Architect* of his reelection. And here at the thirty-second annual Conservative Political Action Conference, there was glossy confidence that he was the architect of something larger and more sustaining, an enduring majority.

Rove said there'd been a political sea change in the four decades since Lyndon Johnson won the presidency in a landslide. In 1964, Democrats held 68 Senate seats, 295 House seats, and 33 governorships. Now, in the vibrant accomplishment of victory in 2004, everything was reversed. Republicans held 55 Senate seats, 232 House seats, and 28 governorships. And the GOP had won seven of the last ten presidential elections.

"We have seen the rise of a great cause and a powerful movement," he said, igniting thunderous applause that rang through the atrium of the federal building named for the icon of modern Republicanism.

He could not resist ridiculing the losers. "Next time one of your smarty-pants liberal friends says to you, 'Well, he didn't have a mandate,' you tell him this delicious fact: This president got a higher percentage of the vote than any Democrat candidate for president since 1964."

Rove was all triumph and self-confidence. "As the governing party in America, Republicans cannot grow tired or timid," he said. "We have a future to make, a nation to renew, values to protect and an agenda to enact."

Karl Rove had reason to boast.

The central insight of his considerable success is not that he's blended politics and policy but that he's obliterated the line between the two. Politics *is* policy. As Governor George W. Bush's chief political strategist in

Texas, Rove remained an outside consultant with an office west of downtown Austin on Shoal Creek, but he regularly attended senior-staff meetings at the capitol, where he helped direct the affairs of government. During Bush's first term as president, Rove advised Bush on everything from stem-cell research to Iraq from his upstairs White House office as political chief. In the second term, he moved downstairs next to the Oval Office. The relocation officially confirmed what he long had been doing, which was guiding every policy by its political advantage.

The making of a majority took place in bits and pieces over time, part strategic planning and part serendipity. Winning was a process, not an event, as Rove liked to say. Walter Dean Burnham of the University of Texas, the nation's leading theorist of political realignment, said the 2004 election was historic because it consolidated years of Republican gains.

"The whole approach was, we don't want to bother doing the squishy-soft middle-of-the-road stuff to try to lure the median voter to our side. That's been orthodox doctrine for political scientists and also for politicians for many decades. And in 2004, it seems this doctrine was simply overthrown."

Success required rallying the troops for a big turnout, which both sides accomplished, but Rove Inc. won. Burnham, who has spent a career deconstructing presidential politics, was impressed. "What Rove and his friends did this time is say, Let's go out and mobilize the base and forget about the middle, and they were very successful in that. This mobilization of the base represents a clean break with successful political strategies that go back all the way to the early part of the twentieth century. Typically, when you have that kind of thing, you have very high turnouts. You get this sense that you're in Armageddon fighting for the Lord."

When Rove was a fledgling political operative for Republican Texas governor Bill Clements in the early 1980s, he sometimes spoke to small groups of Republicans outnumbered in the staunchly Democratic South, peppering his presentations with quotes from Teddy Roosevelt. A favorite was, "We stand at Armageddon and we battle for the Lord." Roosevelt meant it, and Rove understood it, in the context of the underdog facing long odds. Now, the Republicans were very much in charge and, with the foundation Rove had laid, seemed destined to stay that way.

"If Republicans keep playing the religious card along with the terrorism card, this could last a long time," said Burnham.

Rove's formula, the winning formula, was a contemporary twist on the old lyric "Praise the Lord and pass the ammunition." And with it, everything had fallen into place. Over time, trial lawyers had been hobbled by caps on awards, draining money away from the Democratic Party. Unions were divided, and membership was dwindling. The Republican Party, under Rove's political direction, had demonstrated a durable, if unlikely, alliance between Christian conservatives and economic conservatives. Outside, allies such as Grover Norquist and his small-government, antitax confederacy held enormous influence in Washington. On K Street, friends such as Jack Abramoff and Ralph Reed rode the crest of the lobby corps, and Majority Leader Tom DeLay exerted political muscle in Congress. The influential Richard Land of the Southern Baptists and even James Dobson, who was once skittish of Bush 43, were comfortably on board. Campaign staffers had moved on and were now directing independent groups touting administration policy. There was even a new college training the next wave to guide the Republican majority.

It was a campaign without end.

Michael Farris and the work he did were typical of the organizations driving GOP success. He was a national homeschool activist and founded Patrick Henry College of Purcellville, Virginia, in 2000 with the purpose of training a new generation of Christian politicians. A majority of the student body was homeschooled. Unlike Bob Jones and Jerry Falwell's Liberty University, which emphasize the ministry, Patrick Henry prepares its students specifically for "careers in public service and cultural influence." Most are government majors, and many have been hired as interns and staffers by conservative members of Congress and in the White House, including Rove's office. Among the school's benefactors is James Leininger of San Antonio, a Rove ally and one of the many Lone Star moneymen he cultivated two decades ago to finance an emerging GOP in Texas. Now Leininger was one of many pieces in a much larger game.

By seizing on the twin themes of Christianity and patriotism, of moral values at home and strength in the global war on terror, Rove Inc. found a formula that had reshaped the American electorate. Ronald Reagan won landslide victories in 1980 and 1984 by attracting middle- and working-class white voters. Bush won many of the same voters in 2004, but with a difference. A generation ago, the working-class voters were "Reagan Democrats." Many now call themselves Republicans.

A Pew Research Center poll found that Republicans in 2005 held a majority over Democrats among white voters in virtually every income bracket. Only among those making $19,000 or less were Democrats a majority. The implications were both clear and disturbing to the Democrats. The very income groups most likely to be union members or targets of membership drives were now on Rove's side. Republicans had made inroads among the very voters Democrats needed to win. In no small part, the values message had proved attractive in wooing new voters as part of the base. Rove counted on the support of values voters to help drive the Bush agenda in the second term, especially on appointments to the Supreme Court and support of the war on terror.

There was, however, something else.

Simon Rosenberg, who ran for chairman of the Democratic Party against Howard Dean and founded the New Democrat Network, suggests that the Republican Party has found the money necessary to build a communications infrastructure that ensures political power.

"Look, the conservatives invested billions and billions in alternative infrastructure," he said, "because they had neither the U.S. government nor any other way to communicate their values. They built a magnificent machine to communicate, and they used it to take over the government of our country. They have a very robust infrastructure, and we have neither government nor infrastructure. Too many of our answers as Democrats have been tactical and not understanding that the game has been changed. We have to work on changing that by doing some investing of our own."

The conservative Christian network was a significant part of that Republican infrastructure. It provided the political support necessary to confirm judicial nominees whom Rove, in private conversations with his friends on the religious Right, would vouch for as sufficiently conservative on abortion and religious expression. As for the war, there was another synergy at work. Many evangelicals supported the war for religious reasons. To more than a few, the American military was exercising God's will by engaging a millennial enemy, Islam.

That's what the Reverend Richard Lee believed. He was also certain that it was long past time the Christian church got political. Outside the reverend's church in suburban Atlanta was a huge globe and a Bible made of bronze open to Matthew 28, Christ's great commission to convert the world. Inside, on the wall of his church office, there were framed photos of Lee with George W. Bush, Dan Quayle, and Attorney General John Ashcroft.

"If I were to say that because of my calling as a pastor that I shouldn't be involved in the political process, I would be basically giving up my citizenship," he said. "I'm not going to give that up for anybody."

Lee was a tall man with white hair, and in French cuffs and a black suit, he had the iconic look of a Pilgrim. First Redeemer was a growing church in the expanding exurbs of Bush country. It had a television ministry and an active congregation, which Lee exhorted to get involved in the democratic process.

"Politics is merely people," he said.

Like many evangelicals who counted themselves part of Bush's base, Lee fervently supported the president and the war on terrorism. This backing was strengthened by a belief that the enemy was the infidel and that America was engaged in a crusade. It wasn't an isolated idea. Many Christian evangelicals who've rallied to Bush's side see the conflict as part of a thousand-year war between Christians and Muslims, the Children of Light against the Children of Darkness. When the president said that Islam was a religion of peace and that we all pray to the same God, Lee shook his head.

"That's not true. There's only one God, and as a Christian, that is the God that we reach through Jesus Christ."

Asked why he thought Bush had described Islam as a religion of peace, Lee said knowingly, "He had to do that." It was politics, and Lee didn't hold it against the president. Bush needed allies in the Arab world, and, Lee concluded, he couldn't be totally honest about his belief that America was engaged in a divine drama in which evil was not simply an abstract force but an entity on earth. Lee was not alone. A number of evangelical leaders shared his view.

Whatever the reality, it was all good politics to Rove. The Christians were with him, and as long as the economy stabilized, economic conservatives would remain on his glory train as well. In his first postelection news conference, Bush claimed a mandate and in his subsequent inaugural address and State of the Union advanced a big agenda—improved health care and education here at home and freedom and democracy in the Middle East. He promised conservative judges who wouldn't legislate from the bench, which was code for judges who'd curb abortion and homosexuality. He pledged success in the war on terror. The centerpiece of the domestic agenda, which Rove developed with considerable attention, was to change Social Security under the grand rubric "Ownership Society," which he hoped would become a transcendent phrase like the "New Deal" or the "Great Society."

It was an ambitious, if difficult, agenda in the best of times. As the administration opened its second term amid the early flush of optimism, the political historian Walter Dean Burnham gauged its prospects of success. Every postwar president has faced a second term worse than the first. Clinton was nearly undone by a sex scandal, Reagan embroiled in the Iran-contra scandal, and Nixon forced to resign over Watergate. Truman and Johnson had problems. Second terms are like conquering a mountain. After winning, the slope is always downward.

"Might something come along that might blow up the paradise that Mr. Rove thinks he's got?" Burnham wondered. "Two major factors I can think of at the moment: the war and everything it implies, particularly whether it might go on ad infinitum with no way for American troops to get out of Iraq in the foreseeable future. And second, the extreme profligacy of his ideologically driven policy having to do with taxes and other things," he said. "Whether that is going to play out or not, I don't know. But it's not too difficult to imagine a situation in which either or both of these things comes home to roost."

Burnham was as much a prophet as an analyst. Within months of Rove's triumphant speech to the conservatives, everything was falling apart.

Social Security was supposed to be the big idea of the second term. It was a perfect Rove concept, full of political synergy and pop. If successful, more and more Americans would look to the stock market and private investments, rather than to a government program, for the basic part of their retirement income. Social Security, the single most popular legacy of the New Deal, would no longer be the great Democratic Party link to the most reliable group of voters: senior citizens and those approaching retirement. Young people, increasingly dubious about the future of Social Security, would be drawn to the program of private investment accounts and, in the process, cement their loyalty to the Republican Party for decades. Even before President Bush touted the plan as a top priority in his State of the Union address, Rove had calculated its political benefits.

In a January 5 White House memo, Rove deputy Peter Wehner wrote, "Increasingly the Democratic Party is the party of obstruction and opposition. It is the party of the past. For the first time in six decades, the Social Security battle is one we can win—and in doing so, we can help transform the political and philosophical landscape of the country."

Publicly, the president's plan for changing Social Security was a matter of policy. The White House memo made it clear something else was at work: electing Republicans.

Rove was in charge of selling the policy to Congress and the American people. And he did it, as he did all things, as a political campaign. Rove sat down with Wehner and others in his office and drew up a plan to target key constituencies, marshal the apparatus of the Republican Party, enlist outside allied groups, tap big-dollar business contributors, and prepare negative attacks on opponents. The campaign would place op-eds in local newspapers and call in to radio shows on behalf of Bush's plan. Colleagues say Rove pursued the task with typical hyperkinetic optimism, a phone at one ear, barking orders, working his BlackBerry to message lobbyists and members on Capitol Hill.

During the reelection campaign, independent 527 committees were barred from coordinating with Bush-Cheney, but not now. Groups could work in lockstep with the White House on behalf of issues. Progress for America, which had spent $35 million pummeling John Kerry in the 2004 campaign, now became part of the coordinated campaign to sell Bush's Social Security plan. It was a measure of Rove's perpetual-motion machine that it worked so efficiently. The weapons of politics became the instruments of Republican policy and, presumably in the next campaign, the weapons of Republican politics again.

The Republican National Committee started holding meetings every Friday to coordinate strategy among the White House, the GOP, and friendly business groups, including Progress for America. Another group, Compass, was created and financed by Bush allies, the U.S. Chamber of Commerce, the National Association of Wholesaler-Distributors, and others. Terry Nelson, who'd been Rove's national political director in the 2004 campaign, was tapped to run the group. In coordination with the White House, Compass prepared a $20 million television and grassroots pressure campaign and hired APCO, the public relations firm whose top executive, Neal Cohen, had worked with Rove since the early 1990s.

Rove and Republican National Committee chairman Ken Mehlman

imbued the early weeks of the campaign with the swaggering exuberance of a smash-mouth political contest. At the RNC, there was even a
war room.

"We are working with a lot of the same tools we used in the '04
campaign—a research operation, a booking operation (to schedule
interviews) . . . the ability to place op-eds and a grass-roots organization," said Mehlman.

Progress for America prepared a multimillion-dollar TV ad campaign,
hired public relations professionals in twenty-five states, and "generated"
letters to the editor. The organization was ostensibly independent, but its
message came directly from the White House. On its website, the group
declared it was "forcing the media to report the facts about President
Bush's common-sense conservative agenda." Following instructions from
Rove and Mehlman, allied groups applied pressure to members of Congress whose votes the White House needed. Compass "mobilized" thousands of advocates to attend town hall meetings with members of
Congress and placed opinion pieces in newspapers in ten local markets,
according to a White House memo.

The real fireworks came from USA NEXT, whose approach was modeled on the tactics of Swift Boat Veterans for Truth. Several alumni signed
up with USA NEXT, among them the two strategists who had handled
the Swift Boat Veterans' attack ads, Chris LaCivita and Rick Reed.

A chief obstacle to the White House plan was AARP, the 35 million–
member senior citizens' lobby that opposed privatizing Social Security.
Charlie Jarvis, a former deputy interior secretary in first Bush administration and USA NEXT's president, decided to make AARP the issue. "They
are the boulder in the middle of the highway to personal savings accounts," he said. "We will be the dynamite that removes them."

In an Internet ad, USA NEXT dispensed with the policy questions and
went directly to the sensational charge that AARP supported same-sex
marriage. The spot included a picture of two men kissing at what appeared to be a wedding and the words "The real AARP agenda."

In fact, AARP had no position on gay marriage. USA NEXT based its ad
on AARP's opposition to the wording of the same-sex marriage ban on the
Ohio ballot. AARP feared the amendment might affect legal recognition of
any union, even older heterosexuals living together. The White House
publicly distanced itself from the effort. But USA NEXT's approach had a

familiar look: a well-funded, third-party group; an agenda consistent with the Rove agenda; the use of gay marriage as a wedge issue; and a searing attack to tar the enemy.

There were actually lots of enemies. Democrats and organized labor fought the idea. Business was skittish about the short-term economic disruption the plan could cause and unconvinced that diverting payroll deductions to private investment accounts would keep the system solvent. In fact, the federal government would have to borrow trillions of dollars to make up for lost revenue, which concerned fiscal conservatives.

Ultimately, Republicans in Congress, reflecting the wariness of voters back home, were reluctant to sign on. As it turned out, the middle-income and lower-middle-income voters Rove had enlisted on the Republican side were financially risk-averse and reluctant to embrace an idea fraught with so many unknowns. Rove had counted on a cadre of Republicans in Congress who, it turned out, did not relish the idea of stumping for a Social Security overhaul during the 2006 elections. He'd made a rare political miscalculation.

Months after President Bush called on Congress to create personal accounts and shore up Social Security, Rove's grand sales job sputtered. Even the surrogates lacked conviction.

When Treasury Secretary John Snow visited a prominent New York investment house, an executive asked why the White House was putting Social Security reform ahead of other, more pressing fiscal problems such as the weak dollar and soaring federal deficit. According to one person in the room, Snow had one response: Social Security was the president's priority.

Rove arranged public appearances in town hall settings where President Bush pitched his personal accounts concept with lively enthusiasm, as if the idea were still alive. In fact, the proposal was dead, and everybody seemed to know it except Bush. One House Republican recalled a summertime meeting in the Roosevelt Room in which the president went on at length about reforming Social Security.

"I got the sense that his staff was not telling him the bad news," the lawmaker said. "This was not a case of him thinking positive. He just didn't have any idea of the political realities there. It was like he wasn't briefed at all."

By fall, Senate Finance Chairman Charles Grassley said Social Security would have to wait, and in his 2006 State of the Union address, Bush didn't even mention the idea. Bush's big initiative was adrift. For once, Rove was off his game, but the worst was yet to come. There were storm clouds gathering, and as it turned out, they were real storm clouds. More than New Orleans was about to be battered and busted up.

After Katrina hit the Gulf Coast, it was painfully obvious to Republicans and Democrats that the White House was off stride. Matthew Dowd, the Bush team's pollster, messaged Rove on his BlackBerry, wondering what was wrong. They exchanged notes in brief, staccato bursts. Dowd was in Austin and Rove in Washington or somewhere, but certainly where there was television, which was filled with increasingly horrifying images of New Orleans engulfed in black, toxic water. And looting. And flames. And people on rooftops with sheets bearing scrawled pleas for help.

Bush did not hurry to New Orleans. He remained at his Texas ranch and wrapped up his summer vacation, choosing instead to fulfill a commitment in California and then fly over the Crescent City and view the hurricane's aftermath on his way back to Washington. Rove, showing a kind of political tone deafness no one thought he'd ever display, summoned photographers to the front cabin. The photo of Bush gazing out the window in the gentle half-light, amid the security and considerable comfort of Air Force One, peering down on a city lost and ruined and rapidly descending into chaos, dominated the front pages the next morning. It was among the most damaging photos of his presidency. The president appeared detached and powerless, unable even to comprehend how he might use the government to help his own people. Worse, the picture conveyed no sense that the president cared or was worried about the catastrophe unfolding beneath the aircraft's big wings.

Matthew Dowd was baffled by the response to Hurricane Katrina. He swapped messages with Rove. Why was it taking so long? Why did the White House seem so slow-footed?

"Who's in charge?" Dowd frantically tapped into his BlackBerry. "WHO'S IN CHARGE?"

Silence. Nothing. Rove quit responding.

"I guess I pissed him off," Dowd said.

Rove might have been angry at getting such a question from a close ally. Clearly, he was under great stress even for a man accustomed to dealing with weighty affairs. A federal grand jury investigation appeared to be focusing on him, and he'd reportedly been dealing with health problems related to kidney stones. Nonetheless, Rove didn't like letting down a president who willingly admitted he needed the architect at his side.

That Bush would flounder at the start of a crisis before finding his voice was not without precedent. He stumbled initially after 9/11 before recovering to rally the nation in his finest hour. But Katrina was different. It took days before the White House seemed to grasp the enormity of the problem, and for all of Rove's vaunted political acumen and ability to multitask, its response was misstep after misstep, which were succeeded by insensitivity and a political tumble.

In the immediate aftermath of the storm, top Bush advisers spent forty-eight hours arguing over legal niceties about who was in charge, the Pentagon or FEMA or the National Guard, which was under the control of the governors. Lawyers for the Justice Department and the Pentagon quibbled over whether the president ought to federalize the guard, according to administration officials. Defense Secretary Donald Rumsfield objected to sending active-duty troops as cops. There were questions of legal liability, of states' rights, of who should ultimately be in charge. A paralysis fell over the White House.

Three days after the storm had made its devastating landfall, communications counselor Dan Bartlett compiled network newscasts of the storm on a DVD for the president to watch aboard Air Force One on his first trip to the Gulf Coast. When Bush arrived, he, too, sounded tone-deaf. The president praised hapless Federal Emergency Management Agency director Michael Brown—"Brownie, you're doing a heck of a job"—and expressed confidence in the recovery of New Orleans, with an odd observation about his old drinking days in the party city. In Mississippi, he promised to rebuild Senator Trent Lott's house. "Out of the rubble of Trent Lott's house—he's lost his entire house—there's going to be a fantastic house. And I'm looking forward to sitting on the porch."

Bush's assurances seemed oddly out of touch, the kind of political calibration that had previously seemed impossible under Rove's guidance. Given the conditions Bush was witnessing in almost every direction he looked, his remarks were more than clumsy. They sounded almost oblivious. CNN was broadcasting an aerial shot of a New Orleans under water and on fire. That morning, there'd been a predawn explosion, and the sky was blanketed with thick, black smoke. The Superdome was finally empty and the National Guard had arrived, but there were still thousands of homeless around the convention center area. In retrospect, it was clear that the reaction to Katrina was a massive failure of government at every level, and amid the destruction and suffering, it didn't take long for the finger-pointing to begin.

"I'm outraged by the lack of response from our federal government," declared Representative Carolyn Kilpatrick, a Democrat from Michigan, opening a deluge of criticism.

At the White House, Rove moved to contain the political damage, not solve the problems of New Orleans. He and the White House communications director, Dan Bartlett, drew up a public relations plan to dispatch cabinet members to storm-damaged communities on the Gulf Coast and to have the president return repeatedly. Rove instructed administration officials not to respond to Democratic attacks, fearing it would look partisan at a time when national unity was of greater importance. Surrogates would handle the criticism of political opponents. On the Sunday talk shows, officials avoided getting into exchanges about problems of the past week, focusing instead on what the federal government was doing now. Rove's plan had one goal, and it was readily apparent without reading internal White House documents. He intended to shift the blame for poor response from the White House to officials in New Orleans and Louisiana, who were Democrats. Karl Rove was campaigning, as always.

When Tim Russert asked Homeland Security Secretary Michael Chertoff why the federal government had been so slow in responding, he was on a message Rove and his team had developed.

"The responsibility and power," Chertoff insisted, "the authority to order an evacuation rests with state and local officials. The federal government comes in and supports those officials."

Reliable Rove ally Grover Norquist led a chorus of partisan surrogates, blaming the chaos on "looting in a Democratic city run by a Democratic mayor and a Democratic governor."

Among the Rove/Bartlett talking points was the charge that Louisiana officials failed to commandeer hundreds of school buses to evacuate people. Radio talkers Laura Ingraham and Rush Limbaugh quickly took up that part of the message.

On his cable TV show, Bill O'Reilly made passing reference to the administration's tardiness but focused his attack directly where Rove wanted it to go, and that was to criticize New Orleans mayor Ray Nagin and Louisiana governor Kathleen Blanco.

"Most city buses stood idle and on low ground and were quickly flooded by Katrina. Even though the mayor opened the Superdome to thousands, there was not nearly enough security inside, nor enough food and water. Mayor Nagin still has not explained why a mandatory evacuation is not mandatory. What say you, Mayor Nagin?" said O'Reilly. "Like the mayor, Gov. Blanco has no explanation."

On his FOX News show, Sean Hannity denounced Nagin. "He likes to point the finger at everybody else and throw temper tantrums on national TV, but why didn't he use those buses right there to evacuate the people in his city?"

The GOP communications infrastructure was humming. Although Rove had been slow to catch the significance of the hurricane, he found himself on more familiar ground in framing the response as if it were a political campaign. In truth, all sides—federal, state, and local government—had botched the response to Hurricane Katrina. It had been a colossal failure fed by hesitancy, bureaucratic rivalries, and bad luck. But for Bush, Katrina had damaged the fundamental reason for his political success. The central message of the 2004 campaign was that Bush was a strong and decisive leader capable of protecting America against hostile forces. Now that was gone. The inability of federal agencies to respond effectively began to reveal the results of massive Bush budget cuts. And partly as the result of cronyism, there'd been a loss of experienced key personnel, which meant a loss of institutional knowledge about how to respond to a hurricane of this strength.

As Rove and others gathered in the White House situation room on Saturday morning, the first weekend after the storm struck, the president was visibly angry. He told his aides the government's bollixed-up response was unacceptable. In spite of the fact that Rove and Bartlett were well into their plan to shift the blame, there was no doubt that something very precious had been lost. The talk around the table was that if this disaster were a dress rehearsal for response to a terrorist attack, Team Bush had failed the test. The president and the political party that Rove had worked so hard to cast in iron as strong and efficient and worthy of continued command now looked wobbly and inept.

The politics of Katrina were as toxic as the lingering floodwaters. Bush's leadership had been sorely impugned. The massive commitment to rebuild would inevitably drive up the deficit, antagonizing the party's fiscal conservatives. And now Rove's plan to attract minorities to the

Republican Party had also been dealt a severe blow. In watching the hurricane victims plucked from rooftops and slogging through waist-deep water on the TV newscasts, it was impossible to miss the subtext of race. The victims were poor and mostly black. And so it was only a matter of time before black leaders questioned whether the response would have been faster had the victims been mainly white. At the heart of Rove's hopes for a sturdy Republican majority was the need to attract more minorities to the party. Rove was under no delusion that African Americans would suddenly flock to the GOP in big numbers, but the party had made significant advances. Katrina had just washed that all away.

After winning only 9 percent of the black vote in 2000, President Bush won 11 percent in 2004. And in Ohio, where the gay-marriage initiative had motivated a large African American turnout, the president got 16 percent of the black vote. The combination of a values message and White House programs that dispensed faith-based money to black churches had begun to pay dividends. Black churches had long been the comfortable domain of Democrats, but they were perfect places for Republicans such as Bush to advocate the role of Christian charity in dealing with social problems such as drug addiction and alcoholism. Rove sought to cultivate a growing number of black pastors, many of them recipients of government funds for faith-based programs. Increasingly, they felt called to publicly praise the Republican Party. A year before reelection, the president joined the Reverend Tony Evans, the black pastor of Oak Cliff Bible Fellowship in Dallas, for a combination prayer meeting/ pep rally. Evans and fellow Dallas evangelist T. D. Jakes became emissaries for Bush and the GOP among African Americans.

At the same time, David Barton of Texas was pursuing a less-conspicuous appeal to black voters on behalf of the GOP. In Ohio and other states with gay-marriage bans on the ballot in 2004, the Texas GOP vice-chairman and religious activist was among a coterie of national GOP figures flown in by the RNC to promote the party's values agenda. Barton's exhortations in church sanctuaries against gay marriage were important to Bush's success in the 2004 race, especially in Ohio. But it was his appeal to black voters that had the most long-term potential for building the Republican Party. Barton was white but spoke with an evangelical zeal about the long history of African American oppression at the hands of one political party and liberation at the hands of another. Barton's message, which he delivered with a store of documents and a Power-

Point presentation, accused Democrats of fostering slavery and praised Republicans for trying to abolish it.

"The KKK was not started by an independent group; it was started literally by the Democrats," he told predominantly black congregations.

In his presentation of American history, Barton claimed Republicans were the rightful authors of civil-rights legislation from the Civil War through the 1960s. Routinely, he substituted *Democrats* for *the Klan* and *Republicans* for *the church*. He said Democrats committed lynchings, opposed the education of blacks, and promoted the policies of segregation. Barton concluded his history lesson by asking African Americans to reconsider their view of the political parties and to embrace candidates who most reflected their Christian values.

Republican National Committee chairman Ken Mehlman, who'd put Barton on the payroll, declared a year after the president's reelection that Bush "has been a model" of how the GOP and blacks could "restore their historic bond." Republican Party leaders' long-held goal of attracting black voters was showing some progress, thanks in no small part to Rove's organization and the GOP's culturally conservative message.

Following the devastation of New Orleans, though, Rove's hopes of a black Republican resurgence had capsized. Bush's approval ratings among African Americans fell to 2 percent. African Americans believed that race had played a factor in the slow federal response to Katrina, and whatever the truth, the haunting visuals of black refugees on rooftops, outside the civic center, and in the Superdome, desperately pleading for help, would be hard to erase.

The debacle also tarnished another attribute associated with Bush. Loyalty was both a strength of his administration and its most dangerous weakness. FEMA director Michael Brown became the poster boy for the failure after Katrina. The government response was flawed on many levels, but much of the immediate outrage focused on the hapless figure of Michael Brown. He was seen as a Bush loyalist whose main qualification for the job was a recommendation from his pal and predecessor Joe Allbaugh, a member of Bush's early political team in Texas. Allbaugh had followed Bush to Washington to head FEMA, then left to lobby for companies with government contracts in Iraq and, following Katrina, the storm-damaged Gulf Coast. Brown and Allbaugh had given loyalty a new name: cronyism. Suddenly there was the presumption that undeserving Bush pals were everywhere in the administration. Bush's poll numbers, already battered by growing questions about the war in Iraq and rising oil prices at home, continued spiraling downward. The shiny MBA presidency with all its metrics and efficiency had assumed the creaky look of Tammany Hall, which only fed public doubts and deepened Bush's problems in what had become a horrible September.

"They've clearly lost their mojo," said Don Sipple, the president's longtime Republican ally.

Sipple had feared this moment would come, but for reasons less strategic than psychological. Sipple knew Bush well, and he'd worried that, having achieved his goal of reelection, the president might become less engaged. Sipple had long recognized in Bush a deep impulse to redeem the father's defeat by achieving what his father never could.

"A good deal of motivation on the part of this president was to avenge his father's failed presidency," Sipple said. "His definition of a failed presidency is the failure to get reelected, okay? I know that was a strong motivator for him from the first time I met him. And so if you're out to avenge your father's presidency, everything goes into reelection, because that's the tipping point. It's almost as if the whole predicate for his presidency was reelection, ahead of any agenda or anything."

Sipple wondered whether the president and his guru might now be on different paths. For Bush, the endgame was winning reelection. For Rove, it was always something beyond that, the enduring majority.

"The failure of his presidency began shortly after his reelection. It was almost like that's what he was there for, and now he's on autopilot or sleepwalking," he said. "I think that's a partial explanation for the lack of vigilance and planning, of thinking ahead."

Inside the Beltway, there were other explanations. Rove was distracted and had lost his touch. Bush, who took pride in ignoring the Washington buzz machine, was not just insulated but ill informed, a captive of the bubble. *Newsweek* made it the cover: "Bush in the Bubble."

In fact, Bush felt quite comfortable in the bubble. He made it clear that he didn't watch television news or read the newspapers other than to catch up on sports, which was largely true. Once, while flying to a campaign appearance, Bush approached a reporter and asked what he was reading. Looking up to see Bush's face in front of him, the reporter urged, "Here, you need to read this column in the *New York Times*."

Bush recoiled as if struck by lightning. "No way!" he said.

No president can escape the bubble. And for all the criticism that he was out of touch, Bush felt he was thoroughly informed. A packet of news clips was prepared daily, and he was briefed with crisp efficiency by staffers who decided what he needed to hear. As his poll numbers fell and bad news piled up, though, Bush's instinct was to pull his inner circle closer, especially Rove, who was having his own problems with the emerging CIA leak investigation. It was a formula for disaster: the president was isolated and his guru was distracted.

One thing had gone right, however, with the confirmation of John Roberts to the Supreme Court. In that, and in the false confidence of the bubble, Bush felt emboldened to make his next appointment, which would be one of the biggest mistakes of his presidency.

FIFTEEN

THE POWER EXCHANGE

Miers, Abramoff, and Media Management

O, it is excellent to have a giant's strength. But it
is tyrannous to use it like a giant.
—William Shakespeare

Karl Rove was on the phone, working the wackos. That's what George W. Bush sometimes called the Christian conservatives, *the wackos,* and the term had wide currency among Rove's circle of Republican allies. Lobbyist Michael Scanlon told partner Jack Abramoff they had to "bring out the wackos" to help fleece Indian casino operators. Economic conservatives, having little in common, were equally condescending toward the religious Right. But the Christians were a potent political constituency, and Rove recognized their value as a reliable army that could be motivated time and again on behalf of a candidate or an issue.

So on the Sunday before President Bush announced his appointment of White House counsel Harriet Miers to replace Sandra Day O'Connor on the Supreme Court, Rove was on the phone with James Dobson, the influential Christian broadcaster, assuring him of her evangelical bona fides.

"She is from a very conservative church, which is almost universally pro-life," Rove told Dobson.

Dobson didn't seem convinced. Rove needed to present more evidence. "I want you to talk to Nathan Hecht," he said.

Hecht was a Republican on the Texas Supreme Court and a member of Miers's church. Hecht and Miers had dated, and it was Hecht who had encouraged her to join Valley View Christian Church in Dallas, where she taught Sunday school and was on the missions committee. Rove hoped Hecht, a conservative jurist and committed evangelical, would ease Dobson's concerns.

Throughout the 2004 campaign, social conservatives made it clear that a friendly appointment to the U.S. Supreme Court was their highest priority. They viewed past Court rulings on prayer in school, abortion, and homosexual rights as creeping secularism in a culture war that began in the 1960s—and believed that the only solution was the appointment of judges who'd reverse the tide. On radio and in the pulpit, Christian conservatives denounced judicial activism and praised strict constructionism. The phrase *strict constructionist* was code. It meant opposition to abortion. What they wanted was for the courts to overturn *Roe v. Wade,* the 1973 ruling that legalized abortion.

Miers was Bush's choice, not Rove's, although the president's adviser was actively involved in her selection. The president saw in Miers a compelling personal story, that of a woman who'd broken barriers in Texas and proved herself loyal. Rove knew that loyalty could be used for political effect, which was no minor asset in Rove's estimation. In Texas, Bush took great pride in advancing the career of Alberto Gonzales, the son of migrants, by appointing him attorney general. And now he'd do much the same thing for Miers, whose competence and steadfast loyalty Bush saw as equally worthy of recognition.

Bush believed Miers's status as a woman of achievement would be helpful with moderates. And he felt her lack of judicial experience was no problem. After the contorted political dance necessary to win approval of John Roberts, who had a conspicuous paper trail for Democratic critics to seize on, Harriet Miers seemed a perfect choice for a second selection to the high court. She had no paper trail. She was trustworthy and, in Bush's mind, a known quantity. Bush valued few things more highly than loyalty, and Harriet Miers had long ago proved herself a devoted aide, both as a legal adviser to his campaigns and as his appointee to the Texas Lottery Commission, a volatile agency where associates say she ran a disciplined shop and guarded against anything that might damage Bush's political rise. There was no question that Harriet Miers would be Bush's surrogate on the Court, that her decisions would reflect the president's political will in every regard—which Rove tried to reinforce with Christian leaders.

Miers had been managing partner of a prestigious law firm in Dallas and part of Rove's anti–trial-lawyer network to curb lawsuits against business. "She is real close to Karl, very tight," said a former Bush adviser from Texas. In 1995, she wrote a letter to Governor Bush in her capacity as former president of the State Bar Association complaining about contingency fees, a big source of trial-lawyer money. She expressed concern about a bill limiting the ability of the Texas Supreme Court to cut contingency fees "at a time in its history when Justice Priscilla Owen's election to the court placed a majority of the seats in Republican hands for the first time." Rove, the architect of the GOP takeover of the Texas court, had steered Owen's election. And now he was determined that the state's legislature curb trial-lawyer fees that might be used to support the Democratic Party. Miers was an instrument in that mission.

But Miers's portfolio as a political adviser and an advocate of business interests was no way to sell her appointment to the Supreme Court. Rove's method was always the same: divide the field, consolidate the base, and energize the troops for war. Rove knew he had to bring in the religious Right to sell Miers, so he devised a plan to package her as a devout evangelical. Rove's call to Dobson on Sunday, the day before the president's announcement, opened an aggressive effort to rally the Christians to her side.

On Monday morning, he called his reliable ally Richard Land of the Southern Baptists, offering reassurance that if Miers were ever to rule against Bush's political wishes, "it will be seen as an act of gross personal betrayal both by her and by him. And there is nothing lower than somebody who betrays their friends." Land was on board.

Later that day, Rove made arrangements for Hecht and federal judge Ed Kinkeade, a Bush appointee from Dallas, to join a conference call with members of the Arlington Group, the secretive alliance of influential religious conservatives. Among those on the line were Gary Bauer of American Values, Donald Wildmon of the American Family Association, Paul Weyrich of the Free Congress Foundation, and Richard Land.

Dobson introduced the Texas jurists.

"Karl Rove suggested that we talk with these gentlemen because they can confirm specific reasons why Harriet Miers might be a better candidate than some of us think," Dobson said.

According to notes kept by one of the participants, the conversation moved from same-sex marriage to Miers's conservative credentials to the evils of an activist judiciary. But the issue that motivated them most was abortion.

"Based on your personal knowledge of her," someone asked, "if she had the opportunity, do you believe she would vote to overturn *Roe v. Wade?*"

"Absolutely," said Kinkeade.

"I agree with that," said Hecht. "I concur."

It was the perfect message delivered in exactly the right forum. The White House could offer indirect assurance that Miers would side with Christian conservatives in their long-sought goal of banning abortion, but because of strict rules of secrecy, nobody in the Arlington Group could talk publicly about exactly what was said.

The conference call was one of a half dozen that day arranged by Rove, Republican National Committee chairman Ken Mehlman, and Rove acolyte Ed Gillespie. More meetings and conference calls followed all week. There was a lot of selling to be done. Miers was not at all what the religious Right wanted or the party's conservative intellectual elite had expected. "She was a political lawyer," said the former Bush adviser from Texas.

But that's not how Rove would pitch her. His instinct was to make it a base war, to motivate the religious conservatives and have the party's business elite follow. Rove's first step was to wrangle public endorsements from big-name evangelicals such as Dobson, and he succeeded. Two days after the conference call, Dobson went on his radio show and praised Miers to his *Focus on the Family* audience.

"When you know some of the things that I know—that I probably shouldn't know—you will understand why I have said, with fear and trepidation, that Harriet Miers will be a good justice," he said.

What happened next, Rove did not anticipate. Miers proved to be a terrible advocate for herself in meeting members of the Senate. "She's not what you would call an intellect," said a Texas associate. With each succeeding visit to a member of the Senate, she lost support. Worse, Rove's plan to motivate the base and wage war against moderates, Democrats, and the inveterate critics of the Bush administration began falling apart. In retrospect, the strategy was a huge miscalculation. Many social conservatives saw the emphasis on Miers's religion as patronizing; many economic conservatives viewed it as clumsy.

The religious wing was never sold on Miers, but for reasons that should not have been a surprise to Rove. Some big names in the Christian influence network—Gary Bauer, Paul Weyrich, Phyllis Schlafly of the Eagle Forum, and conservative fund-raising pioneer Richard Viguerie—all made their opposition clear. Eventually, even Dobson dropped his support. They wanted another Scalia, another Thomas, someone to signal a strong right turn for a Court that had drifted into the treacherous shoals of secular humanism. They wanted a lightning rod, somebody they could stage a fund-raising appeal around. And Harriet Miers was not it.

"They couldn't make money with her," explained a national figure on the religious Right, who didn't want to be identified because of his relationship with the White House. "Look who was against her. They couldn't go to their members and get them stirred up for contributions."

On both the Left and the Right, Washington influence groups depend on alarmist appeals to raise money. Private assurances that Miers was an ally on abortion were all well and good. But what the social-conservative groups really needed was someone to ignite an ideological battle—a liberal who threatened the moral order or a Scalia II imperiled by the forces of secularism. Either alternative was money in the bank, but Miers was too pastel a figure to rouse the troops.

As for the rest of the party's base, the business and conservative elite, Miers had even less support. To push her appointment, Rove had Vice President Dick Cheney go on Rush Limbaugh's radio show with personal assurances that Miers "has a conservative judicial philosophy that you'd be comfortable with." He tried to have his converted 527s—Progress for America and the Judicial Confirmation Network—beat the drum on her behalf. But few in the conservative chattering class were buying it.

Rove kept getting calls from senators after meeting with Miers, saying they were underwhelmed. Reports from the murder boards, the confirmation prep sessions, were not good. Finally, there was the release from the Texas archives of her syrupy letters to Bush as governor. "All I hear is how great you and Laura are doing. Keep up all the great work. Texas is blessed!" she wrote. In another, she scribbled, "You are the best governor ever!" These were not the messages of a loyalist or even a crony, but of a sycophant. Harriet Miers was simply not up to the standards of the conservative media elite, which turned on her with a vengeance. Columnists George Will and Charles Krauthammer, former White House speechwriter David Frum, and William Kristol of the *Weekly Standard* led a public revolt that ultimately killed the nomination.

The lesson was not lost on Rove. Uniting the conservative base in spite of its differences required that everybody get something. In the case of the Miers nomination, nobody did. Bush appointed his loyal general counsel because he trusted her and believed his supporters should, too. After five years of a president's acting in ways inimical to many of his conservative allies—a soaring budget, a costly prescription-drug program for seniors, the imposition of tariffs on foreign steel, amnesty for illegal immigrants—the reservoir of trust was not particularly deep. The president had kept the base in line through the 2004 campaign with a promise to transform the Court. With Miers, he'd broken his promise.

After twenty-four days, Miers withdrew her name. Bush huddled with Rove and others and moved swiftly to nominate Samuel Alito, an appeals court judge whose conservative credentials were considerably more to the liking of the base.

Around the lobby shops and political eateries of Washington, an odd defense of *Rove Agonistes* emerged. There was talk that had Rove been at full strength, the Miers debacle might not have happened. *Time* magazine picked up the theme: Rove was bedeviled during the period by kidney stones and distracted by the growing federal investigation into the leak of CIA operative Valerie Plame's identity. Barely a week after Miers's appointment, Rove made his fourth appearance before a federal grand jury investigating the leak. For all his vaunted ability to multitask, the president's guru was clearly distracted by his own legal problems, according to friends.

In fact, selling the Miers appointment would have been difficult in the best of circumstances. And circumstances in October 2005 were anything but good. Social Security, Katrina, rising gasoline prices, and questions about the war in Iraq had all taken their toll on Bush's approval ratings, which were the lowest of his presidency. What's more, the Republican Party that Rove had envisioned as a base of support appeared to be mired in questions about overreaching and corruption. It was as if the lesson of absolute power had been lost on the newly ascendant GOP.

Suddenly, media outlets were filled with stories about Republican miscues such as Tom DeLay's indictment in Texas, corrupt Republicans in Ohio, Randy "Duke" Cunningham's confession of wrongdoing in California, and a growing lobby scandal in Washington featuring Rove's erstwhile friends Jack Abramoff, Michael Scanlon, and Ralph Reed. It was not the best background noise for resurrecting the poll numbers of a president who'd come to office with a promise to restore honor and integrity to Washington.

A week before Harriet Miers withdrew her appointment to the Supreme Court, Tom DeLay walked into the sheriff's office in Houston and presented himself for booking on felony charges involving the violation of campaign finance laws and money laundering. The former House majority leader, whose tactics were often guided by Karl Rove through lobbyist Jack Abramoff, was fingerprinted and photographed. He was wearing a light blue shirt, dark jacket, and red tie, and his hair was neatly combed. When a deputy arranged him in front of a screen for his mug shot, DeLay smiled broadly as if he'd won the lottery.

By showing up unannounced in Houston rather than Austin, DeLay avoided the media horde that hoped to film the perp walk. The only picture would be a booking photo, which was no small problem. DeLay and his aides discussed how to deal with the prospects of a mug shot floating around, appearing in every newspaper and on TV and most likely on T-shirts and coffee mugs and other partisan bric-a-brac. There would be a mug shot. The only question was what it would look like. The solution was to smile, making the picture look as innocuous as possible. And it worked. The shot looks like an official campaign photo.

DeLay was accused of steering corporate contributions to the campaigns of several GOP candidates for the Texas legislature in 2002. The legislators then redrew congressional boundaries at DeLay's instruction, adding five more Republicans to the state's thirty-two-member congressional delegation. To accomplish the task, DeLay had to get around two things: state law that makes it illegal to use corporate contributions to elect political candidates and the long-standing tradition of redrawing congressional districts only once a decade after the census.

To circumvent the corporate ban, DeLay created a political action committee that collected $190,000 in corporate money and relayed it to the Republican Party in Washington, which returned $190,000 in donations to the DeLay-backed candidates in Texas. DeLay's lawyers said the transaction was legal. Prosecutors called it money laundering.

As for the tradition of redistricting only once a decade, DeLay told the governor and GOP legislators he didn't like the map adopted in 2001 because it protected too many Democratic districts and he wanted it changed. And he wanted it changed now, at a time when the results would further strengthen his hold on power. He said there was no law against redrawing the lines to favor Republicans. Democrats tried to stop the effort by fleeing the state, but DeLay persisted, at one point calling the FAA and invoking homeland security in an effort to track an airplane carrying Texas Democrats.

In a sense, DeLay completed the work Karl Rove had started two decades earlier to build a Republican majority in Texas. With the election of business-minded Republican judges in the late 1980s, Rove began the political transition toward GOP dominance. The election of the DeLay-backed legislators finished the task, ending the Democrats' century-long control of statewide politics. But if DeLay and Bush were both Texans and members of the same party, they weren't close allies. Privately, Bush viewed DeLay as a bully who could be counted on only when the administration's interests overlapped DeLay's own interests in Congress. Rove knew the best way to influence DeLay was through their mutual friend— lobbyist Jack Abramoff.

Abramoff had a brash style and outsize ambitions, and he lavished money, trips, favors, and tickets to Washington Redskins games on key members of Congress and, in exchange, built strong alliances in the corridors of Republican power. After organizing college campuses in Massachusetts for Ronald Reagan in the 1980 election, Abramoff moved to Washington and teamed up with antitax crusader Grover Norquist to take over the College Republicans. A decade earlier, College Republicans had given Rove his political start, and now there was a new group of young turks in town. Abramoff and Norquist teamed up with a baby-faced fellow collegian from Georgia, Ralph Reed. They were soon attracting media attention with tactics such as burning a Soviet leader in effigy and demolishing a mock Berlin Wall in Lafayette Park. The real target, of course, was Democrats and liberals.

"It is not our job to seek peaceful coexistence with the left," Abramoff declared. "Our job is to remove them from power permanently."

Abramoff's fortunes took off with the Republican takeover of the House in 1994. Abramoff went to work as a GOP lobbyist and shortly thereafter met Tom DeLay at a fund-raiser on Capitol Hill. At the time, DeLay was working his way up in House leadership, and Abramoff, a conservative young lobbyist with a showy confidence that is the currency of K Street, offered to help. Edwin Buckham, DeLay's chief of staff, told the Texas congressman, "We really need to work with Abramoff. He is going to be an important lobbyist and fundraiser."

Abramoff's climb took him through a checkered set of clients. He helped lobby Congress for the Nicaraguan contras and worked on behalf of apartheid South Africa. But it was the casino-rich Indian tribes that fueled his jet-set lifestyle. Between 2000 and 2003, a half dozen tribes paid Abramoff more than $80 million to represent their gambling interests. He brought in as a partner DeLay aide Michael Scanlon to do public relations work, and also Ralph Reed, who organized pastors to block or shut down competing casinos run by rival Indian tribes.

Money bought access, and access purchased influence. Abramoff arranged overseas golf outings for members of Congress and provided skybox tickets to sporting events. Along the way, he assured his connections to power by hiring congressional staffers, including Scanlon. His executive assistant, Susan Ralston, went to the White House to work for Rove, guaranteeing easy access to the president's guru. He became one of George W. Bush's fund-raising Pioneers, raising more than $100,000 for Bush's reelection campaign. He'd been with Bush at the White House and at other functions nearly a dozen times, had chatted up his children with the president, and had the pictures to prove it. He earned a swaggering nickname, Casino Jack, and attracted some of the town's most powerful players to his Capitol Hill restaurant, Signatures.

Once Bush took office and Rove was in the West Wing, Abramoff dispatched his lobby team to press the new administration for friendly hires at federal agencies and protection from trade and minimum-wage legislation that would harm his garment-industry clients in the Northern Mariana Islands. The reception Abramoff's team got from the Bush administration was in stark contrast to the cold shoulder it had received when Clinton was in the White House. Public documents show that Abramoff's team had extensive access to top policy advisers to the vice president, attorney general, interior secretary, U.S. trade representative, and others. In the first ten months of the Republican administration, there were nearly two hundred meetings. But it was Congress that was Abramoff's richest target.

One day in 2002, Abramoff told a client, Marc Schwartz of the Tigua Indian tribe, that he intended to fly to Las Vegas for a Republican political fund-raiser. He invited Schwartz along.

"You gonna be in Nevada?" Abramoff asked. "Why don't we play some golf?"

To Schwartz, it sounded interesting.

"As a matter of fact, John Cornyn will be there," said Abramoff. "It gives us a good chance to network because our friends have been helping him."

Schwartz was stunned. As attorney general, Cornyn had led a very public battle to close Indian casinos in Texas, including the Tiguas' Speaking Rock Casino in El Paso. Now he was running for the Senate as an antigambling crusader.

"He just shut down our casino," Schwartz sputtered.

"You need to set that aside. You need to forget that," Abramoff said. "That was a battle. The big war hasn't been won yet."

The big war, Abramoff assured, was his effort to use influence in Washington to reopen the Tigua casino in El Paso that Cornyn had closed.

Unbeknownst to the Tiguas, Abramoff was making millions by working both sides of the issue. In 2001 and early 2002, Abramoff represented an Alabama Coushatta Indian tribe in a state neighboring Texas, and they wanted the Tiguas shut down. He hired Ralph Reed, who stirred up Texas pastors in opposition to the Texas Tigua casino. At one point, Reed recommended "doing patch-throughs to Perry and Cornyn," a technique using phone banks to locate antigambling voters and connect them directly with the offices of Cornyn and Governor Rick Perry.

Cornyn said he does not recall working with Abramoff or Reed. But in e-mails subpoenaed by a Senate committee, Reed assured Abramoff that he was working with officials in Cornyn's office to help make sure the shutdown happened.

In November 2001, Reed sent Abramoff an e-mail urging the lobbyist to "get me details so I can alert Cornyn and let him know what we are doing to help him."

Before the attorney general succeeded in closing the casino in February 2002, Reed reminded Abramoff that they needed to remember Cornyn in future campaign contributions.

"I think we should budget for an attaboy for Cornyn," he said.

Abramoff wasn't finished, however. In an audacious move, he turned around and pitched the Tiguas on his ability to reopen their operation. At the time, Schwartz and the Tiguas had no idea Abramoff had worked with rival tribes to shutter their operation. All they knew was that Abramoff, exuding the promise of considerable influence in Washington, was offering to help. Abramoff told Indian leaders he had influence with the president and access to the White House, which was almost true. He had Karl Rove.

The Tiguas, desperate, broke out their checkbook. And Abramoff, his blood running with a moneyed frenzy, sent an e-mail to his partner, Michael Scanlon, revealing that their primary purpose was not reopening the Tiguas' Speaking Rock Casino.

"I'm on the phone with Tigua! Fire up the jet, baby. We're going to El Paso!!" Abramoff wrote.

Scanlon responded, "I want all their MONEY!!!"

"Yawza!" Jack Abramoff wrote back.

First, however, the lobbyist had to win the confidence of the Tigua tribal leaders. In the summer of 2002, Schwartz said that Abramoff was all bonhomie and grand assurance, spinning stories about how money and influence work in Washington. When Schwartz said he was surprised that Cornyn, the antigambling crusader, was being fêted by gambling interests, Abramoff laughed.

"It has to do with this giant old game called moving money around," he said. "If someone is in a very conservative district, he can't take gambling money. Well, we can get gambling money contributed. How? We launder it through these other people's PACs, and they make contributions directly to the candidate."

The Las Vegas event included a golf outing and a reception at the home of singer Wayne Newton. Nevada gambling interests contributed to the Battle Born political action committee of Republican senator John Ensign, which then provided it to senators. According to federal records, Cornyn and three other Republicans divided nearly $80,000 in campaign contributions from the Battle Born PAC.

In the brio of the moment, Abramoff told Schwartz, "There's a virtual[ly] unlimited supply of capital, contributions" fueling a partisan takeover of Congress. And he said something that Schwartz has never forgotten.

"He said, 'It's called wealth redistribution, Republican-style.'"

No member of Congress benefited more than Tom DeLay from Jack Abramoff's practice of wealth redistribution. Abramoff wined, dined, and flew members of Congress overseas for exotic golf junkets, including a trip accompanying DeLay to the exclusive Saint Andrews Links in Scotland and a visit to the South Pacific, where news footage showed

DeLay, a hat of fresh flowers on his head, giving his lobbyist friend a bear hug upon arrival. Abramoff provided money to Republican candidates from myriad sources and was a staunch adherent of the K Street Project, DeLay's pet project in which he insisted that lobby firms hire Republicans if they wanted to do business with Congress.

"If you want to play in our revolution," DeLay openly declared, "you have to live by our rules."

Abramoff was the apotheosis of Rove's ideal: the corporate partisan lobbyist.

He gathered in rivers of money from clients and channeled that cash to Republicans, perpetuating the growing dominance of the GOP. Everybody got something. Rove considered Jack Abramoff a point of influence with DeLay. And Abramoff felt he had a friend in the White House.

One of Abramoff's clients was the Northern Mariana Islands, and he was concerned in December 2001 about the potential appointment of Angela Williams to an Interior Department job overseeing the U.S. territory. He asked Reed to weigh in with the White House.

"Any ideas on how we can make sure she does not get it?" Abramoff asked in an e-mail. "Can you ping Karl on this?"

Reed replied, "I am seeing him tomorrow at the White House to discuss it with him as well."

Williams did not get the job. A spokeswoman at the White House told *Time* magazine that Rove "does not recall any of these incidents."

A few months later, Abramoff wrote that he needed some "serious swat from Karl" to get the Justice Department to free $16.3 million for a jail that a client, the Choctaw Indians, wanted to build in Mississippi.

Reed fired back on his BlackBerry: "Am at lunch with Rove at the [Republican National Committee] meeting and just talked with the AG [John Ashcroft]. Will report the substance shortly."

The Choctaws got their jail. The White House said the decision was made on the basis of merit, not influence.

With Rove occupying an office in the West Wing of the White House and DeLay ascending to the post of majority leader in 2002, Abramoff's star was blazing over K Street. He even extended his reach to the news media, secretly paying conservative columnists to write articles favorable to his clients. For several years, Abramoff paid Copely News Service columnist Doug Bandow, a scholar at the Cato Institute, $2,000 per article to boost the lobbyist's interests in print. He also paid a second scholar, Peter Ferrara of the conservative Institute for Policy Innovation. After the practice became public, Copely dropped Bandow's column. Ferrara was unrepentant, saying he takes money from lobbyists "all the time." Abramoff was following the practice of the Bush administration, which paid for favorable news coverage. Armstrong Williams, the conservative columnist and television host, received payments from the federal Department of Education at a time when he was promoting the Bush administration's education policies. The Government Accountability Office concluded the payments amounted to illegal "covert propaganda."

To Abramoff, buying the media must have seemed a logical extension of his ruminations with Karl Rove about controlling the press. Rove's idea, which he'd expounded in 2002 at the Washington deli, was all about using leaks and denying access to manage the media. Abramoff's method was simpler: buy them.

The lobbyist had secured his place as one of the brightest stars in the Republican constellation and appeared set for a very long run. Abramoff's questionable methods, however, eventually caught up with him. A rival lobbyist contacted the *Washington Post,* which, in early 2004, published a detailed account of Abramoff's lobbying. After that, there was a chain reaction of scandals involving powerful Republicans. Some were related to Abramoff and some were not, but they had the cumulative effect of jeopardizing the party's monopoly claim on power.

After a year's investigation, the dominoes began falling. In September 2005, federal prosecutors charged the White House procurement officer, David Safavian, with lying about his dealings with Abramoff. Safavian had been a lobby partner in the 1990s and joined Abramoff and Ralph Reed on a 2002 golf junket to Scotland with Ohio representative Bob Ney, one of several lawmakers targeted in the widening probe. Prosecutors said Safavian concealed his efforts to help Abramoff gain control of two government-run properties in Washington.

In November 2005, Michael Scanlon pleaded guilty to conspiracy to bribe government officials and cheat Indian tribes. Scanlon's plea bargain provided prosecutors with inside knowledge of Abramoff's business dealings, including the questionable purchase of a fleet of casino boats for $147 million. Scanlon said he persuaded Congressman Bob Ney to insert comments into the *Congressional Record* that helped get favorable terms for the sale to Abramoff and partner Adam Kidan. In December, Kidan pleaded guilty to fraud charges in connection with the purchase and agreed to cooperate with prosecutors.

With the circle closing around him, Abramoff cut a deal with prosecutors in January 2006, pleading guilty to defrauding Indian tribes of tens of millions of dollars, bribing government officials, and evading taxes. When he arrived at federal court in Washington in a black trench coat and fedora, he looked like one of the figures in the *Godfather* movies he'd mimicked for friends with such precision. Life was imitating a very dark art.

Abramoff had the potential to bring down a dozen members of Congress and aides. Maybe more. Republicans moved quickly to distance themselves from the disgraced lobbyist. President Bush and members of Congress scrambled to return campaign contributions. Tom DeLay, who'd once called Abramoff "one of my closest and dearest friends," said he had no idea what the lobbyist had been doing. But the history of DeLay's ties to Abramoff appeared evident in the prosecutors' investigations of government for sale. DeLay had taken three overseas trips with Abramoff, including the golf junket to Scotland, and three of his former aides had been enriched by the lobbyist. For DeLay, fighting money-laundering charges in Texas, Abramoff's guilty plea seemed to doom any prospects of winning back his leadership position. Early in 2006, DeLay decided not to seek reelection as majority leader after GOP House members began circulating a petition saying it was time for new leadership that adhered to ethical standards. Facing prospects that he might lose reelection, DeLay announced in April he was resigning his congressional seat.

The Abramoff affair highlighted an audacious nexus of money, power, and influence that fuels Washington politics. Even episodes unrelated to Abramoff were part of a larger tableau of wrongdoing and questionable conduct. Ethics scandals were like land mines, erupting everywhere.

It was not just Tom DeLay in Texas. In California, Republican representative Randy "Duke" Cunningham resigned from Congress after pleading guilty to accepting $2.4 million in bribes from two defense contractors, including a Rolls-Royce and a $7,200 antique Louis-Philippe commode.

The Securities and Exchange Commission and the Justice Department were investigating Senate Republican leader Bill Frist's sale of stock in Hospital Corporation of America (HCA), a hospital chain that his family founded, shortly before its stock price plunged. Frist maintained he did nothing wrong, but the tawdry appearance of the transaction opened the way for Democrats to denounce what they called the "Republican culture of corruption."

In Ohio, the birthplace of the McKinley realignment model admired by Karl Rove and the bellwether state of Bush's reelection victory, the Republican majority was suddenly struck by scandal that threatened the party's hold on power going into the 2006 elections. Governor Bob Taft, the state's most famous political namesake, pleaded no contest to accepting secret gifts from prominent Republican fund-raiser Tom Noe, whose practice was to lavish money and attention on politicians. The state of Ohio accused Noe of stealing millions from the state's rare-coin funds, which he managed. A grand jury indicted him on charges he illegally funneled $45,400 in campaign contributions to President Bush's reelection campaign, and a widening inquiry threatened to snare other presiding figures in the state's GOP.

The problem was not that the Republicans were corrupt and the Democrats were not. It was that the Republicans were in charge; they had a monopoly on power and, with it, wide opportunities for graft. Power corrupts, and Karl Rove's aspiration had long been to lift Republicans to positions of absolute power.

"When you win as big as they did in 2004, something kicks in that the Greeks knew something about, a thing called hubris," said presidential scholar Walter Dean Burnham. "We might also call it election excess. And election excess on the part of the majority party has always been a good source for a rollback or kickback."

The 2006 elections, according to Rove's design, were supposed to advance long-term Republican rule. The machinery of victory—an alliance of corporate interests and religious conservatives, the South as a rock-solid voter base, a perpetual money machine lubricated by friendly forces on K Street—was in place. The Republican Party's status as protector from terrorism was established. The Congress was safely in Republican hands. But a year of administration miscues and growing questions about the war in Iraq had shredded Bush's poll numbers, and Rove's vision for a Republican era was suddenly being jeopardized by a modern-day version of the Gilded Age crooks.

Rove, the student of history, looked to his McKinley ideal. McKinley, he said, had steered around "the Gilded Age crooks" by casting the GOP as "the party of the new reform-minded generation, which is going to be able to confront the new industrial America with a Republican agenda." In much the same way, Republicans had seized control of the House in 1994 with an anticorruption platform. Bush himself came into office promising a higher standard. But now, scandal threatened to erase that advantage and give Democrats an opportunity to paint the GOP as corrupt. Worse, the White House itself was under investigation by a federal prosecutor over the leak of a CIA operative's identity. And Rove, who'd always evaded responsibility for such dirty tricks, was suddenly the focus of attention.

In campaign after campaign, Rove had used an unfailing template for victory. He won by smearing the opposition. But he never left fingerprints. This time, he did. It was the biggest political miscalculation Karl Rove had ever made.

And it had the potential to ruin him.

SIXTEEN

TO COME UNDONE

Lying, Leaking, and Leading

Karl knows how to win the game before you start. I wouldn't
play chess with Karl. It would be futile. He has a brain
that thinks years ahead of most people.
—Ken Luce, GOP political consultant

Rocco Martino, according to the FBI, was simply trying to make a buck. When he met with Elisabetta Burba, a reporter for Italy's *Panorama,* he'd asked her for fifteen thousand euros for his copies of documents showing Iraq had tried to purchase yellowcake uranium from Niger, Africa. Martino was a former agent of Italy's SISMI intelligence service, maintained important relationships within the agency, and had been making a living by selling secrets to anyone who would buy. Burba, however, was not interested. Martino quickly dropped his price and then completely gave up his demand for money and turned the documents over to the journalist, who was working for a publication owned by Italy's prime minister and Bush ally Silvio Berlusconi.

When he was exposed as the person who was conveying the forgeries, Martino began to portray himself as a victim who was used by the Italian spy agency, SISMI. His version of events outlines possible official involvement of the Berlusconi government in an attempt to influence U.S. foreign policy. In a closed-door meeting of a special committee of Italy's parliament, the explanation was that the government had no involvement in the forgeries and, regardless of how he acquired them, Rocco Martino was acting on his own in a scheme to do little more than earn himself some money.

Martino's story is considerably different.

"I received a call from a former colleague at SISMI," he said. "I was told a woman in the Niger embassy in Rome had a gift for me. I met her and she gave me the documents. SISMI wanted me to pass on the documents but they didn't want anyone to know they had been involved."

According to a series of investigative reports published in the Italian newspaper *La Repubblica,* Martino maintained a friendship with Antonio Nucera, a SISMI chief in WMD counterproliferation and technology transfers for Africa and the Middle East. Nucera reportedly arranged for Martino to meet a SISMI contractor who worked at the Niger embassy. She was told only that she was to help Martino and not that there was any involvement by SISMI. The woman, who apparently had keys to an apartment at the Niger embassy, helped stage what was reported to police in Rome as a burglary on New Year's Day 2001.

The letterhead, official stamps, and signature samples that were taken were used to create the forgeries of contracts, letters, and a memorandum of understanding between Niger and Iraq for the sale of uranium yellowcake. (There were also letters involving an alleged Muslim and Arab alliance against the West.) The amateurish fakes appeared to be based on a 1999 trip to Niger by Iraq's envoy to the Vatican, Wissam al-Zahawie, whose visit was not a secret. His picture had been published in the Niamey paper in Niger, and the U.S. ambassador to the African nation at that time, Charles O. Cecil, had filed a routine report on the news with Washington. The Iraqi ambassador was later reported to be traveling to Africa to look for countries that would contract to take toxic waste.

Even though the fraudulent dossier contained the signature of a Nigerian foreign minister who had not held office since 1989, Rocco Martino began to shop it around to the French, Germans, and British after his SISMI friend Nucera had helped him acquire the materials. *La Repubblica* reported the French paid for copies and then tossed them as obvious garbage. Eventually, a few months after 9/11, Martino got the dossier into the hands of the British intelligence agency MI6 long before he took the materials to an Italian reporter.

Martino later claimed he did not know he was passing around bogus materials. "It's true I had a hand in the dissemination of those [Niger uranium] documents, but I was duped. Both Americans and Italians were involved behind the scenes. It was a disinformation operation."

And U.S. intelligence agents with years of experience in Italy believe that SISMI was also directly involved. They point out that when Nicollo Pollari, the SISMI chief, was in Washington with his country's prime minister, the dossier he gave to the CIA about Niger was not taken seriously. The CIA station chief in Rome had completely ignored the obvious forgeries when they were shown to him. Frustrated, Pollari apparently spoke with Italy's defense minister, Antonio Martino (unrelated to Rocco Martino), who suggested Pollari contact Michael Ledeen. Ledeen was in Rome for his December 2001 unofficial meeting with the Iranians and had brought along Harold Rhode and Larry Franklin from the Pentagon's rogue intelligence operation, the Office of Special Plans. Pollari and Antonio Martino also ended up in that conference with the Iranians.

When he was queried via e-mail as to whether he'd met with Martino or Nucera, Ledeen was insistent he had not. "Never met either one of them," he wrote. "Note that I am suing *La Repubblica*."

Regardless, a new, parallel intelligence channel was ultimately established with Italy. When Elisabetta Burba refused to write about the documents for *Panorama*, her editor, Carlo Rosella, ordered her to deliver the dossier to the U.S. embassy. Mel Sembler, who later was to head a fundraising effort to pay for Scooter Libby's legal fees, was the U.S. ambassador to Italy when the documents were cabled directly to Washington, thereby bypassing normal intelligence channels. They arrived relatively unimpeded in the vice president's office and on the desk of the national security adviser and had not even been vetted within the embassy in Rome. The embassy's lack of scrutiny may have owed itself more to relationships than protocol. Sembler accounted for millions in fund-raising for both President Bush and his brother Jeb, the governor of Sembler's home state of Florida. Sembler is also a close friend of Vice President Cheney and would have had direct access to his office.

Despite the fact that intelligence professionals in the CIA had dismissed them as nothing more than poor fakes, the Niger forgeries were suddenly being taken seriously in the highest reaches of the U.S. federal government. Circumstantially, at least, there is a logical case to be made that a coordinated effort was under way to get the White House information that it wanted to be true and needed to make a public case for war against Iraq. As preposterous as that idea is to most Americans who believe in the relative honesty of their country's government, some of the most experienced CIA agents in the United States believe that it was a huge deception. One of them is Vincent Cannistraro, who served as Rome station

chief as well as the CIA's head of counterterrorism operations and was director at the National Security Council under Ronald Reagan.

"I do believe there has been a case of a very broad fraud committed in
which U.S. government officials were clearly involved," Cannistraro said.
"I don't think that any of them were so stupid as to believe all of that silly
crap in those documents. SISMI has lied about this not only in Parliament but publicly. I think there is very little else we can believe other
than there was an effort to promote this as intelligence documents. And
the Brits don't have another source. That's just bullshit."

Evidence indicates the United States either knew about the fraudulent
intelligence or was at least complicit in its distribution well before October
2001, which was when the dossier without the forgeries was first delivered
to Washington. The former vice director of the French intelligence agency
DGSE, Alain Chouet, said the CIA transmitted parts of the dossier to them
in the summer of 2001 before the 9/11 attacks. Chouet said the American
interest in Iraq and African yellowcake uranium deals was based on the trip
of Iraq's Vatican ambassador, who'd very publicly traveled to Africa a few
years earlier. According to a transcript of Chouet's comments published
in an Italian newspaper, he dispatched agents to Niger and Namibia and
found no trace of any deal between Iraq and a uranium-producing country in Africa.

Chouet, who told his story from retirement, said the answer was apparently not what Washington wanted to hear. "The CIA knocked on our
door once again, with the story of the uranium, only in late spring 2002
[after Cheney had asked for the allegations to be checked out].

"Compared to the previous year, the Americans were more precise.
They named a country, Niger. Gave a number of details. They actually
handed us all the information, which only later we found—I'm stressing
'only later found'—were from Rocco Martino, and which we had never
heard about till then. As standard procedure, Langley [CIA headquarters
in Virginia] held back the source."

Chouet said he dispatched five of his best men to check the story. The
trip took place a few months after former ambassador Joseph Wilson
had also gone to Niger at the request of the CIA. "They told me a very
simple thing," Chouet said. "'The American information on uranium is
all bullshit.'"

According to Chouet, the CIA did not relent and was intent on proving the claims of an Iraq-Niger uranium deal. He told *La Repubblica* that, in the summer of 2002 (four months before the actual forgeries surfaced in Washington, having been delivered to the U.S. embassy by Italian reporter Elisabetta Burba), DGSE received copies of the documents in a sealed envelope from the CIA. This was not the original file Martino had sold to DGSE agents, which was merely a summary of allegations. The sealed pouch from the CIA included the forgeries.

"I can remember there were no more than a dozen pages," he explained. "There was a short introduction where the CIA explained the meaning of the documents, I would say. After a quick scrutiny we decided it was all rubbish. Gross fakes."

Chouet's story is complicated by SISMI's claims that Rocco Martino worked for DGSE. The French intelligence agency has not officially denied a relationship with the operative, although from retirement, Chouet said DGSE did not know of Martino until he knocked on its door trying to sell the fake dossier for US$200,000. The French government has called SISMI's and the Italian Parliament's insistence that DGSE was involved with Martino and the forgeries "scandalous."

Chouet's claims were impossible to verify, as were Martino's. The former SISMI agent had said he sold the dossier of forgeries to DGSE, which Chouet appeared to deny. There is, however, no shortage of evidence implicating U.S. government officials in a scheme to get the fraudulent contracts and other documents into American intelligence channels. The Bush administration, led by Vice President Cheney, whipped the CIA and other U.S. intelligence agencies into a frenzy demanding information on Iraq's alleged efforts to acquire yellowcake and to prove connections between Saddam Hussein and Al-Qaeda. Visiting CIA headquarters with his senior staff, Cheney cultivated a pressure-filled atmosphere in intelligence corridors that made it more likely bogus evidence would receive consideration—bogus evidence that, under normal circumstances, would never get beyond an analyst's desk. Standard protocols were either willfully violated or ignored. Information that normally would have been sent to the CIA first was instead given to the Pentagon's Defense Intelligence Agency (DIA), which was much friendlier to data supporting Iraqi intransigence. Often, that intelligence, as corrupted as it might have been, was disbursed into the federal bureaucracy before the CIA even had a chance to give it independent analysis. After facilitating a corrupted intelligence process, and possibly being complicit in introducing fraudulent data into that system, the president and vice president later blamed the decision to invade Iraq on "flawed intelligence."

Former counterterrorism chief Vince Cannistraro pointed out the irony of what occurred. "The case was that this was not a fact-based policy that the U.S. government adopted," he said. "It was a policy-based decision that drove the intelligence, and not the other way around. And that's, of course, the reverse of the process. You had a lot of people who played along to get along, and they understood that in that kind of administration, you couldn't say exactly what it is you really believed."

Cannistraro, as well as most of the professionals within the intelligence community, easily ascertained what the White House was doing to manipulate facts. He has, however, only suspicions about the source of the Niger forgeries. During an interview with Ian Masters, a talk show host on KPFK radio in Los Angeles, Cannistraro suggested involvement by "Rove's brain":

"The Italian intelligence service—the military intelligence service—was acquiring information that was really being hand-fed to them by very dubious sources. The Niger documents, for example, which apparently were produced in the United States, yet were funneled through the Italians."

Masters interrupted Cannistraro. "Do we know who produced those documents? Because there is some suspicion—"

"I think I do, but I'd rather not speak about it right now, because I don't think it's a proven case. . . ."

"If I said Michael Ledeen?"

"You'd be very close," Cannistraro said.

Ledeen immediately responded to the former agent's broadcast accusations. In spite of his decades of involvement with Italy's SISMI, his timely meetings in Rome with operatives from the Pentagon, SISMI, and Italian defense; as well as neoconservative relationships in Washington, Ledeen e-mailed KPFK and Ian Masters to proclaim his innocence.

"I have absolutely no connection to the Niger documents, have never even seen them," Ledeen said in a statement posted on Masters's website. "I did not work on them, never handled them, know virtually nothing about them, don't think I ever wrote or said anything about the subject." In a note to KPFK producer Louis Vandenberg, Ledeen added, "I have left a voice mail for Cannistraro suggesting he should apologize and retract right away. I think you should get back to him and ask him if he didn't just make it up, or was repeating gossip. There can be no credible evidence for the claim, and you will not wish to be associated with it, I'm sure."

Regardless of who manufactured the forgeries, their specious allegations were destined to become a part of American history in the president's State of the Union speech prior to the Iraq invasion. Nonetheless, two weeks before Bush was to tell Congress about the Nigerien yellowcake uranium supposedly bound for Iraq, an analyst at the State Department's Bureau of Intelligence and Research (INR) indicated the Niger documents were forgeries. Oddly, the CIA did not officially receive its copies of the materials in the dossier until a few days later, and it sent them over to the State Department for translation from the French, in which they were composed.

Inside the CIA, the analytical operation known as Weapons, Intelligence, Nonproliferation, and Arms Control (WINPAC) looked at the Niger docs and offered a previously undisclosed assessment that there was "fragmentary reporting" on Iraq's attempts to acquire uranium from "various countries." Wanting the president's address to the nation to be as powerful and convincing as possible, Bush's staff pressured intelligence agencies for authorization to use the Niger story in Bush's text. The head of WINPAC, Alan Foley, and a senior White House staffer, Robert Joseph, gave the approval for the president to use the Niger allegations in his speech but indicated that he should do so by referring to the public dossier that had been issued by the British. The U.K. intelligence has never been shown to have come from any source other than the forgeries delivered by Rocco Martino.

That the forgeries had quickly made it to Vice President Cheney's desk but not the evidence—from Joe Wilson and others—to dispute them is, to say the least, troublesome. The improbability of this suggests that the administration was involved in a deception and that there was something more going on than bureaucratic bungling. There were simply too many Ph.D.'s in the Bush administration with decades of experience in government, foreign politics and culture, and intelligence for them not to know the Niger documents were obvious forgeries. The unavoidable conclusion is that they were involved in using the fraudulent materials for political ends. And leaking a CIA agent's name was a tactic to protect an awful truth.

"I think there is a much bigger story," said former CIA agent Philip

Giraldi. "But I think the much bigger story is that the OSP [Office of Special Plans] in the Pentagon was more heavily involved and definitively involved in the transmission of false information to make the case for war. When you think about that it is the kind of issue that can bring a government down and it is a Nixonesque issue. I don't buy that it's a petty act, this leak. You aren't going to get someone at Libby or Rove or Cheney's level involved unless there is a vital interest of the administration at stake."

If true, the fraud was uncovered when the International Atomic Energy Agency (IAEA) said only six weeks after the president's speech that the Niger documents had been proved forgeries in a matter of minutes using nothing more than the Google search engine on the Internet. The director of the IAEA, Mohamed ElBaradei, who was to win the Nobel Peace Prize in 2005, told the U.N. Security Council that the Niger documents were "not authentic" and "these specific allegations are unfounded." Even Secretary of State Colin Powell acknowledged, a week before the U.S. invasion of Iraq, that the Niger papers might be fakes.

Many CIA agents and Ambassador Wilson appeared to be angered by the administration's complete obliviousness—or was it willful denial?—regarding the ambassador's report on Niger. After the invasion of Iraq, the president kept up his public outcry concerning WMD potential in Iraq despite the fact that both Wilson and a contingent of CIA agents—at least, those who'd maintained their apolitical objectivity—had delivered information contrary to the WMD arguments. Through late spring and early summer, as the U.S. military became bogged down in Iraq, a series of newspaper articles began to appear describing the Niger yellowcake story as phony.

The first was in early May 2003 by Nicholas Kristof in the *New York Times* and described the journey of an unnamed former ambassador who'd traveled to Niger and reported on the lack of proof about Niger and Iraq. A month later, two stories a week apart followed a similar tack of questioning the sixteen words in the president's State of the Union address that made the Niger yellowcake assertion. A *Washington Post* story identified a "retired ambassador," and the *New Republic* offered a quote from a source similarly characterized as a former ambassador who'd been to Niger and said that the administration "knew the Niger story was a flat-out lie" and that there was circumstantial evidence Vice President Dick Cheney was aware of that fact.

Inside the office of the vice president, I. Lewis "Scooter" Libby, Dick

Cheney's chief of staff, launched an effort to find out the name of the unidentified ambassador. A request to an undersecretary of state yielded an "interim oral report" that named Joseph Wilson. The same undersecretary (believed to be Marc Grossman) confirmed that Wilson's wife worked at the CIA and was said to have been involved in planning his trip. At the time he received that knowledge, Libby had already gotten classified faxes from the CIA, which did not name Wilson. Libby, however, wrote "Wilson" and "Joe Wilson" on the sheets of paper. Before the first press inquiry came into the vice president's office, Libby had spoken with a CIA officer who confirmed that Wilson's wife worked at the agency and was involved in arranging the Niger trip.

When Walter Pincus of the *Washington Post* called Cheney's office to ask about Niger, Libby was involved in a discussion of how to respond. The vice president had told his chief of staff that Ambassador Wilson's wife worked in the Counterproliferation Division of the CIA, information Cheney had acquired directly from the CIA. By the time Libby met with a briefer from the CIA a few days later, he was using the name "Valerie Wilson" in his conversation and complained to the agency official that the CIA was making comments to reporters that were critical of the vice president.

Libby was clearly struggling with how to handle the identities of Wilson and his wife. Until late June, the discussions had remained within the vice president's office, and Libby was aware of the sensitivity of the issue. When a senior member of the staff asked him about sharing details with the media concerning Wilson's trip, Libby acknowledged there'd be complications with the CIA if names were disclosed. He resisted a temptation to further discuss the matter on a "non-secure" phone line.

Nonetheless, in a matter of days, Libby was meeting with his friend Judith Miller, a reporter for the *New York Times* who'd written a number of articles that had the effect of generating political support for the war. In his conversation with Miller at a Washington hotel, Libby complained about "selective" leaking by the CIA. He also told the reporter that Wilson's wife might work at the CIA. Miller, for reasons she didn't disclose, never wrote about the information and her meeting with Libby, and her notes from the conversation weren't made public until they were leaked to other journalists more than two years later, in October of 2005, after a story about her appeared in her own newspaper. Eventually, Miller's refusal to tell investigators about her talk with Libby would put her behind bars for almost three months and result in the loss of her prestigious job with the *New York Times.*

Joseph Wilson had no idea what was transpiring in bureaucratic and political circles. But he saw in the media and in statements from the White House that the Bush administration was perpetuating the Niger uranium falsehood as a justification for the war. Wilson apparently decided that he'd waited long enough for the record to be corrected and that his background conversations with journalists hadn't sufficiently chastened the president and his political team. Someone with firsthand knowledge had to tell the truth, he felt. On July 6, 2003, he published an op-ed in the *New York Times* and provided an interview that was the basis of an article on his trip, which was printed the same day in the *Washington Post.* He also appeared on NBC's *Meet the Press* and said that, based on his understanding of the way government works, the vice president's office would have been informed of what he "didn't find in Africa."

And then the attacks began.

Wilson suspected that Scooter Libby was the administration official who was working behind the scenes to discredit the politically unpalatable Niger report. In his book *The Politics of Truth* (Carroll and Graf, 2004), Wilson named Libby as the person who gave reporters the name of his undercover CIA wife. All along, however, he suspected a political attack that was orchestrated by the president's senior adviser Karl Rove.

"The act of leaking the name of a national security asset to the press was a political act," Wilson said. "The White House, in which resides the president, has a political office, and that political office is headed by Karl Rove. Now I can't tell you—the investigators will ultimately tell you, I hope—who actually leaked or authorized the leak; I can't tell you that it was Karl Rove, but what I can tell you is that in the days following Mr. Novak's article which exposed the identity of my wife, Karl Rove, among others, was orchestrating a campaign to push that story on the press. And so, even if Karl Rove was not the leaker, potentially liable or vulnerable for criminal activity, at a minimum you have to ask yourself if that is the sort of ethical treatment that one expects out of one's federal government. That their senior officials would be dragging the wife of somebody they perceived to be an opponent out into the public square to administer a beating. After all, this president said that he was going to change the tone in Washington, and if he's changed it, it's for the worse."

When Valerie Plame Wilson's identity was initially made public in Robert Novak's syndicated column, causing speculation about who'd provided the information, Karl Rove was a logical suspect. The president's political adviser had been fired by the president's father for leaking information to Novak during the 1992 presidential campaign. Rove was working as a direct-mail consultant for the George H. W. Bush for president Texas campaign. Texas political reporters began to hear from Rove that there were functional problems within the campaign's organization. Speaking on background, Rove kept prompting Texas journalists he'd worked with through the years to examine mismanagement of the campaign. As was his practice, Rove refused to go on the record when he described the failures of the campaign's leadership. No one in the Texas press published anything, but Rove didn't stop.

In 1988, as a consultant to the first Bush presidential campaign, Rove had been paid the entire direct-mail budget to handle Texas fund-raising and voter-persuasion efforts. The reelection campaign in the president's home state in 1992 was given to a new manager, Rob Mosbacher of Houston, and he had his own ideas about how to spend the direct-mail money.

"I thought another firm was better," Mosbacher said. "I had a million dollars for direct mail. I gave Rove a contract for $250,000 and $750,000 to the other firm."

Rove was stung by the decision. And with Texas reporters refusing to write about a stumbling Bush campaign, Rove got the information to Robert Novak. Novak quickly wrote a column saying, "The president's reelection effort in Texas has been a bust." Novak described a secret meeting in Dallas that he claimed, wrongly, had removed Mosbacher from the job of Texas state campaign manager for Bush. According to his column, the gathering also included the president's son George W. Bush, as well as U.S. senator Phil Gramm, Texas Republican Party leader Fred Meyer, and "political consultant Karl Rove, who had been shoved aside by Mosbacher."

Rove was fired for the leak to Novak.

"I said Rove is the only one with a motive to leak this," Mosbacher explained. "We let him go."

As obvious as the connection appeared to Texas political observers, both Novak and Rove have denied it through the years. In fact, as the invasion of Iraq was launched in March of 2003 and about three months before he was to have a telephone conversation with Novak about Joseph

Wilson's wife, Karl Rove was still denying the 1992 Novak leak allegation in a flattering profile published in *Texas Monthly* magazine.

"As far as I know," Rove said, "[Rob] Mosbacher still thinks I am the one who did it."

Rove's longtime relationship with Novak, though, is not the only reason to believe he provided the columnist with Valerie Plame's identity. Those who've watched Rove over the years say it's consistent with a long pattern of behavior. During his time in Texas and the Bush presidential campaigns, Rove earned a reputation for leaking, lying, and working through surrogates and "cutouts" to accomplish his dirty work and smear political opponents as well as former professional colleagues with whom he had disagreements. His allies in this regard range from high-profile organizations such as the Swift Boat Veterans for Truth, used to defame John Kerry, to clandestine "boiler rooms" where phone banks conduct "push polls" to spread rumors about political opponents under the guise of being legitimate questions: "Would it change your opinion of the candidate if you knew he had a mixed race child outside of his marriage?"

No one understands Rove's tactics more intimately than his former business partner John Weaver. A man with a soft voice and an undetectable competitive intensity, Weaver left Texas for Washington and eventually ended up managing John McCain's run for president against Bush. After defeating the Texas governor in the 2000 New Hampshire primary, Weaver expected South Carolina to be tough. But not as tough as it was. Because McCain was likely to win the other early primaries, in Michigan and Arizona, a victory in South Carolina had the potential to derail the cash-rich Bush machine. And Karl Rove wasn't about to let that happen.

Whispers and phone calls moved through South Carolina political discourse with the speed of viral pandemic. People began to wonder whether John McCain, who'd adopted a child with dark skin from Bangladesh, had been unfaithful to his wife, Cindy, with a woman of another race. Of course, how could he be completely blamed for such an indiscretion since Cindy had admitted she was addicted to prescription drugs? And what about all of those years he spent in solitary confinement? Surely that had affected his mental stability and made him a questionable presidential candidate.

McCain's prospects in 2000 were destroyed by such allegations, which began as tens of thousands of phone calls from Bush supporters and operations aligned with Rove. Both campaigns picked up and moved on to

Grand Rapids, Michigan, for the next primary, taking the army of political reporters with them. The defining pattern of a Rove campaign—anonymous attacks decimating an opponent—had played out yet again. And again, Rove had left no fingerprints.

In those rare moments when John Weaver will consent to talk about that primary, he won't mention Karl Rove by name, though Weaver will acknowledge that harm had been done to the process as well as to his candidate.

"It's gotten to where you have to actually try to destroy—not just defeat, but destroy—your opponent," Weaver said as he slowly shook his head. "And not just destroy him or her politically, but destroy them personally, professionally; drive them not only from the political battlefield but from being able to be gainfully employed, try to get them indicted, attack their family. That's beyond winning and losing. That's about destruction. Some of that is evil, pure evil, and some of it is amoral at the very least."

The idea of leaking an undercover CIA agent's name to exact revenge on her husband, discredit him, and protect the fraudulent pretext for war is consistent with the kind of hardball political tactic Rove has often deployed. Whether the plan originated in the White House with Rove or was born of Scooter Libby's obsession with Israel, Iraq, and protecting the vice president may not even be known after court testimony. Karl Rove's résumé is proof, however, that he wouldn't have hesitated to suggest such an unlawful act in the interest of concealing a greater crime. On balance, leaking Valerie Plame's identity to reporters was of considerably less risk than exposing the possibility that an American president had misled the country into a war.

Those who know Rove and his temperament best are best equipped to judge Rove's role in the leak. Bill Israel, who considers Rove a "dear friend" and taught a graduate class with him at the University of Texas, is confident Rove is capable of ignoring all ethical concerns, and possibly even the law, to protect his clients and their interests.

"I think Karl takes attacks on himself better than attacks on his candidate," Israel said. "Work for him comes first, before family as far as I can see, before anything; so attacks on him aren't nearly as important as attacks on his candidate. So you attack his candidate and you're toast. He's not someone who thinks, in my view, in ethical terms. He thinks in terms of honor, personal honor. But he's not reluctant to be ruthless."

The origination of the plan to attack Ambassador Wilson by exposing his wife may have occurred in meetings of the White House Iraq Group (WHIG)—the cabinet-level and senior staff organization that handled prewar messages—or it might have come independently from Libby or Rove, who were both members of the WHIG. The accumulated evidence indicates that, regardless of the genesis of the leak idea, it was largely managed out of the vice president's office by Scooter Libby.

The relationship between Rove and Libby has long been described as slightly awkward. The two have great respect for each other's skills, but there are complications of influence and territoriality that make their interdependence a kind of administrative dance. After the vice president informed Libby about Plame's CIA role, it's a virtual certainty he discussed the information with Rove, who, knowing Libby's focus on protecting the war's politics, may have suggested an old tried-and-true tactic to impugn Wilson's reputation and his findings. If Libby were to handle the leaking of the information, Rove and the office of the president would be protected because Rove would then be in the position of playing the secondary role of confirming Plame's identification by being quoted as an "unnamed senior administration official," his most frequently used title.

The possibility that Karl Rove was neither included in the scheme to execute the leak nor involved in its planning contradicts his reputation. Rove is always, always in charge, according to Bill Miller, an Austin political consultant who's worked with Rove on several projects.

"He really needs to be the top guy," Miller explained. "It's sort of understood. You may want to nudge him and try to get an equal position. But it really doesn't work out that way. At the end of the day, Karl is gonna do your work and his work as well. And he'll accommodate you. But he's gonna be the top guy."

Regardless of how the leak was set into motion, the findings of the special prosecutor, Patrick Fitzgerald, allege there was a campaign from within the administration to inform journalists of Valerie Plame's background. The day after her husband's op-ed in the *New York Times,* the vice president's chief of staff, Scooter Libby, had lunch with White House press secretary Ari Fleischer and informed him that Plame worked at the CIA and that the information was "not widely known." The next day, Libby had breakfast with his friend reporter Judith Miller of the *Times* and shared with her the background on Plame's work at the CIA. Later that day, July 8, 2003, Libby asked David Addington, then the legal counsel to the vice president, what paperwork might exist at the CIA "if an employee's spouse undertook an overseas trip."

Rove's involvement with the leak, predictably, had a connection to Robert Novak. Only a day after Libby met with Judith Miller, Rove spoke to columnist Novak. While it's not clear if Novak initiated the call, reports have indicated Novak had telephoned Rove several times previously about another story he was writing on a Bush appointee. Given the nature and history of their relationship, Rove had to know that if the information about Plame was circulating, he could expect to hear from Novak. When he was called before the investigating federal grand jury by prosecutor Fitzgerald, Rove reportedly testified that Novak said he'd heard about Plame and the fact that she worked at the CIA, and Rove responded with, "I heard that too." Novak is said to have told investigators that Rove said, "Oh, you know about it." Rove spoke with Libby in the vice president's office and informed him that Novak was going to be writing a story about Plame and her husband, the former ambassador.

Libby, meanwhile, spoke with NBC's Tim Russert the same day to complain about press coverage of the vice president's office. In a matter of a few days, he was to contact Matt Cooper of *Time* magazine and Judith Miller, confirming for both of them that Wilson's wife worked at the CIA and was involved in arranging his trip to Niger. Over the course of the next week, a number of reporters received phone calls from administration officials informing them about Valerie Plame. One of the journalists, Chris Matthews of MSNBC's *Hardball,* told Ambassador Wilson, "I just got off the phone with Karl Rove and he says your wife is fair game."

When Novak published his column identifying Plame on July 14, 2003, he cited "two senior administration officials." They were undoubtedly Rove and Libby. The vice president's chief of staff was eventually indicted by the federal grand jury for obstruction of justice, perjury, and making false statements. Prosecutor Patrick Fitzgerald had taken testimony from reporters who'd spoken to Libby about Plame—including Tim Russert, Matthew Cooper, and Judith Miller—and they all contradicted Libby's sworn description of events. The three testified that they'd originally heard about Plame from Libby, who insisted before the grand jury that the initial information came into the vice president's office from various reporters and that, as he testified, he was only repeating what he'd been told in conversations with informed journalists. Under questioning on March 5, 2004, about his conversation with Cooper on July 12, 2003, Libby said, "I was very clear to say reporters are telling us that because in my mind I still didn't know it as a fact. I thought I was—all I had was this information that was coming from reporters." Libby, of course, had actively sought the information on Plame through the CIA and had also heard it directly from Vice President Dick Cheney.

Although he wasn't indicted on the day charges were lodged against Libby, Karl Rove also had a lingering issue connected to Matt Cooper. Various published reports have said Rove told the grand jury during his initial appearance in February of 2004 and under questioning by FBI investigators in October of the previous year that he did not begin speaking to reporters concerning Valerie Plame until after he read about her in Novak's column, which was patently untrue; Rove had talked about Plame with both Novak and Cooper in advance of Novak's column.

Rove's rhetorical talents were, for the first time in his life, of no service to him as he testified. Rove's penchant for parsing words and limiting information often left reporters and opponents with false or incomplete versions of reality. This particular ability is precisely not what is needed in front of a federal grand jury. Rove could be expected, however, to negotiate the legal distinction between willfully lying to a grand jury and simply omitting relevant information.

He had done it before.

In fact, Rove had failed to tell the truth under oath to a Texas grand jury. As a consultant in Texas for Senator Kay Bailey Hutchison, Rove was called to testify at a pretrial hearing for his client. Hutchison had been indicted by a grand jury in September 1993 on charges she misused her office as state treasurer. Prosecutors claimed workers on her payroll made campaign fund-raising calls on state time and used a state computer to keep track of contributions.

Rove was part of a public relations effort aimed at discrediting district attorney Ronnie Earle (who was to indict House Majority Leader Tom DeLay in 2005) by creating the impression that the DA was using the Hutchison case to garner publicity and advance his political career. In that effort, Rove took the stand and testified that reporters had been tipped in advance about a raid by prosecutors on Hutchison's office.

Responding to questions by defense lawyer Dick Deguerin, Rove said he was told by a *Dallas Morning News* reporter that he'd received an advance call from prosecutors. It wasn't true. The *News* did not get advance word but instead learned about the raid the same way the rest of the press corps did, which was from Hutchison employees once the raid was already under way. But Rove was successful in inserting the false information into the record.

Fitzgerald, for his part, must have immediately had his suspicions about what he was hearing from Rove and Libby. A few months after he'd taken over the investigation of the leak, Fitzgerald wrote the man who'd appointed him to the post, then acting attorney general James Comey, and asked that his legal purview include the authority to investigate not just the leak itself but also perjury, obstruction of justice, destruction of evidence, and even intimidation of witnesses. Comey readily granted Fitzgerald the additional authority.

Rove's difficulty with Fitzgerald and the grand jury emanated from an e-mail that wasn't produced under an earlier subpoena. The grand jury wanted any communications or other evidence related to contact between the White House and two dozen journalists named in the subpoena. There'd also been a previous directive from White House General Counsel Alberto Gonzales that all such material be gathered and provided to the FBI as the investigation was getting under way. Neither the subpoena nor the order from Gonzales turned up a critical e-mail from Rove to then deputy national security adviser Stephen Hadley. The e-mail specifically mentioned a conversation with Matt Cooper of *Time* and was sent prior to the publication of Robert Novak's column; it was a piece of evidence that directly contradicted what Rove had already told the grand jury.

Hadley was under the same orders as Rove and everyone else working in the White House. If he delivered a copy of the e-mail to Fitzgerald and Rove did not, that fact could be used to provide the foundation for obstruction-of-justice charges against Rove. Fitzgerald might have had Hadley's e-mail from Rove as evidence when Rove testified, which had the potential to place the presidential adviser in serious legal jeopardy. In his appearance before the federal grand jury in February of 2004, Rove conceded that he'd spoken to reporters about Plame but not until he'd read about her in Novak's column. The e-mail to Hadley gave the lie to that statement.

In the hours before the Libby indictments were announced, Rove's attorney, Robert Luskin, met with special prosecutor Fitzgerald and offered an explanation as to why Rove changed his testimony during his

October 15, 2004, grand jury appearance. A year earlier, under oath with the FBI, Rove had said nothing about talking to Matt Cooper or Robert Novak, and, according to Luskin, it was simply because Rove had forgotten. This would have been a historic failure of Rove's legendary memory. At a minimum, it reflected a level of disingenuousness that placed him at legal risk. A man who can remember precinct results from presidential elections more than a century ago, and details such as historic demographic breakdowns of voter turnouts in obscure locales such as remote counties of the intermountain West, seemed unlikely not to recall that he spoke with two high-profile reporters for major publications about what was, at that moment in time, the most critical matter confronting the president of the United States, who happened to be Karl Rove's only client.

An explanation for Rove's failure to surrender the Hadley e-mail confirming the conversation with Cooper was essential to avoid an indictment. And attorney Robert Luskin offered one to Fitzgerald. Luskin said Rove didn't remember talking to Cooper until his memory was jogged by Luskin's conversation with another *Time* reporter, Viveca Novak. (She is not related to the columnist.) According to Novak's published account of their conversation over drinks, Luskin said, "Rove did not have a Cooper problem." Novak said that she'd heard differently around *Time*'s offices and that Rove and Cooper might have spoken about Plame in advance of Robert Novak's column outing the CIA agent.

Luskin later told the prosecutor that the innocent cocktail chatter with Viveca Novak prompted him to send Rove back to conduct an exhaustive search, which produced the previously "unknown" e-mail to Hadley. Left unexplained was why the two previous searches, under the subpoena from Fitzgerald and the grand jury and the directive from the White House counsel, weren't equally exhaustive. As a defense tactic, however, Luskin's assertion may be difficult for Fitzgerald to disprove. Luskin will nonetheless be challenged with having to explain why this one particular interaction stirred Rove's memory when a series of other more significant developments in the Plame story failed to do so. Watching White House spokesman Scott McClellan get hammered on by reporters every day and reading the almost daily articles about the leak, especially those related to Matt Cooper's involvement, ought to have concentrated Rove's mind in a way that should have rattled loose his famously thorough recall. Instead, Rove didn't remember until it appeared the grand jury and prosecutor Fitzgerald were going to require Cooper to testify about his sources for his follow-up story to Robert Novak's outing of Valerie Plame.

Understandably skeptical, Fitzgerald called both Rove attorney Robert Luskin and *Time* reporter Viveca Novak to testify under oath. This happened only days after Fitzgerald had spent hours bringing the grand jury up to date on all of the evidence he'd presented to its predecessor jurors. Immediately, official Washington's thinking was quickened by speculation that Fitzgerald would not be taking the time or trouble to press the information on the jurors unless he had a goal in mind of an indictment against Karl Rove.

Fitzgerald's persistence meant the Bush administration and the president's longtime friends and advisers were forced to contemplate a nearly unimaginable scenario.

"It's hard to imagine the White House without Karl," former Democrat and Bush media consultant Mark McKinnon said. "And I think it would be very difficult for him to be away from the White House and not be involved. Because he's been working on this so long; it's been a lifelong pursuit, so for him to disconnect, I think he would find it difficult."

Perhaps it will not be necessary to either imagine or manage a White House without Karl Rove. A contest is unfolding between two formidable opponents. The prosecutor has struggled mightily to get beyond the lies to his investigators. Hidden behind the deception are likely the facts related to the forged Niger documents and how they got into the U.S. intelligence system. Fitzgerald, a dogged and apolitical investigator, appears unwilling to surrender.

But Karl Rove is equally determined. Television cameras greet him each morning on his front lawn as he climbs into his car and heads to the White House. The media attention seems to have changed nothing. The president says he and his adviser are "as close as ever." Rove is still as influential as he's always been, guiding President Bush with decisions that affect the lives of everyone in America. Karl Rove still hadn't been laid low. The law of the land hadn't stopped or changed him.

Not yet.

SEVENTEEN

THE ROVE GOES ON FOREVER

"If you're going through hell, keep going."
—Winston Churchill

K arl Rove had avoided public appearances for months, but here he was at center stage, beaming like a Buddha. Above the ballroom the chandeliers blazed, casting a gold light over the elegantly dressed crowd, which applauded Rove as a homecoming hero. He was still under investigation in the CIA leak case, but the furious media frenzy had died down and there was a sense both in the Rove camp and here among eight hundred Texans gathered for a festive evening in January 2006 that the president's guru had escaped one more time.

Things were looking up. He hadn't been indicted, not yet at least, and the Samuel Alito nomination was cruising toward confirmation and the worst year of the Bush presidency was over. Confronted with the suddenly urgent controversy involving warrantless wiretaps, Rove knew exactly how he intended reframe the issue going into the 2006 elections: Keep fear alive. It's the terrorism, stupid. Quickly, he took the lexicon of the media, which referred to the wiretaps as "domestic spying," and renamed it "terrorist surveillance."

So on this night, Rove was in a pleasant mood. The lights glistened high on his forehead and he searched the crowd and discovered many familiar faces. The boy wonder had agreed some months earlier to be the object of a political roast sponsored by Austin's prestigious private dining club, the Headliners. The gold-embossed invitation to the state's top politicos and business figures described the evening as a "Roast of Karl Rove by Distinguished Luminaries," which on the Republican side meant Mark McKinnon and Mary Matalin.

On giant screens that flanked both sides of the stage, McKinnon, the campaign's media whiz, showed pictures of Rove making goofy faces, wearing funny hats, and lying under the wheels of Air Force One, which, McKinnon joked, was where the president tossed Rove after his Social Security initiative went down in flames. Matalin's jokes were mostly at the expense of her Democrat husband, James Carville. She jabbed one of the Democrat roasters, a former state officeholder, as "my kind of Democrat. One that holds no elected office."

In fact, it was rare to find a Democrat elected to anything in Texas. No Democrat had won statewide office in the state since 1994, the year Rove guided Bush's election as governor and implemented a plan to sweep the Democrat Party from power. When Matalin, in a backhanded tribute, called Rove "a head-busting political operative," the room erupted in cheers from a hometown crowd that knew Bush's Brain long before he conquered the Beltway.

President Bush made an appearance on video, asking that Rove "autograph the first edition of my new book, *Karl's Brain*." It was an odd comment, both dismissing the idea of Rove as the Machiavelli behind the throne and, at the same time, embracing the notion. Both the central tenet and tension of their relationship was that Bush was the boss and Rove was the genius who got him the job as leader of the free world.

The spiciest partisan fare of the night came from longtime Texas Democrat Lowell Lebermann, a businessman who made the most direct references to Rove's involvement in the CIA affair. "During the Clinton administration, there was a light scandal," Lebermann said of Monica Lewinsky. "The similarities seem to be they involved two pudgy people in the White House who couldn't keep their mouths shut."

Matalin frowned. Some Republicans squirmed in their chairs. But Rove grinned like a boxer who had taken a shot without effect.

"I asked my pastor," Lebermann said, "what's the difference between God and Karl Rove. And my pastor said, 'God doesn't want to be Karl Rove.'"

The joke was a reminder, as if this crowd needed one, of Rove's ascent and the breadth of his ambition. When it was his turn at the microphone, a recorded chorus of angelic voices and harp music filled the room, rising to a crescendo.

During the evening, McKinnon had showed a video of Rove on the campaign trail engaging the media in a furious snowball fight, strutting back and forth in an icy parking lot like a target at a shooting gallery.

"Not a single snowball got within five feet of me," Rove proudly assured the crowd after taking the podium.

Rove won that battle, like so many over the years. He did not lose, not often anyway, and on this night he taunted his roasters as if they were the latest in a line of political adversaries he has beaten over the years.

"Is that the best y'all could do?" he said, smiling triumphantly.

Rove had reason to feel confident. Every day without an indictment bearing his name was further indication that the prosecutor was hesitant or did not have the evidence to bring him to grief. His lawyers had done a good job and he had every conviction that he would escape unscathed. And so when the audience leaped up and offered a standing ovation, it seemed like yet another triumph in his accomplished career of electoral legerdemain.

Circumstances were considerably different for people Rove had worked with to advance the causes of the Bush administration. I. Lewis "Scooter" Libby began 2006 by preparing for his trial on charges he had lied to the grand jury investigating the CIA leak. Florida developer Mel Sembler, who had raised millions for both presidents Bush, was leading an effort to generate major donations for the Libby defense fund. Sembler was the U.S. ambassador to Italy in Rome at the time the forged Niger documents were cabled to the vice president's office and the State Department from the embassy. Sembler had recruited former presidential candidates Steve Forbes and Jack Kemp to join the effort along with former senators Fred Thompson and Alan Simpson. James Woolsey, a past director of the CIA, and Jeanne Kirkpatrick, a previous U.S. envoy to the United Nations, had also become a part of the group. Libby, meanwhile, had not lost his ability to pay his bills. The conservative Hudson Institute hired him as a senior consultant focusing on the war on terror.

Meanwhile, the special prosecutor investigating the CIA leak wrote Libby's attorneys that some of the evidence in the case appeared to be missing. According to a letter from Patrick Fitzgerald, not all of the e-mails from the president and the vice president's office had been properly archived, though he did not expect the deficiency to affect his case against Libby.

"We are aware of no evidence pertinent to the charges against defendant Libby which has been destroyed," he wrote. "In an abundance of caution, we advise you that we have learned that not all email of the Office of Vice President and the Executive Office of President for certain time periods in 2003 was preserved through the archiving process on the White House computer system." Oddly, an estimated 250 e-mails from the vice president's office were turned over to investigators a few months after the prosecutor had sent that note to Libby's legal team. The retrieval might have been a sign that people within the administration who had been protecting Cheney had abandoned their allegiances to take care of themselves.

Nonetheless, Fitzgerald's note was yet another reason to wonder if any e-mails relevant to Rove's possible involvement in the leak had been deleted, by design or accident. Court documents released in early 2006 also revealed that Libby claimed some of the leaking he did was at the behest of his boss, Vice President Dick Cheney. A delay in any indictment of Rove led some analysts to speculate the special prosecutor might be going after the vice president and needed Rove's testimony as part of a deal yet to be arranged and finalized.

Libby, though, was hardly the only Bush official in hot water. Some of the operatives who had attended a meeting in Rome with conservative activist and political operative Michael Ledeen also had problems. Larry Franklin, a father of five who had been working in the Pentagon as an Iran expert, pleaded guilty to passing U.S. government secrets to employees of the powerful lobbying organization the American Israel Public Affairs Committee (AIPAC) and also directly to an Israeli government official in Washington. A man with a doctorate in East Asian studies and fluent in six languages, Franklin found himself parking cars, tending bar, and waiting tables while he arranged a deal with federal prosecutors to testify against two staffers of AIPAC. In January 2006, he was sentenced to twelve years in prison.

Franklin had been at the table in Rome during the December 2001 meeting involving Michael Ledeen, Harold Rhode, the head of Italy's spy agency SISMI along with that country's defense minister, and several people from Iran, including arms dealer Manucher Ghorbanifar. Ledeen, Franklin, and Rhode had all been intimately involved in the Office of Special Plans (OSP), the counterintelligence operation run by the Pentagon that sent uncorroborated data to the president and the vice president to build the case for invading Iraq. Although Ledeen was an external consultant, he reported to Defense Department Undersecretary Douglas Feith, as did Rhode and Franklin. In late 2005, the Pentagon's inspector general agreed to investigate whether Feith's office manipulated intelligence to build political support against Iraq. Rhode and Ledeen appeared certain to undergo intense scrutiny.

Although his name recurs in numerous stories about the forged Niger uranium documents, Michael Ledeen continued to insist he had no involvement in their creation or movement through U.S. intelligence channels. As 2006 began, however, Ledeen acknowledged that he had written various articles for *Panorama,* the glossy magazine published in Italy by the country's then prime minister and Bush supporter Silvio Berlusconi. Ledeen told Larisa Alexandrovna of *Raw Story* in an e-mail that he had written a column for the publication about twice a month "a couple of years ago." Ledeen was also reported by UPI's Intelligence correspondent to have been a paid consultant for *Panorama* at the time of the 2001 meeting in Rome. Both time references for Ledeen's writing and consulting place him in a relationship with the Italian publication precisely when the Niger forgeries, including fake contracts with Iraq, were delivered to *Panorama* reporter Elisabetta Burba. Even though she considered the dossier to be filled with gross forgeries, Burba, nonetheless, delivered the materials to the U.S. embassy in Rome. They were then cabled directly to Washington in violation of protocols requiring they first be vetted by the CIA station chief in Rome, who had previously been shown the papers by operative Rocco Martino and dismissed them as bad fakes.

The forgeries were receiving renewed interest from the FBI. Originally, federal investigators had concluded that they were probably the solitary creations of Rocco Martino. FBI agents believed the former SISMI agent, who had done freelance work for the Italian intelligence service, manufactured the documents in order to sell them and make some money. Even though Martino had long-standing relationships with SISMI agency chiefs, the FBI reached its conclusions about the Niger forgeries and Martino without interviewing him. Journalists Joshua Micah

Marshall, Laura Rozen, and Paul Glastris, writing for *Washington Monthly,* spoke with Martino after they flew him to New York City. Throughout 2005, Martino continued to insist that he had been used by operatives from the United States and Italy in a disinformation campaign. There is no way of knowing if his claims gained traction within the U.S. federal government but late in 2005 the FBI announced it was reopening its investigation into the creation of the Niger forgeries.

In January 2006, another piece of damning evidence surfaced regarding the claims that Niger had sold Iraq yellowcake uranium. A State Department memo, written more than a year before President Bush made his allegations in the State of the Union address, claimed that it was "unlikely" the transaction between the two countries would have occurred simply for logistical reasons. According to the analysis, Iraq would have had to use twenty-five ten-ton trucks, which would have had to be driven one thousand miles with the uranium cargo and cross at least one international border. The memo was obtained by the conservative organization Judicial Watch through a Freedom of Information Act lawsuit. The Bush administration's response to the declassified memo was that the White House was "not an intelligence gathering operation." Bush officials said the president had acknowledged data on Iraq was wrong and that intelligence-gathering protocols had been improved. The White House had not changed its approach to the failure: the fault did not belong to the Bush administration.

To whom did it belong, then? Such a profound mistake in an administration replete with experts seemed improbable. Besides, the forgeries were such crude fabrications they did not pass the scrutiny of low-level bureaucrats. Nonetheless, the American public was asked to believe all the president's men and women had been duped. Certainly, someone was fooled. The evidence indicates it was the citizens of the United States and not the Bush administration.

As the midterm election year began, there were new distractions for the media. The Niger fraud was slowly fading as reporters chased the bribery and influence-peddling scandal involving lobbyist Jack Abramoff. His plea bargain and cooperation with federal agents had the potential to destroy the political careers of many Republicans with whom he had worked. The White House political shop, with Rove at the controls, scrambled to round up every contact with staffers and all photos of the president that included Abramoff and to seal them from public view. In

February, however, the *New York Times* published a photo of the president shaking the hand of one of Abramoff's Indian clients from Texas as the lobbyist and Karl Rove smiled from off to the side.

Rove's mission, nonetheless, was to distance the administration from Abramoff. Spokesman Scott McClellan, who once wrongly insisted that Rove had not spoken with reporters about the CIA's Valerie Plame, now argued the president did not know Abramoff. In fact, Bush was acquainted with Abramoff, as was Rove. Abramoff was a Bush "Pioneer" and had raised hundreds of thousands of dollars for the president. He had attended fund-raisers and White House gatherings. More than that, despite McClellan's press room assurances to the contrary, Rove and Abramoff had a working relationship. The lobbyist had been used by Rove to carry messages to House Majority Leader Tom DeLay. And in cautious fashion, Rove had met with Abramoff outside the White House in ways the lobbyist said would avoid detailed record-keeping.

Abramoff's relationship with Republicans loomed as a threat to the GOP in the 2006 elections. In Georgia, Ralph Reed, a Rove and Abramoff ally, was tarred by the scandal in his race for lieutenant governor. Twenty-one of the state's thirty-four Republican senators signed a letter asking him to withdraw from the race because he was too closely connected to Abramoff and was harming the entire GOP ticket in Georgia. Reed had been paid more than four million dollars by Abramoff to fight gambling interests in states like Texas that were in competition with the lobbyist's casino clients.

With the lobby scandal unfolding at home and growing questions over the war in Iraq abroad, the political landscape for Democrats was the most promising since Bush took office. The 2006 midterm elections approached and Democrats, armed with a message that the GOP majority had imbued Washington with a "culture of corruption," were looking to retake seats in the House and Senate, perhaps even win back control in one or both chambers. When House Majority Leader Tom DeLay decided not to run for reelection because of poor poll numbers caused by his indictment in Texas and his association with Abramoff, Democrats began to believe public sentiment was turning in their direction.

Rove had to change the equation, or, more precisely, he had to reestablish the equation that had assured Republican victory since September 11, 2001. Republicans would protect us from the terrorists, Democrats would not. The GOP made historic gains in 2002 on the issue, and Bush successfully used it again to secure reelection. When the *New York Times* disclosed that the government was monitoring domestic phone calls and e-mails from those suspected of having links to Al Qaeda, Bush did not retreat in the face of questions about legality. Let the Democrats quibble about civil liberties; Rove would paint them as weak on national security. Rove's method was always to divide the field, polarize the base, and energize the troops for war. From his assiduous reading of polls, Rove knew that if he framed the argument right—as a contest between civil liberties and pursuing terrorists—the White House would win.

Still, Bush continued to stumble, like a gambler on a bad streak. The administration quietly approved a business deal to have a company from Dubai, United Arab Emirates, manage several major U.S. ports. It was a politically untenable arrangement. The UAE had been home to two of the 9/11 hijackers, the source of the terrorist plotters' money, and a nation that had provided sanctuary and health care to Osama bin Laden when his kidneys began to fail. When members of Congress in both parties rushed to kill the deal, Bush threatened the first veto of his administration.

As the political furor rose, the White House began looking for a way to salvage the deal. Rove went on a national broadcast to suggest the White House was willing to consider a cooling off period of forty-five days to allow members of Congress to examine the agreement with the Dubai company. But it was too late. Both Republicans and Democrats in the House and Senate, feeling a firestorm of opposition from home and resentful the president had not accorded them that courtesy in the first place, were in no mood for compromise.

For nearly five years, Bush and his key adviser had warned Congress and the nation against the rising threat of terrorism coming from the Arab and Muslim world. Having been whipped into an ethnocentric, anti-Muslim frenzy after 9/11, Americans were in no mood for anything that looked like a compromise to their safety.

With their erstwhile allies on talk radio and in Congress against them, it was clear the White House would lose. But why? Was it ineptitude or hubris born of belief in their invincibility? Theirs was a Republican-conservative machine designed to dominate politics for a generation, to campaign, win votes, raise money, frame issues, and knock down opposition. But the Dubai ports deal revealed that Rove's efficient creation might have birthed a few uncontrollable monsters. Bush and Rove had grown perhaps so confident in the power to win that they seemed to believe they didn't need approval of either the public or Congress. If you can convince a nation to go to war with inaccurate or cooked intelligence, aren't all other political endeavors easier by comparison?

The White House had leaked information and framed the debate against its enemies to great effect. Rove had built a political tower so strong and tall that, from his high perch, he could not see the cracks forming at the base. Congressional candidates began separating themselves from the president as his approval ratings tumbled to Nixonesque levels in the wake of the Dubai controversy, the domestic spying story, and the prospects of civil war in Iraq. Rove remained under investigation in the Plame affair well into the 2006 election year. After building an infrastructure to neutralize the Democratic Party and advance GOP hegemony for a generation, Rove suddenly faced the possibility his grand design might actually consume itself.

A week after he had laughed himself through his evening roast in Austin, Rove took the stage at the midwinter 2006 gathering of the Republican National Committee in Washington. A rapt audience wanted its general unbowed by the controversies attending the Bush tenure in the White House. And Rove did not disappoint. Although still under the cloud of the CIA leak investigation, he was in full bravura about the state of the party and about its prospects for 2006. He described Bush as one of history's "consequential" presidents and said he was both a great "liberator" and "domestic reformer." If history was years from making its judgments, Rove understood the essential lesson that it is the winners who write history.

The only concession Rove made to the Democrats during his luncheon speech was that they were not "unpatriotic." He did say, however, they were profoundly wrong about the war on terror and the economy and the judiciary. We face "a ruthless enemy," he said, and "need a commander in chief and a Congress who understands the nature of the threat and the gravity of the moment." He encouraged Republican candidates to use differences over the Patriot Act and Iraq and constitutional protections to portray Democrats as weak on national security. He quoted Abraham Lincoln on the need to turn out voters in 1840. The task, he said, was no less important today. Against the succession of presidents and wars and issues consuming the nation state, there was the fundamental impulse of politics: victory. He kept the faithful focused on the work required to achieve their mutual dream of GOP realignment and control of the government for decades.

"We now have sophisticated polls, complicated computers, detailed voter databases, the Internet, and more," Rove explained. "But the basics of winning remain what they were. We have to make the perfect list of all the voters, and see to it that our supporters are brought to the polls by someone they hold in confidence. That depends on what you do, and the passion and energy you bring to our great cause. Nothing in politics is foreordained."

With Rove, everything is a campaign. Even the implementation of policy, which officially became part of his portfolio in the second term, was an act of politics. In pushing Social Security and immigration reform, the driving factor was how those policies would energize political support for the GOP. They were pieces of a larger architecture, like a grand machine rising toward some distant goal—but crumbling at the base. Rove had created from its various parts a winning majority and now the majority he'd built was turning against itself.

As 2006 quickened toward the fall campaigns, Rove's primary areas of concentration for the GOP were immigration, the courts, and Social Security. Before midyear, Rove had bungled all three. The evangelicals were demanding conservatives on the court who, they hoped, would overturn *Roe v. Wade,* but the Miers appointment had rankled much of Bush's support on the right. Social Security, which was designed to lure more young voters into the GOP by giving them personal accounts, was a nonstarter in Congress.

Immigration reform, and with it Rove's hopes of achieving both policy and political ends for the president, ignited a civil war within the party. The consequence of this particular stumble was potentially fatal, not just to Rove's dream of Republican hegemony but also to the more immediate goal of retaining control of the White House and Congress. In truth, the anti-immigration forces in the GOP, highlighted by Representative Tom Tancredo of Colorado, were working against the long-term interests of the party. Rove knew that the increasing Hispanic population was a potential engine for future Republican growth. And, much as McKinley had appealed to a new generation of European immigrants, Bush had made significant inroads among Hispanics, long a reliable constituency of the Democratic Party. That task was impossible if Republicans were seen as hostile. Inside the White House, Rove sought to balance the competing impulses within the party—both for strong enforcement of the border and for sensitivity to the plight of the desperate immigrant crossing the Great Sonoran Desert on foot in pursuit of the American dream.

It was an intractable problem, and in many ways, one of Rove's own political making. Having ridden the traditional Republican support for law and order (illegal immigrants were breaking the law) and sounding election-year alarms against the imminent threat of terrorism (a porous border was a danger to the country), Rove saw the very constituencies that had worked so well to elect a Republican majority now working to divide and dismantle it.

With the resignation of White House Chief of Staff Andrew Card, his successor, Josh Bolten, made a change that reflected a cold political calculus. Bolten, the president's former budget director, almost immediately took policy responsibilities away from Rove and handed the job over to thirty-something wunderkind Joel Kaplan. In the 2000 election, Kaplan was a leader in the "Brooks Brothers Riots" during the Florida recount and was seen on tape banging on doors of county clerks' offices demanding favorable results for the Bush campaign. The naming of Kaplan, who has two degrees from Harvard and is a former Marine, was viewed by Democrats and White House critics as a sign the federal investigation of Rove was having an impact on his performance.

In fact, the reassignment was a recognition that without the success of politics in 2006, there would be no policy for the remainder of the Bush administration. Rove's considerable skills were needed to focus full time on the midterm elections. With the president's public approval rating tumbling to 29 percent in at least one poll and only a few points higher in several others, GOP leadership became palpably frightened they were about to lose control of Congress. Many Americans interpreted the increase of sectarian violence in Iraq as evidence a civil war had begun and the president had no plan for either resolving the crisis or for withdrawing U.S. troops. Domestically, three-dollar-a-gallon gasoline had also angered voters who associated much of the dramatic rise in cost with the president's close ties to the energy industry.

The task confronting Rove in November was clearly going to demand his full range of skills. Democrats, struggling for a focused message, needed fifteen seats to take back control of the House and a net gain of six seats to seize the Senate. If the Democrats were to take control of either chamber, the president faced potential impeachment. At the very least, a Democratic majority in the House or Senate would mean investigations, subpoenas, hearings, and, effectively, the end of the president's hopes of accomplishing anything in his final two years.

It was imperative that Rove focus his full attention on the politics of the 2006 midterm elections. The media characterized Rove's new assignment as a demotion; in fact, it was actually a recognition that his supreme talent was winning political campaigns. In that task, there was one rather large potential impediment, which was the grand jury investigation into the CIA leak. Criminal charges would most certainly take Rove out of action. His opponents suspected Rove was worried about his legal situation when he volunteered to appear for a fifth time before the federal grand jury investigating the CIA leak case. Rove answered questions for more than five hours concerning how he happened to forget he had spoken to two prominent reporters about the undercover status of agent Valerie Plame. Initially, Rove said he didn't talk with journalists until after reading her name in the newspaper. In fact, court filings indicated he had, indeed, had conversations with journalists before Plame's name became public. Patrick Fitzgerald, the special prosecutor, sought to determine if Rove had lied and obstructed justice or had simply forgotten.

The blogosphere was rife with Internet postings about a potential indictment of Rove. One reporter for an Internet publication actually wrote that Rove had been secretly indicted for perjury and obstruction, prompting a furious scramble among mainstream reporters to check with Rove's lawyer, who denied it. The Internet site eventually issued a partial apology, but the episode underscored the deep anxiety that had gripped Washington with the advent of the elections. Facts were hard to come by and theories proliferated: that Fitzgerald had discreetly indicted Rove, that Rove was cooperating, that the master of the game would emerge triumphant.

Experienced Rove watchers put their money on the architect's escaping indictment. Still, some Republicans viewed Rove as toxic to the party and hoped he'd step down. In Texas, Rove's longtime adversary and former chairman of the Texas Republican Party Tom Pauken had insisted that Rove's influence "has been negative for the conservative movement, negative for the Republican Party and not good for the country."

"The problem with Karl is that it's always about the next election; it's always about power; it's always about getting the money from the big boys so you can control the process. It's not about principle; it's not about issues—issues are used to gain and keep political power, not to advance the interests of this country," Pauken said.

Rove's answer to his critics was that he'd served his country faithfully as well as his party and his president. And as the summer of 2006 unfolded and the master strategist threw himself completely into the process of reestablishing Republican dominance in the fall elections, nothing substantial emerged to make an incontrovertible case against him. On the contrary, after all the speculation, in early June, prosecutor Patrick Fitzgerald informed Rove's attorney that the government *wouldn't* be seeking an indictment against Rove. Once again, Karl Rove had succeeded in defeating his enemies and critics. Once more, he'd followed the pattern that marked his political rise: attack, but escape culpability.

Or had he? Might there still be a damning piece of evidence lying around somewhere, destined to be stumbled upon and yet lead to the operative's political downfall? His opponents and journalists who've watched him doubt Rove has made such politically fatal mistakes. Besides, it hardly seems to matter. Karl Rove would almost certainly design a plan to make his problems disappear.

The architect never runs out of ideas.

Notes

I: AMERICAN DREAMER

7 **"Really?" Schwartz asked:** Interview with Marc Schwartz, June 11, 2005.

7 **Schwartz was in the midst:** Ibid.

8 **"They've got movement logs . . .":** Ibid.

8 **"You recognize him?":** Ibid.

8 **"We've got a problem, Jack":** Ibid.

9 **"Jack just told me . . .":** Ibid.

9 **"We're not stupid":** Ibid.

9 **"That's the weirdest . . .":** Ibid.

9 **five different federal agencies:** Susan Schmidt, "Paper Shows Tribe Paid to Try to Sway Bill," *Washington Post,* Nov. 18, 2004.

10 **what he and the Tigua:** David D. Kirkpatrick and Phillip Shenon, "Ralph Reed's Zeal for Lobbying Is Shaking His Political Faithful," *New York Times,* Apr. 16, 2005.

10 **"I wish those moronic Tiguas . . .":** Ibid.

11 **Republican Bob Ney:** Michael Isikoff, "A Washington Sand Trap," *Newsweek,* Oct. 3, 2005.

12 **Rove has indicated that a political party can:** Nicholas Lemann, "The Controller: Karl Rove Is Working to Get George Bush Reelected, but He Has Bigger Plan," *New Yorker Magazine,* May 12, 2003.

12 **"It can be drowned in a bathtub":** Steven Leigh Morris, "Shipwrecked: Swimming with the Sharks in a Sea of Arts Funding," *LA Weekly,* June 27, 2003.

13 **"What's happening is . . .":** Interview with Linda Lipsen, June 17, 2005.

14 **identifying themselves as members of unions:** Interview with David Swanson, June 15, 2005.
14 **more than $200 million:** Ibid.
14 **an "all-out attack . . .":** Interview with John Ryan, July 1, 2005.
14 **"Absolutely, I do . . .":** Interview with Swanson.
16 **In one article:** Lemann, "The Controller."
16 **"Well, I think it's a plausible . . .":** Ibid.
17 **"not a Christian":** Interview with Bill Israel, Rove associate at the University of Texas School of Public Affairs, Apr. 13, 2005.

2: GOD IN THE MACHINE

19 **From his operations:** Linda Feldmann, "The Kingdom and the Clout of Ralph Reed," *Christian Science Monitor,* Sept. 8, 1995.
21 **"He's learned . . .":** Melinda Henneberger, "Driving W," *New York Times,* May 14, 2000.
21 **"I got very . . .":** Interview with Richard Land, Feb. 22, 2005.
22 **"I think that Karl . . .":** Ibid.
22 **And Bill Israel:** Interview with Bill Israel, Aug. 7, 2005.
22 **Religion was:** Henneberger, "Driving W."
23 **"He [George W.] was just . . .":** Interview with Doug Wead, Jan. 10, 2005.
23 **"He's got the stuff . . .":** Ibid.
24 **"Christian conservatives . . .":** Sam Attlesey, "Religious Voters Called Key in GOP Success," *Dallas Morning News,* Nov. 11, 1994.
24 **"I gotta tell . . .":** Interview with Don Sipple, Apr. 21, 2005.
25 **"Sip, my man . . .":** Ibid.
25 **"My precinct . . .":** Interview with Ralph Reed, Nov. 25, 2003.
26 **Reed's path:** Ralph Reed, *Active Faith: How Christians Are Changing the Soul of American Politics* (Free Press, 1996).
26 **"My candidate . . .":** Ibid.
27 **Every third Tuesday:** Jeffrey H. Birnbaum, "The Gospel According to Ralph," *Time,* May 15, 1995.
27 **"The advantage . . .":** Erin Saberi, "From Moral Majority to Organized Minority," *Christian Century,* Aug. 11, 1993.
27 **Pat Robertson . . . told a private:** Richard L. Burke, "A Tape Reveals Pat Robertson, the Politician," *New York Times,* Sept. 18, 1997.
28 **when a GOP colleague:** Interview with Ken Luce, Aug. 12, 2002.
29 **"Ralph was very, very . . .":** Sidney Blumenthal, "Fall of the Rovean Empire," Salon.com, Oct. 6, 2005.
29 **For $380,000:** Joe Stephens, "Bush 2000 Adviser Offered to Use Clout to Help Enron," *Washington Post,* Feb. 11, 2002.
30 **"It depends . . .":** Interview with Land.
31 **"I'm supporting George Bush . . .":** Interview with Bobbie Gobel, June 8, 1999.
31 **"It was absolutely amazing . . .":** Ibid.
32 **"Oh yeah?" Bush said . . .:** Conversation with George W. Bush aboard campaign plane, May 18, 2000.

3: THE GOSPELS OF KARL

33 **Patrick Guerriero spotted:** Interview with Patrick Guerriero, Aug. 2, 2005.

33 **During that campaign:** "Religious Right Has Firm Bond with Bush Candidate's Agenda," *USA Today*, July 27, 2000.

33 **In April:** "Santorum Says Homosexual Acts Are Threat to the American Family," Associated Press, Apr. 22, 2003.

34 **"Mr. President . . .":** Interview with Guerriero.

34 **"The only thing . . .":** Ibid.

35 **The meeting was:** Interviews with members of the Arlington Group.

35 **"If the president . . .":** Interview with Kelly Shackelford, May 7, 2005.

36 **"It felt like . . .":** Interview with Guerriero.

36 **Buchanan on the *Today*:** *Today* show transcript, Feb. 5, 2004.

36 **Ted Haggard:** Interview with Ted Haggard, Nov. 24, 2003.

36 **Mark Mead understood:** "Bush Urges Gay Marriage Ban," Associated Press, Feb. 25, 2004.

37 **"I thought it was a joke . . .":** Interview with Ann Richards, May 5, 2005.

38 **Years later:** "Little Did We Know," *Texas Monthly*, Nov. 2004.

39 **"It worked . . .":** Interview with Don Sipple, Apr. 21, 2005.

39 **"That's not an issue . . .":** "Bush Distances Himself from Remarks," Associated Press, Aug. 27, 1994.

39 **The Richards camp:** Interview with Chuck McDonald, Aug. 2002.

39 **"If I had . . .":** Interview with Sipple.

40 **"Fear is . . .":** Interview with Richards.

41 **So in 1994:** "Karl Rove Honed His Skills in Alabama," Scripps Howard News Service, Oct. 29, 2004.

41 **Perkins said he heard:** Interview with Joe Perkins, Sept. 4, 2005.

41 **"Mark is not . . .":** Joshua Green, "Karl Rove in a Corner," *Atlantic Monthly*, Nov. 1, 2004.

42 **"We were trying . . .":** Ibid.

42 **Through much of the politics:** David Richards, *Once upon a Time in Texas* (University of Texas Press, 2002), 5–14.

43 **"The core of it . . .":** Interview with Richards.

43 **Rove complained:** Rove conversation with author.

43 **The next morning:** Interview with Anne Marie Kilday, May 1994.

44 **"There's not . . .":** Interview with Mark McKinnon, Dec. 13, 2004.

45 **"It's a great . . .":** Interview with John Green, Nov. 19, 2003.

45 **"All things flow . . .":** "Gay Issue May Energize GOP," *Cincinnati Enquirer*, Sept. 14, 2004.

45 **"The president's campaign . . .":** Blackwell letter to supporters, Aug. 2004.

46 **"I was a paid . . .":** Interview with David Barton, Feb. 2, 2005.

46 **In Wisconsin:** "Homo Hate," *LA Weekly*, Nov. 5, 2004.

46 **In Kentucky:** "Mongiardo Has Come Far," *Lexington Herald Leader*, Oct. 30, 2004.

46 **Phil Burris:** Interview with Phil Burris, Mar. 4, 2005.

46 **"Vote your Bible!":** Interview with Dallas Billington, Oct. 14, 2004.

46 **"the most horrific . . .":** "Same-Sex Marriage Ban," *Columbus Dispatch*, Oct. 30, 2004.

47 **On street corners:** Interview with Dan Trevas, Jan. 26, 2005.

4: DEVILISH DETAILS

49 **Bush volunteered an anecdote:** Conversation with reporter Ken Herman, July 12, 2005.

50 **To resolve their modest dispute:** Ken Herman, "Bush Trip Steeped in History," *Austin American-Statesman,* Dec. 1, 1998.

50 **Herman had no idea:** Conversation with Herman.

50 **Bush was criticized:** Michael Kinsley, "Go to Hell," Washington Post Newsweek Interactive Company, July 24, 1999.

50 **never became a major campaign issue:** Herman, "Bush Trip Steeped in History."

51 **"We had exchanges . . .":** Ibid.

51 **"I want to remind both of you . . .":** Ibid.

51 **"troubled if people misinterpreted . . .":** Eric J. Greenberg, "Heaven Can't Wait," *Ethnic Newswatch, The Jewish Week,* July 30, 1999.

51 **"Listen, I have this problem":** Herman, "Bush Trip Steeped in History."

51 **"You need to deal with it":** Ibid.

52 **"As a Christian, he believes . . .":** Ibid.

52 **"put this behind him . . .":** Ibid.

52 **"regrets having said it . . .":** Ibid.

52 **Bush wrote a personal letter:** Ken Herman and Mark Sherman, "Bush Digs In," *Austin American-Statesman,* Mar. 7, 2000.

52 **During a Republican governors' conference:** Conversation with Herman.

53 **Bush goofed up again:** "Report: Bush Asked to Clarify 1993 Remarks," Associated Press, Dec. 1, 1998.

53 **"You know what I'm gonna tell those Jews . . .":** Ibid.

53 **"I'm tellin' . . . all going to hell":** Ibid.

53 **"You know what he just said to me? . . ."** Conversation with Herman.

53 **"Well, you can't write that . . .":** Conversation with *Dallas Morning News* reporter Wayne Slater, July 18, 2005.

54 **the quote was buried deep:** Conversation with Herman.

54 **"So, what, am I in trouble here?"** Ibid.

54 **"You know, I could have kept you . . .":** Ibid.

54 **"Religion is serious . . .":** "Report: Bush Asked to Clarify 1993 Remarks."

55 **wore a traditional:** Ibid.

55 **"abruptly cancelled":** Ibid.

55 **Upon Bush's return:** "Welcome to Washington," *Forward Magazine,* Dec. 11, 1998.

55 **"I regret the concern caused . . .":** Ken Herman and Mark Sherman, "Bush Digs In," *Austin American-Statesman,* Mar. 7, 2000.

56 **"God Almighty does not hear the prayer of a Jew":** Alan Cooperman, "Among Evangelicals, a Kinship with Jews," *Washington Post,* Jan. 8, 2006.

56 **distributed to every member:** Interview with author-researcher Frederick Clarkson, July 19, 2005.

56 **conspiring to create communism:** Pat Robertson, *The New World Order* (W Publishing Group, Sept. 1, 1991).

56 **"[But] the minute you turn the document . . .":** *The 700 Club,* Christian Broadcasting Network, Dec. 30, 1981.

57 **published a book-length report:** Bill Berkowitz, "Strangers in a Strained Land," Conservative Watch, *ZMagazine* 15, no. 11 (Oct. 2002).

57 **"describes the rise of the Christian Right . . .":** Patrick Buchanan, "Bellicose Barrage of Christian-Bashing," *Washington Times,* June 15, 1995.

57 **"if a Christian group . . .":** Ibid.

57 **"instead of debating the issues . . .":** Don Feder, "ADL Attack Discredits Organization," *Boston Herald,* June 16, 1994.

58 **"I think what we are seeing . . .":** Interview with Max Blumenthal, Apr. 22, 2005.

58 **a national meeting of the:** Ralph Reed, "From Confrontation to Cooperation," speech to the Anti-Defamation League, Washington, D.C., Apr. 3, 1995.

59 **have been "insensitive and have lacked . . .":** Ibid.

59 **"It was an extraordinary moment . . .":** Interview with Clarkson.

60 **"Are you going to kill him?"** Interview with Bush friend and confidant.

5: NOT AS I SAY

63 **Karl Rove began working with Ken Mehlman:** Thomas B. Edsall, "Bush Taps Campaign Manager to Lead Party," *Washington Post,* Nov. 16, 2004.

63 **knocking on doors for Ronald Reagan:** Ibid.

63 **A graduate of Harvard Law School:** Ibid.

63 **ending up with the chairmanship:** Ibid.

63 **In Ohio, Mehlman worked closely:** Eric Resnick, "Bush Campaign Connected to Ohio Ban Amendment," *Gay Peoples' Chronicle,* Sept. 24, 2004.

64 **"I think the best way of phrasing it . . .":** Interview with John Aravosis, June 9, 2005.

64 **Aravosis had run successful:** Ibid.

64 **"biological errors . . .":** StopDrLaura.com (website).

64 **"the president believes a marriage . . .":** Adrian Brune, "Bush Campaign Mum on Any Openly Gay Staffers," *Washington Blade,* May 28, 2004.

64 **"We don't know if . . .":** Interview with Aravosis, June 9, 2005.

65 **"You just don't get to act . . .":** Interview with Mike Rogers, Mar. 11, 2005.

65 **"We're a big tent . . .":** Mike Rogers, "Randi Rhodes on Ken Mehlman and the GOP Leadership," Blogactive.com (website), Dec. 2, 2004.

66 **"if you drive a Volvo . . .":** Michelangelo Signorile, "Out and About to Get Ugly," *New York Press* 17, no. 47, Nov. 23, 2004.

66 **"Since he's so confident . . .":** Ibid.

66 **off the record that Mehlman was straight:** Interview with Rogers.

66 **"background only":** Ibid.

66 **if he thought homosexuality was a choice:** Interview of Ken Mehlman by Tim Russert, *Meet the Press,* NBC, June 5, 2005.

67 **"And that's . . . irrelevant to the question of the public definition of marriage . . .":** Ibid.

67 **"is going to use my private life . . .":** Jake Tapper, "Hot for Gay Republicans," *GQ* magazine, Apr. 2005.

67 **"Ken Mehlman is not gay":** Ibid.

67 **"What Mike Rogers is doing . . .":** Ibid.

67 **editor Chris Crain decided:** John Byrne, "Staff: Editor of Washington Gay Paper Thwarted Story Outing RNC Chair Mehlman; Editor Asserts He Was Offered Schrock Tapes," Raw Story, Mar. 22, 2005.

68 **the editor of the *Harvard*:** Mike Rogers, "Take Action: Is He or Isn't He? What the *Washington Blade* Hasn't Told You," Blogactive (website), Nov. 30, 2004.

68 **"... as young political activists":** Ibid.

68 **"Chris would confirm it ...":** Ibid.

68 **"I don't think you can report ...":** Ibid.

68 **the Christian Coalition had given:** Mike Rogers, "Time to Look in Some Closets," Blogactive (website), Aug. 19, 2004.

69 **"You're in the showers with them ...":** Jon Glass, "On the Issues: Candidates Sound the Same but Differences Emerge," *Virginia-Pilot,* Oct. 22, 2000.

69 **repeatedly calling the offices:** "Va. Congressman Drops Re-election Bid after Outing Claim," *Washington Blade,* Aug. 27, 2004.

69 **"a little too aggressive":** Interview with Rogers.

69 **provided with audio recordings:** Mike Rogers, "Schrock Faces Accusations: Cancels Congressional Campaign," Blogactive (website), Aug. 30, 2004.

69 **"... he can go down on me ...":** Mike Rogers, "Schrock Ignores Past Sexual Liaisons with Men: Casts Vote for Federal Marriage Amendment," Blogactive (website), Sept. 30, 2004.

70 **"facing the nation and our region":** Michael D. Shear and Chris L. Jenkins, "Va. Legislator Ends Bid for 3rd Term," *Washington Post,* Aug. 31, 2004.

70 **"Schrock is the archetypal ...":** Interview with Aravosis, June 9, 2005.

70 **"I think, at this point ...":** Interview with Patrick Guerreiro, Aug. 2, 2005.

71 **When ... Jeffrey Kofman broadcast:** Antonia Zerbisias, "TV Man Is (Shock) Gay and (Horror) Canadian," *Toronto Star,* July 19, 2003.

71 **"Asked about it, Drudge said ...":** Ibid.

71 **"Hugs, kisses to the cheek ...":** Mark Karlin, "Matt Drudge: A Gay Who Backs the Gay Bashers," Buzzflash (website), July 13, 2004.

72 **"Drudge picked me up ...":** David Brock, *Blinded by the Right: The Conscience of an Ex-Conservative* (Crown Books, 2002).

72 **"What does Drudge do ...":** "Most People Didn't Know Drudge Was Gay," interview transcript from Alan Colmes radio show posted at Blogactive (website), Apr. 19, 2005.

72 **"No, I'm not gay ...":** Ibid.

72 **Drudge is not the only:** Kevin Naff, "Out, Out Damn Celebs," *Washington Blade,* Oct. 21, 2005.

73 **"Smith once chatted ...":** Ibid.

73 **GOP consultant Arthur Finkelstein:** Frank Rich, "Just How Gay Is the Right?" *New York Times,* May 15, 2005.

73 **Gurley had a profile posted:** Mike Rogers, "Gurley Admits: Yes That Was My Gay.com Screen Name," Blogactive (website), Nov. 16, 2004.

73 **"just looking for good sex ...":** Mike Rogers, "RNC Staffer Seeks Others for Unsafe Sex," Blogactive (website), Nov. 16, 2004.

74 **claimed it had been stolen:** Rogers, "Gurley Admits."

74 **"In some ways ... a community in collusion ...":** Interview with Aravosis, June 9, 2005.

74 **party was responsible for the mailer:** David Kirkpatrick, "The 2004 Campaign: The Tactics; Republicans Admit Mailing Campaign Literature Saying Liberals Will Ban the Bible," *New York Times,* Sept. 24, 2004.

75 **"Are you out at work?"** Lou Chibbaro Jr., "GOP Officials Announce They're Gay," *New York Blade,* Oct. 15, 2004.

75 **"So you have no crisis of conscience ...":** Ibid.

75 **"You can come up with a top-ten list of . . .":** Interview with John Aravosis, Mar. 12, 2005.

75 **second term to tell him he was gay:** George Rush and Joanna Molloy, "Out of the Closet and into the Cabinet," *New York Daily News,* June 25, 2005.

75 **Allen's chief of staff:** Mike Rogers, "The Gayest Office on Capitol Hill," Blogactive (website), Dec. 7, 2004.

76 **"Pro-family conservatives throughout . . .":** "The Truth about George Allen and Homosexuals," Family Policy Network (website), June 2005.

76 **"If someone is going to run . . .":** Jody Brown, "Commentary and News Briefs," Agape Press–Christian News Service, Dec. 6, 2004.

6: TIN SOLDIERS AND NIXON'S COMING

77 **"Congratulations . . .":** Interview with Janet Creighton, Jan. 26, 2005.

78 **"I'm the only . . .":** Ibid.

78 **"We have done . . .":** Ibid.

78 **For the 2002:** Paula Dwyer and Lee Walczak, "The Invisible Campaign," *Business Week,* Sept. 2, 2004.

79 **"They laid their plan . . .":** Interview with Creighton.

79 **"We've been watching . . .":** Interview with Creighton.

79 **"We won by . . .":** Byron York, "Dems Showed Soros Secret Rove Plan," *National Review,* Apr. 6, 2005.

79 **"We failed to . . .":** Martha Brant, "West Wing Story: A New GOP," *Newsweek,* Dec. 13, 2001.

80 **Under Rove's direction:** Interview with Matthew Dowd, Dec. 3, 2004.

80 **"It was, like . . .":** Ibid.

81 **"We were talking . . .":** Interview with Bob Klaffky, Jan. 25, 2005.

81 **In his briefcase:** John F. Dickerson and Karen Tumulty, "The Love Him, Hate Him President," *Time,* Dec. 1, 2003.

81 **"In 2000 . . .":** Interview with Matthew Dowd, Oct. 11, 2005.

81 **"The deal was . . .":** Interview with Bob Bennett, Jan. 26, 2005.

82 **"You guys really . . .":** Ibid.

82 **"Karl Rove is . . .":** Dick Polman, "Conservatives Turn on Each Other and Bush," *Philadelphia Inquirer,* Oct. 24, 2005.

83 **"Just looking at . . .":** Interview with Herb Asher, Jan. 11, 2005.

83 **"Here we are . . .":** Interview with Rocky Saxbe, Jan. 12, 2005.

84 **The company's chairman:** Texans for Public Justice, "The Bush Pioneer-Ranger Network," Oct. 1, 2004.

84 **"It's a roll-up-your-sleeves . . .":** Transcript of President Bush's remarks in Canton, Ohio, Apr. 24, 2003.

84 **A year later:** John McCormick, "Ohio Town Faces Bleak Job News," *Chicago Tribune,* May 30, 2004.

85 **"We spent a lot . . .":** Interview with Dowd, Dec. 3, 2004.

85 **In 2000:** Ibid.

85 **Coors beer and:** Thomas B. Edsall and James V. Grimaldi, "GOP Got More Bang for Its Billions," *Washington Post,* Dec. 30, 2004.

85 **The Bush campaign:** Katharine Q. Seelye, "How to Sell a Candidate to a Porsche-Driving, Leno-Loving NASCAR Fan," *New York Times,* Dec. 6, 2004.

86 **Dowd said the information:** Interview with Dowd, Dec. 3, 2004.

86 **Bush's conservative allies:** John C. Green et al., "The Battle for Ohio: The 2004 Presidential Campaign," monograph, University of Cincinnati, University of Akron.

86 **Mark McKinnon:** Interview with Mark McKinnon, Dec. 13, 2004.

86 **Many of the contributors:** Federal Election Commission, Internal Revenue Service filings.

86 **Progress for America:** Peter H. Stone, "The Business Blitz on Social Security," *National Journal,* Jan. 22, 2005.

87 **"I'm telling you . . .":** Interview with Dowd, Jan. 3, 2004.

87 **"If it were . . .":** Mark McKinnon presentation at Lyndon B. Johnson School of Public Affairs at the University of Texas, Oct. 30, 2005.

87 **McKinnon's media team:** Interview with McKinnon.

89 **"We see John . . .":** *Hannity & Colmes* transcript, FOX News network, Jan. 29, 2004.

89 **"You can't trust . . .":** "Special Report," FOX News network, Jan. 29, 2004.

89 **"He flip-flops . . .":** *FOX News Sunday,* FOX News network, Mar. 21, 2004.

89 **Radio commentator:** Hugh Hewitt, "The Things They Kerry'd," *Weekly Standard,* Feb. 12, 2004.

89 **By the time:** Jennifer Loven, "Bush Talks Up Economic Leadership," Associated Press, Mar. 4, 2004.

90 **"The whole thing . . .":** Interview with Chad Clanton, Apr. 23, 2005.

90 **In the case of:** Swift Boat Vets and POWs for Truth filings with Internal Revenue Service, PoliticalMoneyLine.

90 **All three were:** Campaign finance reports with Texas Ethics Commission, *Dallas Morning News* database.

90 **The group's lawyer:** Interview with Ben Ginsberg, Nov. 15, 2005.

90 **The chief strategist:** Center for the Study of Elections and Democracy conference, Brigham Young University, Feb. 7, 2005.

91 **Rove had always:** Jim Vertuno, "Rove Touts Republicans as Tougher on Terrorism," Associated Press, Jan. 18, 2002.

92 **The campaign cultivated:** Interview with Jo Ann Davidson, Jan. 24, 2005.

92 **"You think . . .":** Interview with Tom Erney, Jan. 14, 2005.

92 **An early Bush:** Interview with McKinnon.

93 **With Bush:** Ibid.

7: LAPSED VOTERS

95 **"I kept the . . .":** Speech to American Alternative Foundation dinner in Washington, Nov. 8, 2001.

96 **"We kidded . . .":** Interview with Deal Hudson, Mar. 2, 2005.

96 **"Catholics—at 50 million . . .":** "The Mind of the Catholic Voter," *Crisis,* Nov. 1998.

97 **"The reality . . .":** "The Catholic Vote: Does It Swing?" *Crisis,* Nov. 1998.

97 **Rove was on:** Interview with Hudson.

99 **He struck out "Bible":** Ibid.

100 **When the state:** "Bush, Moses Defend Curriculum Plan," *Dallas Morning News,* July 10, 1997.

101 **"I view my religion . . .":** Interview with George W. Bush, Apr. 16, 1999.

101 **In February:** *Life Today* (television program), Feb. 15, 1999.

102 **"I can't believe . . .":** Conversation with George W. Bush aboard campaign plane, Feb. 27, 2000.

103 **"The election . . .":** Lewis Gould, *From Canton to the White House: The Presidency of William McKinley* (Regents Press of Kansas, 1980).

104 **As Rove prepared:** Interview with Karl Rove, Mar. 1999.

105 **One day:** Interview with Hudson.

105 **"Hudson," he said . . .:** Ibid.

106 **Rove shook his head:** Ibid.

106 **By the 2004:** National exit polls, Roper Center.

107 **A few years:** Interview with John Hays, Jan. 19, 2005.

107 **"No! No! No!"** Interview with Karl Rove, Oct. 19, 2004.

8: FOR DADDY IN OHIO

110 **"How we doin'?":** Interview with Doug Preisse, Jan. 25, 2005.

110 **From the stage:** Scott Lindlaw, "President's Stump Speech Gets Constant Adjustment," Associated Press, Oct. 30, 2004.

110 **Kerry pollster Mark Mellman:** "Down to the Wire," *Newsweek*, Nov. 15, 2004.

111 **"I'm not sure . . .":** Terence Hunt, "Two Wars Shadow 2004 Election," Associated Press, Oct. 27, 2004.

111 **"Coalitions that get . . .":** Interview with Walter Dean Burnham, Jan. 7, 2005.

112 **"They had reports . . .":** Interview with Jo Ann Davidson, Jan. 24, 2005.

112 **"Twice we did . . .":** Ibid.

113 **"There's no way . . .":** Interview with Lee Leonard, Jan. 23, 2005.

113 **"What churches were . . .":** Matthew Dowd presentation at Lyndon B. Johnson School of Public Affairs, University of Texas, Oct. 25, 2005.

114 **"All the Issue One . . .":** Interview with Bob Bennett, Jan. 26, 2005.

114 **An e-mail went out:** Carol Eisenberg, "An E-Mail Appeal," *Newsday*, June 4, 2004.

114 **In keeping with:** Alan Cooperman, "Churchgoers Get Direction from Bush Campaign," July 1, 2004.

115 **"The Bush campaign's . . .":** Interview with John Green, Aug. 9, 2004.

115 **Names, addresses, phone numbers:** Ken Herman, "Bush Effort among Churches Draws Criticism," Cox News Service, July 1, 2004.

115 **"What happened?":** Interview with Deal Hudson, Mar. 2, 2005.

115 **"Well, first of all, . . . I called . . .":** *Capitol Report,* CNBC transcripts, July 2, 2004.

116 **"It was astounding . . .":** Interview with Gary Marx, May 11, 2005.

116 **"They stole God . . .":** Interview with Tom Erney, Jan. 11, 2005.

116 **"Religion is . . .":** Interview with Don Sipple, Apr. 21, 2005.

117 **"I want to be . . .":** Barbara Slavin, "Onward Christian Soldier," *Los Angeles Times,* May 1, 1995.

117 **"The Republican Party is not a church":** Sam Attlesey and Wayne Slater, "GOP Begins Session; Leaders Stress Unity," *Dallas Morning News,* July 11, 1994.

117 **Pauken's first action:** Interview with Tom Pauken, June 2002.

117 **"That's when I . . .":** Ibid.

118 **Former White House:** David Frum, *The Right Man* (Random House, 2003), 36.

118 **"We had religious . . .":** Interview with Davidson.

118 **"And a light . . .":** Interview with Preisse.

119 **In an internal:** Byron York, "Dems Showed Soros Secret Rove Plan," *National Review,* Apr. 6, 2005.

120 **"What's interesting here . . .":** Interview with Herb Asher, Jan. 10, 2005.

120 **Bush had a rule:** Interview with Rob Schuler, Jan. 28, 2005.

120 **"We've been to . . .":** Interview with Karl Rove, Oct. 22, 2004.
121 **The day before:** Interview with Preisse.
121 **When Springsteen took:** John Soeder, "Vote for Change Tour Serves Cleveland a Double-Shot Concert," *Cleveland Plain Dealer,* Oct. 3, 2004.
121 **"I'm in a row . . .":** Interview with Dan Trevas, Jan. 26, 2005.
122 **made 1.8 million telephone:** John C. Green et al., "The Battle for Ohio: The 2004 Presidential Campaign," monograph, University of Cincinnati, University of Akron.
122 **"Karl Rove was . . .":** Interview with Republican campaign ally in Columbus, Jan. 26, 2005.
122 **"Time will tell . . .":** Interview with Davidson.

9: A FEW SIMPLE QUESTIONS
126 **"For our community . . .":** Interview with Eric Resnick, July 21, 2005.
126 **a married father and closeted gay man:** Sarah Fenske, "The Godfather in the Closet," *Cleveland Scene,* June 11, 2003.
127 **Resnick was making:** Interview with Resnick.
127 **"I knew Ken Mehlman . . .":** Ibid.
127 **Secretary of State Kenneth Blackwell:** Interview with Herb Asher, Jan. 22, 2005.
127 **"I actually came home . . .":** Ibid.
128 **When the vice presidential debate came:** Eric Resnick, "Gay Marriage and Mary Cheney Are Topics in Vice Presidential Debate," *Gay People's Chronicle,* Oct. 8, 2004.
128 **Arshinkoff was enduring publicity:** Sarah Fenske, "The Godfather in the Closet," *Cleveland Scene,* June 11, 2003.
128 **stopped by police in Akron:** Ibid.
128 **Arshinkoff . . . was not arrested:** Ibid.
129 **"Most people are aware . . .":** Ibid.
129 **he ran into Arshinkoff:** Ibid.
129 **"If there's anything I can do . . .":** Ibid.
129 **"live up to his end of the bargain":** Ibid.
129 **"I've just decided he's . . .":** Ibid.
129 **Resnick . . . lingered . . . after Ken Mehlman . . .:** Interview with Resnick.
129 **"I shook his hand . . .":** Ibid.
130 **" . . . canned, standard answers":** Ibid.
130 **"That's inaccurate":** Eric Resnick, "GOP National Chair Avoids Questions about His Sexuality," *Gay People's Chronicle,* Mar. 25, 2005.
130 **"What do you mean?":** Interview with Resnick.
130 **"What they are saying . . .":** Ibid.
130 **"You mean you are not . . .":** Ibid.
130 **"You have asked a question . . .":** Resnick, "GOP National Chair Avoids Questions."
130 **known as "Mehlmania":** Interview with Resnick.
130 **"I just went in there . . .":** Ibid.
130 **"I am extremely angry . . .":** Ibid.
131 **had received an offer:** Interview with Karl Rove, July 2002.
131 **"This was a great job":** Ibid.
131 **"He's my stepfather . . .":** Ibid.
131 **"Oh, I have no idea . . .":** Ibid.
131 **"The theory was . . .":** Ibid.

132 **one friend estimated:** Interview with Joseph Koons, Aug. 28, 2005.

132 **"I thought of him as my brother . . .":** Ibid.

132 **"Louie didn't hide the fact . . .":** Ibid.

133 **appeared to be uncomfortable:** Interview with mutual friend of Joseph Koons and Louis Rove, July 10, 2005.

133 **"We are just an innocuous . . .":** Ibid.

133 **at the Rainbow Cactus:** Ibid.

133 **"These were very public, openly gay . . .":** Interview with Koons.

133 **"He was a sad and lonely . . .":** Interview with mutual friend of Joseph Koons and Louis Rove.

133 **habit of nightly drinking:** Interview with Koons.

133 **"No, . . . I don't recall that there was . . .":** Ibid.

134 **Neighbors of Louis Rove:** Interview with mutual friend of Joseph Koons and Louis Rove.

134 **and another on the mantel:** Ibid.

134 **"That's my son . . .":** Ibid.

134 **"This was well before . . .":** Ibid.

134 **"He [Karl] obviously was hurt by the divorce . . .":** Ibid.

134 **vacationed with him in Santa Fe:** Karen Tumulty, "The Rove Warrior," *Time*, Dec. 19, 2004.

134 **found their biological father:** Ibid.

134 **to send money:** Ibid.

135 **his mother's 1981 suicide:** Ibid.

135 **"Again, it's hard to figure out . . .":** Ibid.

135 **took his father to Norway:** Ibid.

135 **coordinated emergency efforts:** Ibid.

135 **"I think they were reasonably close . . .":** Interview with Koons.

135 **Karl was executor:** Tumulty, "Rove Warrior."

135 **in a star-shaped frame:** Ibid.

135 **"He lived life . . .":** Ibid.

135 **Louis Rove passed away:** "Federal Social Security Death Index."

10: LAWYERS, DUNS, AND MONEY

137 **Calad thought she'd:** "Catie Couric Interviews Ruby Calad," *Today*, NBC News, Nov. 4, 2003.

137 **"You have to leave":** Ibid.

137 **"But I can't even . . .":** Ibid.

138 **Calad's insurance company:** Interview with George Parker Young, Sept. 8, 2005.

138 **further corrective surgery:** Ibid.

138 **Davila was in constant:** "HMO Nightmares," *National Law Journal*, Mar. 1, 2004.

138 **The appropriate prescription:** Ibid.

138 **a less-expensive generic:** Interview with Young.

138 **given seven units:** M. Gregg Bloche, "Bush Turns His Back on Fight for Patients' Rights," *Los Angeles Times*, Mar. 22, 2004.

138 **the Managed Care Responsibility Act:** "Setting the Record Straight," Bush-Cheney campaign news release, Aug. 20, 2000.

139 **bragged about his involvement:** "St. Louis Presidential Debate Transcript," George W. Bush, Oct. 17, 2000.

139 **"I do support . . .":** Ibid.

139 **was vetoed by Bush:** Charles Lane, "A Flip-Flop on Patients' Right to Sue?" *Washington Post*, Apr. 5, 2004.

139 **"It was the easy thing . . .":** Paul Burka, "Bad Medicine," *Texas Monthly*, Aug. 1995.

139 **without Bush's signature:** "Sharp Shootin' Texas Doctors Put HMOs in the Malpractice Target Zone," Wayne J. Guglielmo, *Medical Economics Magazine*, Dec. 22, 1997; "A Patient's Given Right to Sue HMOs," by Polly Ross Hughes, *Houston Chronicle*, May 23, 1997.

139 **"I said, 'You cannot afford to veto . . .'":** *Washington Post*, Feb. 17, 2000.

140 **"I can't make them happy . . .":** "Taking Credit for Patients' Rights Where It's Not Necessarily Due," *New York Times*, Oct. 18, 2000.

140 **"the potential to drive up health care . . .":** *Medical Economics Magazine*, Dec. 22, 1997; *Houston Chronicle*, May 23, 1997.

140 **"In 1997, Bush *signed* . . .":** "Setting the Record Straight."

140 **his name on four . . . new laws:** Bush speech at Southern Methodist University, Dallas, Tex., Aug. 19, 2000, and Texas Legislative Records, SB 382, 383, 384, 385.

141 **took George W. Bush at his word:** Interview with Young.

141 **Linda Lipsen sat:** Author's notes and transcript from attending ATLA meeting, Mar. 2, 2005.

142 **a well-known Republican lobbyist:** Ibid.

142 **John Weaver, a former:** Ibid.

142 **spends about $300 million:** Paul Braverman, "The Stealth Campaign: When the Chamber of Commerce's Stanton Anderson Puts On the Gloves against ATLA's Linda Lipsen, the Fight for Tort Reform Isn't Always about Tort Reform," *American Lawyer*, Oct. 1, 2004.

142 **spent more than $112 million:** Ibid.

142 **"This is a very broad terrorism bill . . .":** Author's notes and transcript from attending ATLA meeting.

142 **"God, this is just . . .":** Ibid.

142 **"Don't we need to . . .":** Ibid.

143 **first order of business:** John F. Harris and William Branigin, "Bush Signs Class-Action Changes into Law," Feb. 18, 2005.

143 **a series of qualifying criteria:** Ibid.

143 **"coupon lawyers":** Interview with Ken Vest, ATLA communications consultant, May 1, 2005.

143 **sought to put a federal limit:** Sarah Lueck and Jeanne Cummings, "Bush to Push Plan to Limit Awards for Malpractice," *Wall Street Journal*, July 25, 2002.

143 **"We know that the current tort . . .":** Transcript of speech by Treasury Secretary John Snow to the American Tort Reform Association, Mar. 18, 2004.

144 **"Go back and look . . .":** Interview with Carlton Carl, ATLA media executive, Mar. 2, 2005.

144 **A group of doctors from:** Author's notes and transcript from attending ATLA meeting.

145 **"He now has the doctors . . .":** Interview with Linda Lipsen, Mar. 2, 2005.

145 **"Our badly broken medical . . .":** Scott Lindlaw, "President Backs National Malpractice Caps as Way to Rein In Health Care Costs," Associated Press, July 25, 2002.

145 **siding with "pregnant mothers . . .":** Ibid.

145 **met privately with:** Braverman, "Stealth Campaign."

146 **"Confronting the New Health Care . . .":** Stephanie Mencimer, "Malpractice Makes Perfect: How the GOP Milks a Phony Doctors' Insurance Crisis," *Washington Monthly,* Oct. 1, 2003.

146 **"Harming Patient Access . . .":** Ibid.

146 **delivered to the House floor by:** Ibid.

146 **"I will have to stop . . .":** Ibid.

146 **his annual rate had gone:** Ibid.

146 **three years of criminal probation:** Ibid.

146 **Roberts did not mention:** Ibid.

147 **"This . . . is the equivalent of a convicted drunk . . .":** Scott Finn, "Malpractice Speaker Left Out Drug Record," *Charleston Gazette,* Jan. 3, 2003.

147 **Eighteen doctors:** Ibid.

147 **Dr. Zaleski's photo:** Mencimer, "Malpractice Makes Perfect."

147 **"on the brink":** *Connie Chung Tonight,* interview with Dr. Robert Zaleski, CNN, Jan. 2, 2003.

147 **a personal invitation to attend:** Mencimer, "Malpractice Makes Perfect."

147 **he was addicted to:** Ibid.

147 **cited court documents:** Ibid.

147 **sued fourteen times:** Ibid.

147 **West Virginia Board of Medicine:** Ibid.

147 **a surgeon who had cut:** Ibid.

148 **left a clamp:** Ibid.

148 **more than $6 million:** Ibid.

148 **Two dozen surgeons in four hospitals:** Gavin McCormick, "West Virginia Surgeons Leave Jobs in Protest," *Pittsburgh Post-Gazette,* Jan. 2, 2003.

148 **Practice areas are banded together:** Interview with Lipsen.

148 **"If I sideswipe another . . .":** Ibid.

148 **According to the General Accounting:** Mencimer, "Malpractice Makes Perfect."

148 **"Some reports of physicians . . .":** Ibid.

148 **"Many of the provider actions . . .":** Ibid.

149 **National Practitioner Data Bank:** Sidney Wolfe, M.D., "A Free Ride for Bad Doctors," *New York Times,* Op-ed, Mar. 3, 2003.

149 **accounted for 54 percent:** Ibid.

149 **more than 60 percent:** Andrew Jacobs, "Behind Walkout by Doctors, Chronic War with Lawyers," *New York Times,* Feb. 3, 2003.

149 **thirty-five thousand doctors with two:** Wolfe, "Free Ride for Bad Doctors."

149 **"Amid the uproar . . .":** Ibid.

149 **passed the Medical Injury Compensation:** "How Insurance Reform Lowered Doctors' Medical Malpractice Rates and How Malpractice Caps Failed," Foundation for Taxpayer and Consumer Rights, Mar. 7, 2003.

149 **Over the next twelve years:** Ibid.

149 **of Proposition 103:** Ibid.

150 **In the twenty-five states:** Jacobs, "Behind Walkout by Doctors."

150 **National Association of Insurance Commissioners:** Ibid.

150 **"Falling Claims and Rising Premiums . . .":** Jay Angoff, "Falling Claims and Rising Premiums in the Medical Malpractice Industry," Center for Justice and Democracy, July 7, 2005.

150 **remained flat from 2000:** Ibid.

150 **"the increase in the premiums . . .":** Ibid.

151 **HCI is reported to:** Ibid.

151 **"Doctors and consumers deserve . . .":** "New Study on Rising Insurance Rates and Dropping Claims Leads Attorney General to Proclaim, 'No Excuse' and 'A Matter of Life and Death,' " Center for Justice and Democracy news release, July 7, 2005.

151 **defensive medicine costs were "negligible":** "Defensive Medicine and Medical Malpractice," Congressional Office of Technology Assessment, H-602, 1994.

151 **"there is some coordination":** Mencimer, "Malpractice Makes Perfect."

151 **the West Virginia Care Coalition:** Ibid.

152 **gave the coalition $200,000:** Ibid.

152 **More money came from:** Ibid.

152 **A computer analysis by:** Ibid.

152 **verdicts against doctors:** Ibid.

152 **More than 80 percent of all litigation:** Interview with Lipsen.

152 **"It's ridiculous . . .":** Ibid.

153 **"I don't care what you call . . .":** Interview with Carl.

153 **"Don't talk about . . ."** Neal Cohen, Public Affairs Council Speech, Feb. 1994.

154 **"You ask people if they want to . . .":** Interview with Ed Lazarus, Mar. 2, 2005.

154 **A busy trauma center:** Joelle Babula, "Trauma Center: Facility at UMC Set to Close," *Las Vegas Review Journal,* July 3, 2002.

11: IT'S HARD WORK

155 **took over the project:** Michael King, "Battle on Town Lake," *Austin Chronicle,* Mar. 6, 2002.

155 **fired Guy's:** Ibid.

155 **all of Guy's union:** Ibid.

155 **had been trying to unionize:** Carl F. Horowitz, "Toxic Grains: Inside Organized Labor's Salting Campaign," National Institute for Labor Relations Research, Oct. 2004.

156 **IBEW accused:** King, "Battle on Town Lake."

156 **"This here's a union job . . .":** "Testimony of Ty and Shelly Runyan," Committee on Education and the Workforce hearings, May 10, 2004.

156 **"Hey, . . . one of our people arrested . . .":** King, "Battle on Town Lake."

156 **filed criminal trespass:** "Statement of David Van Os, Esq.," Committee on Education and the Workforce hearings, May 10, 2004.

156 **self-made millionaire:** "Testimony of Ty and Shelly Runyan."

156 **half-Hispanic minority:** Ibid.

156 **"great lawyers":** Interview with Ty Runyan, Jan. 14, 2005.

156 **"This union mentality . . .":** Ibid.

157 **illegal for employers to exclude:** "Statement of David Van Os, Esq."

157 **protection to the "salts":** Horowitz, "Toxic Grains."

157 **the company hired 48:** "Testimony of Ty and Shelly Runyan."

157 **back of a 1971 Dodge:** Ibid.

157 **"We have had a death threat . . .":** Ibid.

157 **Local 520 filed:** Interview with Runyan.

157 **workers . . . were videotaped:** General Counsel Barry J. Kearney, "Advice Memorandum," National Labor Relations Board, Apr. 29, 2003.

157 **refused employment for being:** Ibid.

157 **"These guys gloated . . .":** Interview with Runyan.

158 **ruled in favor of:** Kearney, "Advice Memorandum."

158 **"government agency . . . ostensibly an independent . . .":** "Testimony of Ty and Shelly Runyan."

158 **who he knew were union members:** Pargen Robertson, administrative law judge, "United States of America before the National Labor Relations Board Division of Judges," Jan. 17, 2003.

158 **settled out of court:** "Statement of David Van Os, Esq."

158 **Hispanic Businessman of the Year:** David Whitford, "Minority Entrepreneurs: New Voices," *Fortune,* Dec. 26, 2003.

158 **"We were attacked . . .":** Interview with Runyan.

158 **minority set-asides create:** Whitford, "Minority Entrepreneurs."

158 **"We look at the certification . . .":** Ibid.

159 **representative of the Republican Party:** Interview with Runyan.

159 **"I was talking with . . .":** Ibid.

159 **"I said I might be interested, and . . . I wrote a check . . .":** Ibid.

159 **"Now, having spent a half a million dollars . . .":** Ibid.

159 **unions had spent about $200 million:** Interview with David Swanson, Feb. 18, 2005.

160 **"We assume you've consulted . . .":** Interview with Jon Hiatt, Sept. 9, 2005.

160 **"I assume you've done your homework . . .":** Ibid.

160 **"I know you guys aren't happy . . .":** Ibid.

160 **"He was wearing his DOL hat . . .":** Ibid.

161 **"For years, . . . unions have created trusts . . .":** Mark Tapscott, "Transparency: Bad News for Big Labor?" *Capitalism Magazine,* Aug. 6, 2005.

161 **"This was done purely to harass us . . .":** Interview with Hiatt.

162 **Gingrich sent a memo:** Memo from Newt Gingrich to Lynn Martin, Congress of the United States, author's copy, Feb. 19, 1992.

162 **delayed implementation:** Interview with Hiatt.

162 **Every receipt of each expense:** Anita Gallagher, "White House Hand Is behind Labor's Troubles," *Executive Intelligence Review,* Aug. 26, 2005.

162 **". . . do that for employers, too . . .":** Interview with Hiatt.

162 **advocacy of specific candidates:** "Labor HHS Subcommittee Hearing: Statement of Jonathan Hiatt," United States Senate Committee on Appropriations, July 31, 2003.

162 **more than five thousand unions:** Gallagher, "White House Hand Is behind Labor's Troubles."

163 **Gordon S. Heddell accused:** Steven Greenhouse, "Labor Dept. Is Rebuked over Pact with Wal-Mart," *New York Times,* Nov. 1, 2005.

163 **"jointly develop news releases":** Ibid.

163 **people enforcing laws:** David Moberg, "Under the Microscope," *In These Times,* Mar. 8, 2005.

163 **A 15 percent budget increase:** Ibid.

164 **forty of those new bureaucrats:** Ibid.

164 **in their offices "for months":** Interview with Hiatt.

164 **"There's been a strategy . . .":** Moberg, "Under the Microscope."

164 **"My God, Karl Rove is all over this . . .":** Interview with John Ryan, July 1, 2005.

165 **"We have some concerns . . .":** Chairman Battista and members Walsh and Meisberg, "Shaw's Supermarkets and United Food and Commercial Workers' Union

Local 791, AFL-CIO, Case 1-RM-1267," National Labor Relations Board, Dec. 8, 2004.

165 **"The current board . . .":** Jonathan P. Hiatt and Craig Becker, "The Bush National Labor Relations Board and the Attack on Employee Rights," congressional testimony, Sept. 13, 2004.

165 **"It's kind of funny . . .":** Interview with Per Bernstein, Mar. 1, 2005.

165 **"The four executive orders . . .":** "Bush Issues Four New Executive Orders," *Braun Consulting News* 6, no. 1 (Spring 2001).

165 **"employees cannot be required . . .":** "Notification of Employee Rights Concerning Payment of Union Dues or Fees," *Federal Register*, Feb. 22, 2001.

166 **"collective bargaining, contract administration . . .":** Ibid.

166 **The council had required managers:** Kellie Lunney, "Bush Dissolves Labor-Management Partnership Council," GovExec.com, Daily Briefing, Feb. 19, 2001.

166 **"Bush was so intent . . .":** "American Federation of Government Employees," Joe Henderson's blog, undated.

166 **Under the Clinton regulation:** "Revocation of Executive Order on Nondisplacement of Qualified Workers under Certain Contracts," *Federal Register*, Feb. 22, 2001.

166 **also overturned a Clinton order:** "Preservation of Open Competition and Government Neutrality towards Government Contractors' Labor Relations on Federal and Federally Funded Construction Projects," *Federal Register*, Feb. 22, 2001.

167 **Chao met with:** Mark Gaffney, "The Election's Deleterious Effect on Labor," speech, Jan. 2001.

167 **"We want to work with you . . .":** Ibid.

167 **She brought with her a book:** Interview with Bernstein.

167 **"It was real insulting . . .":** Ibid.

167 **McCutcheon reached out:** Interview with Hiatt.

167 **Hiatt offered to arrange:** Ibid.

167 **"I told her . . .":** Ibid.

168 **"This is what I was told to do":** Ibid.

168 **More than 90 percent:** Harold Meyerson, "Labor's Civil War," American Prospect Online, May 25, 2005.

168 **"It's a cause for considerable worry . . .":** Interview with John Judis, Mar. 25, 2005.

168 **estimated 6 million doors:** Chip Reid, "Democrats Worry about Rift in Big Labor," MSNBC News, July 25, 2005.

169 **AFL-CIO broke apart:** "Teamsters, SEIU Split from AFL-CIO," Associated Press, July 25, 2005.

169 **They were joined by:** Ibid.

169 **"Things are grim . . .":** Interview with Swanson.

169 **exempt tens of millions:** "Department of Labor Rule Change Undermines Overtime Pay Protections," National Organization for Women (website), June 12, 2003.

169 **graduate students were not:** "Bush's Labor Board Denies Graduate Students Rights of Workers," AFL-CIO (website), July 5, 2005.

169 **A group of disabled janitors:** Chairman Battista and members Liebman, Schaumber, Walsh, and Meisburg, "Brevard Achievement Center, Inc. and Transport Workers Union of America, Local 525, AFL-CIO, Case 12-RC-8515," National Labor Relations Board, Sept. 10, 2004.

170 **The White House attempted:** Cynthia Green, "Bush on Labor: Worse Than Ronald Reagan," AFL-CIO (website), Mar. 27, 2003.

170 **has also used executive authority:** Ibid.

170 **"I'll be honest with you . . .":** Interview with Ryan.

171 **"The NLRB had been . . .":** Interview with Runyan.

171 **"We have tickets . . .":** Ibid.

12: A GREAT GRIEVANCE

173 **jumped aboard Air Force One:** "Bush Presses for Caps on Malpractice Awards," Associated Press, Jan. 5, 2005.

173 **had dubbed Collinsville:** Ibid.

174 **President Bush met with:** Ibid.

174 **Illinois trial lawyers:** Ibid.

174 **Congressional democrats insisted:** Ibid.

174 **lawyers spent $250,000:** Ibid.

174 **"It wasn't lawyers who switched . . .":** Transcript of Linda McDougal commercial, Association of American Trial Lawyers document, author's copy.

174 **a few thirty-second runs:** Interview with Ken Vest, ATLA communications consultant, Mar. 2, 2005.

174 **"We don't want to have to see pregnant mothers . . .":** "Bush Presses for Caps on Malpractice Awards."

175 **"Medical malpractice?"** Interview with Linda Lipsen, Mar. 2, 2005.

175 **president signed the class-action:** John F. Harris and William Branigin, "Bush Signs Class-Action Changes into Law," *Washington Post,* Feb. 18, 2005.

175 **"malpractice suits are driving really fine . . .":** Ibid.

175 **costing the economy $250 billion:** Ibid.

175 **they'd considered $8 million:** Interview with Vest, Mar. 2, 2005.

176 **American voters believed:** "Attitudes toward Trial Lawyers and the Civil Justice System," Peter D. Hart Research Associates, May 14, 2005.

176 **"persistent attacks by opponents . . .":** Ibid.

176 **broadcast another medical mistake:** Interview with Carlton Carl, ATLA communications executive, Mar. 2, 2005.

176 **aired in a rotation right up:** Interview with Vest, Mar. 2, 2005.

176 **mother, Christine, was pregnant:** Background briefing document provided by ATLA, Mar. 2, 2005.

176 **He lived four years:** Interview with Ken Vest, Nov. 16, 2005.

176 **family won $4 million:** Ibid.

176 **decided to spend:** Ibid.

176 **for unspecified reasons:** Ibid.

176 **to confront doctors:** Interview with Lipsen.

176 **airing the Dylan Malone ad:** Interview with Vest, Nov. 16, 2005.

176 **hotel's management refused:** Ibid.

177 **A larger coalition of organizations:** "A Message to Members of the American Medical Association," newspaper print ad, *USA Today,* Mar. 14, 2005.

177 **a couple of trucks:** Interview with Vest, Nov. 16, 2005.

177 **victims of medical errors:** Ibid.

177 **whose heart was damaged:** ATLA documents for Mar. 2005 news conference at Mayflower Hotel, authors' copies.

177 **debilitating heart attack:** Ibid.

177 **spent close to $400,000:** Interview with Vest, Nov. 16, 2005.

177 **strictly local coverage:** Ibid.

177 **"It's pretty simple . . .":** Interview with ATLA official.

178 **After bringing aboard:** Interview with Vest, Nov. 16, 2005.

178 **Mather set up a "war room":** Author visit to ATLA headquarters, Georgetown.

178 **"Real Legal Reform":** ATLA draft document on reform strategy, authors' copy.

178 **"In addition to protecting the legal rights of American families . . .":** Ibid.

178 **"identify for consumers . . .":** Ibid.

179 **"The tipping point . . .":** Interview with Lipsen.

179 **tobacco companies agreed to pay:** "Texas Reaches $15.3 Billion Settlement with Tobacco Industry," CNN, Jan. 16, 1998.

179 **"We had to . . .":** Interview with Ralph Wayne, Oct. 7, 2005.

180 **The beginning:** Ibid.

181 **One of Rove's:** Interview with Karl Rove, Mar. 29, 1996.

181 **In Washington:** Multinational Monitor (website), Mar. 2003.

181 **A tobacco industry:** Ibid.

181 **Rove agreed:** Interview with Jon Opelt, July 5, 2005.

182 **"Is this going . . .":** Ibid.

182 **"I sort of . . .":** Interview with Karl Rove, Aug. 17, 2002.

182 **appropriate $7.1 billion:** Diedtra Henderson, "Bush Flu Plan Eases Firms' Liability," *Boston Globe,* Nov. 8, 2005.

183 **"What I've seen with liability . . .":** Ibid.

183 **the hypocrisies and contradictions:** Interview with George Parker Young, Nov. 8, 2005.

183 **raise money to help George W.:** Ibid.

183 **"I was very disappointed . . .":** Ibid.

184 **Ruby Calad and Juan Davila:** Charles Lane, "A Flip-Flop on Patients' Right to Sue?" *Washington Post,* Apr. 5, 2004.

184 **the ERISA statute:** Ibid.

184 **medicine by sending her home:** David Savage, "Patients' Right to Sue HMOs before High Court," *Los Angeles Times,* Mar. 24, 2004.

184 **had been given a generic drug:** Ibid.

184 **Bush's solicitor general:** Department of Justice website, Theodore B. Olson biography page.

184 **one of the country's most powerful:** Judy Sarasohn, "Olson to Return to Gibson, Dunn," *Washington Post,* July 8, 2004.

185 **his former law firm:** Savage, "Patients' Right to Sue HMOs."

185 **"They're not managing care . . .":** M. Gregg Bloche, "Bush Turns His Back on Fight for Patients' Rights," *Los Angeles Times,* Mar. 21, 2004.

185 **Aetna and CIGNA prevailed:** Ibid.

185 **"correctly concluded . . .":** Michael Graczyk, "Court Rules for HMOs in Patient Lawsuits," Associated Press, June 22, 2004.

185 **"The big story is . . .":** Lane, "Flip-Flop on Patients' Right to Sue?"

186 **"continued to support . . .":** Ibid.

186 **"This decision takes away . . .":** "American Families Lose to HMOs in U.S. Supreme Court," ATLA statement from David Casey, June 23, 2004.

186 **in September of 2003:** Allison Wollam, "Medical Insurance Rates Roll Back," *Houston Business Journal,* Oct. 2003.

186 **"They pretty much did away with . . .":** Interview with Young.

186 **"a regulatory vacuum exists":** Lane, "Flip-Flop on Patients' Right to Sue?"
186 **"very real problem of HMO accountability":** Statement from law offices of George Parker Young, June 21, 2004.

13: ROVE'S BRAIN

187 **It was early December:** Joshua Marshall, Laura Rozen, and Paul Glastris, "Iran-Contra II: Fresh Scrutiny on a Rogue Pentagon Operation," *Washington Monthly*, Sept. 2004.
187 **three representatives of the U.S.:** Ibid.
187 **arranged by Michael Ledeen:** Ibid.
187 **"creative destruction":** John Laughland, "Flirting with Fascism," *American Conservative*, June 30, 2003.
187 **consultant for Douglas Feith:** William O. Beeman, "Who Is Michael Ledeen?" Pacific News Service, May 8, 2003.
187 **had accompanied Ledeen:** Marshall, Rozen, and Glastris, "Iran-Contra II."
187 **considered himself a protégé:** Knut Royce and Timothy M. Phelps, "Secret Talks with Iranian Arms Dealer," *Newsday*, Aug. 8, 2003.
187 **Assigned to the Pentagon's:** Jeffrey Goldberg, "Real Insiders," *New Yorker*, June 27, 2005.
188 **consternation of civilian advisers:** Robert Dreyfuss and Jason Vest, "The Lie Factory," *Mother Jones*, Feb. 2004.
188 **Rhode is fluent:** Ibid.
188 **"no bartering in the bazaar . . .":** Ibid.
188 **clear out nonbelievers:** Interview with Karen Kwiatkowski, Nov. 29, 2005.
188 **"were mostly from . . . and pro-Likud operations":** Ibid.
188 **"handler" of Ahmad Chalabi:** Richard Sale, "FBI Probes DOD Office," United Press International, Aug. 28, 2004.
188 **almost lived out of:** Ibid.
188 **"mind-boggling":** Ibid.
188 **security clearances had been suspended:** Ibid.
188 **a "regular bureaucrat":** Interview with Kwiatkowski.
188 **busily generated the information:** Ibid.
188 **"Those who speak . . .":** Dreyfuss and Vest, "Lie Factory."
188 **"James Bond":** Interview with Kwiatkowski.
188 **an Iran specialist:** Justin Raimondo, "The State of State Secrets," *American Conservative*, June 20, 2005.
188 **A close friend of:** Michael Ledeen, "An Improbable Molehunt," National Review Online, Aug. 31, 2004.
188 **well connected with . . . (AIPAC):** Raimondo, "State of State Secrets."
189 **all reported to Douglas:** Brian Bennett, Elaine Shannon, and Adam Zagorin, "A Web of Intrigue," *Time*, Sept. 13, 2004.
189 **also a hard-liner:** Stephen Green, "Serving Two Flags," *CounterPunch*, Feb. 28, 2004.
189 **conservative policy wonks of:** Ibid.
189 **every international peace treaty:** Ibid.
189 **At the direction of:** Jim Lobe, "Pentagon Office Home to Neo-con Network," Inter Press Service, Aug. 7, 2003.
189 **Office of Special Plans (OSP):** Ibid.
189 **Shulsky had been working:** Green, "Serving Two Flags."

189 **overseen by William Luti:** Ibid.

189 **Luti managed:** Ibid.

189 **as a Feith consultant:** Jim Lobe, "Veteran Neo-con Advisor Moves on Iran," Asia Times–Inter Press Service, 2003.

189 **overthrowing Arab regimes:** Laughland, "Flirting with Fascism."

189 **makes Bush a great president:** Michael Ledeen, "Iran-Contra Revisited?" National Review Online, Aug. 14, 2003.

190 **"Faster, please":** Ibid.

190 **already evident twenty-four minutes:** Entry on Free Republic (website) chat room by Ledeen, Sept. 11, 2001.

190 **arranged for his Pentagon colleagues:** Marshall, Rozen, and Glastris, "Iran-Contra II."

190 **acted as a double agent:** Lawrence E. Walsh, independent counsel, "Final Report of the Independent Counsel for Iran-Contra Matters," Aug. 4, 1993.

190 **reported that Nicolo:** Marshall, Rozen, and Glastris, "Iran-Contra II."

190 **a former member of:** Ibid.

190 **"We need to sustain . . .":** Michael Ledeen, "How to Lose It," National Review Online, Dec. 7, 2001.

190 **"Rove's brain":** Clayton Hallmark, "Indictments: Karl Rove's and Others' May Expose War's Fake Causes," *Oklahoma Independent Media Center,* Oct. 24, 2005.

191 **"one of the most honest . . .":** Jim Lobe, "Veteran Neo-con Advisor Moves on Iran," *Asia Times,* June 26, 2003.

191 **been unable to pass:** James Risen, "How a Shady Iranian Kept the Pentagon's Ear," *New York Times,* Dec. 7, 2003.

191 **"burn notice":** Marshall, Rozen, and Glastris, "Iran-Contra II."

191 **Ledeen wrote back:** Author's e-mail exchange with Michael Ledeen, Dec. 1, 2005.

191 **"fool's gold":** Ibid.

191 **"midlevel Iran experts . . .":** Ledeen, "Iran-Contra Revisited?"

192 **the Pentagon had not notified:** Marshall, Rozen, and Glastris, "Iran-Contra II."

192 **"I'm not going to comment . . .":** Knut Royce and Timothy M. Phelps, "Secret Talks with Iranian Arms Dealer," *Newsday,* Aug. 8, 2003.

192 **managing to promote his new book:** Ledeen, "Iran-Contra Revisited?"

192 **"ask our diplomats . . .":** Ibid.

192 **the CIA was reported to have just received:** Laura Rozen, "*La Repubblica*'s Scoop Confirmed," *American Prospect,* Oct. 25, 2005.

192 **also shared with France:** Carlo Bonini and Giuseppe D'Avanzo, "Berlusconi behind Fake Yellowcake Dossier," *La Repubblica,* Oct. 25, 2005.

192 **considered the intelligence unreliable:** Ibid.

192 **rolled it into a dossier:** "The Iraq Dossier," Ray Suarez interviews David Allbright, *Newshour,* PBS-TV, Sept. 24, 2002.

193 **ordered them to stop:** Marshall, Rozen, and Glastris, "Iran-Contra II."

193 **informed the U.S. embassy:** Ibid.

193 **Repeated warnings:** Ibid.

194 **Private White House dinners:** Interview with Jewish Bush supporter, Apr. 2005.

194 **most influential of the Bush choices:** Green, "Serving Two Flags."

194 **with his wife, Meyrav:** Dreyfuss and Vest, "Lie Factory."

194 **"A Clean Break . . .":** Ibid.

195 **Wolfowitz was once investigated:** Green, "Serving Two Flags."

195 **related to the sale of U.S. arms:** Ibid.

195 **pushed for the export:** Ibid.

195 **belief in "technological cooperation":** Ibid.

195 **picked up on an FBI wiretap:** Ian Masters interviews Philip Giraldi, KPFK-FM radio, University of California at Riverside, Dec. 18, 2005.

195 **leaking of a classified CIA:** Ibid.

195 **"Nearly every one of the people . . .":** Ibid.

195 **A founding member of the board:** Tom Barry, "Is Iran Next?" *In These Times,* Sept. 28, 2004.

195 **"an agent of influence . . .":** Edward Herman and Gerry O'Sullivan, *The Terrorism Industry* (Pantheon, 1990), 161.

195 **Ledeen was working out of:** Interview with Kwiatkowski.

195 **"Anytime you have a good idea . . .":** Thomas B. Edsall and Dana Milbank, "White House's Roving Eye for Politics; President's Most Powerful Adviser May Also Be the Most Connected," *Washington Post,* Mar. 10, 2003.

195 **he faxes Rove every:** Ibid.

195 **either policy or rhetoric:** Ibid.

196 **suggested in his 1972:** Laughland, "Flirting with Fascism."

196 **charges of plagiarism:** Sidney Blumenthal, "Journal in Turmoil," *Washington Post,* Feb. 16, 1987.

196 **"Any suggestion that my scholarship . . .":** Charles R. Babcock, "Ledeen Seems to Relish Iran Insider's Role," *Washington Post,* Feb. 2, 1987.

196 **"He seemed . . . the work of somebody else":** Ibid.

196 **"breaking the law . . .":** Michael Ledeen, *Universal Fascism: The Theory and Practice of the Fascist International, 1928–1936* (H. Fertig, 1972).

196 **"enter into evil . . .":** Michael Ledeen, *Machiavelli on Modern Leadership: Why Machiavelli's Iron Rules Are as Timely and Important Today as Five Centuries Ago* (St. Martin's Press, 1999).

196 **changes in legal restrictions:** Michael Ledeen, "Intelligence? What Intelligence?" *National Review,* Sept. 20, 2002.

196 **documents from the 1980 trial:** Herman and O'Sullivan, *Terrorism Industry,* 161.

196 **Pazienza was convicted:** Ibid.

197 **Ledeen was paid $120,000:** Jonathan Kwitny, "Tale of Intrigue: Why an Italian Spy Got Closely Involved in the Billygate Affair," *Wall Street Journal,* Aug. 8, 1985.

197 **used the code name:** Ibid.

197 **consulting firm ISI:** Ibid.

197 **"may well have been . . . I can't remember":** Ibid.

197 **"I had . . . personal account in Bermuda":** Ibid.

197 **"risk assessment":** Ibid.

197 **"I've said to every journalist . . .":** Babcock, "Ledeen Seems to Relish Iran Insider's Role."

198 **in almost total control of P2:** Blumenthal, "Journal in Turmoil."

198 **bombing of the Bologna:** Ibid.

198 **authorized by Henry Kissinger:** Barbara Honneger, *The October Surprise* (Tudor Books, May 1989).

198 **identified in . . . Pazienza's:** Blumenthal, "Journal in Turmoil."

198 **"a well-known American Italianist":** Ibid.

198 **worked "in collaboration":** Ibid.

198 **"succeeded in extorting . . . published—in the international press . . .":** Ibid.

198 **was gathered by the P2-controlled:** Ibid.

198 **Ledeen's coauthor:** Ibid.

198 **was an "intriguer":** Herman and O'Sullivan, *Terrorism Industry,* 161.

198 **"transparent crap":** Ibid.

199 **for the United States in 1983:** Green, "Serving Two Flags."

199 **Koch learned:** Ibid.

199 **"agent of influence . . .":** Ibid.

199 **Exhibiting a habit:** Ibid.

199 **alphanumeric designators:** Ibid.

199 **"just ceased coming to work":** Ibid.

199 **supervisor was marine colonel:** Ibid.

199 **"Israeli contacts might be . . .":** "Senate/House Iran-Contra Investigative Committee Report; Chronology of Events: U.S.-Iran Dialogue," Nov. 18, 1986.

199 **role to that of messenger:** Green, "Serving Two Flags."

199 **downgraded his security clearance:** Ibid.

199 **"periodic polygraph examinations":** Ibid.

199 **suspected that Ledeen and operative:** Ibid.

200 **Clarridge had been intimately involved:** "Iran-Contra Final Report," *United States v. Duane R. Clarridge,* Aug. 4, 1993.

200 **and close associate of Ahmad:** Ken Silverstein, "Former CIA Agent Looks for Financial Links to Hussein," *Los Angeles Times,* June 26, 2004.

200 **close enough as friends:** "The War against the Terror Masters: How We Got There, Where We Are Now, How We'll Win," American Enterprise Institute (website), event announcement, Sept. 10, 2002.

200 **"The connection to all of these people . . .":** Interview with Philip Giraldi, Dec. 12, 2005.

200 **on New Year's Day 2001:** Marshall, Rozen, and Glastris, "Iran-Contra II; Bonini and D'Avanzo, "Berlusconi behind Fake Yellowcake Dossier."

200 **"République du Niger":** Barton Gellman, "A Leak, Then a Deluge," *Washington Post,* Oct. 30, 2005.

200 **based on the forged documents:** Rozen, "*La Repubblica*'s Scoop Confirmed."

200 **has denied any involvement:** Landay, "Italy Provided U.S. with Faulty Uranium Intelligence."

200 **the prime minister was anxious:** Bonini and D'Avanzo, "Berlusconi behind Fake Yellowcake Dossier."

200 **delivered to MI6:** Jonathan S. Landay and Warren P. Strobel, "Indictment Doesn't Clear Up Mystery at Heart of the CIA Leak Probe," Knight Ridder Newspapers, Oct. 31, 2005.

201 **Giraldi believes it is possible Michael Ledeen:** Interview with Giraldi.

201 **"Ledeen goes way back . . . up to their eyeballs in this":** Ibid.

201 **dismissed within a few days:** "Report on the U.S. Intelligence Community Prewar Intelligence Assessments on Iraq," Select Committee on Intelligence, United States Senate, Section II, "Niger Reporting," July 7, 2004.

201 **"lacking in detail":** Ibid.

201 **The central criticism:** Ibid.

201 **one of the two mines . . . was flooded:** Ibid.

201 **large stock of uranium oxide:** Ibid.

201 **such a deal was "possible":** Ibid.

201 **The French and the Germans:** Bonini and D'Avanzo, "Berlusconi behind Fake Yellowcake Dossier."

201 **informed either the CIA station chief:** Marshall, Rozen, and Glastris, "Iran-Contra II."

201 **Mel Sembler, an old:** Ibid.

201 **only a consultant:** Green, "Serving Two Flags."

202 **was sufficiently embarrassed:** Marshall, Rozen, and Glastris, "Iran-Contra II."

202 **sent another report to Washington:** Landay and Strobel, "Indictment Doesn't Clear Up Mystery."

202 **describes as "embellishments":** Interview with Giraldi.

202 **the verbatim text:** "Report on the U.S. Intelligence Community Prewar Intelligence Assessments on Iraq."

202 **"Iraq is probably . . .":** Ibid.

202 **given the DIA's report:** Landay and Strobel, "Indictment Doesn't Clear Up Mystery."

202 **Both agencies had been made aware:** Gellman, "A Leak, Then a Deluge."

202 **"[My wife] was in no way political . . .":** Interview with Joseph Wilson, Oct. 2003.

202 **expressed concern to NSC:** Marshall, Rozen, and Glastris, "Iran-Contra II."

202 **Tenet spoke directly:** Ibid.

202 **Hadley called DOD:** Ibid.

203 **informed the U.S. ambassador:** Ibid.

203 **transfer or fire employees:** Interview with Kwiatkowski.

203 **"They wanted nothing to do with the professional staff . . .":** Green, "Serving Two Flags."

203 **was David Wurmser:** Dreyfuss and Vest, "Lie Factory."

203 **"Iraq Needs a Revolution":** Ibid.

203 **cosigned a letter:** Ibid.

203 **"Securing the Realm":** Ibid.

203 **The purpose of the intelligence operation:** David Morgan, "Pengtagon Agrees to Probe Feith's Role in Iraq Intel," Reuters, Nov. 17, 2005.

203 **"In 1998, we went . . .":** Dreyfuss and Vest, "Lie Factory."

204 **a former navy aviator:** Ibid.

204 **"makes Ollie North look like a moderate":** Ibid.

204 **where she closely observed:** Interview with Kwiatkowski.

204 **Luti was a direct conduit:** Ibid.

204 **"Luti was permanently locked into . . .":** Ibid.

204 **"Yes, they were cherry-picking . . .":** Ibid.

205 **"I had never heard of Scooter . . .":** Ibid.

205 **briefed two CIA officers:** Interview with Wilson.

205 **given a grade of "good":** "Report on the U.S. Intelligence Community Prewar Intelligence Assessments on Iraq."

205 **lost in the "bowels":** Frank Rich, "Follow the Uranium," *New York Times,* July 17, 2005.

205 **exchanged a number of faxes:** Marshall, Rozen, and Glastris, "Iran-Contra II."

205 **an unnamed "high-level":** Ibid.

205 **again not informed:** Ibid.

206 **working with the Iranians:** Ibid.

206 **Ledeen unmistakable instructions:** Ibid.

206 **a "courtesy call":** "Press Briefing with National Security Advisor Stephen Hadley," transcript at WhiteHouse.gov, Nov. 2, 2005.

206 **owned by Italian prime minister:** Carlo Bonini and Giuseppe D'Avanzo, "Yellow-cake Dossier Not the Work of the CIA," *La Repubblica,* Oct. 25, 2005.

206 **a disgraced former SISMI:** Ibid.

206 **possession of stolen checks:** "Key Judgments from National Intelligence Estimate," Iraq's Continuing Programs for Weapons of Mass Destruction, White House background briefing, July 18, 2003.

206 **receiving a stipend:** Ibid.

206 **Although Burba trusted Martino:** Bonini and D'Avanzo, "Yellowcake Dossier Not the Work of the CIA."

206 **the file to the U.S. embassy:** Ibid.

206 **appeared to be "expected":** Philip Giraldi, "Forging the Case for War," *The American Conservative,* Nov. 21, 2005.

207 **"saw that they were fakes":** Gellman, "A Leak, Then a Deluge."

207 **for exactly a month:** Bonini and D'Avanzo, "Yellowcake Dossier Not the Work of the CIA."

207 **landed quickly . . . in the U.S.:** "Report on the U.S. Intelligence Community Prewar Intelligence Assessments on Iraq."

207 **"funky Emb. of Niger . . .":** Landay and Strobel, "Indictment Doesn't Clear Up Mystery."

207 **"is intelligence that Iraq has sought . . .":** "Iraq Dossier," Suarez interviews Allbright.

207 **"A foreign government service . . .":** "Key Judgments from National Intelligence Estimate."

207 **The White House Iraq Group:** Giraldi, "Forging the Case for War."

207 **"mushroom cloud":** Wolf Blitzer, "Search for the Smoking Gun," CNN, Jan. 10, 2003.

14: THE UNRAVELING

209 **Karl Rove stepped:** Interview with Marc Schwartz, June 10, 2005.

210 **Rove would help:** Ibid.

211 **"Four decades . . .":** Transcript of Karl Rove speech to the Conservative Political Action Conference, Feb. 17, 2005.

212 **"The whole approach . . .":** Interview with Walter Dean Burnham, Jan. 5, 2005.

212 **When Rove was:** Papers of Governor Bill Clements, Texas A&M University.

212 **"If Republicans keep . . .":** Quoted in Fred Barnes, "Realignment, Now More Than Ever," *Weekly Standard,* Nov. 22, 2004.

213 **Patrick Henry prepares:** Patrick Henry College website.

213 **Most are government:** Hanna Rosin, "God and Country," *New Yorker,* June 27, 2005.

213 **Among the school's:** David Kirkpatrick, "College for the Home-Schooled Is Shaping Leaders for the Right," *New York Times,* Mar. 8, 2004.

214 **A Pew Research:** "GOP Makes Gains among the Working Class," Pew Research Center for the People and the Press, Aug. 2, 2005.

214 **"Look, the conservatives invested billions . . .":** Interview with Simon Rosenberg, Mar. 15, 2005.

215 **"If I were . . .":** Interview with the Reverend Richard Lee, Dec. 3, 2003.

216 **"Might something . . .":** Interview with Burnham.

217 **In a January 5 White House memo:** Peter Wehner, White House director of strategic initiatives, "Memo on Social Security," Jan. 5, 2005.

217 **target key constituencies:** Brendan Murray, "Rove Uses Campaign Playbook to Mastermind Social Security Fight," *Bloomberg News,* Mar. 3, 2005.

217 **Progress for America:** Mark Silva, "Business, RNC Lend Hand to Bush Blitz," *Chicago Tribune,* Mar. 14, 2005.

217 **In coordination with:** Thomas B. Edsall, "Conservatives Join Forces for Bush Plans," *Washington Post,* Feb. 13, 2005.

218 **"We are working . . .":** Silva, "Business, RNC Lend Hand."

218 **The real fireworks:** William M. Welch and Jim Drinkard, "USA Next Campaign Targets AARP," *USA Today,* Feb. 28, 2005.

218 **"They are the boulder . . .":** Glen Justice, "A New Battle for Advisers to Swift Vets," *New York Times,* Feb. 20, 2005.

219 **When Treasury Secretary:** Tom Hamburger, "Trade Groups Join Bush on Social Security," *Los Angeles Times,* Apr. 11, 2005.

219 **"I got the sense . . .":** Evan Thomas and Richard Wolffe, "Bush in the Bubble," *Newsweek,* Dec. 19, 2005.

219 **By fall:** Mary Dalrymple, "No Social Security Change until 2009," Associated Press, Nov. 9, 2005.

220 **Matthew Dowd . . . messaged:** Interview with Matthew Dowd, Oct. 11, 2004.

221 **Lawyers for:** Evan Thomas, "What Went Wrong," *Newsweek,* Sept. 12, 2005.

222 **"I'm outraged . . .":** Press conference with members of the Congressional Black Caucus, Sept. 2, 2005.

222 **Rove instructed:** Adam Nagourney and Anne E. Kornblut, "White House Enacts a Plan to Ease Political Damage," *New York Times,* Sept. 5, 2005.

222 **"The responsibility and power":** Transcript of *Meet the Press,* NBC News, Sept. 4, 2005.

222 **Reliable Rove ally:** Richard Wolffe, "Yet Another Gulf War," *Newsweek,* Sept. 12, 2005.

222 **On his cable:** Transcript of *O'Reilly Factor,* FOX News, Sept. 6, 2005.

223 **On his FOX:** Transcript of *Hannity & Colmes,* FOX News, Sept. 8, 2005.

223 **The talk:** Judy Keen and Richard Benedetto, "Under Fire, President Attempts to Gain Sense of Equilibrium," *USA Today,* Sept. 6, 2005.

224 **After winning:** 2004 presidential election exit polls, Roper Center.

224 **A year before:** William McKenzie, "White Evangelicals, Black Churches Could Reshape Politics," *Dallas Morning News,* Nov. 4, 2003.

225 **"The KKK was . . .":** Presentation by David Barton at Harvest Time Church, Houston, Tex., Mar. 11, 2003.

225 **Republican National Committee:** Michael Fletcher, "GOP Plans More Outreach to Blacks,"*Washington Post,* Aug. 7, 2005.

225 **Allbaugh had followed:** John Riley, "FEMA's Bumpy Bid Solicitation," *Newsday,* Sept. 22, 2005.

226 **"They've clearly lost . . .":** Interview with Don Sipple, Nov. 23, 2005.

226 **Once, while flying:** Author conversation with George W. Bush.

15: THE POWER EXCHANGE

229 **Lobbyist Michael Scanlon:** Scanlon e-mail to Kathryn Van Hoof, a former outside lawyer for the Coushatta tribe, U.S. Senate Committee on Indian Affairs.

229 **"She is from . . .":** Kimberly Hefling, "Specter Says Bush Getting Unfair Pummeling," Associated Press, Oct. 11, 2005.

229 **Hecht was a Republican:** Joyce Saenz Harris, "Dallas Native Picked for High Court Seat," *Dallas Morning News,* Oct. 4, 2005.

230 **After the contorted:** Joseph Curl, "Rove Played an Active Role in Selection of Miers," *Washington Times,* Oct. 6, 2005.

231 **In 1995, she wrote:** Miers's June 11, 1995, letter to Governor George W. Bush, Texas State Archives.

231 **On Monday morning:** Interview with Richard Land, Oct. 6, 2005.

231 **Later that day:** Steve Thomma and James Kuhnhenn, "Miers Denies Revealing *Roe vs. Wade* Opinion," Knight Ridder News Service, Oct. 18, 2005.

231 **"Karl Rove suggested . . .":** Ibid.

231 **According to notes:** John Fund, "Judgment Call," *Wall Street Journal,* Oct. 17, 2005.

232 **The conference call:** "Confirmation Process," *National Journal Hotline,* Oct. 4, 2005.

232 **"She was a . . .":** Interview with Miers associate in Texas, Oct. 10, 2005.

232 **"When you know . . .":** Mike Littwin, "Dobson Awaiting Final Word on Court Nominee," *Rocky Mountain News,* Oct. 6, 2005.

232 **"She's not what . . .":** Interview with Miers associate in Texas.

233 **Eventually, even Dobson:** "Reactions from Colorado Official on Harriet Miers' Withdrawal," Associated Press, Oct. 27, 2005.

233 **"They couldn't make . . .":** Interview with Christian religious leader, Oct. 27, 2005.

233 **To push her:** Joseph Curl, "Bush Taps Harriet Miers for Court," *Washington Times,* Oct. 4, 2005.

233 **"All I hear . . .":** Miers's Oct. 27, 1997, letter to Governor George W. Bush, Texas State Archives.

234 **There was talk:** Nancy Gibbs and Mike Allen, "A Time to Regroup," *Time,* Nov. 7, 2005.

235 **The former House:** R. G. Ratcliffe, "DeLay All Smiles for Photo at Booking," *Houston Chronicle,* Oct. 21, 2005.

235 **to get around:** Wayne Slater, "Two DeLay Associates Indicted in Misuse of Corporate Funds," *Dallas Morning News,* Sept. 14, 2005.

235 **As for the tradition:** Interviews with Texas legislative leaders, 2003.

236 **Democrats tried to stop:** Suzanne Gamboa, "FAA Spent 8 Hours Searching for Texas Legislators' Plane," Associated Press, July 11, 2003.

236 **After organizing college:** Susan Schmidt and James V. Grimaldi, "The Fast Rise and Steep Fall of Jack Abramoff," *Washington Post,* Dec. 29, 2005.

236 **"It is not . . .":** Thomas B. Edsall, "Abramoff Allies Keeping Distance," *Washington Post,* Nov. 8, 2004.

237 **Edwin Buckham:** Schmidt and Grimaldi, "Fast Rise and Steep Fall of Jack Abramoff."

237 **He'd been with Bush:** E-mail from Jack Abramoff to Kim Eisler, national editor, *Washingtonian,* Jan. 18, 2006.

237 **He earned:** Peter H. Stone, "K Street Stumble," *National Journal,* Mar. 27, 2004.

237 **The reception:** Sharon Theimer, "Controversial Lobbyist Had Close Contact with Bush Team," May 6, 2005.

237 **One day:** Interview with Marc Schwartz, June 10, 2005.

238 **Cornyn said he:** Michael Hedges, "Senate Panel Seeks Records," *Houston Chronicle,* Apr. 22, 2005.

238 **In November 2001:** Reed e-mail to Abramoff, U.S. Senate Committee of Indian Affairs, Nov. 30, 2001.

238 **Before . . . the casino:** Interview with Schwartz.

239 **"I'm on the phone . . .":** Reed e-mail to Abramoff, U.S. Senate Committee on Indian Affairs, Jan 6, 2002.

239 **"It has to do with . . .":** Interview with Schwartz.

239 **According to federal:** Federal Election Commission filings.

239 **In the brio:** Interview with Schwartz.

239 **news footage showed:** *World News Tonight,* ABC, Jan. 2, 2006.

240 **"If you want . . .":** David Maraniss and Michael Weisskopf, "Speaker and His Directors Make the Cash Flow Right," *Washington Post,* Nov. 27, 1995.

240 **"Any ideas . . .":** Abramoff e-mail to Ralph Reed, U.S. Senate Committee on Indian Affairs, Dec. 5, 2001.

240 **told *Time* magazine:** Adam Zagorin, "An Unholy Alliance," *Time,* Oct. 31, 2005.

240 **some "serious swat . . .":** Abramoff e-mail to Reed, Jan. 18, 2002.

240 **For several years:** Finlay Lewis, "CNS Suspends Bandow for Payments from Lobbyist for Favorable Columns," Copley News Service, Dec. 16, 2005.

241 **He also paid:** Eamon Javers, "Op-Eds for Sale," *Business Week,* Dec. 16, 2005.

241 **Abramoff was following:** Government Accountability Office report, Sept. 30, 2005.

241 **Rove's idea:** Interview with Schwartz.

241 **A rival lobbyist:** Schmidt and Grimaldi, "Fast Rise and Steep Fall of Jack Abramoff."

241 **Safavian had been:** Peter H. Stone, "Ensnared in the Abramoff Probes," *National Journal,* Nov. 12, 2005.

241 **Scanlon said he:** Toni Locy, "Lobbyists, Prosecutors Close to Deal," Associated Press, Dec. 31, 2005.

242 **DeLay had taken:** Steven Thomma and Alison Young, "Lobbyist's Guilty Plea Rocks DC," *Philadelphia Inquirer,* Jan. 4, 2006.

242 **In California:** Charles R. Babcock and Jonathan Weisman, "Congressman Admits Taking Bribes," *Washington Post,* Nov. 29, 2005.

242 **Frist maintained:** Jonathan M. Katz, "Probe into Frist Stock Sale Continues," Associated Press, Dec. 11, 2005.

243 **Governor Bob Taft:** Pete Slevin, "Ohio Scandals May Give Democrats a Life," *Washington Post,* Nov. 27, 2005.

243 **"When you win . . .":** Interview with Walter Dean Burnham, Jan. 5, 2005.

243 **McKinley, he said:** Interview with Karl Rove, March 1999.

16: TO COME UNDONE

245 **trying to make a buck:** Peter Wallsten, Tom Hamburger, and Josh Meyer, "FBI Is Taking Another Look at Forged Pre-War Intelligence," *Los Angeles Times,* Dec. 3, 2005.

245 **euros for his copies of documents:** Michael Smith, "The Spy Story That Has Enmeshed Bush," *Sunday Times of London,* Nov. 6, 2005.

245 **former agent of Italy's SISMI:** Tom Regan, "Italy Denies Faking Niger Documents," *Christian Science Monitor,* Nov. 4, 2005.

245 **turned the documents over:** Carlo Bonini and Giuseppe D'Avanzo, "Yellowcake Dossier Not the Work of CIA," *La Repubblica,* Oct. 25, 2005.

245 **owned by Italy's prime minister:** Seymour Hersh, "The Stovepipe," *New Yorker,* Oct. 27, 2003.

245 **Martino began to portray himself:** Wallsten, Hamburger, and Meyer, "FBI Is Taking Another Look."

245 **His version of events:** Nicholas Rufford, "Italian Spies Faked Documents on Saddam Nuclear Purchase," *Sunday Times of London,* Aug. 1, 2001.

245 **the explanation was:** Jonathan S. Landay, "Italy Provided U.S. with Faulty Uranium Intelligence, Officials Insist," Knight Ridder Newspapers, Nov. 4, 2004.

246 **"I received a call . . .":** Rufford, "Italian Spies Faked Documents."

246 **friendship with Antonio Nucera:** Carlo Bonini and Giuseppe D'Avanzo, "Berlusconi behind Fake Yellowcake Dossier," *La Repubblica,* Oct. 24, 2005.

246 **worked at the Niger embassy:** Ibid.

246 **keys to an apartment:** Interview with former CIA agent Philip Giraldi, Dec. 2, 2005.

246 **used to create the forgeries:** Bonini and D'Avanzo, "Berlusconi behind Fake Yellowcake Dossier."

246 **based on a 1999 trip:** Hersh, "Stovepipe."

246 **published in the Niamey paper:** Ibid.

246 **to take toxic waste:** Carlo Bonini and Giuseppe D'Avanzo, "Nigergate, French Spymaster Debunks SISMI Version," *La Repubblica,* Dec. 1, 2005.

246 **not held office since 1989:** Hersh, "Stovepipe."

246 **began to shop it around:** Bonini and D'Avanzo, "Berlusconi behind Fake Yellowcake Dossier."

246 **Nucera had helped him acquire:** Ibid.

246 **tossed them as obvious garbage:** Bonini and D'Avanzo, "Nigergate."

246 **into the hands of the British:** Smith, "Spy Story That Has Enmeshed Bush."

246 **"It's true . . . a disinformation operation":** "Italian Ex-Spy Discusses Own Role in Iraq-Niger Uranium Traffic Hoax," *Il Giornale,* Milan, Sept. 21, 2004.

247 **SISMI was also directly:** Interview with Vince Cannistraro et al., Dec. 13, 2005.

247 **station chief in Rome:** Bonini and D'Avanzo, "Yellowcake Dossier Not the Work of CIA."

247 **Pollari contact Michael Ledeen:** Ibid.

247 **Ledeen was in Rome:** Joshua Marshall, Laura Rozen, and Paul Glastris, "Iran-Contra II: Fresh Scrutiny on a Rogue Pentagon Operation," *Washington Monthly,* Sept. 2004.

247 **Martino also ended up:** Ibid.

247 **her editor . . . ordered her:** Hersh, "Stovepipe."

247 **was the U.S. ambassador to Italy:** William March, "Tampa Republican to Take Charge of Scooter Libby's Legal Defense Fund," *St. Petersberg Times,* Nov. 24, 2005.

247 **had not even been vetted:** Hersh, "Stovepipe."

247 **accounted for millions:** March, "Tampa Republican to Take Charge."

247 **close friend of Vice President:** Ibid.

248 **"I do believe there has been . . .":** Interview with Cannistraro et al.

248 **dossier without the forgeries was first delivered:** Barton Gellman, "A Leak, Then a Deluge," *Washington Post,* Oct. 30, 2005.

248 **transmitted parts of the dossier:** Bonini and D'Avanzo, "Nigergate."

248 **Iraq's Vatican ambassador:** Ibid.

248 **"The CIA knocked on our door . . .":** Ibid.

248 **"They told me a very simple thing . . .":** Ibid.

249 **"I can remember . . . no more than a dozen pages . . .":** Ibid.

249 **Martino worked for DGSE:** Smith, "Spy Story That Has Enmeshed Bush."

249 **fake dossier for US$200,000:** Bonini and D'Avanzo, "Nigergate."

249 **"scandalous":** Elaine Sciolino and Elisabetta Povoledo, "Source of Forged Niger-Iraq Uranium Documents Identified," *New York Times*, Nov. 4, 2005.

250 **"flawed intelligence":** "Bush Tries to Deflect Blame for Flawed Iraq Nuclear Claim," Agence France-Presse, July 11, 2003.

250 **"The case was . . . not a fact-based policy . . .":** Interview with Vince Cannistraro, Dec. 13, 2005.

250 **". . . being hand-fed to them . . .":** "Ian Masters Interviews Former CIA Agent Vincent Cannistraro," KPFK radio, Los Angeles, Apr. 3, 2005.

250 **"You'd be very close":** Ibid.

250 **"I have absolutely no connection . . .":** E-mail from Michael Ledeen to Louis J. Vandenberg posted on Ian Masters's website after interview of Vincent Cannistraro, Apr. 10, 2005.

251 **an analyst at the State Department's:** Jonathan S. Landay and Warren P. Strobel, "Indictment Doesn't Clear Up Mystery at Heart of CIA Leak Probe," Knight Ridder Newspapers, Nov. 4, 2005.

251 **translation from the French:** Ibid.

251 **"fragmentary reporting":** Ibid.

251 **The head of WINPAC:** Ibid.

251 **referring to the public dossier:** "Ian Masters Interviews Philip Giraldi," KPFK-FM radio, University of California at Riverside, Dec. 18, 2005.

251 **"I think . . . a much bigger story":** Ibid.

252 **more than the Google:** Landay and Strobel, "Indictment Doesn't Clear Up Mystery."

252 **director of the IAEA:** IAEA Director General Dr. Mohamed ElBaradei, "The Status of Nuclear Inspections in Iraq: An Update," statement to the United Nations Security Council, IAEA.org, Mar. 7, 2003.

252 **"these specific allegations are unfounded":** ElBaradei, "Status of Nuclear Inspections in Iraq."

252 **Powell acknowledged:** "U.S. within Striking Distance on Iraq," CNN.com, Mar. 9, 2003.

252 **Kristof in the *New York Times*:** Nicholas Kristof, "Missing in Action: Truth," *New York Times*, May 6, 2003.

252 **a "retired ambassador":** Walter Pincus, "Bush Cited Iraqi Uranium Bid after Investigator Concluded Documents Forged," *Washington Post*, June 12, 2003.

252 **"knew the Niger story was a flat-out lie":** John B. Judis and Spencer Ackerman, "The Selling of the Iraq War: The First Casualty," *New Republic*, June 19, 2003.

253 **launched an effort:** "*United States of America v I. Lewis Libby*," in the United States District Court for the District of Columbia, five-count indictment, Oct. 28, 2005.

253 **"interim oral report":** Ibid.

253 **The same undersecretary:** Ibid.

253 **gotten classified faxes:** Ibid.

253 **Before the first press inquiry:** Ibid.

253 **called . . . to ask about Niger:** Ibid.

253 **The vice president had told his chief:** Ibid.

253 **Cheney had acquired directly from the CIA:** Ibid.

253 **using the name "Valerie . . .":** Ibid.

253 **complications with the CIA:** Ibid.

253 **"non-secure" phone line:** Ibid.

253 **complained about "selective" leaking:** Ibid.

253 **appeared in her own newspaper:** Howard Kurtz, "Reporter, *Times* Are Criticized for Missteps," *Washington Post*, Oct. 17, 2005.

253 **Miller's refusal to tell:** Ibid.

254 **he published an op-ed:** Joseph Wilson 4th, "What I Didn't Find in Africa," *New York Times*, July 6, 2003.

254 **printed the same day:** Richard Leiby and Walter Pincus, "Ex-Envoy: Nuclear Report Ignored," *Washington Post*, July 6, 2003.

254 **would have been informed:** "Joe Wilson Interviewed by Andrea Mitchell," *Meet the Press*, NBC-TV, July 6, 2003.

254 **"The act of leaking . . .":** Interview with Joseph Wilson, Oct. 2003.

255 **leaking information to Novak:** Rick Casey, "Karl and Bob: A Leaky History," *Houston Chronicle*, Nov. 7, 2003.

255 **began to hear from Rove:** Authors' conversations with Karl Rove, fall 1992, various dates.

255 **refused to go on the record:** Ibid.

255 **given to a new manager:** Casey, "Karl and Bob."

255 **"I thought another firm . . .":** Ibid.

255 **"The president's reelection effort . . . has been a bust":** Ibid.

255 **"I said Rove is the only one . . .":** Ibid.

256 **"As far as I know . . .":** S. C. Gwynne, "Genius," *Texas Monthly*, Oct. 2003.

256 **"Would it change your opinion . . .":** Author television interview with voter who claimed to have been asked the question during a telephone interview with a polling firm, Feb. 2000.

256 **Weaver expected South Carolina:** Interview with John Weaver, Nov. 2003.

256 **child with dark skin:** Ibid.

256 **tens of thousands of phone calls:** Author television interviews with voters and political operatives, Feb. 2000.

257 **"It's gotten to where . . .":** Interview with Weaver.

257 **"I think Karl takes attacks . . .":** Interview with Bill Israel, Nov. 2003.

258 **both members of the WHIG:** Barton Gellman and Walter Pincus, "Depiction of Threat Outgrew Supporting Evidence," *Washington Post*, Aug. 10, 2003.

258 **described as slightly awkward:** Murray Waas, "Why Novak Called Rove," *National Journal*, Dec. 16, 2005.

258 **"He really needs to be . . .":** Interview with Bill Miller, Sept. 2003.

258 **information was "not widely known":** *"United States of America v I. Lewis Libby."*

258 **breakfast with his friend:** Ibid.

259 **"if an employee's spouse undertook an overseas trip":** Ibid.

259 **Rove spoke to columnist Novak:** Ibid. (Rove confirmed as "Official A" named in Libby indictment); Waas, "Why Novak Called Rove."

259 **telephoned Rove several times:** Ibid.

259 **"I heard that too":** Ibid.

259 **"Oh, you know about it":** Ibid.

259 **going to be writing a story:** Waas, "Why Novak Called Rove."

259 **complain about press coverage:** Ibid.

259 **confirming for both of them:** *"United States of America v I. Lewis Libby."*

259 **a number of reporters received phone calls:** Ibid.

259 **"I just got off the phone . . . your wife is fair game":** Vicky Ward, "Double Exposure," *Vanity Fair*, Jan. 17, 2004.

259 **"two senior administration officials":** Robert Novak, "Mission to Niger," Creators Syndicate, July 14, 2003.

259 **contradicted Libby's sworn description:** *United States of America v I. Lewis Libby.*

260 **"I was very clear . . .":** Ibid.

260 **was patently untrue:** Jim Vandehei and Carol Leonning, *"Time* Reporter Testifies about Contacts with Rove," *Washington Post*, July 14, 2005.

260 **failed to tell the truth under oath:** Rove testimony in Travis County District Court, *State of Texas v Kay Bailey Hutchison*, Dec. 22, 1993.

260 **a public relations effort:** Interview with Travis County district attorney Ronnie Earle, June 2002.

260 **Rove took the stand:** Author present in courtroom, Dec. 22, 1993.

260 **received an advance call:** Author's notes from reporting on raid.

261 **asked that his legal purview:** Letter from acting U.S. Attorney General James B. Comey to Patrick Fitzgerald, special prosecutor, Feb. 6, 2004.

261 **Comey readily granted:** Ibid.

261 **turned up a critical e-mail:** John Solomon, "Rove E-Mailed Security Official about Talk," Associated Press, July 16, 2005.

261 **Rove changed his testimony:** Carol Leonnig and Jim Vanderhei, "Grand Jury Hears Summary of Case on CIA Leak Probe," *Washington Post*, Oct. 27, 2005.

262 **because Rove had forgotten:** Viveca Novak, "What Viveca Novak Told Fitzgerald," *Time*, Dec. 19, 2005.

262 **Rove didn't remember:** Byron York, "Will Rove Be Indicted?" National Review Online, Dec. 14, 2005.

262 **until his memory was jogged:** Novak, "What Viveca Novak Told Fitzgerald."

262 **"Rove did not have a Cooper problem":** Ibid.

262 **might have spoken about Plame:** Ibid.

262 **conduct an exhaustive search:** Carol Leonnig and Jim Vandehie, "Rove Team Cites Warning from Reporter," *Washington Post*, Dec. 3, 2005.

263 **Understandably skeptical:** Ibid.

263 **"It's hard to imagine . . .":** Interview with Mark McKinnon, Oct. 2004.

17: THE ROVE GOES ON FOREVER

265 **was in a pleasant mood:** Author's notes from attendance of Rove roast, Austin, Jan. 12, 2006.

266 **". . . holds no elective office":** Ibid.

266 **"Karl's Brain":** Ibid.

266 **"God doesn't want to be . . .":** Ibid.

267 **Florida developer Mel Sembler:** William March, "St. Petersburg Developer Takes Charge of Scooter Libby Defense Fund," *Tampa Tribune*, Nov. 24, 2005.

267 **The conservative Hudson Institute:** "Lewis Libby Joins Hudson Institute," *US Newswire*, Jan. 6, 2006.

268 **"We are aware of no evidence pertinent . . .":** Joel Seidman and Norah O'Donnell, "White House E-mails Missing in CIA Name Case," MSNBC, Feb. 2, 2006.

268 **an estimated 250 e-mails:** Jason Leopold, "Details Emerge in Latest Plame Emails," Truthout.org, March 1, 2006.

268 **his boss Vice President:** "Bush, Cheney, Directed Libby's Leak Campaign On Iraq, Critics, Court Papers Indicate," Associated Press, April 7, 2006.

268 **to twelve years in prison:** "Pentagon Man Jailed Over Spying," BBC, Jan. 20, 2006.

269 **In late 2005:** David Morgan, "Pentagon Agrees to Probe Feith's Role in Iraq Intel," Reuters, Nov. 17, 2005.

269 **articles for *Panorama*:** Larisa Alexandrovna, "American Who Advised Pentagon Says He Wrote for Magazine That Found Forged Niger Documents," *Raw Story*, Jan. 17, 2006.

269 **solitary creations of Rocco:** "FBI: Niger Documents Fraudulent," CBS News Web site, Nov. 5, 2005.

270 **spoke with Martino:** Joshua Michal Marshall, "The FBI's Review of WMD Forgeries Looks Like a Sham," *The Hill*, July 28, 2005.

270 **another piece of damning evidence:** Eric Lichtblau, "2002 Memo Doubted Uranium Sale Claim," *New York Times*, Jan. 18, 2006.

271 **one of Abramoff's Indian clients:** Philip Shemon and Lowell Bergman, "Photograph Shows Lobbyist at Bush Meeting with Legislators," *New York Times*, Feb. 12, 2006.

271 **Twenty-one of the state's thirty-four Republican:** Bill Sizemore, "Ralph Reed's Questionable Coaltion," *Virginia Pilot*, Feb. 12, 2006.

271 **had been paid more than four million dollars:** Susan Schmidt and James V. Grimaldi, "Panel Says Abramoff Laundered Tribal Funds," *Washington Post*, June 23, 2005.

272 **manage several major U.S. ports:** "Bush, Congress Clash Over Ports Sale," CNN.com, Feb. 22, 2006.

272 **two of the 9/11 hijackers:** Dafna Linzer, "A Year Later, the 19 Hijackers Are Still A Tangle of Mystery," Associated Press, Sept. 12, 2002.

273 **to Nixonesque levels:** "Bush's Approval Ratings Slide to a New Low," CNN, April 25, 2006.

273 **a rapt audience:** Chris Cilliza, "Karl Rove: Back From the Missing," *Washington Post*, Jan. 21, 2006.

274 **". . . have sophisticated polls . . .":** Ibid.

275 **Kaplan was a leader:** Peter Baker and Jim Vanderhei, "Rove Gives Up Policy Post in Shakeup," April 20, 2006.

275 **two degrees from Harvard:** Ibid.

275 **tumbling to 29 percent:** "Bush's Approval Rating Hits 20s for the First Time," *Editor and Publisher*, May 11, 2006.

276 **appear for a fifth time:** Jim Vanderhei, "Rove Testifies Fifth Time On Leak," *Washington Post*, April 27, 2006.

276 **Rove had been secretly indicted:** Jason Leopold, "Karl Rove Indicted on Charges of Perjury, Lying to Investigators," Truthout.org, May 13, 2006.

276 **influence "has been negative . . .":** Interview with Tom Pauken, May 12, 2006.

Index